PAST AND FUTURE OF
ETHICS

Past and Future of
ETHICS

By

M. A. R. TUKER

*Y a-t-il rien au monde de plus caché
que la verité*

OXFORD UNIVERSITY PRESS
LONDON   NEW YORK   TORONTO
1938

OXFORD UNIVERSITY PRESS
AMEN HOUSE, E.C. 4
London Edinburgh Glasgow New York
Toronto Melbourne Capetown Bombay
Calcutta Madras
HUMPHREY MILFORD
PUBLISHER TO THE UNIVERSITY

PRINTED IN GREAT BRITAIN AT THE UNIVERSITY PRESS, OXFORD
BY JOHN JOHNSON, PRINTER TO THE UNIVERSITY

CONTENTS

v

35870

CONTENTS

CONTENTS

CONTENTS

CONTENTS

CONTENTS

reformed by the outward'—as such, men have not the 'specifically human' qualities—justice—cruelty—vanity—humility—courage, physical and moral—fear—jealousy—envy—hypocrisy—inconsistencies and incompleteness—temperament—life and conflict—the law of life—the prevention that 'the old is better'.

SECTION I
THE NATURE OF ETHICS

SECTION I

THE NATURE OF ETHICS

INTRODUCTORY

IN the world in which we live the certitudes that compassed the life of our forebears have crumbled on every hand; astronomy geology biology physics, historical and literary exegesis, have removed the bricks one by one, and nothing now remains of the structure that was there: the results have been purely destructive, disintegrating. Amidst this mass of ruins what of universal significance remains standing? Conduct remains. Man [Conduct] is an ethical animal, and his acts, mental or physical, are reflected in the lives and circumstances of other animal life. Whatever else we may cease to do we cannot cease to behave; whatever else man might lose he cannot lose this characteristic necessity—conduct. For life itself is a matter of conduct, life and conduct are inseparable, and satisfaction in life must depend in the first place on the actors in this great drama. Here is man's great reality, his great interest, the value that is permanent in life. And its instrument is character: conduct and character are the [Character] solid mental reality, the permanent structure beneath our feet and before our face—the things which cannot be shaken. But how is this true? Is not conduct the most fluid of 'values', do not its standards vary almost as much as the characters which are its vehicle? There could be nothing to say about ethics if this were not so. Conduct and character are only the raw material of ethical life, man's business is to fashion them. Nevertheless they are his as no other possession. Not because his power over them is unlimited—the contrary is true—but because every step of the way requires the one and expresses the other.

Someone who heard I wanted to write on ethics

3

exclaimed "I thought there was nothing more to be said about it!" It appeared to be a matter summed in the 10 commandments. But no subject so little lends itself to limitation by 'thou shalt not' and 'thou shalt' as this; and the prevention that morality is a code given once-for-all, a branch of religion, unchangeable, immovable, cut-and-dried, has sterilized not only the canons of conduct but the development of character. Wings have been given to other activities of the spirit, room has been made for their inspiration and aspiration, but ethic has been regarded as something grey and stereotyped, the thing which you ought to do and do not want to do. The moralists have themselves approached their subject from an armchair, as though the experience of life could bring no enlightenment, as though there could be no suspicion that in ethics the problem *solvitur ambulando*.   In my *studium* days I had recognized that ethic must depend upon psychology; the psychological factors are determinant, and the moral sentiment can never be formed on 'a pattern in heaven'. There could be no cruelty if we had no nervous system, if animal life were insentient; and the facts of moral or mental cruelty are on the same footing for if there were impassible beings they could not be injured by wickedness or unkindness. Moral life therefore is related to the power to feel and its goodness is decided by the kinds of conduct possible to sentient beings. Outside these facts there is and can be no ethic. But behind psychology lies biology; and a very recent modern attempt to get behind biology, to substitute the phenomena of physics for the phenomena of biology, is singularly unreal: biology is the workshop of ethic and no truths of physics can oust the significance of the great biological process. This—did it take place or not? and if it took place how can it be helped that it should influence the ethical and teleological problems of life?

One of the strangest facts in man's history is that there

4

have been so few ethical geniuses; the spiritual and the intellectual genius have both been far more common. Moral passion then has been, with one great exception, a rare experience. There is not much evidence that the human intelligence has evolved since the great days of Greece and there is evidence that men in the mass have learnt to respond to subtler moral suggestions; but today it is still true that there is no equation possible of man's ethical achievement with his material and mechanical achievement.   Why has man's moral sense never grown up? The first reason, I think, is because moral principles themselves have been largely not ethical at all but fetichistic and legal; and whatever progress is made in other directions no one can be moral-minded who believes that fetichism and legalism are to command real moral assent. Ethical instinct and ethical fineness cannot grow in that soil.[1] And in fact the things obtained by such standards in the past have not brought moral or spiritual security. We are the heirs today of the insecurity they have produced. This false direction of morals is paralleled by a general mediocrity of sentiment itself, which is the greatest of all the enemies of conduct.[2] For conduct demands perhaps more fineness than any other spiritual activity. In the third place there has been the universal rule of force. It would not be disputed that we have hitherto governed ourselves almost entirely by physical force and fear, by the coercion of the fist or by a mischievous moral coercion: opinions sentiments beliefs have all been maintained by forces which were not ethical forces. And then there is the further fact that the amount of ethical thinking even among the intelligent and the good has been so small. From one end of the world to the other men's reflection on moral conduct has been infinitesimal compared with their reflection on the tabus behests and mysteries of their creeds: if we included the

[1] See *infra*, pp. 8–9.   [2] See *infra*, p. 10.

more primitive races of men this would not be strange; but it is just as true when they are excluded. For moral thinking is beset by a disability which does not affect scientific and philosophic thinking, since mediocre minds are not occupied with these things: they are however occupied freely with religion and the conventions of conduct and a flood of foolish and unjust thought about them has always prevailed.

The ethical view of life then has always been rare; it has been much more rare than the spiritual, and religion, only, (and in the sense in which it is generally understood) has been a wide-spread moral idealism—a common human experience whose writ runs in all lands. But the importance of these three idealisms is in proportion to their rarity. The paradox must be accepted that in ethics the *modus* of the ideal is the sense of reality—which operates as a moral instinct. And it is the lack of ethical reality in his moral activities which has belittled man's social and religious life and his political philosophies.

Supremacy of Conduct If man had all beauty and all knowledge, if he adored his gods and believed he was pleasing to them, if he had the perfect use of all things mechanical and material—if with all these things he had not conduct what would life be and what could he himself be? He himself is of course its product, for it is conduct, not religion, not spirituality, which creates him a person. And conduct alone can ultimately make life worth while to ourselves or our fellows. We may be going towards a material and chemical transformation of the world: what is the anchorage in a storm-tossed sea of world change and uncertainty? It can be found in nothing but the growing recognition of the place of human conduct and human character as both the machinery and the spirit of life. Without the balance this brings life is a frightful thing. Or let it be supposed[1] that man's brain development

[1] As it has been.

6

might one day exceed what it now is as much as ours now exceeds that of an amoeba; he would still be left with the two universal inescapable conditions of character and conduct: no possible mental or ontological activities would supersede the necessity and the importance of conduct and therefore of character. There can be mind without character but there cannot be character without mind and the not unusual combination of superior intellectual development with inferior ethical (or character) development is one which makes real human progress impossible.   Which leads one to reflect what it is that constitutes human greatness and personal success. Some of the greatest men have hoped that their work would live in the memory of their species. But in the history of the globe, some day, near or distant, your name and your memory will be blotted out—the aeons remember nothing. Your 'success' if it means a 'name' associated with a work is confined within narrow boundaries of centuries—and a great personality who brought gifts to the world 3 or 4,000 years ago might as well be known as the Man of Crete or the Unknown Writer of the Law as by any personal name for him which might have come down the ages. For a personal memory can only survive as long as there is a setting for it with which living persons are in touch—a cultural setting of history and literature common to both periods. If, then, we cannot insure though we work for a future age that our memory will be projected into it, such a possibility cannot be regarded as the measure of human 'success'. But there is another measure. The value and success of life as an experience depends on the character reactions of the individual to the circumstances which his life presents to him. Nothing humanity can get besides will ever be equal to this kind of achievement—that at the moment it is asked for the right response is given in life or in death. If we picture a giver of gifts to his age and to ages unborn whose

7

character response to life was always in default while he lived, we picture what from the point of view of life—his own and others' lives—was a continual failure. But a fine character response is real and direct life response—the one thing without which—whatsoever else man achieves or can achieve—there can be no happiness or nobility in the experience of life.

What are known as 'moral' considerations do not exhaust the content of ethics. The latin word *morality* points to the role of custom, but the greek word *ethic* points to that of character. Many people no doubt think that we ought to mean by the word moral largely that which is sanctioned by custom;[1] but what makes the difficult beauty of moral action is that it depends upon fineness and facilities of character, and that there is nothing either stereotyped or of herd quality in the idea of the ethical.   Meanwhile it is obvious that we are all at different stages of maturity and no one among us has quite grown up morally, so that the idealisms with which we try to lighten our darkness are themselves born amid misty things and live by turning a blind eye to the real. But the true idealism demands no such blindness; it will live (which I think is not the destiny of those we see about us) because it has courage to find the ideal not in the mist but in the light.

Men have looked for a word which should save the world. There is no such word. Or if the buddhas have found the word it has not saved. There is no such word; for men must save themselves. Good is not made out of bad, something out of nothing, and no word can be anything but a seed. Now it is not the seed which decides the harvest but the soil in which it is sown.

[Falsity of human sentiment.] Take such moral judgments as that a man capable of suicide would therefore be capable of murder. Or that birth control is more heinous than any lechery. Or that

[1] Or by law.

8

something moral has been effected if the mother of an illegitimate child is persuaded to marry the father. Or that it is more wicked to dissect human dead bodies than to cut open the living bodies of other animals. Or that greater turpitude was shown when a man took his *caffè cappuccino* before saying his mass than when he violated the niece of the brother-priest in whose house he was 'preaching a mission'.

The fellow of a medical college speaking at a meeting for medical research on "the modern conflict between reason and sentiment" told his hearers that while no society exists for the protection of atoms which may be "bombarded exploded and tortured in every possible way without evoking a protest", when it is proposed to experiment on "sentient living matter" "an additional factor" enters: "feeling" is evoked in the mind of the experimenter "as well as in that of the onlooker" (but not, apparently, in the "sentient living matter" which is no doubt too much preoccupied with the reasonableness of its situation). The lecturer, who wished to justify vivisection of living bodies, naturally introduces the analogy of dead bodies, when people had been "dominated by the feeling that the dead were sacred" and that "dissection was a ghoulish practice". To a thinker of this profundity the conflict of reason and sentiment in the case of ex-sentient matter would of course suggest how we ought to proceed in dealing with "sentient living matter", as to which his candid mind would no doubt have us become as 'reasonable' as we are when 'torturing' atoms in a laboratory. Nevertheless, when reason has come into its own we are allowed to see that there would still be a refuge for sentimentality, for this is the peroration: "if there is need of a society to save animals from unnecessary suffering, there is still more need for a society to save scientific men from the cruelty (*sic*) of misrepresentation and injustice." A fortnight later, when flogging was called for in the case of a blackguard who had beaten eight dogs to death, a socialist member of parliament inquired whether the flogging of a man was to be regarded as a more moral action than the beating of a dog. No, these 2 persons had no moral sense; and we have here the very charlatanry of morals.   In the House of Commons (in a debate on equal divorce in 1923) a clergyman said that he could conceive of no graver crime and no more abominable situation than that a husband might have to cherish and maintain the child of another 'man'. It is perhaps because—even in the courts of the temple— it has been impossible to conceive greater crime or greater abomination than this, that ethics have been and are in such a parlous state.

All these people who may have had excellent notions of theology or politics had no notion of morals.

[Mediocrity of human sentiment.] In the leading press of this country editors who are never tired of saying that patriotism is a sacrosanct duty eulogized a deceased politician because he listened to the call of patriotism and refused office though this had involved "loss to himself"; and it was declared that a prominent living statesman deserved eternal credit because he had "put patriotism before party" at a crisis in his country's history. But why is the small grocer blamed for sanding his sugar?

CONDUCT-CUSTOM

Perhaps they will say that long-established custom sanctions the practice. Then it is those who originated it who should be blamed? PLINY TO CELER

Vulgus ex veritate pauca ex opinione multa aestimat.
(The vulgar esteem little because it is true and much because it is the common opinion.) CICERO

WE have seen that the universal mark of organic beings is a faculty for conduct, or is behaviour; behaviour which affects the individual and all with which it comes in contact. There are two kinds of behaviour, the one immediately subserving material processes, the other directly affecting us as psychical beings—it is this only which is 'moral' or 'ethical'. The most noticeable thing about conduct of either kind is its tendency to resolve itself into habits, habitual conventions—customs. Customs which affect man in his moral relations I shall call conduct-customs as distinguished from technical customs whose immediate object is the attainment of some material end. When the olives are pressed and the '*posa*' obtained it is a technical custom; but the charms used to avert the ill-luck of spilled oil are conduct-custom: when corn is stacked into cocks we have a technical custom; but when the reapers bringing home the harvest hold up their reaping forks as is done in Devon and shout "We have 'en, we have 'en", it is a conduct-custom.

Now ethic is in the beginning nothing but conduct-custom. Our notions of moral conduct originated as the very words 'ethic' and 'morals' show, in our customs. And the conduct-customs of man are as various as his ignorances, his passions, superstitions, hopes, needs, lusts, and fears. Such a fact must indeed be recognized by all who consider the origin of mankind and it is well understood by the anthropologist. But the philosopher's knowledge of moral history is not what matters, what matters are the moral thoughts and knowledge of mankind at large, and it is certain that the part played in the formation of man's moral life by the pressure of custom is neither realized generally nor understood. It is not understood that 'moral actions' which we are here calling conduct-customs are of the same original character as caste law, as the weird and superstitious obligations imposed on himself by primitive and savage man, and as the habits and conduct-customs of all other animals. The herd instinct and the subaltern instinct, which we share with many other animals, and which are probably reciprocal instincts, weld these conduct habits and customs into our life so that we have no power to distinguish the right from the customary, the good from the conventional or habitual: our judgments of ultimate right and wrong run in no other groove than that made by the actions imposed on man by man through custom. Family sex and marriage lore have provided age-long material for customs and beliefs which may have no better sanction than the outlook of the savage.[1] These become shrined in law and receive the sanction of religion which in its turn has nowhere and at no time proved as strong as custom. Consider the caste law which obliges a man to warn others of his approach lest he pollute them, and has made poor creatures die of starvation in a famine rather than touch food prepared by a superior caste; or the suttee

[1] This has been noticed by Frazer, *Golden Bough*.

which sends Hindu widows to burn on their husbands' pyre; or the strange sense of insult felt by the Tesee woman if she is offered an egg which an old custom of this Gold Coast tribe has forbidden women to eat. It is clear that the conscience responds with the same alacrity to such artificial or mischievous absurdities and moral falsehoods as to the finest spiritual perceptions of the human spirit. It requires a finer spirit to respond to these but not a stouter conscience. Adultery, we are told, is a heinous wrong; but how many who believe this would not rather commit it than leave a gambling debt unpaid, or appear clothed in a blanket on some important occasion? Not moral ideas but customary ideas hold sway with us; the really moral notions are never customary, they have never been among our habitual recognitions. And the point for us to seize here is not that man is naturally imperfect and may prefer pleasant vices to any sort of virtue, but simply that habit and custom are the constraining 'moral' force with him; that customs not moral ideas actually do duty for morality. And to fit them with the most complete authority over our conduct it is not necessary for these customs to have any but a surface moral character. Man is now an animal who wears clothes, and derelictions in this matter would certainly obtain less toleration than most breaches of the chief moral commandments. Mill points out that the notion of a married priest is disgusting to a catholic; and it is as difficult for the catholic not to feel that a priest who marries does what is grossly immoral as it is for the protestant not to prefer a fancy sabbatarianism before weightier matters of the divine law. As we are morally horrified at what is not immoral so we all laugh together at what is not absurd, while no matter how absurd a thing may be to which we are accustomed, no one laughs. For us the 'respectable' is ever more urgent than the good; we are ashamed to ostracize the rich swindler while we consent to the punishment of the needy one. The majority of men are willing, in each case, to approve what it is thought respectable to do, however immoral. And it is the characteristic effect of custom-morality to make the worse appear the better reason; for moral sentiment belongs to the few, herd-custom instinct to the many, and the human herd instinct is on obvious grounds much less trustworthy than the same instincts in the other animals.[1]

The great power wielded over us by the sense of shame is a running commentary upon this. For shame is universally aroused not by moral obliquity but by offences against what our congeners deem respectable or suitable, or when a man is found out in some breach of the conventions of the community to which he belongs. The dog, in contact with us, easily learns this sort of shame; but indeed most animals afford an example of herd-morality in the making, for a dog will feel shame if he fails to come up to some expectation of his congeners, be it only for his awkwardness in missing a rat. "La honte fait plus que la conscience."[2] Bind upon men some burden however horrible and unnatural and they will feel outraged by the attempt to remove it. Take away a right however natural, however necessary, however pleasant, and the defrauded man will meet all efforts to restore it to him with 'respectable' indignation. The slaves of custom hug their chains. Nothing but a phenomenon of this sort explains the virulence of the hold of caste lore, while it is a measure of the difficulties besetting all moral and political development. As the roman word for morality expressed the origin of the morality around us, so the greek word expressed the idea of conduct formed upon character. The cure for gregarious morality is character morality. The cure is respect for idiosyncrasy, eccentricity, that individualism which is the power of acting

[1] As has been noticed by Frazer in the *Golden Bough*.
[2] George Sand.

out of the circle made by the crowd, of thinking apart from it as well as acting apart from it—the capacity to shake ourselves free of mass morals. Where there is no audacity of thought there cannot be moral fineness, and nothing is more certain than that every ethical ideal has originated in one mind or few, never with the crowd. So that what was admirable in a man is precisely that which was cold-shouldered when he displayed it: it is the originality condemned while it was with us which is extolled when we are no longer there. We naturally approve in the character of units of the species what yields to us, makes no demands, and never turns and rends. At the same time we are well aware that these characters may be neither the most useful nor the most estimable. Man tries to coerce his fellow into offering him no resistance, but he despises the compliance he has provoked. Even the idealist who feels the full greatness of originality in history and romance looks askance at it enacted before his eyes. And not only does the moral judgment usually fail in the presence of the unusual but ordinary men can be got to do and endure for custom what only extraordinary men brave for the sake of principle and virtue. How then are we to tell from age to age whether we are following real or ruck morality? Are the safe paths never the well worn ones and is the only highroad that along which no one has yet travelled? Is what the mass of men think always wrong, and is there not rather a pragmatic sanction attaching to our use of highways trodden *ubique* and *ab omnibus* that has in its nature more validity than the vista splendid of a path opening before the few but which no one knows for certain may not end in a *cul-de-sac*? The instinct in gregarious animals to do what our fellows deem suitable is not and cannot be altogether misplaced. But it is no general rule for moral conduct; and it is because this instinct takes up in human life a preposterous share, and because organic beings as such are framed to regard the customary as the right and proper, that it is all-important to ethical life to establish an antidote.   Someone has said that duty developing out of generalities and divorced from nature and common sense becomes fatalism. That is true. And the mistake we make is to confuse the real exigence of group needs with the supposed exigence of group customs and opinions. Whether or not we are following ends that are moral will depend entirely on what we are to find is the nature of morality—what are moral ends and what quality or qualities make them so. But meanwhile the value of traditional customs is subject to a simple test. We must look at the hole of the pit from which they were digged. For a very large portion of conduct-custom it would be utterly impossible to show that any attempt had been made in the ages which framed it to inquire what was good true or just; and the criterion of these things and the knowledge and information which must underlie such a criterion have always been inadequate and defective. If, for these causes, ethic has no finality we may at least preserve for it the moral unities obscured by traditional customs; for what unity or finality can have been prepared in the witches' cauldron of human thoughts and habits from which we have derived our moral notions?

Custom instead of being the respectable staple of moral ideas is of all the sources of conduct the first which should be questioned. It does not contain the stimulus to any ethical thought; and there inheres in all mere customary morality something subaltern, an intellectual and moral abjection which belongs to things that ask nothing from us but acquiescence. So a crowd can be got together to follow a leader which could not be got together to champion the finest cause in the world.

UNITY OF ORGANIC LIFE

THE sentiment of human solidarity is due, we are told, to the gospel. That solidarity can be conceived in two ways—as a theoretical doctrine following upon a common origin and destiny, or as a practical precept binding men as such to mutual service and charity. But there is a vaster solidarity—the solidarity of all organic life—revealed to us by biology and psychology, which profoundly modifies the previous conceptions of ethic. This recognition of solidarity is among the most momentous of modern times and it is very difficult to realize that it should have come so late in human history. Galileo upset our notion of the world's place in the universe and Darwin upset our notion of man's place in the world. But Darwin's seed fell on better ground than Galileo's, and we may expect in the course of the xxth century that the two mighty recognitions of the xvith and xixth will finally be assimilated by mankind who will then understand that the theogony or the ethic which took no account of them must perforce undergo radical restatement.

The moral sentiment of solidarity as an asset of species life, in so far as it at present exists, was, as it were, recovered in the case of mankind. For unlike most species of living beings man has always been hostile to man; the more complex brain process has accentuated the antipathies—the causes and the skope of antipathies—which the invididuals of a species may feel towards one another: tribal, racial, theological, and class and political opinion divide man and destroy his solidarity in a way that has no parallel among other animals. Hence interspecies hate, jealousy, envy, intrigue, malice, bitterness, and all the reaches of self-interest, play a prominent part in human life and a comparatively small part in the life of most other species. Christianity has not achieved human solidarity; the war of 1914–18 between christian and 'civilized' peoples is the sufficient proof: but what theological dogma has been unable to create in man's breast may yet be evoked through the fundamental psychological instruments of morality once their role is recognized; for it is, as I conceive it, a psychological law that the poverty of the natural sympathies cannot be supplied by a call on the supernatural; and conversely that it is because these natural sympathies have been so undervalued that the supernatural sympathies which man has been asked to embrace have done so little to reform him. Man's supernatural is built on the natural, however it may be outside this planet.

When this planet on which we live had cooled sufficiently for fluids and solids to appear on it we may picture slime as the abounding primal substance. Viscid agglutinative and agglomerative the primordial slime was the basis of all those subsequent changes which constitute the world as we see it. The primordial slime individual had latent The primordial the powers of accretion, secretion, excretion; it consisted individual of that mixture of albumen and perhaps carbon which made contraction possible and hence movement. The serpent which contracts its head and its tail moves on no other plan than the simplest mass of living substance when it shrinks from a contact or than the muscles of a highly trained man in a Marathon race or in the performance of the most delicate of operations. It was "living matter" and we speak of it as 'protoplasm'. It Protoplasm had function but not structure; structure came when a nucleated mass of protoplasm was formed within it which we call the 'cell'. As long ago as 1838 it was known that and the a 'cell' was the common elementary organism in plants cell whose various tissues were nothing but combinations of these cells. This simple statement describes the nature of all living things including man who begins his fœtal life, like all other living things, as a unicellular organism. When these elementary organisms we call cells are

Death   destroyed, tissues are destroyed. For the cell is that which brings with it the power of segmentation and growth, it splits up, segregates, reforms, and transforms; it is a living nucleus and workshop of change and growth and life.

There is a characteristic of this primal substance which appears to be the root of every subsequent transformation. Irritability This characteristic is irritability. It is this which explains both sensitiveness to surroundings and reaction to stimuli. And in fact the earliest of all organs to appear in a unicellular individual is what is known as 'the simple reflex arch' of Haeckel—a sensitive spot or primitive organ of touch which conveys any stimulus it receives across the unicellular body to a fixed spot at the other end of the cell, causing contraction.[1] Here we have already present the primitive elements of psychical activity—sensation and movement; these two spots are elementary sensory and motor nerves. Later we get two types of cells focussing these two functions of sensation[2] and movement, a filament between them making a psychic bridge which conveys the stimulus from one to the other. But the distance between such primitive psychic activity as this and the lowest form of consciousness is not spanned until the advent of a third and intermediate cell (the 'adjustor' of the anatomist), which first receives the stimulus from the point of sensation (the sensory cell) and then conducts it to the other cell which is the primitive representative of muscular movement. Was this third cell which appears intermediately between the sensitive points and the reactions of an individual mass of plasm, itself a result of the stimuli and reactions already existing—a psychological outcome of that irritability which is the con-

[1] Recently it has been suggested that the conveyance of this stimulus across the cell may be due to a difference of potential between the 2 regions involved.

[2] Not sensation, and not sensory, in the later psychological meaning of something present in consciousness—but a sensitive point, a stimulus.

18

stant characteristic of protoplasm? For this intermediate mechanism was the register of a stimulus. By means of it—of such a halfway house along the sensory-motor bridge—we get that 'presentation' of an object to a subject—that 'perception' of an object by a subject—which the psychologist recognizes as the foundation of consciousness. It was unconscious presentation, but the larger number of reactions to stimulus in our own daily life are themselves reactions to unconscious presentation. The phenomenon of presentations and reactions which never come on to the level of conscious life, and are therefore called subconscious, was a discovery of the second half of the xix[th] century, and since this time it is no longer possible to restrict the notion even of advanced psychical activity to conscious activity.[1]

The same psychophysical genealogy is traceable in the development of organs—*foci*—of sense. Those primitive sensitive spots and filaments were themselves a step in advance of the first psychoplasm where every part was equally sensitive. The rudimentary basis of sensation is reaction to touch, that is, a sensitiveness to contacts. From the sense of touch, from the vibrations underlying tactile reactions, the other senses have been developed, beginning with sight which in its primitive condition is a pan-sensitiveness to light—the whole body being sensitive

Organs of sense

---

[1] See *infra*, pp. 26–8.

Words and names which arise in the mind with no conscious mental act are examples of unconscious cerebration. Dreams are a special mode of consciousness; a background is prepared for the dreamer and encountered by him, with sequences in time and space not (as in a daydream) of his conscious devising. And the time which our waking consciousness would take to elaborate the dream is annihilated.

Spencer notes that the regressive stages of consciousness under anaesthesia may be taken to indicate the steps from lower to higher stages of consciousness. (*Principles of Psychology*, vol. i, p. 640, ed. 1881.) And J. B. S. Haldane points out that the origin of consciousness out of unconsciousness in the remote past is no stranger than its origin in the embryo life of each of us. (*The Causes of Evolution* (1932).)

to those 'light-waves' which are concentrated later in a special organ. By the very gradual evolution of special organs pan-sensationism of a poor quality has been turned into keen sensations with distinct centres—our five senses. The sensations of all living things, of the anemone, fish, insect, bird, mammal, man, are all of one texture: we know the world through the same senses as does our dog, see with its eyes and hear with its ears; both have been formed on an identical pattern, physiologically and as a psychical phenomenon there is not the slightest difference. The same vibrations—or light 'waves' and sound 'waves'—the same elements of elektron and motion, the same cellular structures on the superficies of our bodies, the same aeons of time, account for the phenomena in both cases. No being ever planted the eye that we see with or the ear that we hear with.

The next great step in the evolution of psychical life was the passage from invertebrate bodies to vertebrate. In the *vertebral*—the spinal—column there were concentrated ganglia of nerves which both co-ordinated and multiplied psycho-physiological phenomena, making possible their far greater complexity. Of this transition the organ was a new psychical cell which thenceforth accompanies the intermediate or presentation-cell. It has been aptly called 'the will cell', for it was a psycho-physical mechanism that carried a mandate of motion to the muscle-cell.[1] The psychical reaction to sensation became 'volition', or inclination, that is a choice and a mandate.[2] Whether this mandate for a reaction be conscious semi-conscious or subconscious, instinctive, or intelligent, does not matter—what matters is that its mechanism first appears in a well-defined condition with the lower vertebrates; and that the skull which supports and protects the

The verte-brates

and a fourth or inclination cell

---

[1] The motor neuron and the association neuron of the anatomist.

[2] H. S. Jennings indeed holds that the unicellular organism has always possessed a simple volitional apparatus.

20

brain (the final psychic apparatus of living organisms) is nothing else but an extension of the vertebral column which supports and protects the spinal cord, a wonderful anatomical truth first recognized by Goethe.

Now the psychical life of man, his doings and his physical and psychical achievements are, or may be, far in advance of those of any other mammals. All mammals standing on four feet are deprived of the first great The Hand instrument of psychical progress which has developed since the last vertebra of the spine became the mammal brain. No animal, not even the ape, has the real and continuous use of the hand, for it cannot erect itself permanently on two feet. When this became possible the last link in the evolution of organic life was forged. The first subhuman beings which stood permanently on their feet fashioned the road to man as we see him; for the hand had been set free. If we think for a moment of the immense complexity of the things brought by the hand— physical things with strong psychical reactions—we shall not doubt that it was the hand that built the bridge— while the feet trod out the path—between the mammal brain and the human. From throwing a stone and shaping a tool to the wonders of the telegraph and the power engine, from kindling a fire and handling a child to the curiosities and utilities of the kitchen, the tailors' shop, and the surgery—each one depended on the hand, and on the responses which it provoked in the human brain. The feet meanwhile trod out the path: the freeing of the and foot hand had not summed the change, there was the new outlook upon the surrounding world which came with the erect position—then for the first time a mammal looked upon the stars.   When we throw our minds back into the minds of those first users of the hand we The first are constrained to recognize that the things we now think users of the hand of as distinctively human—a conscious pursuit of the and the modern beautiful the good and the true, the spiritual and artistic, soul the inventive and ethical—did not belong to primordial man and are no more propria of man as man than of man as mammal; they were potentialities of mammal and of man. The savage today, like the primitive man then, does not share with civilized man those higher cerebral activities which are impossible to other mammals, with the exception of superstition and, it may be, of deliberate pursuit of the false and evil. The finer activities he has no glimpse of. What he really shares, as a subhuman and primitive ancestor shared them, are these human potentialities.

The xxth century of our era dawned before ordinary men from bishops to artizans began to realize that the tiny changes and processes we have been tracing link the lowliest living organism with the highest organism known on this planet—with that division of vertebrates known as mammalia; and moreover that they link a type of psychical activity which is hardly distinguishable from a physical activity with psychical activities as high in the scale as the love fidelity endurance and intelligence of the higher animals. Those indeed who supposed that man was a separate and spiritual creation had not demanded for these psycho-spiritual marvels of animal life an origin distinct from the feeding bag of the jelly-fish. They were ready in this case utterly to confuse the physical and the psychical.[1]

Matter and mind

But when we have traced these changes are we defining mind in terms of matter and mechanism? we shall see that it is impossible to define mind in terms of matter in the sense in which the attempt has been made to dispose of matter in terms of mind. The 'psychic arch' is not rightly described as a mechanism; for protoplasm does not owe its characters to mechanism and mere gross matter does not describe any organic process. While in speaking of living matter we retain the distinction between

[1] Spencer had to point out that the *psychological* is not confined to human cerebration!

physical and psychical we have to remember that a filament uniting two cells is not a purely physical phenomenon, nor are the phenomena of perception purely
psychical. The true name for the underlying plasm is
psychoplasm. The mental indeed is a power of the psychical; but the psychical is not a power of the physical, it is
a power of living matter, and living matter is a psycho-
physical phenomenon. Take the intention I have to
move my arm—I will to do so and the movement I intend
follows. You say this is a common instance of the power
of mind to act on matter? you think perhaps it is a type
of god's action. But the phenomenon is common to all
conscious animals; and it is clearly a psychological
phenomenon, for how should the one act directly on the
other—mind on matter—unless they had points of contact? We owe the thesis in our theologies that god has
relations within himself, that had god been monadic no
creation could have materialized, to this recognition that
utterly unlike things exert no influence on one another.
We have the frequent phenomenon of the spiritual or
psychical triumphing over the physical, and conversely;
and the truth is that we never know in the case of organic
beings in what proportion these two will affect each other
or react upon each other—soul and body.[1]

[1] The action of mind on *ex. gr.* the sphinctas (the direct mental control
of their physical reaction), and the production of musical notes in the
desired sequence from the vocal cords, would not be possible unless the
original unit were psycho-physical. A goat can and does keep back part
of her milk even from the most expert milker so as to leave some for her
kid. What 'unmaterial' basis is there to the changes of character set up by
excess or defect of certain glands, and the disturbances of a psychological
character brought about by a blow on the head and in certain diseased
conditions? The brains of lunatics and defectives are described respectively
as unhinged and unmatured—the one has never been "a brain in equilibrium" and the other has always lacked certain layers. How can this be
if the mind is a separate gift? How is it that he who has no nose has no
mind? That is putting it the wrong way, you say: his good nose is a sign
of a good mind. But that is just as inexplicable.

The subtlest psychological characteristics, talent, genius, together with

Two salient facts accompany the entire history of life and growth, one is the millions of years of time which have elapsed in which the slightest phenomena, the minutest changes, could be repeated till the next small advance, however pregnant, became fact; and the other is that when we go backwards in the history of life and growth, we always get the simpler forms first—the simplest type of nerve, the simplest sense-organ—and then the more complex. These two facts themselves suggest that higher forms are a gradual development from lower. There has been endless time in which to accumulate minute changes; and no one who realizes these changes can doubt that there has been no break at all either in the physiological process or in the psychological unity. On this planet spirit and body are one not two, however it may be extraterrestrially. Here there is no spiritual change without a physical change, no physical development unaccompanied by development in psychical power. The facts of development impose themselves so inexorably that what the underlying substance may be or what the final causes does not affect in any way the significance of the *pari passu* evolution of 'matter' and

such physical traits as the tilt of the head, the lilt of a voice, a crooked finger, a peculiar growth of the hair, a characteristic gesture, are transmitted, on a physical basis, by the cells of living bodies from one soma to another: such an episode as this cannot be described in spiritual terms. Are all psychical phenomena parcels of soul? If so, then where has the latent quality of a great-grandmother been—as part of what soul-substance—before it emerges in the descendant? How indeed could the wit of an ancestor be passed on if body and soul are not one; for the *soul* of the one did not pass it to the *soul* in an embryo?   Memory and recollection is another example of our psycho-physical constitution. Where are the things we remember stored until we recall them? Ward makes everything sink into a subconscious continuum. But the subconscious self is and must be a psycho-physical compound. Until we recall a memory it is not existing as a psychical activity, and when it is awakened it is along a groove which is both physical and psychical. Moreover mental and physical characteristics are inextricably mingled—physical fineness and psychical fineness go together; neither creates the other.

'mind'—the incidence everywhere and at all times of a complicated mental process where there is a highly organized 'material' process, and also the invariable coincidence of a step forward in the one with a step forward in the other. What appears most like a 'break' occurs just where we have been told not to look for it, within the human species itself where the savage man's intelligence is in contrast with the highest man's. And that correlation of spiritual change with physical which I have said is constant holds true till we come to the sheer brain developments, when such a factor as speech has intervened to evolve powers of thinking beyond all that was possible without it, or where domestication has quickened the emotional and intelligent life of non-human animals.

That man when he began to think should have placed himself outside the unity of the terrestrial process was due to ignorance of that process, and then to a megalomania which led, as only moral causes lead, to deliberate obscurantism. Man, before he thought, had felt his unity with the animal life round him: with the passing of the primitive era he made himself a son of god and called Tangaroa, Jupiter, or Jahveh his immediate author. I do not think mere human ignorance would have kept man so long in the dark about the unity of nature; a moral factor as I say hid the clue, blinding his vision so that he could not see nature and the soul as they are. It has not been realized how largely human megalomania has kept man back from important truths in the spiritual and ethical as well as in the scientific order. In judging the position of man relatively to other animals we have fallen into the error of taking man at his highest. Man as man cannot be judged by his highest development or by his lowest. But his lowest sets a term to his position as a species at his highest. Savage man, still extant in both hemispheres of the globe and on four of its five continents, is the

(margin note: Human megalomania)

representative of primordial man, and between the highest human type and primordial man of a million or fifty thousand years ago or the lowest savage alive today there is a far greater difference than there is between these and the higher apes. Palaeolithic man and the australian native are closer to the ape intellectually and morally than they are to the highest product of the civilized human spirit. Because he has primordial man behind him we cannot regard civilized man as having dropped from the skies; and no one who had seen him would have suggested that primordial man fell from the skies. Hence our ignorances and megalomania have for thousands of years set a bar to human progress. But now at last it is no longer necessary for man to be hag-ridden by his megalomania.

Conscious-
ness

When we throw our minds back to cave-dwelling men we face from a new angle the problem of consciousness and self-consciousness in man, in the bee, in the whale, or the dog. All these have a conscious life and the man the whale and the dog have always had conscious affection for the young at their breast. Consciousness, nevertheless, has appeared to us to be the highest of all manifestations, and in the antiquated psychology which prevailed till a short time ago it was not predicated of any animal below man. We know now that it would be at least as absurd to assert the conscious life of cave-dwelling men and deny it of our comrade dogs as it would be to assert it of the elephant in the jungle but deny it of cave-dwelling man. The great contribution made by Bergson to psychology was his theory that intelligence is only one mode of consciousness. Instinct is clearly another mode. Instinct is itself the reaction of conscious—not intelligent—adaptation; it is hereditary consciousness, hereditary mind with no dependence on experience; whereas intelligence is educable mind, dependent on experience. What then, in terrestrial beings, is the fundamental mode of consciousness? It is feeling. Feeling is what underlies all developments in consciousness, all presentations and therefore all perceptions. We are to see that there has been no more radical mistake in philosophy than that of the rationalist school: for conduct will never depend upon reason and reasoning—always upon feeling and the perceptions brought by feeling.[1] Our teachers are the emotions—desire sympathy love antipathy comradeship. The bases of conduct are to be sought (and found) in these laws of organisms common to all organisms. Reason has not done much to improve conduct—for example, by developing a sense of justice in mankind—and in any case the ultimate sanction of ethic is not reason but emotion. We have gone so short a way *because* we have supposed reason, not feeling not emotion, to be the ethical guide. Man's megalomania made him believe that the point at which he most outdistanced other animals lay nearest to the moral perceptions. And man was wrong.

Feeling then is the original form, and type, of all consciousness: the next step is a form of conscious—not intelligent—adaptation; which led to the phenomenon of instinct-mind. For instinct obtains where conscious **Instinct** life is undistracted by a multiplicity of impressions, it is the result of knowledge and adaptation in creatures having a low degree of *self*-consciousness. The conscious life of creatures with low self-consciousness suffered a definite modification with the creation of instinct-mind, and this instinct-mind has persisted even in the higher animals. It was the evolution of the brain and the arrival of those complex conditions of the central nervous ganglia and reflexes upon which self-consciousness depends—[not necessarily the higher ratiocinative consciousness,[2] the 'I know that I know', but the essential self-consciousness, **Self-consciousness**

[1] Sect. iii, rationalism and progress, p. 403.

[2] We must not assume that there is a 'stuff of consciousness' distinct from other mental 'stuff'; rather consciousness may be conceived as depending on an integration taking place in the brain and as requiring not an organ but an organizing process. See *supra*, p. 19, *n*[1].

'I know that I am I and you are you']—it was the evolution of these which brought into play the conscious intelligence; not the mode of consciousness which in fact covers the larger area of our lives (sensation consciousness and the subconscious) but the one that we have made the mistake of identifying with consciousness itself. The primordial life of man in common with the other animals must have been largely instinctive; now he places less reliance than any other animal upon these hereditary memories, inherited mnemonic records, which we call instinct: because he more than any other animal is compassed about by a psychical manifold the creation of foot, hand, brain, and glottis. And wooed on all sides by experiences his consciousness has grown by what it feeds on. So that man has thus become completely a rational being, by which I do not mean a reasonable being but one who has normally ceased to act in any direction with the certainty—or limitation—of instinct.[1]

Social life   If all the essentials of conscious life exist abundantly in the other animals so also do all the elements of sociable living. The extension of consciousness beyond the self and beyond the sensation of external matter to consciousness of the species as a social group was a late attainment of man who remained for hundreds of thousands of years less sociable than the insect.

THEORIES OF ETHICS

IF we consider the thoughts of man about ethical conduct for the past thirty centuries we recognize three types. One is the greek type, where man is regarded as *politikos*,

[1] Man has also far less reliance on pansensation than other animals; a dog, and a horse, habitually feel atmosphere—the presence of someone or something, and trust a psychical instinct of caution, antipathy, or confidence (the instinctive knowledge of a traitor, a treacherous act, or a friend—and no matter in *what* species) as mankind seldom has power to do.   For instinct and race-memory, see the important recent work of Marais, *The Soul of the White Ant.*

a political being with social obligations and ideas. This type may be traced as early as Homer and is explicit in the Nicomachean Ethics. Another is the primitive type of tabu and obediences under the sanction of a god, which finds full expression in the hebrew bible. And a third is the roman type, which combined ethic and law, and on the whole expects less from man than the two others.   It is the second of these which has most claim to have been concerned with what is natural; for the primitive tabus were largely held to rest upon natural facts, and the behests and sanctions of a divinity were supposed equally to inforce those of nature. The earliest idea of the duties of civilized man, therefore, belongs to the greek type, which is susceptible of great spiritual refinement. The roman type was less spiritual, it made no inherent claim on the greatest gifts of the soul of man, as the other two could do: for there is no supererogation in law.

Two of these three types of ethical thought have received notable accretions of idealism; the one through the conception of abstract justice the other through that of an inner conformity with a holy divine law. To the first is owed every thought which wars against the tyrannies and oppressions of human society, to the second the development of spiritual religion.

The theory of conduct received small attention on the disappearance of the great greek schools, for ethical thought had little skope in a juridic system and perhaps even less in the theological. The theory of ethic is concerned with two main inquiries, Why we call one thing good and another evil, and what it is which constrains a man to do the one and eschew the other. The theological answer has been everywhere the same;[1] and it was not till the renascence of learning and the uprise of scientific knowledge that the western mind again set itself to demand what were the principles of moral conduct. The

[1] See Ethic and Religion, pp. 88, 89; and A Teleology, p. 423.

forthcoming answers were three—materialistic with Machiavelli and Hobbs, idealistic with Plato (and Plotinus), and thirdly utilitarian which was an english clergyman's riposte to the charge that moral theology disregards natural happiness; the riposte consisted in asserting that what god requires has a utilitarian value for man. Kant fathered a metaphysical ethic, Spencer the biological, while our english Shaftesbury was perhaps the first professional ethicist to tell us that the deepest root of moral action is sympathy.[1]   With the metaphysical theory of ethic we shall have nothing to do. The principle upon which Kant based it has no real existence.[2] The materialistic basis for ethic which assumes that man only acts from self-interest and is swayed only by fear of personal consequences is just as false as the theology which employs religion as a moral police and substitutes a man's hope of heaven or fear of hell for moral phenomena. We are on ethical ground with neither.   We come then to the utilitarian which premises that what everyone seeks is happiness, the pursuit of happiness being in the ultimate resort the only possible motive for conduct. The criterion of moral conduct is therefore that which tends to procure the greatest happiness for the greatest number. But there is an obvious lacuna between the first and the second proposition. What makes you believe that you ought to procure the happiness of other

The pursuit of happiness

people? For if happiness be the only possible motive for the individual's choice then some form of self-interest is the only possible motive for the individual choice, and he cannot find in himself another motive, namely the interest of other people. The one motive cancels the other.[3] Unless we distinguish between kinds of happiness

[1] Adam Smith, 50 years after, asserted the same all-important moral principle.

[2] See *infra*, conscience, p. 38.

[3] That some men find their happiness in that of others does not supply us with a general principle.

(which at once introduces further criteria) it is not true either that what men seek is happiness and can be nothing else nor that the sole proper end of conduct is to procure the greatest happiness of the greatest number. The utilitarian theory, in fact, has juggled with two different things—desire and happiness: what each of us wants is what each of us thinks desirable, for to deny this is a contradiction in terms; if man is capable of wanting things it is because he finds one thing more desirable than another, but that he can only choose what he desires does not mean that he can choose nothing but happiness. The idea of happiness is too near akin to the idea of pleasure for the purposes of a true psychological theory: instead of being universally true, and so that the contrary cannot be even conceived, that men and other animals seek their own happiness, nothing in the long history of the human mind is clearer than that some form of desire, some kind of satisfaction, alien altogether from the idea of happiness, is what has swayed man in his tabus, choices, customs, and caste-theories.

The biological basis for utilitarianism put forward by Spencer fails for the same reasons to account for the phenomena. It is not a universal law that we tend to pursue our well-being, nor that the pain which obstructs that well-being is always shunned. Pain may be desirable, and looking back on the past we may say we would not have forgone it or have forgone horrible troubles. If this is true in retrospect why not in prospect? And the motive for the choice here is not ascetic; it is simply that we are able to believe that we have gained—that we shall gain—from suffering that which is better than happiness. But such a choice of pain cannot be described in terms of biological well-being or of the pursuit of happiness. It follows some other law. Neither the sanctions of pain and pleasure nor the instincts which subserve well-being are capable of exhausting the nature of desire. It is

Well-being not a constant motive

31

impossible to confine the acts of a mother within any such scheme; or the love sacrifice of a dog. A man may care greatly more about what will happen to someone else after his death than he cares for any good whatever for himself. A man's most passionate desire may be that others should not get harm from what is harming him; he may die, as Arria did, to save the loved from the bitterness of death.[1] That shame and self-respect should deter men from shirking what others will be required to do in their place; that we can call upon ourselves for the courage and tenacity to go through the horrible task we have undertaken, shows motives at work which have nothing to do with the desire of happiness. The very fact that few things in the world can help a man to bear outrageous circumstance better than the knowledge that he is one of a group of like sufferers brings us face to face with two motives, the biological sense of solidarity[2] and *esprit de corps*, which replace personal motives. Such non-hedonistic motives penetrate all societies of organic beings; savages are as capable as civilized men of dying willingly when they believe their torment will help the community; and the voluntary suicide of the Samurai code in Japan discovers motives far stronger than any desire for happiness for yourself or for others.   The assumption made by the utilitarian is that we reach a fertile proposition about the nature of conduct when we qualify feeling (which itself determines all motives) as pleasureable or painful. But we reach it only by obliterating all the distinctions between pleasures and pains—by admitting a definition of pleasure and happiness which is

---

[1] *Paete, non dolet.* Indeed the very sentiment to which Arria made appeal is non-utilitarian: 'having seen me die it will be easier for him to die'. Pliny in a letter to Macer tells the story of a similar act by an unknown woman on the Larian Lake.

[2] The community of fate is, in fact, the great merger of the personal in the social. Why should my lot be different to theirs? What they can suffer, I can.

not hedonistic at all. When Spencer in the *Data of Ethics* escapes the hedonism of the utilitarian position[1] by pointing to biological well-being as the legitimate goal of conduct, pleasure and pain (which cease to be the only things desirable or undesirable) are retained as signposts on the road. But how far along the ethical road does pursuit of well-being take us? Spencer bids us notice, for example, that it will conduce to prolongation of life; but longevity is as arid an ethical end as freedom from stomach ache. Pleasures and pains as signposts to the path of well-being are also inadequate: not all which serves our well-being is pleasurable nor which is noxious to it painful. On the biological hypothesis there are two supreme types of conduct, the self-maintaining and the race-maintaining; but it is evident that courses which are self-destructive may be enjoyable and that conduct which is of the highest importance to the race may be performed with no pleasure. Spencer realizes that a third kind of conduct must be joined to these before they can reach their highest development. I suggest that this third type of conduct is nothing else than the operation of the sympathy common to all animals and of the human faculty which forms an ideal of personal life and of group life.

Such conduct as that of the solitary fossor wasp is a type of much of the instinctive action of animals; it cannot be said to be performed because the individual receives pleasure from it. It is performed according to some other law of existence. Pleasure or pain, rest or toil, the little or the big animal feels an imperious need to do what it has to do, and in that finds its satisfaction—a satisfaction not to be confused with its pleasure but akin to self-fulfilment in work or to action under the spur

margin notes: Well-being · Pleasure and pain not reliable signposts · We have a type of moral action in instinct and habitual custom

---

[1] The position is enunciated by Bentham in the opening words of the *Introduction to the Principles of Morals and Legislation*: "Nature has placed mankind under the Governance of two sovereign masters, pain and pleasure."

of necessity.[1] This operation of instinct in animals is matched by those cast-iron customs of men which have been formed by habit and are in fact the earliest regulated conduct actions—and happiness is not the sanction or the stimulus in either. It is evident then that in these phenomena of instinct and habitual custom we have another type of ethical action which is non-hedonistic. Among the higher animals the servile desire of others' good opinion may perhaps prove a stimulus to unwelcome habit; but something else is at work—the fixed idea of a thing which must be done or not done, of which a ready example is the savage *tabu*, though we civilized men present many equally striking instances of the operation of habit indistinguishable from instinctive action. For man having dropped instinct has picked it up again as habit.

Those acts which tend to make life better for our fellows are regarded by Spencer as specially 'good' acts,[2] and he supposes the biological basis for such conduct to be *The worth* the persuasion that life is itself worth living. If you did *whileness* not suppose so there would apparently be no moral pur- *of life* pose in assisting things to live. I do not agree that we must think life worth having to wish to do what supports and protects living beings. I think there is no teleological implication in helping others. The fact is sufficient that they are alive, without fire, without medicine, without means, calumniated, unable to defend themselves morally or physically, and the like. It is the ethics of "helping lame dogs over stiles". "Who was neighbour to him that fell among thieves?" There is nothing abstract here at all, there is no generalization; it is action on the model supplied by maternal action; it is individual and particular and grounded in zoological sympathy.

[1] "The Pride of compassing may more than compare with the pleasure of Enjoying." Halifax.
[2] *Data*, ch. iii. 24–5.

The biological ends of life and the pursuit of happiness afford no sufficient mark for the shafts of our desire.

There has indeed been a misprision of the state of Desire desire. It has been assumed that absence of indifference and choice of pleasure or avoidance of pain are the same things. The state of desire—absence of indifference—belongs to all higher organisms; and when Daniel was saluted as a man of desires it did not mean that he had a concern for happiness. That by the nature of things no higher organism can be indifferent is the salient fact about life and the crucial fact for conduct. This state of desire is the ultimate fact underlying behaviour, and controls all choices whatever their quality. It hastens the steps of the Indian to the pyre and thrusts the Samurai sword into a man's own entrails.[1] It is desire which the luster finds so hard to silence, and it is desire which invokes anathema for self that another may be exalted. Out of the kosmic womb desire comes forth, and all indifference ceases. Thenceforth its voice alone is heard in the earth—pain, happiness, self or other-self, are its elements—its playthings—out of which it buys satisfactions. For it is the irreducible motor of psychic life and is in the psychic sphere what irritability is in the physical;[2] like irritability its kinship is not with pain or pleasure as such—it lies behind all pleasure and all pain, choosing the one and the other. It is the recondite principle of all psychical becoming—the logos, emanation and messenger of the soul.

What then brings desire? Clearly if this account of it is the right one the answer is that desire is as manifold as the life complex; that since it is the well-head of the psychosis it has the entire soul as its province. The

[1] If it is urged that these are fanatic phenomena, it would be just as remarkable on the utilitarian hypothesis that such things should ever be desired.

[2] *Supra*, Unity of organic Life, p. 18. Irritability is of course a primitive psychical fact; but it is also a physical fact.

psychosis is indeed determined to action by motives, but the motives to desire are as far to seek as the source of irritability in protoplasm. No general account can therefore be given of what is desirable; and since it is untrue that we can only desire what is pleasurable and must reject what is painful, pleasure and pain are not the stuff of which all motives are made, and we must seek the principle of ethical action elsewhere.[1]

If we could assure ourselves that there is a supreme good, at once a touchstone of values and a standard for all conduct, we should be in possession of the principle of ethical action and of the right ethical motive. For in one sense utilitarianism (based on the criterion of happiness) is of all solutions of the problem the least satisfactory; because the ethical cannot be understood at all apart from the notion of a standard, and utilitarianism supplies no criterion of quality and no right measure of quantity.[2]

In order to reduce the problem to ethical terms it is necessary to substitute 'the greatest good' for 'the greatest happiness', and when we do this we mean that which is desirable for people to have not that which people may happen to want, we go back to the sokratic *summum bonum*. In the minds of those who expounded it it is certain that that *summum bonum*—which man could share in ideating and desiring—was consistent with his highest well-being but its consistency with his nature is not so sure. It would indeed appear that a *summum bonum*

---

[1] Desire is distinguishable from feeling—from all pleasure and all pain —in being active not patient; for of his pleasure a man may be only patient, but his desire is always an agent. I take desire to be not the inactive principle which suffers the discomfort of unsatisfied longings—for this is rather an apathy, a sickness and asthenia of desire; true desire is always an irritant, and the source of all psychical becoming. Hence it is desire which is the ultimate; for if there were no desire there could be no choice. Man then though he may suffer what he does not desire, cannot pursue it. Once he pursues it he desires it, on the balance. Again, pain and pleasure take possession of us, but by desire we take possession.

[2] See Political Government (majorities), p. 366.

(whether with Zeno we place it in virtue, or with Epicurus in the creation of happiness,[1] or whether with Plato it is reached through a combination of the perceptions of goodness and beauty) is as unlikely to be universally enjoyed or sought after as the aspirations of the artist or the mystic. The existence of ideas does not involve the existence of something corresponding to them—to suppose that it is otherwise has been one of the pitfalls of philosophy—and hence lofty spiritual apprehensions may —like the highest art—resolve themselves into realities for none but the finest of men. To Plato the essence of things was goodness and beauty; and it was impossible for a man to help loving the good if he could know it: ignorance alone kept him from it. This is a truth for the exalted spiritual and religious sense but it is in no sense at all a truth psychologically. It is not ignorance but spiritual poverty, or deformity, which keeps us from appreciating a 'highest good'. Nevertheless morality being so much a matter of aspiration it is a hard thing to resign ourselves to reject a supreme and universal good, the inspiration and sum of all possible aspiration; to have to trace instead step by step from dawn to nightfall a path beset with doubts and problems, in his resolution of which—and in that only—a man can come face to face with the ideal. For there is no 'greatest good' by which men may live, the celestial mirage recedes before us as we pursue it: we are wayfarers, and the light is thrown only on our footsteps; the goal is never seen except afoot and on the path before us.

The *summum bonum* or conception of a supreme value and good finds a counterpart in the post-greek conception

[1] Kant writing on the greek *summum bonum* says that there were properly only 2 schools of thought, the epicurean which said, To be conscious that one's maxims lead to happiness is virtue, and the stoic which said, To be conscious of one's virtue is happiness. (*Dialectic of Pure Practical Reason*, ch. ii.)

of a supreme right, a *summum justum*. Its correlative is conscience.

What is conscience?[1]

It is, we are told, a unique faculty possessed by mankind, which recognizes moral commands; it is a voice saying 'this is right', 'that is wrong', and it is an innate sense of moral obligation which can be defied but not stifled. "Two things", wrote Kant, "fill my mind with ever-renewed wonder and awe . . . the starry vault above me, and the moral law within me."

We have here, in my view, an entirely false account of the function we call 'conscience'. For, first, it is not a distinctively human faculty. Then, it does not tell us what is right or what is wrong but only what we have been told is right or wrong. And its office is not to issue moral mandates but to impose obedience to commands. Kant called the action of conscience a kategorical imperative. There is a kategorical imperative, but it has no connexion with a "moral law within us".

Ethical writers and teachers have said little that is either helpful or true on this matter, which instead of being allied to a sound psychology has been subjected to the duress of metaphysical explanation; and the first piece of enlightenment came with an assertion formulated within the catholic church that what is to be obeyed is not any conscience but 'an instructed conscience'.

Conscience itself is not the instructor.

What then is its action, its mechanism?

It is a register of instructions.

Such a register of instructions is part of the texture of animal life, is that which makes possible the formation of habits, the conduct and behaviour which must be ac-

---

[1] Anglo-saxon and the Norman-english which replaced it, unlike the romance languages, both set apart a word to denote the moral conscience as distinct from consciousness. But Shakespeare does not give the word any moral significance in Hamlet's soliloquy.

quired by every living organism sufficiently advanced in the scale to learn from its parent. Thus the origin of conscience is to be found in the primal relation of living creature to parent; without such a faculty the young could not learn on the authority of the older or receive the discipline of training. Not a perfect law but a perfect need belonging of nature to animal life as such lies behind its responses; and what is inexorable and imperative in conscience testifies not to a divine law but to an *arcta necessitas*, something welded in with the biopsychical conditions of living organisms.

It must be clear when we come to think about it that another method of acquiring the life habits is demanded as soon as volition and desire begin to operate, unless indeed instinct in the more highly developed animals were so strong as to override every desire noxious to survival and well-being. But this is not the case.[1] Volition and desire if they are themselves the result of determinate factors yet introduce an individual element into life as opposed to group elements. Hence there comes into operation the psychical factor and faculty of conscience: all organic beings capable of learning possess as such the conscience faculty, for no mother could teach the new-born and utterly inexperienced if the little one could not feel 'I ought' and 'I must'.

Such an account of the origin of conscience explains its purely formal nature, the fact which one would suppose could not escape the dullest among us that it only acts as a formal monitor. It does say 'you shall' and 'you shall not' but it does not inform us why this is good and that is bad. The young organism learns what it has to do and avoid without distinguishing between physical obligation and moral. It does not recognize the difference between

---

[1] The instinctive act is wanted and desired by an animal and is therefore willed; but whereas such action is protective non-instinctive volitions and desires have no such safeguard, but are eccentric.

stepping into the water or biting its baby brother, between eating too much of its own dinner or taking its
brother's dinner. And here is the point: it accepts the
fact that both are iniquities because both are forbidden,
both are to be eschewed; the moral 'ought' of which so
much is made by intuitionists does not correspond to a
moral law but simply to the unconditional because unquestioned and not questionable authority of the parent
lawgiver. The kategorical imperative bears witness not
to an absolute law but to a relative helplessness. Such an
origin, again, accounts for what has been variously felt
to be the 'simplicity' of conscience, its 'instinctive' or
'rudimentary' character, its uselessness in solving moral
problems or questions which demand the processes of
reason.

But if in origin conscience is a response to commands
which are not understood it has assumed a secondary
character as a response to what we have learnt is 'right' or
'wrong'. It has moved from its first absolute simplicity
to a relative complexity. It has not, as is sometimes
thought, become simple automatically as a result of the
constant practice of complex moral judgments; a subconscious judgment has not intervened on judgments
once fully conscious; on the contrary, actions which were
once subconscious and quasi automatic have become conscious and reasoned. The creature grows to discern the
point of view of the lawgiver. The lawgiver, however,
was never infallible except within strict utilitarian limits,
and the conception of morals which man inherits from
man is groping and uninformed, a response for the most
part to custom-morality, to moral prejudices, and to conventions, not the outcome of spiritual instinct or a higher
wisdom of the soul.   What has happened is that
among men and other domesticated animals the original
biological 'ought' with its foundations in the life processes
—a quasi automatic faculty—has been transferred to an

ethical 'ought'—a conscious attempt to respond to the standards of conduct set from time to time by our surroundings. And here what conscience gains in articulateness it loses in cogency. As a conscious register of man's shifting and ignorant judgments it loses the validity of its unreasoned obedience, and exchanges the certain for the uncertain.

But it may be said that this account of conscience though it rakes the intuitionist's position leaves intact the theologian's. That there is in fact a third alternative: conscience if it does not acquaint a man with the nature of the divine law yet testifies to the existence of a divine lawgiver; and because a man has not a moral law within him it does not follow that all moral law is derived empirically and as a bio-psychological phenomenon, for the responses of conscience bear witness to a divine constraint, and answer to a moral command. The onus of proof in such an argument must rest on those who put it forward. If conscience be the response to a divine ruler who wills righteousness and hates iniquity the virtue of obedience to the lawgiver cannot take the place of the value of obedience to the law. And the first criticism of the theological position is the uncertain and contradictory character of the moral response, the moral realizations and appreciation of any age. If conscience were indeed to respond to a divine law outside us, what commands has it received? Man—from the earliest to the latest man, from the primeval to the civilized—goes through his life, and what does he learn about the divine law? Is it not evident that like the fledgling or the puppy he may learn nothing at all about it by obeying his conscience? Is it not evident that what the human conscience responds to is in great part not goodness and badness at all but simply what is sanctioned by custom, precedent, tradition of elders or parents? This is what it would be on my theory of its mechanism and origin.

A fresh element is intruded when we are told that if a man obey his conscience he is a good man, though he choose what is wrong. This distinction between a right motive and a wrong action divides conduct into what is 'materially' good—that is, right in itself—and what is only 'formally' good—what we believe to be right; and it is evident at once that it is incompatible with the intuitionists' theory of morality. For if a man knows by intuition what is moral how can he fail to be 'materially' right when he follows his conscience? And if the moral commands were intuitive why were the 'commandments' necessary? Commandments would be necessary if there were an authority without which we could not know the law. This is the theological thesis and it is the biological. Alike by chick and puppy and child the commands of conscience are obeyed because they are commands not because they are good; so that the scholastic dictum that the divine law is 'holy' because it is god's will not because god necessarily wills what is holy is in truth the root of the biological sanction of conscience.

But is a man always good when he does what his conscience tells him, and can he never be good when he does otherwise? Here we have always had a pitfall spread before us for an answer has never yet been propounded which reckoned with the psychological factors. The sentiment of the inviolability of conscience derives from the apodeictic character of maternal injunctions. Let the sentiment and belief that an injunction is one that should be followed exist, however erroneously, and the 'conscience' is of necessity violated by disobedience. But were a faculty of this sort allowed to stand in the place of instructions given to the intelligence and moral sense, in the place of experience which it is our duty to acquire, of information, existing knowledge, and the processes of reason, it would not be the quickener of goodness but the sepulchre of enlightenment and morality. The immature

living organism is educable because it possesses the
faculty of response to an imperative injunction of conduct.
But moral growth, and the moral sense, do not depend
upon conscience at all and do not follow on our capacity
for following conscience; they depend upon reasons and
sentiments addressed to the intelligence and the sympathies. The faculty of conscience is in fact a passive
power to receive and correspond with conduct impressions, so that the distinction so commonly received between the formally and materially good is as a moral asset
largely fictitious. For if the sympathies be the principal
root of right conduct—as they are—a man who violates
the sympathies is not a good man though he be so con-
structed or instructed that he thinks his cruelty right.
Conscience is as essential to moral life as the artistic sense
to art; but the technique of both—how to use and choose
the material presented—is learnt. When it is learnt—
when the right and wrong way are understood—then the
quality of conscience will count. For it has always been
possible to violate conscience, to disobey the vital injunctions. Conscience presents itself as an apodeictic
faculty—as unfightable and needing no demonstration—
because it is usually disobeyed at the peril of the organism
and because the young are incapable of judging the rule.
Yet some eccentric, some individual with less sense or
greater independence, with a different moral balance to
the rest, will play out of the harmony of the brood or
litter: if we watch young with a mother we shall see the
groundwork of their lives is obedience to her call, and we
shall also see the occasional deflections. It is the same
with the progeny of mankind and the same psychical facts
underlie it.

To recapitulate: conscience in its origin is nothing but
the faculty for responding to conduct instructions, and is
therefore akin to the 'formally' right not to the 'materially'
right. It is an imperative regarding conduct and the

thoughts which lead to conduct without being in any sense a guide to what is moral and not moral. Obedience to a mother's instinctive injunctions first gave this sense of a thing in conduct—as distinguished from the technical obligation in art or craft—that must be done and a thing that must not be done: 'right' and 'wrong' at first are simple imperative propositions in the form 'ought' and 'ought not'. And if it be true that there is this original sense of obligation in conduct quite apart from the material quality of the conduct (and who that considers the imperative customs of the savage can doubt it?) there must always also have gone with it the sense of wrong and right. When the creature comes to discern for itself a quality in conduct the same conscience mechanism of the immature creature is behind the new consciousness. And as cerebral life increases in complexity man judges the social and moral acts in precisely the same way as he judges wrong or right in art, bad or good in a utensil; they are good or bad in view of ends consciously put before ourselves.

These ends are of great variety, and perhaps the one criterion which they do not satisfy is ideal rightness or wrongness. It is not true that man as man knows he ought to be good, though he has, with other living beings, inherited a conduct conscience which in his case responds to aeons of human tradition. What he knows is that there are conduct acts which will certainly be required of him by other men: from savage horrific custom and cruel caste law to a society of perfect men this pressure is and would be equally felt. It is what the puppy and the colt and the fledgling realize with him. But man, as a whole, is not conscious he was meant to be good, nor has he inherited any criterion of an absolute good. When man comes to reflect on a right and a wrong in his actions the form 'I must follow what I think good' is far less common than the form 'I must follow what I am enjoined'. This is as true of religious duties as of moral or social. The

44

first formula belongs to the highly independent spirit, sometimes to a narrow and obstinate one. As to the second, certain things—I am conscious—are required of me (generally by other men, by parents, or family, or associates) and 'I *must* do so and so'. What I 'must do' varies with the moral perceptions of each age. But since the individual's conscience has been popularly confounded with his knowledge of a real moral law it has done duty in our estimation for moral and psychological experiencer in defiance of which no one can be moral.

Conscience, when untutored, responds as easily to evil instructions as to good. This is true with the single proviso that part of the instructions always received by conscience concern our gregariousness as a species, the presumed or ascertained 'good' of men. Not that there is no such thing as a naturally good conscience but it belongs to the being who answers to the sympathetic and just instincts not the malicious and lusting. It is not conscience which gives him intimation of his good instincts. His conscience merely registers their verdict. There is, however, a strong belief that men do know evil when it is set before them, and good. If a man taught his son that some repulsive practice was right would he develop a conscience in its regard? The answer is that it would certainly be so in the case of a child or a domesticated animal. The thing would be done even in the absence of coercion and though it was disliked, simply under the compulsion of conscience. With the adult it will be different; for he is surrounded by the standards of the gregarious conscience.[1]

This pressure of the group on the unit has been a chief factor in the moral consciousness we call conscience, but

[1] Those who think conscience really responds to moral pabulum, that the child will not respond to evil teaching or think vice 'right', cannot have the history of man's doings with man in mind—such things as Jesus has in mind when he says that the men who do them will suppose they are doing god a service.

behind the obvious gregarious faculty and the gregarious discipline, both in the case of men and the other animals, there is the moral relation established between mother and young wherever instinct is not the sole guide of conduct. Conscious organic beings might conceivably have acquired all that was necessary to their own well-being and the well-being of their species in some other way. The faculty of conscience might have been replaced by instinct, a coactive imitative faculty, or an equally compelling tendency to adaptation. But none of these things would have satisfied the psychical conditions of the higher animals; they would not have supplied what we mean by training, nor disciplined and developed the individual. Only when the power to do or not do enters in can we 'learn' anything; and conscience is that faculty which responds on the one hand to the power of learning conduct and on the other to the animal habit of imparting it, and of disciplining the young creature. It is the principle of education and discipline because it is the corollary of psychical freedom.[1]

Which does not involve any sort of *liberum arbitrium*. It means that the subject of psychical freedom is not an automaton but has idiosynkratic desires and aversions, that he is a unit not the mere channel of group psychology.

Freewill   Is it true that we are free to do what is bad or what is good, free to do *a* or to do *b*? For freedom of the will must mean that we are free *to will a* or *b*. And nothing can be less true. If I am kind and affectionate I cannot *will* to torture one I love, or to torment an animal; if I am honest I cannot will to do a dishonest act—I am *not* free

---

[1] In the field of conduct the role of the mother is paramount; it is through her that the tradition of inherited experience becomes possible— which is impossible for animals such as reptiles who develop without maternal nurture, and whose experience dies with them. The young everywhere imitate the mother; birds, fowls, and the mammalia receive her definite injunctions; and in many of the higher species she disciplines her young. The otter is known to put her offspring through a complete

to put my hand in another man's pocket. Why then should the evil man be free to do what is good. For your will and his are determined by your motives. I may be physically free to knock a helpless person down, but how am I free morally? Such a will-o'-the-wisp as this would undermine the entire structure of character. I am to be able to 'will' to defraud and betray you and to be able to 'will' the contrary—whichever I choose; the good and the bad man are both free to 'will' both ways. What then will decide action? Not goodness and badness, not motives or past character or past life, but something alien to the actor, so that virtue may spring from vice and vice may overlay virtue.   The will can be nothing but the resultant of the motives and must also depend on mental and moral vigour or the lack of them: so that though we may 'will', whether we give effect to our will or not will depend on strength or weakness, on resolution or irresolution of character. You cannot be strong or firm or reasonable if you are weak vacillating and obstinate; and if the weak man is determined to a course by the stronger he is not the subject of freedom but of coercion. If, then, the will is determined complete ultimate responsibility for our actions does not exist. We see that on the assumption of a free will I must be able to will evil with the same freedom as I will good and the bad man must be able to will good with the same freedom as to will evil.[1] But both these are

education in the arts and crafts of their lives. But not one of these nurturing and teaching mothers—elephant, ape, bear, otter, beaver, mammal or fowl —falters when putting their little ones through perilous experiences: there is the stedfast desire to impart on the one hand and on the other the capacity to learn—a spirit of discipline.

Maternal reproduction gives us not merely educability but educability on the basis 'ought not' and 'ought', the mother's instructions introducing the conception of the forbidden and the allowed.

[1] If though he is free his facility to will good is less than a good man's then his badness is not so bad and his goodness is much better than the good man's. This is the *reductio ad absurdum* of the position.

When a good man says: I am free to do such and such a bad deed *but*

pictures of something which never happens. The good man is precisely the man who cannot will evil with the same freedom as he wills good; and the bad man would be still worse if he could always call up good motives, if he were always free to act at the bidding of a good conscience. The good man is responsible to the affections and constraints of his character, while the bad man eschews the responsibility which another feels. And this fact that a man must always act as his character determines does not alter by one iota the moral problems of his life or what we can or do obtain from him.

Duty
Ethic

For the Stoic and for Kant duty is the essence of the ethical; and *prima facie* it might well rank as the premier moral sense. Kant not only gives it this place but asserts every act to be within our power which is enjoined by the sense of duty, a doctrine which is not more extravagant than the theological one of 'sufficient grace' or than that which assumes the will to be absolutely unfettered. It is clear however that duty, like conscience, carries with it no criterion of moral quality. Its mode of action, of course, is the precise contrary of the utilitarian: duty and conscience both of them suggest that what we have to do is not what we want to do; *prima facie*, at any rate, the ideas of duty and happiness do not march. There could be a right and wrong but there could be no sense of right or wrong if there were not a faculty answering to the sense of duty; and the sense of 'ought' and 'ought not' is therefore fundamentally ethical. But its prominence varies and may decrease to vanishing point with the kind

I shall not do it, this 'shall not' actually means 'I *can not*'—i.e. the will is not free; it is determined by my character: it is my will because *my* will cannot be otherwise. We say: 'if his will is strong enough' to do so and so; but if the will is not strong enough it is not free. There is no escape here. The will, in fact, can only effectively will to do what it is in its power to do. Shall I open this swing door back or forth? But: Shall I go to the stake? Shall I ruin my neighbour by a lie?

of stimulus to action—for example, when this stimulus is
sympathy or love. In ethic, then, the sense of duty simply
represents the 'ought' and 'ought not' which is proper
to every activity where a right and wrong way is discerned; it is hence as incomplete a description of the
moral mind as the artistic 'ought' would be of the artistic.
Here therefore is an answer to the question 'ought all
morality to proceed from the sense of duty?'

The sense of duty is not identical nor co-terminous with
the ethical sense; it does not give a sufficient account
of virtue; it is always auxiliary. Every higher vision of
conduct leaves it behind. Even while proclaiming that
duty is the essential religious sense a French prelate declared from the pulpit of Notre Dame: "Quand l'homme
sera venu à se passionner pour la vertu, c'est alors, alors
seulement, que le devoir sera en sûreté, que l'égoïsme
sera vaincu, que le désintéressement sera complet." It
is on this ground that the creeds meet. Not till we have
the passion for the good are we good; and this passion
waits upon no creed but among all bloweth where it listeth.

There is an important school of thought which sees in
the gregarious instinct of living beings the nucleus and
principle of moral life. Peter Kropotkin set forth this
thesis rich with biological data; but I think he allowed it
to escape his highly socialized mind that gregariousness
is not only the principle of sociality but equally of anti-
sociality. If it breeds sympathy so does it breed antipathy;
it is as much the cause of friction as of forbearance, of
rivalry as of co-operation, and in it are all the seeds of
hate greed and envy. Our gregarious character does not
therefore afford us the principle of moral and social life;
it is rather the necessity for social life which requires us
to choose between gregarious instincts and to call 'moral'
those which make for co-operation and sympathy. Our
gregarious character is in fact of the same quality as our

Gregarious ethic

E

individual—both bring forth good and bad, and offer unsolved problems for ethics. The whole of human history shows that the action of the group on the individual is more often cruel than kind.[1]

[It has been suggested that the congress of the sexes forms a natural social nucleus. But the history of sexual relations does not bear out the supposition that they are a natural root either of sympathy or of social relations. The sex union as a social relation is, in fact, a distinctly modern phenomenon. It was unknown in matriarchal communities and is weak in patriarchal polygamy. This idea presents great difficulty no doubt to the modern western mind, but it is perfectly clear that comradeship and sympathy are not inherent in the sex relation but are developments of it in highly organized societies.]

Speculators on ethics have seen the moral clue in "enlightened self-interest": it is enlightened self-interest precisely which is yielded us by the social impulse—'I must give up Y if I want you to yield me Z', whose primary motive I take to be as definitely selfish as the mother's primary impulse is unselfish.

If we cannot find the principle of ethic in the sentiment of duty or in the group instinct can it be discovered in the range of the aesthetic percepts? Someone has said, We cannot dispense with duty; yet freed of all duteous necessity there burns that enthusiasm for the good and for virtue "which resembles the vivid admiration of the beautiful".[2]   What is good and what is aesthetically

Aesthetic ethic

---

[1] The *à priori* argument: if a being wishes to live with its fellows it *must* learn to give because it wants to take, will not carry us far; because with gregarious animals (ourselves first) the liking for the society of one's species does not prevent our doing it all the harm we can. The type of sympathy felt by other animals in each other's society (Kropotkin notes that it is "sympathy not love")—sociability with your kind—does not lead to sympathetic action. It is egoist. Look at ducks sitting close up together in sympathetic society; but if a piece of food is thrown each will try to get it regardless of the others.

[2] I. Lazzari (missionary priest), *Terza Conferenza*, Naples, 1900.

beautiful resemble each other. They resemble each other in spontaneousness and the absence of all servilism, all opportunism. They resemble each other in the quality of beauty as no two other things in the world resemble one another. The perceptions of the ethical and of the beautiful have developed together. Sokrates would not divide them. Yet the beautiful is not the good? In the country where art attained its perfect development it seemed to one of the most moral of mankind that the perception of artistic beauty had a counterpart in the perception of moral and intellectual beauty. For it is not only aesthetic beauty which we realize it is also beauty of mind and conduct—percepts and concepts of the spiritual being discernible as *beauty* just as we discern them in the mind of the artist as well as on his canvas. There is another psychological likeness between them: ethic is not a science; conduct is always of the nature of an art and like art it has an inner and an outer life, it seeks, that is, expression, interpretation. Like art, once more, our judgment of it cannot be independent of judgment of manner —of the recognition of noble manner, delicate manner, or of courage and an unworldly vision of reality. Both idealize life—art idealizes it as it is, ethic as it should be.[1] So that art is not independent of conduct, as conduct cannot be independent of beauty.

But how far will criteria of beauty carry us. Can the perception of the lovely the fitting and the aesthetically adequate be substituted for the perceptions of the right and good and holy? No such substitution is possible; but commerce is possible, that interpenetration of the two ideas which was the *divinum commercium* discerned by Plato. I am persuaded that no sufficient call upon the ideas of beauty and ugliness in reference to conduct has ever yet been made in any age. Yet these ideas propose to us a higher form of perception than those due to super-

[1] Giovanni Lanzalone, 1908.

stition and religious awe which have played so large a part in determining conduct; and they are less didactic than our set ethical doctrine. We should often say 'this is beautiful' 'that is ugly' rather than 'this is right' 'that is wrong'. The ethical notions of right and wrong must be incardinated in heart and mind, but when they associate indelibly with those of the beautiful and the ugly they reach a fresh and more buoyant soil, they coalesce with delicate and audacious energies in the soul, intimate like feeling, and, like feeling, not derived from argument or imposed from without.[1] Moreover the outraging of beauty has the same elements as the outraging of holiness. What is holiness but spiritual apartness; and apartness is the meaning of the Latin *sanctitas*, apartness from the world, apartness from the self. The beautiful is also apart, apart from the mean and ugly the confused the disharmonious—separated. Its presence rebukes our worldliness, reproaches us for our popular morality, calls upon us to select and refine. It suggests to our spirits that 'this beauty is more than that prejudice', that the beautiful is the real and what we call 'real' the sham.

We are told that the good man is he that has formal goodness, who obeys his conscience and follows a sense of duty. But is there any such goodness? The good man is not this sort of man—he is the man of good instincts of moral fineness sympathies and inborn choices. The moral and aesthetic intuitions are then truly analogical, affinitive, they have a common language and standard of exigence and beauty. And this analogy between them brings out the individual and intimate aspect of ethical sentiment—as having not a group origin but a peculiarly personal one, not in the sense of independence of our

[1] In the *Characteristics* Shaftesbury "combines the beautiful and the good" in one exalted conception, and a certain internal sense (the moral sense) is assumed as perceiving both alike.

group history but in the sense of possessing an intrinsic personal teacher.[1] This personal teacher comes late in A personal instructor human development; individualism is itself a development, it is the savage who is unindividual.

We may say of the search for a single principle of conduct what should also be said of the expectation that an absolute right and wrong exists for every occasion: Why should we expect it? What principles at work, spiritual or natural, need be supposed to have subsumed all actions under an ethical absolute? There is no one principle of conduct and there is no absolute ethic. When I save my loved one at the expense of others, or my baby at the expense of the Sistine chapel, or when I elect to save an unknown B instead of an unknown A there is moral choice, but it is not simple right or wrong which determines it. A gesture of A's or B's, some predilection, some pity, the aesthetic sense even, will decide my conduct, and our life is inconceivable without the operation of such individual appreciations.

The claim that the happiness of others has upon us is not due to an intuition of the principle of duty, we owe it to sympathy. The biological law may indeed be, and is, that we learn what another desires by what we ourselves desire; but it is the alchemy of sympathy to turn this egoism into altruism. This alchemy it is that obtains

---

[1] This intimate instructor is not the bringer of the moral law, is not a conscience, but a tutor of method and fineness. The greater openness to influences, the greater openness to sensibilities in oneself, in epicureanism made possible a culture of feeling which was not possible under the stoic treatment of will. In stoicism the will was a blind transcendent force, in epicureanism sensibility was the transcendent force, and was itself a vision; but the use of the will was neglected.   The relation of the moral sense to the aesthetic sense is by no means constant, and for the argument maintained here need not have been found to be. Aesthetic races have been not ethical races but races with some special moral strength. A race like the italian would feel that that should not be thought of as duty which ought to be a pleasure, which it is fitting or beautiful to do; and with this temperament a man would never shut himself in to a mere duty ethic.

Do as you
would be
done by

recognition in the 'golden rule'[1] which is a call to simple reflection on a natural fact—the fact of feeling; it suggests that the real goal of my feeling is sympathy, feeling is to become feeling-with; we idealize our own sensation as sensation in others. No better axiom of social morality has yet been offered, yet it is clear that it is ethically incomplete; you may *not* owe to another in a given circumstance what you merit yourself, and you may owe him more; your standard of what you may want may be no sort of guide to what is demanded of your conduct to him.

Doubtless civilization demands that I should come to realize that what and how I feel others feel, and in that degree; if I doubt this let me ask myself if I do not recognize such civilization of spirit when another man decides to risk himself to save my loved one. But no civilization of sympathy can take the place of affectional feeling nor oust its discriminations. "Love your enemies, do good to those that despitefully use you." How, then, shall I treat my friends?[2] If sympathy were to become a flat-rate virtue its strength and its enthusiasm would be sapped.

Organic life is a unity. What behaviour of organic beings as such might set us on the path of natural moral conduct? An answer will be found in mother-behaviour which is the most naturally moral of all organic activities and a clue to the nature of ethic. There is in the range of organic life no other propitious moral activity to set beside this wonder of nature the same quality in the same intensity operating in the insect, the mammalian, man.

Life affords 3 types of conduct—our conduct as units, our conduct as members of a group, and maternal conduct. The two first give rise to one of the chief problems of ethics.[3] The third gives rise to no problems, it solves its own. It is the supreme example of an inevitable and inalienable beneficent interaction of self and group, as of inner and outer; it is the most perfectly ethical activity of the world.

[1] See Individual and Species, p. 120.
[2] This was pointed out by Confucius, and again by John viscount Amberley in his *Analogies of Religious Belief* (1876).
[3] See Individual and Species.

BIOLOGICAL SOURCES OF ETHICS

In nearly all organic species, and invariably in the higher, two dissimilar forms coexist: they represent two aspects of the species, in the reproduction of which each has a separate function to perform, and this function is the sole Sexes determinant of the dissimilarity. Such a difference must necessarily be a prominent factor in the conduct we call moral, and in truth moral quality and function have both been determined by it; nevertheless as far as humanity is concerned these distinctions in moral function and quality have not played a normal part. It is only when the origin of sexes is understood that we can understand their difference of ethical quality and the psychological contribution to be expected of each.

In the beginning was the mother. Not in that beginning before there were cells of reproduction but in that beginning where there was no male. The first true procreation of species took place in a femel body. It was not the result of bisexual union, neither was it unisexual; it was not sexual at all, it was maternal. The matrix of all the higher forms of life, the mould which moulded and developed them, is the reproductive cell of a mother. Within herself some chemical-motor principle existed the essential function of which appears to have been to precipitate or at least to facilitate the development of the reproductive cell.[1] Such a chemical-motor cell is found attached interiorly to the mother-soma or cast forth from her body—several of such cells together, which are then carried about, on her back perhaps, for use at the breeding season; the spare ones serving in case of accidents, like the superabundance of pollen in plant life. Very gradually this pollen-cell comes to possess a separate existence as a lowly individual, hardly yet a member of the species.

[1] It may be truer to say: to facilitate that cell division which is precedent to development. Cf. p. 58 *n.*².

This primordial male is much smaller than the mother-individual and possesses few of her species characteristics, and at this stage it has no power of transmitting its individual qualities to the offspring: in fact it has no qualities separate from the femel, for it is a *rejectum* of her body. Even when in the course of organic development males are born from the mother in the same way as femel progeny they are still unable to transmit their qualities and their role is still confined to the chemical-motor function described. Not until the cast-off chemical-motor cell of primordial organisms is builded up—by slow evolutionary stages—into a perfect individual of the species resembling in all points the mother-individual does it become a parent in the sense of a transmitter of its own qualities to the zygote.   This zygote is the cell from which in all higher and in many of the lower organisms a new individual takes its rise, and it is formed from the femel ovum cell after its conjunction and fusion with the male cell. The zygote is therefore the result of bisexual reproduction: it is not clear what decides the sex of the resulting organism; but the competing qualities which seek for expression in every zygote are dominant and recessive towards each other, and sex appears to be a character like these, maleness being recessive, femelness dominant, so that maleness only occurs in the absence of femelness.

Partheno-genesis   This life history of the male is borne out by the phenomena of parthenogenesis. At the present day large numbers of plants and animals remain parthenogenetic, that is they produce their kind without a male, and are organic species consisting of none but femels, or rather mothers. In other species, however, this virgin mother puts forth a certain number of males; in this case there is occasional pollination,[1] and the usual result of such pollination is the production of femels, males being everywhere produced

[1] Here used to = stimulation; see footnotes, p. 58.

by parthenogenetic mothers with no pollination at all. We have then in some species perpetual parthenogenesis where no males exist; and in those species where a male exists the parthenogenetic mother retains the capacity to reproduce without it, as many as 14 unpollenized generations intervening between one pollination and another. In the ants bees and wasps though males are produced the species are each and all characterized by femel dimorphism: a femel, or worker-bee, prepares an egg cell larger than the rest which develops into a mother-bee whose sole office is to reproduce her kind: the femel worker-bee does not reproduce her kind, she spends her life in the work of the community, while the large mother-bee who in time conjugates with a drone or sex-bee replenishes the race. If there is abundance of food the worker-bee will produce males even while the 'queen' bee is in her full vigour, and in the same way if the queen-wasp be removed the workers become fertile and produce parthenogenetically, but only males. Von Siebold who carefully examined drone and worker eggs tells us that in no case did he find "seminal filaments" in the drone egg; the eggs deposited in drone cells are unpollenized eggs. The femel, then, represents the race, is the race; and nature clearly expends care and solicitude upon it as the more precious and complex structure which is never expended on the male.[1]

Bee, ant, and wasp

In the economy of nature the male came last: this is no sort of evidence of inferiority but it is complete evidence of function. Water, in fact, cannot rise higher than its

[1] When animals evolve protective colouring the femel "is a far more effective mimic" than the male; the explanation no doubt is "that it is much more important from the point of view of the species" that the femels should be able to warn off the birds "than that the male should do so, for the latter having once accomplished the fertilization of the eggs, is of no further value to the race". The gall-fly which has alternate parthenogenetic generations over a time cycle of at least two years, produces occasional generations of both sexes, but the greater part of these two years is occupied in perfecting a generation of femels.

57

source, and the male can never be anything but the junior partner in reproduction. This truth has been overlaid and mislaid by ignorance and passion, and hence terms were used and have clung to the birth processes which in no way described the facts. The contribution of the male was called 'seed'[1] and its work 'fertilization' or 'fecundation' or 'impregnation' of the femel, while breeders still speak of puppy or foal as bred "by" the male "out of" its mother. Nevertheless the male contribution is not comparable with seed but with pollen; its share is in its nature contributory—adjunctive and subsidiary—not primary and not creative. In reproduction the egg which is the germ of life is grown in a femel body: there is *no* new life till it is begun in a mother, and the word 'sire' for a racial fountain head, a source and originator of being, belongs essentially, despite its present male connotation, to her.[2] What nature shows is that the part reserved for the male is service of the femel: its action when it is a parasite or reject from a femel body is doubtless what we have called it, partly chemical and partly mechanical; but even where it has a completely separate existence as an individual to all appearance similar to the femel its life is restricted to sex service, the span of life being in some instances limited to one such act of serjeantry—the drone dies after serving the mother-bee.

Parasitism Parasitism is part of the male's life history, and is not confined to 'males' which subsist inside or attached to a larger femel body; it is clear that the male is always more

---

[1] *Semen, sperm, spermatozoon.* "We say that the ovum is *fertilized* by the spermatozoon . . . But . . . 'fertilization' is not a good word to employ . . . for the process is not a one-sided one . . . its very essence is the fusion of two cells". Marcus Hartog. The activation of the egg by the sperm was commonly designated as 'fertilization' or 'fecundation' by early embryologists "who had not the least notion of the real nature of the process". E. B. Wilson, *The Cell*, ch. v, p. 394 (1925).

[2] A more proper description of the life which starts in the womb would be the *stimulated ovum*, see *infra*, pp. 61, 61 *n*.[2], 63 *n*.[1].

dependent on the femel than the femel on the male.[1]
Moreover when the primordial state of dependent physical existence ceases the activity and freedom accompanying the new life stage have still nothing but a sexual
significance; he is free and active only that he may find
a femel.

For in origin the male is not a worker: throughout the $\quad$ The male
lepidoptera—which are among the most ancient of all $\quad$ worker
terrestrial organisms—the femel is a mother-of-all-work
and the male the sex-of-no-work. It is the femel bee who
gathers makes and stores the honey which the drone
feeds on; the femel spider who spins the web and catches
the flies; the femel gall-fly who gives her name to the
species; the femel ant who carries out all those wonderful
operations which make the ants' brain "the most marvellous bit of matter in nature".[2] $\qquad$ When, as happens
among highly developed animals, the status of the male $\quad$ The
is that of a full member of the species he appears before $\quad$ Seeker-sex
us with a marked psychological character, that of seeker-
sex. The primordial unconscious seeker moved by some
chemical necessity has become the conscious seeker
urged by a self-regarding desire; it is this urgent sex
demand which determines male character, and male
activity as such, throughout organic life. For this demand
comes first, and tends to make the male oblivious to the
strength and supremacy of the maternal demands and
functions: if he is male he is still seeker, and in the larger
number of species his only knowledge of parenthood is
from the same angle. The fundamental distinction between femel and male is that this seeks and that gives.
It follows that male tendency is to be self-regarding and
exigent, impatient, reckless, and destructive; these charac-

[1] As he owes his existence to her in a sense in which she does not owe
her existence to him.

[2] So insignificant is the life of the male in the history of these species
that every naturalist takes the femel as the sole representative of the
species for purposes of description.

ters being, nevertheless, completely modified in those few species where he shares all parental cares with the mother. It has been suggested that the proper character of the male *qua* male is protection of the femel; even naturalists write as if this were obvious. It may be confidently said, however, that no moral character has less evidence for it than this.[1] In the desire to recognize this quality in males sexual jealousy has been allowed to pass muster for protection of the femel; but acts done from jealousy are not due to any instinct for protection of the femel, they are purely self-regarding not other-regarding. There is, indeed, among many of the birds mutual defence of the young and of each other. But with the bulls and bucks of species like cattle, deer, seals, and the cocks of many gallinaceous species, aggressive sexual rivalry and combativeness is all we have to note while the mother often adopts means to protect her young from the male parent. In the higher mammalians—lions, tigers, horses, wolves, monkeys, dogs—it should always have been obvious to the observer that the femel is not only the nurturer but the natural protector of her young: in the non-gregarious of these species the male remains with the femel and they conduct life together—for instance, he drives the 'kill' towards her and she does the killing, and he does his share in defending the offspring. Among those wolves which are semigregarious living in couples during the breeding season and in routs when the young are able to travel, both parents remain with the young and the male helps to provide the larder. When (as among ovipari) there is no larder to fill and offspring are born able to pick up their own food the male as a rule does nothing for the mother or her progeny. There are no ferocious carnivores where the male only is pugnacious; the notion that it could be so is indeed an absurd one: it is supposed that the male will protect his mate or at least

Protection not a proprium of the male

[1] See Woman and Werman, history, p. 220.

his mate who is with young; but how are growing femels to get food, or the numberless femels who are not with young? Is it imagined the males return and lay their venison before the femels? That brothers 'support' sisters? The truth is that the femel of carnivores is at least as ferocious as the male, and frequently more so— she fends for herself and above all is a combatant for her young: how indeed could they be protected if the male hunter was their chief protector? As to the pseudo-ferocious species—certain of the herbivores—male pugnacity is here nothing but a sexual manifestation, and has no concern whatever with the protection of mother and young.

We do not know what necessity or what convenience of the mother-body caused it to thrust forth the dynamic male element; and whatever was the original function it performed this had never been strictly essential to reproduction.[1] Moreover in the evolution to the status of a complete member of the species maleness has in fact changed its central function which appears to be no longer that of a stimulus but the not less important one of contributing a second strain to the ovum.[2] In any case a principle of conjugation prevailed widely in nature though it was not sexual conjugation, and it is this principle which

---

[1] A. Dendy, *Outlines of Evolutionary Biology*, remarks of parthenogenetic cynips (gall flies) where the offspring are normally femels though males are occasionally produced, "It must be assumed that in these species the male is useless, the continuation of the species being effected by virgin females although males exist." The phenomena clearly prove, writes E. B. Wilson, *The Cell in Development and Heredity*, "that sexual reproduction . . . cannot be regarded as a fundamental necessity of continued life"; the fusion of the 2 (femel and male) cells, he points out, "is not in itself an act of reproduction" but must be regarded as at most an antecedent condition.

[2] The union of male and femel pronuclei in fact is not to be regarded as necessarily furnishing the stimulus to development: "this union, or amphimixis as Weismann terms it, has another significance and is most probably connected with the transmission of inherited characters from parent to offspring." Dendy, p. 146.

is always represented in dioecious species with the same immense advantage to organic life.[1] It is therefore interesting to realize the evidence for the femel being femelmale in constitution, the male being male-male. The point was made by Bateson as regards certain forms of life.[2] It is of course corroborated by that peculiarity of parthenogetic reproduction described on pp. 56–7. Femels more often change into males than males into femels, and the results of castration in either sex give apparently more pronounced maleness in the femel than femelness in the male. The evidence shows a male latency in the femel which is far more generally operative than the reverse

Anabolic
and
Katabolic

case.[3] It has been said of the ovum that it is the result of a relative preponderance of constructive or anabolic processes, the pollen-cell, on the contrary, being the result of a relative preponderance of disruptive or katabolic processes.[4] And although it has been seen that we are not

---

[1] This is the principle of restimulation called rejuvenescence by some biologists. In the simplest forms of life 2 similar somata, which multiply by simple transverse fission until exhaustion sets in, meet and cling together by the orifice surfaces, and then separate entirely, having undergone "some kind of rejuvenescence whereby their vigour and power of multiplication are completely restored". (Dendy, pp. 39, 91.) What has taken place is an exchange of chromatin material between the conjugants, and there is nothing either gametic or sexual in the phenomenon. Conjugation itself, therefore, is primordially not only asexual, it is conjugation between 2 proto-mothers. Rejuvenescence, then, depends on exchanges of chromatin not upon male gametic action—in its essential nature, that is, it is not a sexual phenomenon though sex agency may come and has come to be used as its channel.

[2] W. Bateson, *Mendel's Principles of Heredity*.

[3] Sex itself is determined by one parent only—the femel. All the chromosomes contributed by either sex are of identical constitution *except* the extra chromosome which determines femelness.

[4] The anabolic is sustained continuous force: the life energy is anabolic; the enhancing energy katabolic. The one is a building up force which delays and sustains, the other precipitates movement and is not sustained, not persistent, but discontinuous. The one is intended for stability and continuity, the other for mobile and spasmodic effort. If there were no anabolic force nothing would maintain itself. Again, the one force accretes, conserves and integrates, the other dissipates disperses and parts with

62

warranted in concluding that this antithetical force (the katabolic) was at any time essential to the reproductive process,[1] we may still find in katabolic agency the male contribution to the life of his species. The male may be considered then as an enhancer of life activities: what he represents is strictly an exuberance of activities,[2] which among the higher animals may be said to consist in the variety and complexity introduced by two strains in the production of each individual. Whether enhancement of life is the role which should be expected of him in nature can best be gauged by regarding other animals than man. And frankly it requires some faith to maintain it. For even in some of the other animals excess of sexual combativeness and jealousy, though it uses up a large amount of surplus energy, obviously does nothing to enhance the happiness or activities of organic and maternal life. Nevertheless it seems to me that there are species in which such a power does exist. We have to judge chiefly by domesticated species, but the courtship of dogs, the chance meeting of dogs of both sexes, and to a certain extent their daily companionship—and the same may hold of such animals as horses and certainly of many birds —are examples of accessory happiness, of an increase of animal happiness and of femel happiness. So that we may perhaps conclude that to heighten and enhance life would be the normal contribution of males and would normally happen whenever excessive sexualism had not distorted the seeker-individual's life relation to the mother-individual and the race. The life history of the male it is clear

Male as enhancer

force. And in the last place the anabolic is that which is served by extraneous forces, the katabolic force is never served, it serves.

[1] The chief element in which process is held to be the reduction of the nuclear cell or cell-segmentation, which would appear to depend on some kind of katabolic action, yet cell-segmentation occurs in matured ova which have not received the so-called 'spermatazoon'. This has been proved in artificial parthenogenesis.

[2] She *ubertas*, he *exuberantia*. (Cf. footnote, p. 62, Rejuvenescence).

marks an evolution from what is at first nothing but a sex life to that of a transmitter of his individual qualities, when his personality becomes of prime importance for the same reasons that the mother's is important. But it is only in a given development of his life that the male can be regarded as an enhancer of race happiness: it cannot be supposed that this is the contribution of the drone who if he does not die when he has served the mother-bee is stung to death by the femel workers, or of the tiny male whom the spider (she who spins the web) eats after conjugation;[1] and it is equally clear that the males of mammals —such as the bull and stallion under domestication or the stags of wild deer—forfeit this character in their turn through excessive sexuality: they serve no purpose in the daily life of the species, their use is only that of breeding tools.[2]

As secondary nourisher

The contribution of the male must be governed by the fact that the entire business of procreation and nurture is performed by the mother, who supplies the material, starts the living zygote, builds up the new life, and nourishes it in her womb and after its birth. It is inevitable that the member of the species which does not inherit these mother occupations should come in some sort to share them and the most obvious way of doing so is when the male becomes a secondary race nourisher. For male evolution had this outcome: it freed the mother from the necessity of doing everything for the life and welfare of her species herself; it brought into operation a second adult individual able to share in the creation and maintenance of the life conditions—shelter, feeding, the simple occupations and arts. This is the only possible

[1] In the life history of hymenoptera, for example, it is the femel evidently who is the enhancer of life activities: the worker-bee is a true femel; the mother-bee does nothing but multiply for among hymenoptera all this is put upon one femel and her role is to replenish the colony; but the male exists in order to perform one act once, which is not even essential.

[2] Under individualization and over sexualization both prevent the role of life enhancer.

division of labour; for bisexual generation which involves a separation of functions is not in any sense a division of labour, though it has been inaptly so called.

That marked psychical polarity of the male which we have seen is involved in being the seeker-sex is indefinitely modifiable, as is shown by the number of instances where he enters into natural mate relations and parental relations, where he is no longer a mere male but the helpmeet and comrade of the mother, sometimes throughout life, sometimes only during the breeding season. The columbines and passerines build the nest together, hatch the young together, turn and turn about, and together feed them. Some little males help to build but do not help in incubating, or they help in the feeding or, like the male parrot, share attendance on the newly hatched young when they issue from the egg. The partridge accompanies the newborn chicks, teaches them, and is "as skilful as the mother" in protecting them when attacked; and the care and love of those little parents who do everything that the mother does except bear the young, with a zeal and patience almost—sometimes entirely—as unwearied as hers is one of the most admirable phenomena of animal life.[1] *Parental love*

There is a second important type of male conduct which, unlike parental love, is sexual in origin. Throughout selfconscious life the tendency of the male is to court the femel when he desires to conjugate. This little act of self-interested self-forgetting has a clear influence on the character of the species: we may see it in the dog whose courting is as attractive as the lechery of a male cat is unattractive. On each occasion—whether dogs are living in pairs or otherwise—the male woos and tries to attract the femel, and the femel who in this species and others has a conjugating season when she is ready to receive a *wooing*

---

[1] The maternal instincts are acquired in these cases just as the mother's are (cf. *infra*, p. 70).

male, protracts the episode, both enjoying this approach to each other, till she decides it is the moment to come together. There are a few curs even among dogs but the rule is to act as described. When, however, male animals are kept under domestication for breeding purposes— stallion horses, the bulls of cattle, the male goat—there is no courtship, and there is none in the polygamous species where the male kills or ousts his rivals. The femel is very conscious of the desire the male has towards her: the rabbit buck courts the doe, but she will not be ready for him, will not let him come to her at once, shuts herself away. He may stamp his little feet but the doe is not impressed; though she has no 'season' she either wants or does not want the buck, and his restless impatience leaves her quite placid. The sex urge is strong and it is callous; and for this alone the femel would be superior, since the maternal modifies physical desire, but nothing modifies it in the male. The cockerel comes out, lusting and destructive; he will even seize a duck. He knows nothing but his own wants, and as these are paramount with him he imagines them paramount in the universe.

Natural ignorance of the male Nevertheless there are always things which the little femel keeps, like Mary, in her heart, things which she knows that he does not know, other factors of their common life which she feels and he does not feel. The arbitrariness and aggressiveness often found in a male animal depend entirely on this ignorance of any motive for action, any meaning to action, but its own. It feels a strong lust incentive and treats the femel accordingly. She on her side defends herself from this overwhelming desire—by escape, by ruses, and subterfuge—that she and her young may have their chance. No one has paid any attention to these facts which must nevertheless be among the most important in the life of higher organisms. The self-importance of the male to be found for example among herbivores and gallinaceae arises from no other cause than this inherent male ignorance of the significance and importance of the femel—from the fact that he knows nothing beyond his own doings and is conscious of no needs but his own. This phenomenon is countered by the psychical phenomenon of wooing, and indeed in no other way than by counter-balancing psychical qualities in the male can such facts be met. To woo, to wait, to attend her convenience, to attract, and to please—what other amenity can there be between lust on the one hand and maternity on the other?

Where the femel has a conjugating season and there is a close time for the sexes there is the happiest solution. It is clear that in species like the polygamous herbivores and oviparians which do not woo and do not share the maternal cares the male is usually farouche, lustful and stupid; and one measure of happiness in organic life is no doubt the amount of comradeship existing between the two types in dioecious species—the mother and male. Animal happiness is greatest where the male is a comfort and resource to the femel, where there is understanding between them; and on the whole this is rare in nature. In too many species part of her anxiety is to keep the male from destroying her young and plaguing herself. When Secondary we consider the life activity of motherhood, the inevitably sex characters lesser sexuality of femels and their many self-protective instincts, we may ask ourselves how nature secures the acceptance of the male by an animal which is free to run away, even where oestrum provides an incentive; for even in these cases it is too often obvious that the femel is the less eager. How then is the male to induce the less eager partner and the one who so often exercises a choice to meet his advances, unless he can do something to make himself attractive? The phenomenon of secondary sexual characters is one of the means. No one can watch the display of the peacock or the antics of male monkeys who have a special sexual colouring without realizing that

67

colours and fine feathers are used by the male to attract
the femel in addition to the olfactory incitement which
doubtless exists universally on both sides. Whatever the
origin of secondary sexual characters[1] in the male he
deploys them to attract the femel, and she does nothing
of the kind. Nature—or sex nature—has evidently
striven if not to provide at least to employ accessory
attractions; and in order to overcome the relative indifference of the mother-sex the mate-sex not only courts
but exhibits the gay feathers, bright colours, and ornaments, which are only developed at the breeding season.

Femel
choice Darwin pointed out that "any female will do for the male",
and many males wage battles for access to a femel; but
when the fight is over the femel who has been sitting on
a bank dispassionately watching it will take possession of
the male who pleases her most and run off with him,
leaving the victor to his dudgeon. This principle of
selection in the femel is a marked and fecund organic
factor. It appears to belong to maternal character and is
akin to the mysterious sympathies and antipathies which
I have noted elsewhere.

The femel must therefore be regarded as leading, not
only by her choices but because of the pre-eminence of
her function. The male is prominent through the strength
of his lust and its very obnoxiousness to choice and insight.
Looked at from another planet such a phrase as "a bull
and his herd of cows" would be ludicrous—the bull's
portion would be seen to be sexual service to cows. It
is as obvious in the largest and most developed creatures
as it is when the simplest male cell comes to meet the
femel ovum. Sex service then it is, with a certain dash or
gallantry or impetuous adventure to propel it, but with
a very definite dependence typified by the helplessness of

---

[1] "Exuberance" in the unemployed male or "sexual selection" by the
femel? When formed, however, by sex exuberance they are used as a
sex adjunct.

the male cell to do more than find the femel cell. She does all the rest, her soma deals with it as it pleases, nothing the male can do can alter it, no responsibility whatever is attached by nature to his act. And this absence of responsibility should be correlated with the fact that psychical character is not as stable a factor in the male as in the mother. Sometimes, as we see, he tends the young, but this is not a principle of male life, its principle is the attainment of his own gratification, and resistance to whatever obstructs it.

<small>Contingent character of male</small>

PART II. THE MATERNAL

Every want a gift. GOETHE, *Die Natur.*

Termine fisso d'eterno consiglio,
Tu se' colei che l'umana natura nobilitasti. DANTE, *Paradiso.*

IF we consider all higher organic evolution we perceive it has been the response to changes in a femel womb. Its course can only be described in terms of changes in the mother—who may be oviparous (putting forth an egg to be matured outside her body),[1] marsupial (where the partly matured embryo passes into a living pouch and is there fed from the mother till it reaches its development), or a placental mammalian where a further evolution of the maternal process permits of the embyro being completely matured within her body, and the mother having put forth a living miniature of herself nourishes it with the mammary secretions we call milk. This femel reproductive process is the most fundamental in nature; and it is always and everywhere the same—the growth of an egg within the body of a living being and the subsequent putting forth of an affiliate which is potentially or

<small>The biological highway</small>

<small>Organic evolution is the unfolding of changes in a mother</small>

[1] The *monotremes*, now almost extinct, which lay eggs but suckle the young when hatched out, are a survival of the change into mammals undergone by some reptiles.

actually a reproduction of the maternal creature.[1] Pre-uterine forms of life exist, but we know of no power to evolve the higher organic forms other than that of the matrix.

Maternity   But there is a psychological process which accompanies this physiological one. The psychological force of the femel is in an instinctive power to defer what is self-regarding to what is other-regarding: it is not a force that attaches to mere gestation but it belongs to those ulterior acts which constitute maternity properly so called. If there had not been maternal reproduction, if the mode by which species is multiplied had been that of fission of viviparous units, or that of fish spawning sperms in the sea which are afterwards drenched with male fluid but have no further contact with the parent, or that of the frog which puts forth a proto-frog that hatches out in its turn and changes from a marine to a land animal all without any aid from a parent, the course of psychical life on this planet would have been profoundly modified. The worm, the fish, the frog, are, like the dragons of the prime before the earth had cooled, neither mothers nor young, they are parent and product.   In the last section we wanted to discover whether there is some reason in nature for morality, whether we get a moral motive for conduct inherent in things as they are, not merely relative to some outside sanction, and to a law outside things as they are. We found such a moral motive in feeling and its correlative the sympathetic faculty. And it is this which leads us on to recognize that there is a moral heart of nature, a natural seat of the sympathetic emotions, which is the mother heart. Man is a self-seeker, greedy, envious, lusting, predatory, violent, a prey to passions, anti-social in desires and fears; what root is there in his nature that can be set against these greeds. What other law is set

[1] The gestation of male forms which are highly dissimilar to the maternal form is not therefore strictly a reproductive process.

in his heart, some *foyer* of the moral instincts, a permanent centre and vestal flame of those things which the race recognizes as in their nature ethical things? Is there in nature a natural moral law and a type of ethical conduct— something surer than the gregarious instinct, deeper than self-interest, and where the mould and matrix of ethics may be seen at work. There *is* a hearth and home of ethics and it is found in motherhood. There is no other source and well-head of these things—if we except natural sympathy and other human felicities which are rarer and cannot cover as much ground—but the maternal source, maternity. With the mother comes all the moral panoply of nature. And our moral nature is incarnate in her.

Inextricably the ethical roots of our life are bound up with the maternal roots of life—the deep root of altro- centricism compared with the biological egocentricism of species; disinterestedness in contrast with biological self- interest; that hidden root of all fine conduct (latent in motherhood) action for its own sake looking for nothing again. There are the two physiological life instincts, hunger and sex; but morality enters with that mother hunger which is a gift rather than a want, a manna not an appetite. For the mothers' hunger is what feeds hunger. It has been observed that hunger in the male is a stronger appetite even than the sexual appetite; but in the femel the maternal instinct is stronger than hunger itself. The immense and singular strength of maternity then in contrast with sexuality is that it is *not* an appetite: what she seeks is the good of her young—he, his pleasure, she the pleasure of the child. Everywhere what the mother does is to subordinate interest to sympathy.[1] The beast that is most ferocious, the one that is most lustful, turns

---

[1] It is evident that the male has less sympathy than the other sex, but it is not evident that this need have been so: for male sympathy might have clung to the relation to the femel.

with self-sacrificing yearning to her young.[1] With the mother you get the sympathetic highly developed and with the sex the appetitive. Nothing can undo that original biological preoccupation of the mother with the not-self and of the male with self. Self-preservation is a third life instinct but in the mother it also is transmuted into a passion to protect her young. The root fact of life cannot be a struggle for subsistence bringing perforce in its train the personal selfish and competitive elements as the decisive factor, for the root fact is the fact of motherhood. So strong is maternal altruism anywhere in nature that the hen will allow chicks—any chicks of course—to take all her food and will not touch the best of food if they cannot get at it; a sick animal lying in great distress will stretch herself out if her kids come near so that they may get her milk. The kind of struggle for subsistence and existence contemplated by our naturalists is exactly reversed in activities which are operating every moment we live.[2] The maternal instinct is also stronger than the

---

[1] Edwin Arnold describes the dying mother tiger which Buddha saw during a severe indian drought:

> "Hunger in her orbs
> Glared with green flame; her dry tongue lolled a span
> Beyond the gasping jaws and shrivelled jowl;
> Her painted hide hung wrinkled on her ribs
> . . . . and at the poor lean dugs
> Two cubs, whining with famine, tugged and sucked
>
> While she, their gaunt dam, licked full motherly
> The clamorous twins, yielding her flank to them
> With moaning throat, and love stronger than want,
> Softening the first of that wild cry wherewith
> She laid her famished muzzle to the sand
> And roared a savage thunder-peal of woe."
>
> Light of Asia, pp. 134–5.

And the point here is not that the male is incapable of such heroic love, but that love like this is shown by the femels of every species; that this love anguish is not the portion of male animals.

[2] Here as elsewhere we owe the mistake to the prevalent maleness of our outlook. Darwin saw conflict everywhere and never counterbalanced it with maternal sympathy. (Cf. infra, pp. 75–6.)

filial; the young animal will quit her side willingly, but the mother's anxiety never ceases, her thought for the little life is always first. Love itself, as we are to see,[1] is founded in the maternal.

These ethical characters are derived indeed from the phenomena of gestation and lactation but they form a femel psychological personality whose first care is life, which is independent of physical motherhood.[2] The protection of helpless life, as such, is the characteristic femel quality; while the male is characterized by a desire to destroy what stands in its way. And what stands in the male's way is what obstructs personal gratification. The femel, too, resists what stands in the way; but what stands in her way is what obstructs her in the protection of helpless life. We need only compare the gesta of mother life throughout nature with the gesta of male life to see that there is a fundamental distinction between the psychological experience of the mother along endless aeons of time— and that of the male. Down through the history of organic life since warm-blooded animals made their appearance mothers have lived and died with one main psychical interest; out in vast spaces where man's foot never trod, by pools in great silences where each animal brings her young, mother-animals, small and great, tend teach and

---

[1] What is Love, p. 155.

[2] For instance, the dog who has not been a mother will show the same motherly protective care to puppies or even kittens. Throughout nature this quality is lavished on young not their own. A cow has adopted lambs, another piglets (which was discovered when the cow failed to give the usual yield of milk); a hare and a hen have each reared kittens; a cat in Wales constituted herself foster-mother to incubated chicken which she had defended with ferocity; another cat reared fox cubs with her own young; a duck brooded an otter kit; and young otters were guarded by a femel lion. When a puppy had been killed in mistake a lion carried back the other to her den, nursing it with the same care as her own. A gazelle hound which had killed a mother gazelle in the chase had her motherly pity touched by the bleating of the young gazelles and brought them up with her own puppies. A picture was taken of her with her charges. This hound continued to hunt gazelles. (Cf. pp. 295–6.)

discipline them. Observe a hen's inducements to a sick chick to come under her and be warmed—her entire self-forgetting thoughtfulness and anxiety; or hear her comforting cluck each time it peeps with pain. We have only to look at a sheep with her lamb, her newborn or sick or dead lamb, and contrast this with any experience in the life of the male mammal, to seize at once the significance of this psychological record of the femel, the imprint it has left upon life. The psychosis which results may be discerned in a greater benignity of expression and *allure* in the femel of all species, as remarkable in a pack of hunting hounds as in the responsible protective and benign expression of a mare with her foal.   We see that the femel of most species is far more of a person than the male and more useful than he—bee, ewe, goat, cow, sow, doe, hen, or duck: people see this, and nothing but the dominance of maleness in human life could make them assume that there is really something in bull and ram boar and buck and in the human male to warrant a natural pre-eminence unobvious in nature. With life comes the mother—nothing in life history is comparable with this fact. With life come the life needs and behaviour, with life comes in time consciousness, individuality, and also the sex consciousness: but deeper than all these and before them and accompanying them there is always the maternal and it is the psychological equivalent of the maternal which explains life best. Life imports the mother in the physical order bringing with her the maternal in the psychical order. The mother lies nearest to life and her psychosis nearest to its needs and necessities.

Not that all femels share what I have called the mother heart which is the heart of nature. That is as untrue as it is unnecessary. What is true is that the individual, as an individual, is always self-regarding and it is the mother alone who introduces an altruistic principle; so that if all species were nothing but self-regarding the mother individual would have introduced what is not so. The truth at the heart of organic nature is that maternity is sympathy and sex is appetite. Nothing can alter the fundamental fact that the sex urge is the strongest thing in male nature and the maternal urge in femel nature. Not that there is nothing appetitive in the maternal; the appetitive is a root process of life, a root necessity of growth and development; we have it in the fundamental facts of nutrition and the mother desires the child to come to her breasts, the babe satisfies a hunger. But in sex the appetite is all and sympathy nothing. In the femel though the nurturing of her young be a natural desire it is also a sympathy. It is evident that even the law "Do unto others as you would they should do to you" is given a more perfect form in the maternal instinct, for there it is the pure impulse to do for the helpless and weak what they have need of, without consideration of consequences to self and untaught by personal exigencies. That we possess the altruistic sentiments—those extra-regarding sentiments which do not imply "enlightened self-interest"—is due chiefly to the maternal form of love: for enlightened self-interest is not given in the maternal instinct at all. The mother *must* feel sympathy; she is the only being in whom this is essential. Hence with the femel the primary motion is ethical, with the male it is non-ethical, and both are spontaneous.

About the first century of our era Epictetus made a diatribe as follows: "Be not deceived, universally nothing is so dear to any creature as his own interest. Anything which seems to hinder this, be it father or child or friend or lover, he will hate and abuse and curse. For nature never made anything so that it loves aught but its own profit; this is father and brother and kin and country and god."[1] But it is not the mother. Is nothing dear to a mother but her own interest, and when nature made the

[1] Epictetus, Bk. iii. ch. 7.

mother was not something made which loved and gave itself without thought of personal profit? During the war in the xx[th] century these words were written by a fine and discerning french writer: "L'être, dans sa chair, souffre toujours solitairement, et c'est aussi pourquoi la guerre est possible."[1] This enlightening and terrific truth is also that part of truth which I think I see the male is generally and everywhere restricted to seeing. For it is not true that because the child suffers alone in its flesh the mother is callous of the sources of pain. Is it not the truth that the maternal introduces the principle which is the exact contrary of this? In *Biology of War* G. F. Nicolai affirms that almost the sole business of animals "is feeding"; "even beasts of prey spend their days in hunting, eating, and sleeping" and when "the time which animals require for the business of love-making and for a certain amount of attention to physical cleanliness" is allowed for "there is hardly any spare time left". The business of motherhood is ignored.[2] "Outside the cares of maternity (in which it almost always shows itself admirable) the insect . . . thinks and cares for nothing but itself." When Fabre penned this sentence he had gathered his knowledge from the femel's life; and it is apparent at once that with the change of venue there is a change in the moral appreciation.[3]

It is in motherhood also that the essential root of
Sociability sociability may be discovered. We saw in the last section how far the gregarious instinct can be regarded as a moral root or otherwise,[4] but we get the principle of

---

[1] Georges Duhamel, *Vie des Martyrs*, 1914–16.

[2] Elsewhere, Nicolai has not ignored it. *Biology of War*, § 91, 92.

[3] Freud makes sex the basic impulse. This again is an essential male judgment.

[4] See Theories of Ethics, pp. 49–50. This sociability is evident in the adult life of femels when it is absent in the adult male. Even among the sociable insects the unselfish toil for the community is done by the femel only.

sociability indelibly imprinted in the mother's consciousness of other-life—the life of her young ones—the
insistent consciousness of it. And it seems to me incon-
testable that the essential root of sympathy (which we The root
must regard as the first of all moral teachers) is placed of social
sympathy
here too. For the mother's instinct as we have seen is
not moved simply by her own young, it is moved by the
phenomenon of helpless life everywhere.   The most
important factor of ethical life is moral responsibility and Responsi-
this is represented biologically in the femel alone; it can bility
never be represented in the male. It is the weakness of
the male (in our own and in most species) that nature does
not allow him to follow up the consequences of his act;
this has to be achieved by extrinsic means. *She* is naturally responsible, he can only be made so, and the moraliza-
tion of the male has to wait until he is made, or he makes
himself, so.[1] The maternal again is a source of the moral
because it alone incarnates force as an instrument of
defence of the helpless. Not the most timorous or the Combative-
weakest mother will fail to protect its young with or ness
without weapons. In her, combativeness is exhibited as
a spiritual force.[2] There is in the femel indeed a union of
authority and service, for that is the method of mother
agency: she represents—in contradistinction to the selfish
tyrannies of the world—deprecable power. For she is the
resultant of a harmony, the union in one person of self-
integration and relation: the male seeks something beyond
what he finds in himself, and hence conflict and dualism.[3]
Finally there is in the femel a notable principle of moral
growth—the intuition of reality, a biological character A touch-
comprising vision and immediateness. The perfunctory stone of
reality
does not satisfy a mother; it cannot do so: and so with the
human mother no sound of words and no pretences do
duty for things and facts.

[1] See p. 271.   [2] Cf. Force, p. 360.
[3] Cf. Individual and Species.

In the maternal therefore we have a workshop of the moral, and the psychological contribution of women is primal in importance for the conduct of life: it is this which has been persistently obscured during the thousands of years that man has had a history. The road trodden by the mother through all ages was nevertheless the ethical way, it gave the key of the arch, the clue we are seeking. What lies before humanity is to get back to this psychical path and retread with nature the maternal highway of life.

The ethical highway

There is then an organic origin and foundation for ethical conduct. Now we are to see how ethical conduct is related to nature, to law, and to religion.

NATURE AND THE NATURAL

Qu'est-ce que la nature? peut-être une première coutume, comme la coutume est une seconde nature.   PASCAL

Naturam sequere (STOIC MAXIM)

WHAT is man's relation to nature; does his moral life require him to follow in nature's footsteps, or to strike out a path of his own?

What is nature?

But what is nature? for it is evident that we use the word in two senses. In one sense everything is natural, it is so, that is, because it is its nature to be so. In the other sense some ways of nature are regarded as 'natural' while others, which are unlike these, are regarded as 'unnatural'. Nature then may embrace all that is, or only what generally and normally is.   Obviously we are not to follow nature in its universal aspect: but neither should it be implicitly followed because it presents the characters of normality. It is because nature has been envisaged as an immutable static fact, fenced about and fencing us about with rigid canons—those 'laws of nature' by which all its ends are held to have been accomplished—that the normal has appeared to our eyes to be the truest

78

representative of the 'natural'; all that is normal being natural and right and what is not normal being 'unnatural' and wrong. But nature is no static immutable fact, it is a fact of flux; its dynamic force is more than its static, it can only be described by its dynamic changes, and it does not register laws but habits. 'Nature' is the result of the way in which things have been done, not of the way in which things must be done.   If we consider such a fact as the long evolution of conduct-habits and of appetites it becomes evident that time may produce a normal which has ceased to be natural when compared with the primitive norm. Use and misuse disfigure the original design. So that 'nature' comports for every individual both that which he cannot help and that which has been constantly modified by his and others' use and abuse. But true laws of nature—where they exist—are laws of necessity, 'if you can't you won't' is as far as they take us. It is not, then, easy—as the moralists affirmed it to be—to set limits to nature. Far from always doing things in one way nature accomplishes the same thing in a great variety of ways; and recent knowledge has brought no new truth more momentous than this—the infinite diversity of nature, the instability of its processes, the fact that there is not a single process or function in the organic world which has not been, and is not, subjected to trial and chance, flux and change; that nature's habits are infinitely varied. If species remain true to their habits the individuals (who form the species) do not; and the higher the species the less the adherence to type of the individuals within it. It was a great celtic saying that "there is a separate wisdom for everything that lives". The individual is constantly departing from the orbit of habits of the species both physical and psychical; discrepancies and the amount of actual idiosynkrasy varying directly with the complexity of the organism. Physical development is itself due to this tendency to vary; and the same is true of psychical development: so that we must look to the abnormal at least as much as to nature in its other moods for our progress. As examples, the direction of progress in male sexual control has come to be a direction along the abnormal; and if the abnormal is unnatural then nothing is so unnatural as genius.

Man's relation to it

The question how far we are to live according to nature is not susceptible of an exact answer since nature itself as we see is the result of the habits it has formed, is itself a seeker after the right way. Nature nevertheless must always remain an ultimate reference. There exists, as we saw in the previous section, a process of nature which is correlated with imperatives of conduct, and ends of nature correlated like this one with an emotion of the ideal are a natural guide to moral conduct. But nature draws us with other cords also. For a proper direction of conduct with the humblest and the highest organisms is to be found in action according to their own nature, which brings with it, *ipso facto*, satisfaction and finality. How is such a dictum to be reconciled with the existence of weak and vicious natures? We may set weakness on one side, for it is but a negation of qualities. Viciousness also is a negative—it is a negation of those emotions of the ideal upon which fine conduct is wholly dependent. According to the sokratic school all evil is a negation, the child of ignorance. But the truth is not this; the truth lies in saying that evil is the negation—the positive negation—of that ideal emotion which makes life lived according to our nature right life.[1]   Our moral life is to be regarded as guided by two criteria not one—by nature and

[1] It seems to me that (wilful) action can obviously be such as to integrate the personality or such as to be disintegrating to personality. Many a vicious propensity though it may be an output of character is not in any sense a reintegrating output; one man makes or preserves what is beautiful, another tries to destroy, to besmirch, to make around him what is ugly and gross. It is not true psychologically that this act is as whole or integrating as that.

by intelligence: man's exemplar is to be sought not only in the best that humanity has offered us but also in an exemplar far more universal. When man looks outside himself he sees that nature's services to organic life are greatly in excess of its disservices, and that it yields more food than thistles; but all over the globe and through all the ages and races of men the benefits which man confers on man are greatly in defect of his disservices, a consequence of that universal greed which serves his own interest and passion at others' expense. Nature may bring the earthquake but man brings war, and his viciousness and stupidity have disturbed the tenour of nature to a much greater extent than his goodness. But nature is wanton only because it is unconscious. And man looking upon nature may determine with himself that living things shall not be harmed by his passage, that he will give not take, serve not exploit.

It was said by Burke that what nature has disjoined in one way wisdom may unite in another; and the converse is true. For nature does not discern, it feels, it does not devise, it gropes; and man's part will always be to inquire rather than blindly to follow—*naturam requirere* rather than *naturam sequere*. If man could not select he would never have achieved a relation like that of sister and brother which reverses the natural and is purely a growth of the mental life in man, in whom what is physically unnatural may become psychologically natural. And it is equally necessary that he should intelligize the data of nature. For nothing is moral only because it is natural. It is no more an ethical process to procreate than to excrete; and the sympathy and altruism of motherhood are moral for a reason which is not their naturalness. The moral then is always the spiritual, its reference is to an ideal end.

When human cerebration began to act it was able to interfere with nature because nature does *not* present a Cerebration and nature

81   G

body of inexorable laws, but only some immutable necessities and a vast collection of more or less fluid habits. But though the term nature is often employed to mean that which exists apart from human intelligence cerebration is as much a natural phenomenon in man as in other animals; and everywhere it is the potential phenomenon of the dynamic and idiosynkratic. Man's reason, when it comes to assert itself, is as much a natural element as the sun which fertilizes the earth, but with far more power than any other natural factor of interfering with nature's processes. Man may devise and carry out both in the mental and in the material world what may defeat the ends of nature and his own ends; he may compass and overpass physical *anangkē*, he may, that is, set his brains against nature, but he cannot insure the results. And as the operations of the brain are capable of transcending nature but are never capable of being their own guarantee man's intellectuality may prove a pitfall like all his imperfections of reason and sentiment: it is not, for example, a natural thing that the young should be reared in the society of intellectual parents, and we do not know whether it is expedient or inexpedient. Man has both followed and flouted nature, distorting it alike by his ignorance and by his knowledge. Nothing has been less a guide to him than nature, not even reason, and our judgments of natural things have never been due to the action of a civilized intelligence.[1]   Hence there has been no true commerce of nature and intelligence. We are heirs of the ancient notion that nature was the finished work of a power which represented destiny, or autokratic will, or perhaps a will all-wise and beneficent. But nature is a kosmic process, one of which it is always more true to say that it is becoming than that it is. Kosmic nature,

---

[1] We were once nature, wrote Schiller, and culture—our reason and our freedom—will bring us back to nature. *Über naive und sentimentalische Dichtung.*

again, is a habit, as organic life is a habit, taken up each day. All young animals enjoy the mere repetition of acts, the young child likes best the oft-repeated tale: for life is repetition, that is how we live it and how we learn it. And we learn from the idiosynkratic as freely as from the usual; even an artificial habit is learnt as easily as a 'natural' one, and as easily by my dog as by myself. There is a truth then that we have always neglected—that adaptation, the idiosynkratic, the ex-centric *is* nature, are its powers. On the other hand, normality of conduct and sentiment may mean nothing but the standard reached by the many, not the right standard, not the best. It may be only what most people are made like, capable of; so that when moral eunuchism is approved in the gospel it is the normal which is flouted, just that normal which possesses no element of progress, no distinction. It is implied indeed in our common notion of originality that the majority of men are copyists. Nature presents certain harmonies, certain felicities, certain detachments, and is the living water of originalities that quicken the soul. Again, it is the stagnant pool of habits which dull it. And so we learn that there is a hearkening to nature which is a way of life, and a serving of the normal which is the way of death.

We have been accustomed to oppose 'nature' and 'man', man's 'nature' and his reason, and even savage *False* nature and our own. But as philosophic distinctions the *oppositions* two first are worthless, and the third, which suggests that what is nearer to the savage is nearer to nature, is totally untrue. The savagery of man—accompanying his whole history—is a thing by itself, a phenomenon which we have not understood and which we have persistently mis-named.[1] Not even are religion and nature opposed. For there is a religion of nature. It cannot be gainsaid that there is a special peace in "living according to nature",

[1] *Infra*, p. 179.

bringing with it the confidence and *pietas* of that old roman religion which was a religion of nature; the happiness it brings being apart from any recognition of nature as the expression of a divine mind, or any vision of ends for myself beyond nature—which is surely a wholly separable and separate consideration. It is probable that the tranquillity born of this union with nature is not surpassed by any form of religious sentiment. Anxiousness, deprecation, fear, spiritual despair, all are absent. Such experiences as the mystic absorption of the soul in its object, the self-forgetting sacrifice of the lover of his kind, and the stranger contentment in the soul of the ascetic, have brought and will continue to bring rest to the souls of those rare types of men; but nature-piety can give the same rest to the soul as these. Nature is a mother and those who live in union with her are her children. But it may be said: religion to be a fine experience must ask great things, and it is not tranquillity which we reap when such a prayer is answered. But those great things are to be *our* gifts—they are gifts which both nature and god require. Both require us to resist our own nature where it clashes with the *pietas* which is their due and which brings their peace. And this is grace.

There is a final lesson which nature sets always in the sight of man, whose foolishness cupidity and false values have rendered him blind and deaf to it: when he listens to this lesson of nature he will have learnt something more of the nature of ethic. 'Civilization' has been marked by the progressive exploitations of man. In a few weeks he can destroy what it has cost nature aeons of time to perfect: he can interfere with seasonable production, disturb the relation of plant and insect life, and bring pest and baneful climatic changes as the result of his activities. And this wilfulness, this heedless lusting destruction of what men have not created and can never recreate is done

A lesson
of nature

for the greed of an hour; nothing is permitted to stand in the way of a momentary gain; man thinks he has the lordship of the globe, and thereupon he violates nature for his pettiest requirements. Nature's lesson is that man's social progress has been too much punctuated by truculence and greed, when what it should produce is a school of respect; and no very high degree of civilization is now possible until we have learnt to respect nature.

Man in his little moment of life disposes of untutored powers of destruction; and the problem before him is whether he is to be always in fact the archexploiter, or the great disciple. In the majesty of organic life—from plant to mammal—as in the august spectacle of the heavens about us, nature is our constant monitor of a certain simplicity, which is friendly to the lavishness that embraces all but resists the vulgarity of the egoism of man.

These then are the permanent links between morality and nature. What is the relation of morality and law? Is there a similar perennial link connecting the moral sentiment with the legal.

ETHICS AND LAW

"The Laws go but a little way." EDMUND BURKE

"*Mere* law is among the weakest of bonds."
ARTHUR, FIRST EARL OF BALFOUR

I THINK it is a common notion that civil law is not only associated with ethic but nearly identical with it. It is regarded, like a ten commandments, as binding the conscience, and men suppose that their moral reactions to the legal code should be direct and unhesitating: perhaps to most men the law appears to be not only a large part of morality but a tutor in determining its nature. The view to be taken here is that law and ethic have scarcely anything to do with one another. Laws were originally imposed to secure the rights of the strong not to protect

85

those of the weak, and every legal code bears witness to the fact that its goal was the organization of the rights of status and property not the organization of justice. So little has law had to do with equity that it has never been true that a good man will not disobey the law or that bad men are good men by obeying it. For its function is to uphold the letter; it has nothing to do with honour or invisible obligations, and no one could be moral who guided his conduct by what it allows or forbids. Nature acts by necessity and has sanctions which are absolute because they are necessary. But law is largely founded not upon necessity but upon force, and it has done continual violence to the natural; such artificialities of the Roman law as the *patria potestas*, for example, being only workable by invoking a *jus gentium*. So that when we turn from nature to jurisprudence—to *lex* and *jus*—we turn from what has natural necessity and natural freedom to an arbitrary absolute.

Since it is the character of law to act as a civil sanction the conception of law is political not ethical, and when the great jurists call upon us to admire its majesty it is as a school of ordered public life and of the self-discipline of the citizen. The reign of law, we are ready to agree, is what separates us from the savage; and had men not conceived the idea of law ruling community life (not as tribal custom and tabu but as a *corpus juris* with a political function and distinct from religion) civilization would scarcely have been realizable. Civil law therefore makes its appeal to moral forces and moral sanctions, for all men of good will are friends to public order and uphold the measure of justice and civic altruism which the laws require: but had bad laws not been broken public morality and decorum would have fared ill; and the notion of law in modern parliamentary times includes the notion of changes in the law as a matter of course.   The era of law was not only a prelude to civilization it ushered in the greatest of all contributions to the political life of man in substituting government by laws for government by a human will.

Now the natural moral code is founded in sympathy—of which even justice is a part—but law is a civic instrument which ignores sympathy and can never make any but a rough approach to justice. The direction of public life along lines of law rather than lines of sympathy may no doubt be debited to the obvious fact that masculine processes of thought have everywhere moulded civil life—processes which include 'red-tape', an artificial and befogging verbiage, and a distaste for the appeal to moral force. Women abide by principles, wers by law, they care about realities not about conventions. They could not have written the book of Leviticus, or been satisfied, like Pilate, by washing their hands, or been upset by the problem of the "egg laid on a festival". But law deals with conduct; and its history—as that of civil government—runs parallel with the history of ethics, and becomes a better history as morals become better.

ETHICS AND RELIGION

> Thou art the Way
> Hadst thou been nothing but the goal
> I can not say
> That thou hadst ever met my soul.
> ALICE MEYNELL

Deus rapit nos a nobis et ponit nos extra nos.
MARTIN LUTHER

VICTOR HUGO wrote a poem which he intitled 'Religions et Religion', and any consideration of religion must start with the paradox that nothing is so unlike it as religions. Religions depend upon certain dogmatic propositions some of which instead of illuminating the soul have dimmed its spirituality. And the origins of religions—

their origins in the soul of man—being what they are, the loss of spirituality has never been regarded as of the first moment. Fear and awe are the sentiments and emotions fundamental to this religious experience; the principal religious act has been placation of the powers which man stood in awe and dread of; and these emotions and sentiments still play not only an active but the most active part in religions today.   It is said that the 3 universal elements of religion are a belief in god free-will and the immortality of the soul. But it is evident that among the great religions of the world each of these has in turn been dispensed with. That these three particular elements are essential to the functioning of the moral sense is a commonplace of christianity which has taught that religion as history reveals it to us is and must be the chief factor in moralizing the life of man whom it provides not only with a canon of morals but with the sanction for its due observance. Can this intimate connexion of religions and ethic be established? The answer I think divides itself into 3 parts (1) no religion has succeeded in modifying the worst instincts of humanity. Even though this be true it would still be open to us to ask how much worse humanity would have been without it. (2) The sanctions of religion—fear of punishment and hope of reward—are not in themselves fitted to operate morally, to effect, that is, a moral disposition of the soul. Religion may therefore make a man do what is materially right without making him in any manner a moral being. (3) Religion does not make a bad man good. If this is true, then the objection that men would have been still worse without religion would seem to fall to the ground. In the christian religion Repentance the idea of repentance has always been set in the forefront; fear and the necessity of repentance being the two salient religious influences brought to bear upon the wrongdoer. For though love is the perfect religious sanction and though Francis de Sales could not admit that any other was tolerable, it is pointed out, unanswerably, that the gospel itself appeals to fear. Moreover it is evident that evil men must be less approachable by an appeal to the love of god than good men. It is apparently never doubted that repentance is the potent factor in experience which we are led to expect by this type of religion; but in spite of the conspicuous place it has thus taken as a religious and moral phenomenon the actual part it has played in the drama of life is a very small one. Men are good or men are bad, or partly good and partly bad. The good "need no repentance". The really bad do not repent.[1] Repentance then as the faculty by which we may insure salvation has never had the power which theology assigns to it. In the case of the partly good and partly bad—that is of the enormous majority of us— repentance is not a very decisive experience; let us hope then that hell is not the place prepared for so large a proportion of human actors. But we are in touch with the spiritual when we say that really bad men do not repent— for the better man does repent. His sins are not unto death, but his repentance is unto life. It is a conspicuous evil thing in otherwise upright characters when there is no power of turning round on yourself, of the moral self-criticism which is implied in repentance, which is a distinctively moral and spiritual faculty. Repentance then has a necessary part in our daily moral life, but has not the value for eternity which religions assume it to have. Let us see how this is: its guerdon is declared to be the divine forgiveness; human repentance and divine for- *and for-giveness*

[1] Barbarous history regales us with extravagant tales of remorse which upsets the character and alters the whole life. Remorse has often affected not the finest but the crudest and most violent specimens of humanity, and like conscience it answers as easily to a false notion of the morally wrong as to the true—it is the reaction to crimes of violence: but among such ill-doers as the malicious, traitors, libellers and malignant liars and those who injure others by sensuality or who (whether as millionaires or otherwise) wreck people's lives by their frauds, there is no remorse at all.

giveness are the obverse and reverse of moral theology, the great points of contact between the divine spirit and man's: but there is no moral parity between the gravest acts of wickedness and this far-off act of cancellation. The treachery betrayal or torture you perpetrate on some sensitive living thing, the life you have lied away, or the happiness and honour of a comrade—all of these, it is said, will be overlooked, if only you 'believe' and 'ask god' to forgive them. But how can such a cancelling of sins cancel their wickedness?[1] We are not offered the restoration of the man we have injured nor the prospect of a more moral world, but only the annulling of the wickedness which the individual works in it. I see in that no eternal values.

The sense of sin

This doctrine of repentance and forgiveness has depended upon the fact that in the non-philosophic religions the theological sense is the sense of sin, of conduct which offends god and imperils your own soul in its relations with god. It has been the opportunity of all priestcrafts. But the ease with which man's 'trespass' in the sight of an offended god could be arranged has always tended to destroy the urgency of the claims which men have upon us; and the emphasis on 'sin' appears everywhere to have encouraged a theological in place of a spiritual mentality, substituting for mere ethical claims a theological *corban* which satisfied the supreme matter of the fate of the soul but checked man's power of revising and developing his moral perceptions. In the philosophic religions the doctrine of sin is replaced by the doctrine that man must free himself from low desires and the trammels and craving of the senses: it is believed that a man can be made to perceive he has duties to his soul—apart from his interest

---

[1] It is remarkable that in Tibetan religion the forgiveness of sins is held to be immoral. And it was not part of original Zarathustranism—only a balance of good works over bad could cancel sin; the judgment of god on the soul could not be altered either by free grace or by sacrifice.

in it—and to the kosmos of which he forms a part. In the non-philosophic religions he must obey the commandments which represent the 'will' of a personal god, and the end is personal reward.

It may be said: What can a man do but repent? What other change in him can there be but to be sorry and remorseful for what he has done and cannot undo? But in the field covered by sins crimes and injuries, small and great, there is a large space for restitution and compensation; and it is an immense ethical weakness to have placed all the emphasis on the forgiveness of the wrong-doer leaving 'restitution' as only a pious ideal. It should be universally recognized that there is no repentance where a wrong which could have been righted is left unrighted.[1] And it is difficult to see what sort of virtue can be ascribed to the recidivist who comes again and again for the forgiveness of his sin. In comparison with the great wrongs which make the unrelieved suffering and ugliness of the world from age to age what importance can the 'forgiveness' of the evil man—as an episode *in foro interno*—possess? The first aspiration towards the morally beautiful is not concerned with the status of my own soul. And that a man should be better for his repentance is not value enough to set against the values he may have stolen.[2] The 'forgiveness' of sins then is a theological not an ethical feature of religions; and the examples of valid repentance for sins against our neighbour have been so few that the world would not have been perceptibly

What can the wrong-doer do?

[1] The case of slander is in point.

[2] The only forgiveness which perhaps might restore him in his own sight would be that of the man he had wronged.

Again, for a man to forgive those who have perpetrated outrageous things—if by forgiveness we mean a material act of reinstallment—is a violation of personality, and it is not evident why such violation should be necessary, or what is the compensating good which our forgiveness has on the evil man's side in comparison with what it wounds in ourselves. But if forgiveness be a merely mental act, formal forgiveness, I do not see what influence it has on anyone.

worse had no one ever repented.　　　But there are the sins which do not drag another with them? Here it is only by a change of mind, by the 'prickings of conscience', by a robust self-criticism, that we can begin to make ourselves better men; and only so that we spiritually live and grow. And here religions have no more to do with us than a score of other influences (within and without) of which example is foremost. Neither can it be considered that the help afforded by religions is due to their paramountcy as a social factor over against the selfish individualistic factors, for they have always made their appeal to the individual's anxiety for his own destiny, and have never represented the unself-regarding instincts as even a principal end of man. Never yet has there been a great religion where perfunctory and superstitious duties did not rank before the obligations of moral goodness.[1]

Three services rendered by religions

Historically and psychologically religions may perform one or other of 3 services to mankind. They may serve (a) as a moral police (b) as a support to the moral nature (c) as a spiritual experience of the soul. (a) The first service is bound up with the idea of religion as affording sanctions of reward and punishment. And it may be argued that as a really evil man will not respond to a holy sanction religion would have no message to the wicked without its police sanctions. We may leave it so. But religion as a police force can only rank as a department of political government, it has and can have no interest for ethics (or for spirituality) as such. The very existence of these sanctions indeed has always appeared to dispense those who exercise religious influence from trying to touch other and higher chords, chords of self-respect, sympathy, and the like. (b) Many things in a man's life are supports to his moral nature. And he may not distinguish between operating through religion and operat-

---

[1] The ideal of religion as a social force was perhaps most nearly approached by the classical religion of Rome.

ing because of it. Religion does not make noble characters
it finds them. Whether it be the egyptian trader greedy
for his rights to immortality or three or four thousand
years later a Sœur Rosalie avid for spiritual beauty with
no thought of rights all the evidence goes to show that
each man makes his own religion; and the saying that
every man is both better and worse than his creed sets
the limits to its power of influencing us for good or ill.[1]
It would be warmly denied by many classes of thinkers
that no religion has succeeded in weakening the worst
moral instincts, or made bad men good. Certain things
which come essentially into the religious purview, we
think, must be banished from the heart when religions
hold sway: nevertheless the practice of religions by be-
lievers has always been compatible not only with the
utmost wickedness of spirit but with the utmost grossness
and triviality also. We have, to take a small but trenchant
example, been called on to admire the influence of the
christian church on modesty and to deplore its absence
when that influence dwindles: but what modesty was
there in the ages of faith? When faith ruled and none
gainsaid discipline what coarseness was banished? It had
not been banished in the xii[th] century,[2] nor two hundred
years later in Chaucer's time; it was not less apparent in
the Venice of the cinquecento than in the England of the
xviii[th] century. And which century between the iv[th] and
the xiv[th] would the church select as the model of an age of
faith?   Religions, then, do not imply religiousness,
for like tabu and custom they are national and racial
institutions, as hinduism in India, buddhism in China,

[1] So difficult has the improvement of man by religions been found to be,
that these have everywhere accepted the vices of the nations. This is the
more noticeable when a religion like the christian is transplanted from an
asian home (and the gospel is completely asian in temperament) to Europe
the place of its development.
[2] See the *Policraticus* of John of Salisbury, and Langland, Text C,
passus xvi, verse 200, ed. Skeat.

christianity in Europe; the men who are drawn to them are drawn by a certain temperament which does not create religiousness but religiosity. It is because religions have been so little confined to the religious that there have arisen in all of them *foyers* of the spirit, of seekers after god and despisers of the easy and perfunctory. None of these has been accepted by the great religions, or if accepted they have very generally ceased to remain spiritual nuclei. For there can be no good religion but a persecuted religion.[1]

(*c*) But perhaps religion ought to be described simply as a spiritual experience of the soul; and it is perhaps best

Religion
a definition

defined as devout action from love. How does this differ from moral experience? It differs I think in the further reference which is peculiar to it: a spiritual element is recognized in my action beyond the value it has for its own sake, and towards which my attitude can only be described as devout. To Marcus Aurelius this spiritual element consisted in putting oneself in harmony with the kosmos. To another it is union with a divine being who commands our reverence and love—the religious sense becomes a sublimated personal relation. And again it is the passion which makes us see in all lovely and righteous acts a fulfilling of goodness for its own sake, helping to unite the soul which has this passion with an invisible kingdom of god, which is mystically in the midst of us. This experience of the soul is the recognition (both stoic and buddhist) of eternal or infinite things which we may touch at certain points through an attitude and through achievements of the spirit. Religion is inadequately described as "morality touched by emotion", for the elements of our ethical life are charged with emotion; and religion, which did not originate as morality, developed as a spiritual realization not as an ethical code. Its perfect work is devout action inspired by love.

Spirituality
a definition

But spirituality as the realization of the religious con-

[1] An exception would be 'Quaker' history since their persecution.

sciousness came late, for it awaited progresses of the
human soul. It does not exist without aspiration for it is
the love of the ideal beautiful, and its perfect knowledge is
that the world is well lost for the vision vouchsafed. The
spiritual man walks by faith not by sight—not by sight
but by vision.[1] And again he walks not by law but by
love. Spirituality and scrupulosity have divergent paths,
they never encounter each other. For there is no spirituality without liberty as there is none without respect.[2]
Being so fine and religious a thing it has suffered from
counterfeits, mere caricatures of spiritual things.[3] There
is only the one spiritual rule, that he that seeks to gain his
life shall lose it, and he that loses his life shall save it.
Anxiety to insure my eternal happiness and the dedication
of my chief efforts to the care of my soul are not religious
or spiritual instincts. It has been mistakenly assumed

[1] Religious faith has never freed itself from its concrete attachments—
faith in facts. But divine faith means something much more essential to the
spirit, and closer to it, than the belief that a supreme being exists. Neither
is the notion that faith is a mental act rather than a spiritual fact countenanced by the gospels.—See the fine parables Matt. xxi. 28–31; xxv. 33.

[2] See the spiritual saying which occurs in verse 4 of Luke vi in the
syriac version of the 4 Gospels (discovered in the monastery of Mount
Sinai, and preserved also in the Codex cantabrigiensis D). Jesus seeing a
man working on the sabbath, says to him: "Man, if thou knowest what
thou doest blessed art thou; but if thou knowest not thou art accursed and
a breaker of the law": if he is spiritual he is free, but if he is only disobedient
he is defying a law which is greater than he.   Augustine says, *Ama,
et fac quod vis.*

[3] A person is said to be 'spiritual' who is assiduous at religious rites, or
'spiritual' because he despises rites and hopes for salvation on more recondite
grounds. But neither dogmatic faith nor sacramental observance can be a
substitute for spirituality. And the kind of spiritual attainment which
'belief in god' may imply can be gleaned from the opinion of Thomas
Browne that "not to believe in witches is a sort of atheism".   Religion,
it is said, by placing heaven before the soul affords an inspiration to it. But
to fear damnation for ill-doing and hope for bliss if you do well is not to be
inspired by heaven but bribed by it.   One of the aberrations of the
'spiritual' in these days comes from assuming that to be 'spiritualistic' is to
be spiritual—as though there could possibly be anything the least more
spiritual in 'disembodied' spirits than in embodied ones.

that the desire to survive death is a religious desire, whereas it is no more religious than the desire to postpone death. The way of the spirit shows that there is in the soul a love and a perception of spiritual riches, and that there are gallantries of the spirit, which disregard the ends of personal survival however magnificent these might prove to be—the soul's quality is such that it can elect rather to be damned in certain conditions—or in certain company—than saved in others; it would buy with itself eternal glory for another; and a man would not wish his creed to prevent him placing his soul where the Frenchman's was when he said: 'my paradise will be on the day when all the gentle patient suffering beasts of burden are led by the lord's angel along green pastures watered by cool streams.' So my survival can never be the supremely glorious goal of the spirit.

Where spiritual life is there is the eternal—that which does not cease to be. It has nothing at all to do with extensity in reference to myself. When Sœur Rosalie was asked how it would be if after all there were no eternal life, her answer was "my eternal life is here". Wherever this conception is substituted for that of our own immortality the things which have eternal value are seen to have an importance so triumphant that the destiny of the individual is of no account by the side of them. A creed so spiritual as Buddha's placed no reliance on the survival of human life as a spiritual weapon; it placed the craving for a future life on the same unspiritual plane as the craving for the 'good things' of this life.[1] It is certain that the least spiritual among us are often the most sure of their 'spiritual' survival, and such an assertion as 'nothing spiritual can be lost' (which does not carry us far[2])

[1] Cf. pp. 436–7 n².

[2] The idea of 'immortality' is not interchangeable with 'something spiritual'; and if by spiritual we mean simply the non-material and psychical then what is spiritually evil exists as well as what is holy.

is confused with the desire for personal immortality. But 'the Something-for-me' is never spiritual. That is not a spiritual desire, the wish to perpetuate myself because it is myself: to be spiritual I must want what is best in the self to survive? And then because this lives, I live? I live, yet not I, but that which was life in me.[1]

"Hadst thou been nothing but the goal" thou hadst *Conclusion* not met my soul. Religion does not seek an end but a path. And it is not a quest of immortality: that the gods (τὰ θεῖα) alone are immortal is a great spiritual truth. Religion is concerned with that spirituality which is both an endowment and an achievement—with nothing more and nothing less; and it is its own end, because the goal of the spirit is the way of the spirit. Die Sehnsucht du und was sie stillt.   In the only sense in which it is transcendent religion is spirituality. None of its other uses or meanings has this supreme character. So it does not consist in any quest of the grail, it is not in self-sacrifice, it is not joy in the temple courts; and it is not hidden in those acts of anxious piety which prompted a Sokrates to distrust the high meanings of music in order to satisfy a scruple with halting verse.

Religions are the most widely distributed influence, the *Religions* most widely distributed of all the mental forces brought *and the moral* to bear upon mankind,[2] and they have had their own way *conscience* with a completeness denied to all others. They have therefore taken wings and reached the butterfly stage of fairness and perfection. But ethics has remained a chrysalis. We cannot ascertain what has ruled in men's hearts, stirred their minds, and nerved their arms, without perceiving that moral considerations have been the least

---

[1] This spiritual or religious truth is clearly also a teleological truth. See pp. 429–30.

[2] With the exception of tribal and kinship influences.

potent of all. This means that they have nowhere been a religious necessity. And in sooth the setting forth of future reward and punishment as the guerdon of conduct here establishes a conscience which is radically immoral; for it signifies that men can never care for goodness for its own sake, *and were not intended to.* The quest of personal salvation then has checked the altruism of the gospel and dimmed our sense of the worthwhileness of the good in and for and by itself. There is no necessary connexion between belief in a 'supernatural' world and the religious sentiment; and the doctrine that a supernatural motive must be present in order to acquire merit is totally false.[1] The religious faculty has in fact provided the crucible and chief focus of superstition, and a much larger part of the religious consciousness is filled in this way than we are willing to imagine. *Our* particular superstition ranks as meritorious; while religious emotion, gratitude, and observance are to a very large extent nothing but symptoms of a materialistic and mercenary self-interest.[2]

Religions and the craving for figurative expression

And when we turn from the end which religions propose to the means they employ we come first to the craving for imagery. The soul is strongly moved by imagery and the need for figurative expression. Among primitive peoples the belief that what is done with his image is done to the person is absolute, and the most cultivated man would shrink from outraging the senti-

[1] For example, if you repent because you have wronged your neighbour it is not sufficient; but if you repent because you fear hell the 'supernatural motive' is present.

[2] A cultivated and very religious catholic said: "if you object to such things as the cult of S. Antony as a finder of lost objects being reckoned as religious I fear there would be very little religion left." The counsel common in the last century to accept 'religion' in case it should be true, simply recognized hypocrisy or a self-interested choice of chances as meritorious. The ethical temperament is incompatible with such a mind as this. And the means for insuring religion have not been any happier: how can a vow secure spiritual and moral qualities or acts.

ment which clings to inanimate objects when these are connected with what we love and reverence. The image or memento is a powerful associator of ideas, keener than memory, and quickly arousing the poignant and tender emotions. So rite and reverence grow; and the sentiment which irresistibly attaches to material objects is a core of that religious instinct which is universal. In some religions mental images take the place of material ones; but the power of every mental image consists simply in the ideas it is able to conjure up; and these ideas are themselves images as strictly representative as the physical.   Later, Interiority we come to interiority. Marcus Aurelius said that the soul is constituted for holiness and for *pietas* no less than for justice. And religions, more especially of the indian and of the european-christian type, have fostered a life of the soul, interiority. Whether or not we are to recognize that the interiority and spiritual intimacy which have so greatly deepened religious experience have helped to endow man and will bring a greater sensibility and depth of feeling to the consideration of morality, I cannot believe that life being what it is spirituality could ever have so noble an office as sympathy.

The world affords a spectacle so contrary to what is humane and spiritual that even those who do not believe in religion invoke it against the greed and cynicism around us. It is easier to invoke it than to point to its fruits. In their essential character religions as we know Religions them cannot be the bulwark against wickedness, for if and
goodness there is an omnipotent god, god is responsible for the wickedness of the men he creates; leaving man face to face with the despair of it. What is wanted is not more 'religion' but more spirituality. And if this is a far rarer thing the coincidence of the common phenomenon of 'religion' with a high standard of goodness is also rare. No really good man would or could become a bad or indifferent man because he came to disbelieve his religion.

And everything will depend on whether a man's goodness is his religion or his religion his goodness.

Is there any other sentiment, any other aspiration, which we can recognize as a fount of ethical conduct and a sanction?

HONOUR MORALITY

"HONOUR is an alliance of the higher egoistic instincts with the social instincts against the baser passions of fear, lust, or avarice . . . it remains, and will always remain, a stronger guarantee of truthful dealing between man and man than any which has been created by theology. No such machinery for crushing the baser power of egoism has ever been invented."[1]

The sentiment of honour is an arcanum of the moral consciousness; it is a fundamental conscience. Conscience we are told stands alone as an inward monitor pointing to a moral law within us: but honour is just as much a "still small voice", only rarer than conscience because it has never depended as conscience has always done on external intimations and sanctions. Conscience is an interior monitor, an inward witness. Honour also is an inward intimation like conscience, a monitor whose monitions are without fear, and a witness that its reward is itself. When I turn to the professional writers on ethic, however, I find that this is not amongst the matters which it is thought necessary to treat of.[2]

Honour is of supreme importance as illustrating the nature of ethic. It is the intimate satisfaction of self-respect and consideration for others. The intimate thing which has no dependence on what is seen or known or lawful. And first of all it is the one emotion which trans-

[1] Dr. John Henry Bridges.
[2] But Rabelais did think it necessary: *Gargantua* lvii, How the Thelemites were governed.

mutes self-love in preserving it. No other emotion turns egoism into the abettor of altruism. Love indeed bridges the gulf between the two for love destroys egoism, but honour sublimates it. Honour is an interior fount of sweetness and beauty, like the love of god or the generosity of any other love. Its character is to teach a man his duty to another by his own experience, like the golden rule; but it goes beyond our own experience and bestows more than it would ever ask. Honour is not only, like conscience, an admonitor it is also an instructor—it knows what ought to be done and forborne. The monitions of conscience do not enter the realm of the spiritual until they are followed from the spiritual motives:[1] but though conscience may thus ally itself with the spiritual, honour has a still greater dependence on a man's spiritual quality. Without self-respect and pride there could be no such sentiment as honour; and honour morality is only possible when duty to self and a scrupulous self-respect are put forward as moral duties, a side of ethics much neglected in the popular presentment of the gospel teaching. In most european countries it is the 'gothic' code of honour which is esteemed as the moral code; self-defence and not the christian code of meekness and forgiveness of injuries. And this gothic or teutonic sentiment of honour is clearly marked off from the classical or latin sentiment. Gothic honour set out to give men something without bargain and without price: in latin countries honour does not mean this, it means primarily the observance yourself and the recognition by others of a certain external 'honourableness'—it is something you think due to you not only from yourself but from other men. This bears no relation whatever to honour morality, and is to be compared with the ecclesiastical notion of 'scandal' which consists not in doing what is inconsistent with your profession but in this fact being noised abroad. In the same way there is

Honour teutonic and classical

[1] See p. 98.

a bogus teutonic 'sense of honour' which works out as disastrously for the moral sentiment.[1] A gambling debt is called 'a debt of honour' because it cannot be legally distrained. But it is clear such a consideration does not and cannot touch the groundwork of the sentiment of honour, and that you cannot compare what is due to a man who decides to stake his money for the sake of the hazard and the game with what is due to the most serious and loveliest responsibilities and ties. Neither is honour the same thing as scrupulous commercial honesty; it may distinguish between degrees of honesty but its unique office is to throw light on the secret places of the soul and show it the perfect ways.   When we fail in the sympathy that should move us to action how are we to meet the moral claim on us. There is Kant's sense of 'duty', and there is the duty of obedience to religious principles; but I think honour would be the best guide and the most acceptable to a recipient—honour which is self-honour as well as regard for the honour and dues of others; which has nothing of the mercenary outlook of reward, and perhaps for that reason is more akin to sympathy, and is often less apt to wound than charity. Charity which is a general element of eastern religions is the special doctrine of the christian, and it includes sympathy with distress and the duty of relieving it. This is a doctrine of the poor and suffering and has its assured place in the world at all times; but we may hope that with a fair distribution of the world's wealth and a lessening of the ravages of disease honour will be called for more and more as a quality of spirit, giving to moral conduct a discrimination and fulness which it has lacked under all the systems of the past. For honour is an adytum and hidden fount of moral feeling and delicacy. Working without disquietude or fear its only sanction is an intimation of base and noble.

<small>Charity</small>

---

[1] James I referred to his 'honour' when making a bogus plea for his mother's life.

It neither warns nor menaces. Instructing without words like a garden flowering with lovely things, it is peculiar to honour that its breaches are neither noticed nor condemned by any religious teaching.

In its aspect as a sanction it may be compared with the sanction of eternal spiritual values. One person says: I will do my duty by my neighbour, will not despoil him nor betray him nor take advantage of him, because of the sentiment of honour. And another person says: But I will do these things in pursuit of a spiritual ideal which has eternal value. I think the idea of spiritual value will always leave too much unnoticed; it will never be sufficiently close to the ethical ends of life: no spiritual ideal would be sufficient without sympathy; and spiritual value with eternal significance must remain in some sense detached from life, without warmth enough for its needs. The 'spirituality' which means the power to live by eternal values[1] is as much a temperamental gift as the mystic's or the artist's; it never can be for all, as conduct can and should be. It is strange how little this class of truth is recognized. *(Spiritual sanctions and honour)*

Ricasoli said that the real poverty of the poor is a moral poverty; and honour cannot be developed as a practical basis for ethics until the circumstances of human life are consistent with a greater self-respect.

CONCLUSION

There is then no single answer and no final answer to the question, Why do we think one thing morally good and another morally bad; and progress in moral civilization and in moral idealism is possible because large tracts of conduct can be removed from the ken of blind custom and superstition into the keeping of sympathy and reason; because new moral realizations are possible. The material *(No single answer)*

[1] *Not* theological values, a belief in which and in their sanctions is in most people's power.

offered by human qualities remains always the same, what can be changed is the balance between them. And it must be recorded that the selfish interests of mankind cannot be so prominent as past social systems have made them appear to be, because in the natural activities of half the race self-forgetting love is the predominant fact. When the light from this most ancient of all organic facts is thrown upon our moral data we may begin to look for a higher social development.

Spencer said that in a perfect society the life of the individual and that of the society are identical, pure egoism being as impracticable as pure altruism, and a hindrance to personal happiness: and Renan declared that devotion is as natural as egoism to the man of fine race. This simply means that the higher type of being is a moral being; and so it undoubtedly is. He alone represents the full conditions of life, the interaction of self and not-self; and illustrates to the full society's gifts to the individual, the gifts, in his turn, of the individual *quā* individual to society, the advantage to him of a social instinct and to society of a respect for individuality— which is to say that by ethical conduct man does not abnegate himself but integrates himself. His gifts should follow the analogy of the maternal gift. Where love and sympathy have sway though there is cost it is not counted and though there is sacrifice it is not felt. It is only a certain kind of self-sacrifice which is self-fulfilment, and if we reject self-fulfilment as an ethical end we do too great a violence to the conditions and character of organic life, which are themselves the very source of conduct.

Altruism and egoism The preference of others to self is not intrinsically virtuous: that it may be virtuous I must be preferring something which can be regarded as good in itself, such as the legitimate happiness or ends of others. That is why altruism cannot be a perfect measure of conduct, and why, as an abstract idea and apart from any further definition of the good, Spencer calls it "rather a method than an end". The same argument applies to duty. All the iniquities are possible with a deep sense of duty and a dutiful nature. What, in fact, is the relation of Kant's dictum as to duty and the pauline "If I have not love I am nothing"? It is that while the pauline touches the real substance of moral disposition, Kant's is nothing but a remedy when that disposition fails. 'Don't you *want* to help him?' 'No.' 'Then I tell you it is your duty.' But this sense of obligation is not the root of ethical instinct. Would Kant have thought a man moral who avoided cruelty because he felt it to be his duty? The point of that great teaching "If I speak with the tongues of men and angels and have not love, it profits me nothing" is that the good man is the one who wishes to do what is good from some sentiment which is not the sentiment of duty, and which is as unlike action from moral force as from physical. We come, I think, to the permanent moral factor in duty with the sense of personal responsibility. When it is coupled with the sense of personal responsibility the sense of duty makes a vigorous moral character, but coupled with the habit of obedience it makes a servile one.   Duty being a means or method for the performance of right conduct rather than morality in itself it is dependent in turn on each moral quality for its own quality. A world moved by sympathy would be a more moral world than one moved by duty, and the roots of responsibility itself are not to be found in duty but in sympathy. Nevertheless we cannot say that the supreme moral duty is sympathy; the ground of moral conduct is not covered by acts done out of sympathy—including most of the ground covered by duties to self, and the qualities necessary to insure the performance of the dictates of sentiment. But sympathy plays a far larger part in the moral life than has ever been discerned for it among mankind.

[marginal note: Duty and the sense of responsibility]

[marginal note: Duty and sympathy]

Sympathy and the pursuit of happiness

It may be objected to the criticism of utilitarianism (*supra*, pp. 30-4) that the satisfaction of sympathy is itself happiness; but sympathy is the motive which seeks in the first instance the happiness of others and not first the satisfaction of sympathy. Sympathy is a non-hedonistic motive.[1] Clearly I might be happier if I had less sympathy; but no sympathetic man ever limited his sympathy on this account. Clearly sympathy brings pain as well as pleasure—without thereby creating any dualism or conflict of motive.

Moral material

Moral material—sympathy, self-respect, the sense of justice, personal responsibility, love and honour—responds to what enhances not to what represses. And the proper function of ethic, as Grote said, is "to animate rather than restrain".

[1] Consider such examples as consenting to die or even to be tortured to save another: or the case when a man says 'I have no one who will suffer if I die—you save yourself first.'

SECTION II
PROBLEMS OF ETHICS

SECTION II

PROBLEMS OF ETHICS

I. INDIVIDUAL AND SPECIES

Selfishness is suicide. The selfish man withers up like an isolated
sterile tree; but self-love in its quality of an effective effort towards
perfection is the origin of everything great.   TURGENIEV

If I am not for myself, who is for me? And if I am for myself
alone, what then am I? And if not now, then when?
                                                            HILLEL

THROUGHOUT the activities of living things we come
across a double source of conduct, the acts of an
individual towards himself and his acts as member of a
group: nature always presents us with the individual and
the species. This dual spring of conduct actions is not an
instance of the antitheses so familiar to ancient thought,
good and evil, flesh and spirit, femel and male; what it
points to fundamentally and essentially is not antithesis
but adaptation. The belief that the world presents on all
sides evidence of the dualism of opposing forces and that
this is paralleled by a necessary permanent dualism in
the human agent has coloured moral theory and philosophy; yet this belief records no essential verity but an
elementary stage in human thought. In place of dualisms
there is underlying unity (the original essential unities—
of life itself, of animals and men, of assimilation and
reproduction), there is change and development, and there
are the very different stages and values of psychical life
within the same species, a fact more marked in the
evolution of man than elsewhere. These things—unity
of origin, the phenomena of development, the wide differences of inter-special capacity—constitute the actual
material with which we have to deal, and taken together
they signify that adaptation and not conflict is the supreme

organ of nature. Adaptation not antagonism is the law of life. If there is conflict between some species there is adaptation everywhere and adaptation is the more fundamental—it is the essential factor. If this is a truth it is evidently a standard truth, and it operates both in the realm of self-development and of group conduct.

Nature, indeed, always presents us with the unit and the group, but the relation between these is subject to extreme variation: in the bee and the ant the individual is sunk in the society, among cats and frogs the society has no influence at all. With animals which are neither social nor entirely solitary a group is sometimes formed during the breeding season consisting of the mother with her male partner and her young; such a family group is sometimes constant. The difference in the disposition of animals and in their organic habits would make the pressure of group life upon the individual or, per contra, the freedom of the individual from such pressure, vary with the hundred circumstances of species. Amongst the most important of these differences are the initial facts of procreation: the bee society is produced by one mother, whereas the frog is a developed form of the tadpole and has no mother; and dependence upon a mother—or upon both parents—for rearing and food obviously introduces a social aspect to species life, assistance on one side, dependence on the other. But the primeval facts of maternity though they underlie the altruistic and loving instincts which are essential to moral life, however regarded, do not determine the moral relationship we are now considering, they do not determine whether individuality is more important than sociability or whether moral weight must be said to attach most to self-regarding or to group-regarding conduct. Beneath this great inquiry there lies always a conviction and an uncertainty; the conviction that what is moral and good means mainly what is unself-regarding and altruistic, and the uncertainty as to the comparative value of the individual and the group to which he belongs. Neither can be neglected, and we will take the second first.   The thoughts by which the race lives are the thoughts of individuals not group-thought. What even the lowliest types of life exemplify first and foremost is individuality, for every cell is an individual. The individual often seems of small, or no, account in comparison with the life of the species and its exigencies; nevertheless it is in order to produce the individual that the entire biological process exists. With conscious life it is evident that we come to a new and the most potent principle of individuality; we come eventually to those thoughts by which the race lives, when the idea of one man may be dominant over centuries of caste tyranny, a more real more living more fundamental thing. Man owes the greater part of his psychical life to the not-self, but he does not owe it to the group, to the species as distinct from individuals; and the human society, like the individual, is debtor to its units not to its masses. Now the supreme need of the individual in order that he should bring his gifts is liberty: the primordial fact of individuality, for which the biological process exists, has two facets—liberty and self-discipline, and no truths about our relation to ourselves can by any means be more important than these. The individual is the real end of existence and its fine flower, the society can only be fine because of him: and it would not be too much to say that in reaching the great truths of the world no force has been so strong as a man who stands in a minority of one. It is no doubt an experience common to all who stand in advance of their kind to be looked at askance by moral inferiors. The price of individuality is a certain solitude, and original personalities must not kick against the pricks, for their value depends on standing apart from the crowd; yet it belongs to the hope which is inherent in all idealism, and to sympathy when this has been their

Man owes the larger part of his life to the existence of other men —but this is owed to individuals not to groups

teacher, that they should believe that understanding must and will be possible which is not possible.

Exotic
friendships

That individuality plays a great part is patent throughout nature; exotic friendships—profound zoological sympathies—exist everywhere, a foxhound fraternizing with a little fox, a cat with a pigeon, a gander leaving its own species to companionize a cow which returned all its affection, or the friendship seen in a London park for many years between a dog and a cormorant. One chick of a brood will attach itself to the ducks, another is reared by a partridge with her young; everywhere is evidence of the idiosynkratic. To say that this should not be encouraged, that a given 'sport' hen will not make a good fowl and that its reason in life is to be a fowl and to multiply, is not very good reasoning after all. Clearly this is not what most matters when you come to mankind, for moral artistic and intellectual excellence matter much more, and these can only be produced by 'sports'. But even among cows and hens it is nothing but the commercial outlook which allows us to argue against individuality, to regard reproductive powers as paramount; though it is obvious that quality of the species and quality in the species must always be of greater moment than quantity. In all cases of friendship outside the group it is the tremendous force of individuality which shines out, widening and enriching organic life and quickening organic powers. It is a profound loss in our own species when we are unable to recognize this.[1]

Self-fulfil-
ment or
self-abnega-
tion?

This account of the relative values of group and indi-

[1] See The Other Animals, pp. 193, 194 and n.[2]. It is remarkable that the emotional life seems to be stimulated by these idiosynkratic friendships. In the case of the donkey and cat the cat died the day after its friend, and when its friendship with a Labrador was ended by death its kitten lover refused food and died. This heightening of life is not to be attributed to abnormality and eccentricity but to a development of personality which is made possible to those individuals of a species which are not driven by the sex complex.

vidual brings us nearer to a solution of the other problem, whether man's action is good in proportion as it is unself-regarding. Self-sacrifice is a means. It is not an end in itself, and it is not good in itself. If everyone were un-selfish it is obvious there would be none to profit by it; what happens therefore is that the unselfish sacrifice themselves to the selfish. Evidently this is not the road to any moral progress and therefore the justification for it that it increases our own merit is itself selfish. But, putting aside the reward, even the beauty and perfection of our character are not things so great that they can be bought at such moral loss. Self-sacrifice to the selfish whims of others may be called self-perfecting or amiability or un-selfishness of disposition; but its name is not virtue. Or if we look at group action not one in many thousands of all the deaths died at the behest of the community has served any end it was worth while to serve. Civic self-sacrifice has followed from the arbitrary claims of society, and private self-sacrifice is often due to a parallel absence of standard.

The great gift to the group of the individual who is worth anything is self-fulfilment. Nothing that he can give us is worth having at the expense of this; but self-fulfilment is not the same thing as happiness. If a man with a genius for friendship sacrifices his gift in order to meet family or other group convenience he may not be unhappy but he misses self-fulfilment, and he has given to society his poorest gift not his richest. The end of personal life is not happiness, but the end *is* self-fulfilment: in the scheme of organic life the place and gifts of indi-viduals come first, and are the gradual realization of the highest forms of conscious life.

Sacrifice is not then the best gift of the unit to the group. Does a man's relation with himself differ in this respect? Is all virtue a conflict and is there a necessary dualism of flesh and spirit; what should be the relation of *The argument transferred to the forum internum* the soul to the body, and how does virtue emerge from this relation. Men, we say, have nourished the conviction that what is good is in the first place what does violence to one's own interests. But the teaching of religions and philosophies does not bear out such a doctrine of pure altruism. The christian teacher has told us that man's first business is to save his own soul and the buddhist that the evil of personal existence is to be met by an exercise of mental and carnal detachment. Neither christianity, then, nor buddhism deemed that the simple practice of altruism fulfilled the moral requirements. The truth is that self-cultivation to the extent of putting the interests of one's own soul first has been the salient tenet of the world's creeds. Wherever the welfare of the soul has been the staple of religion self-cultivation has been an *askēsis*, an ascetic exercise, and has implied an absolute superiority of the 'spiritual' over the 'bodily'. This emphasized a moral dualism in human nature which has been not an integrating force but a disintegrating one; it did not seek to harmonize the elements of life it antagonized them. Behind us lies an age-long tradition of self-suppression, resumed in such a saying as "Take up your cross": from India to Palestine, from fakir to monk, the duty, ay and the blessedness, of self-crucifixion have been exalted: and social life has not been behindhand in demanding from men a complete subservience through tabu and iron custom to the will of societies. These two tabus are to be read together; they are not the products of social and moral wisdom but both are examples of the despotic element which has predominated in human Asceticism society. The only genuine meaning of the counsel to take up the cross is that you should be ready to take up *your* cross, the one that is in your path. There is no obligation to seek one. Life offers every skope for self-denial, and ascetic practices are not a substitute for this life discipline: the charge to be brought against voluntary asceticism that it is no preparation for the discipline of life is its condemnation. "Touch not, taste not, handle not" bans all life as unclean and makes the achievement of any critical standards impossible. What belongs to organic beings in a world of objects—appreciation, selection, criterion—is laid aside as useless paraphernalia, and all that you have to do in their regard is to do nothing. "I take no notice" says the ascetic of the food or other material that is set before him—good or bad for its purpose it is the same to him. What shall we say of this attitude? We shall say that there is no virtue in not requiring that the things we use should be fitting and fine of their kind, that without this requirement no aesthetic choices, no standard, no taste or fastidiousness, no knowledge or discrimination about the life around us is possible. We shall say that the question of virtue does not enter until we are required to prefer more important goods to these or not to enjoy them at the cost of another's abstinence: then what we substitute is a different beauty, a higher standard of beauty.   Asceticism, itself for itself, is not a product of the civilized mind, it is a mean between the natural and the civilized and it has the strength and the weakness of savagery. It is indeed the one device constantly to be found no matter how primitive the scale of savagery or barbarism. The first resort of the savage is self-maceration—so he serves his tribe, stiffens his courage, startles his enemies and friends. To be macerated or to macerate yourself is the method of ethics in primitive human society, where it takes the place which belongs of right to all the forms of free self-cultivation and therefore of true self-discipline. That a thing should be only black or white and that you should be called upon to do all or nothing are easier precepts than selection and the higher ways of self-restraint. We know the roman contempt for ascetic practices, the scorn with which the filthy ascetics were received in the ivth century, and how repulsive to the civilized Roman or Greek was the oriental notion that maceration was a gift acceptable to gods. No doubt to require such acts in others has encouraged cruelty and a despotic temper from which the practice of self-maceration is itself not free in some of its forms— they appeal to that evil love of power which makes us wish to tyrannize over the bodies as over the souls of men. Despotic methods with oneself or with others destroy that true spirit of discipline which always keeps close to the spirit of education. Asceticism does not teach the selfish man to meet life unselfishly, and it is not required to teach the unselfish to do so.

The infelicitous majority

Nevertheless the role of asceticism in the past has not been merely barbarous nor merely inimical to a truer self-cultivation: it has been consciously adopted to redress a balance. The majority of men feel a war in their flesh; to repress appetite and satisfy sympathy does not take the form of a higher satisfaction but of a conflict. Moral natures, I think, are to be found chiefly among those who are sensible of no such constant war in their members, to whom goodness is a delight not a burnt offering, whose soul and body work together as one, in whom the psychophysical life is a harmony not a discord. But the great majority of mankind is not moral in this sense; most men feel no harmony within themselves, what we feel is conflict and evil desire and, not least hostile, the calls upon our own pettiness: what we are is not moral man but immoral man. And in as far as we are immoral there is conflict about the great things of life. The men in whom this conflict exists can be divided into the two classes of those who have in themselves a source of self-discipline and those who have none. These are the refuse, the evil hearted of whom the gospel found nothing more to say than that it were better that a millstone should be hanged about their necks and good had they never been born. Mankind then having within its ranks not only the naturally moral and the naturally evil but the naturally teachable, all the resources of selection and education should be concentrated on the men of good will. Such a man may be good but not naturally moral, and when he disciplines himself he effects reforms but never effects the essential reform, which is natural morality.[1] A man burdened with bad heredity, always watching himself, always fighting the war in his members, gives evidence of considerable moral endowment; in so far he is naturally moral: but the distinction holds between the felicity of moral acts in those who not only desire to do them but feel natural happiness in the moral choice and those for whom the choice is always painful and may always involve conflict.

There is the man who has suffered the slings and arrows of outrageous fortune, who has known what it is to stretch out his arms on a cross bound there by the malignity of his fellows or by the blindness of circumstance. For him, as for the man who feels the conflict within himself, life must often appear as a battle-field, and the true gospel one which recognizes that conflict is indeed the measure of life, and spiritual combat or resignation its principal duties. Nevertheless this man who experiences the malignity of men and the ironies of circumstance is not the victim of a death struggle set in the midst of life—Ormuzd and Ahriman, god and devil—but of forces which resemble the ignorance and guile of the savage or the catastrophe of a falling mountain. *The sufferer's gospel*

It remains true that no man who is naturally moral will consent to say "I die daily" unless the nails are driven by outer circumstance not by inner conflict. Is it then no part of a good man's experience to deny himself, take up his cross, and follow where the divine light leads? I think the answer is that for those with natural goodness there may be and is conflict in the little things—in meeting the *The denial of the good man*

[1] Human Character, pp. 386, 395-6.

117

sloth, the temper, the self-covetousness, the overbearing will, or the weak will, of every day; but if we have to look after these pence the pounds take care of themselves— there is not conflict in the great things, those great things which are the source of conflict in the immoral man. If you have natural moral fibre there should not be wrung from you the cry "O! wretched man that I am who shall deliver me from the body of this death!" For the body of the good man is not death; it is his instrument of life. Those who think the secret of Jesus was 'dying to live' will always despise aesthetic and other activities which demand not dying but living more abundantly: and since the great business of life is an appraisement of values, when we are told that 'spiritual value is always the greater' we should demand real answers to the question, What is spiritual value. Is my spirit always of more account than my body; is inclination always a danger signal warning us that duty lies the other way. Do not sympathies, on the contrary, point a better way than mere altruism? I ought to regard what my own moral sympathies and affections dictate because they are my affections and sympathies; and the altruism which takes no account of affections and specific endowments—altruism which wages war with what we feel to be the rights of love and of art— should never by itself dictate our allegiance. It will perhaps not be denied that if the artist sacrifices himself to the aged parent the group is not on the whole the better for it: in what high sense can the parent be bettered by it? As to the artist he has done violence to the best he had to give. But if he loved, he would not hesitate? Ah! there we touch the core of the ethic which is bound up with self-fulfilment. He would not hesitate, and the world might be the poorer, but I think the individual is not born for the world against self-fulfilment. It is never part of moral duty to persuade a person to do violence to the sympathies, which is always done at the risk of moral

shipwreck. This is also true of the violence done to antipathies and moral hatreds.

Spiritual and moral values cannot then be decided
either by opposing inclination and claims, or by creating a necessary cleavage between body and spirit which
corresponds with no psychological facts. The fleshly appetites may urge, but the faculties of the soul also crave
evil; jealousy and spiritual murder are not sins of the body
but sins of the soul, and so we have the devil set beside
the flesh as a second enemy. It was Catherine of Siena
who rightly discerned the relation which obtains between
body and spirit when she called the one the disciple of the
other, "*il discepolo dello spirito*".[1] The 'body' is a disciple
and therefore a co-operator, a fellow traveller of the soul
and in its turn a messenger of truth. When by 'spirit' we
mean that which is highest within us a discipleship subsists; but in our daily life body and psyche live together
as co-workers and co-learners, co-sufferers, co-evangelists.
This truth is partly discerned even in ascetic theology for
christianity has not hesitated to call a pure body the temple
of the holy ghost. The psyche learns of the physical—
its strengths, endurances, resiliences, its skills chastities
harmonies adaptations, suggest these things to the soul
and also show it a way: the aesthetic choices among things
being other spiritual educators. It is when we understand
this true relation of spirit and body that we know that self-
love is not so vile a thing as self-neglecting. But there will
always be those who go away disappointed when they
hear this gospel, for it may demand a rare harmony and
men are often ready to do something costly to themselves
who will not be moved by the counsel to care for the
body—Go, wash in Jordan: the conflict in our members
cries to us for effort and we demand that our creed should
prepare us for the fight. Nevertheless there can be no

*Spiritual
value*

---

[1] Cf. Hadrian's description of the soul as 'guest and comrade of the
body'—*hospes comesque corporis.*

magna pacis majestas in the ethical realm except in the terms of this harmony—that body and spirit are one and **The golden** that each learns of the other. The golden rule itself **rule** teaches the same lesson, it does not make its appeal to asceticism. For it supposes an amenity in our relations with ourselves which serves as a measure for our conduct towards our neighbour. It is a self-liking precept by which I am taught that what I like others like also. "Whatsoever" you like to receive like also to render. This, too, is the secret of sympathy—its roots are in the individual's power of feeling; an indifferent person is an indifferent sympathizer. And love is another teacher— because it is warmer and nearer than group sympathy and than self-love, so that we understand that what sub- serves the group cannot be the only thing worth while. Love is a strictly individual experience but an all-sufficient motive, and it is here also that there is least element of **Personal** conflict. We come then to see that spiritual values always **value and** imply a regard for personal values. Self-cultivation and **spiritual** self-development are every whit as necessary as senti- **value** ments which are more directly other-regarding. Love, friendship, and group life, all these require our indi- viduality and only through this regard for our individuality can the personal end of organic life be attained, which is self-fulfilment. Many of the self-denying qualities are those which run smoothly along lines of least effort and least resistance, and the mass is a hard taskmaster just because it is so easy to follow him. Sacrifice of self in one direction may lead not only to the loss of our own soul but to our hurting where we can hurt most, where our own acts and affections have called forth in others the power to be hurt.

Spiritual values require us to regard personal value for another reason: every gift is not, and should not be, equally acceptable from all. If I give the gift which another is better fitted to give, my own proper gift will not be given though it may be just as important as that for which I sacrificed it. There are divers gifts but the same spirit—and this spirit is a preparation of yourself to give what you can give best. The good man must settle with himself what sacrifice he may withhold, what gift he must give. For it is fatally easy to say "You would suffer less than I" and "This is a case in which I ought not to give". If the battle come to our doors, all must fight; if the persecutor offers each his life if he recant, all must be ready to die; there are causes and circumstances which demand the selfsame gift from all, the same sacrifice. But in the general lives of men all sacrifices have not equal value and the spirit of the gift has not equal value. The truth that in every great cause of the world there has been need of the one kind of martyrdom—the martyr's way of fixing men's attention and seizing their hearts—does not mean that this is the only holocaust. When the finest artist idealist writer poet philosopher discoverer may have to die for some cause which is not his own, we are to understand that such confusions of parts pertain to stress and storm and the sooner they are over the better. Because the poet must on an occasion give the same gift as the navvy navvies and poets have not the same value. Quality not quantity is the goal all through, and it is because the real question at stake in the greatest causes is quality of life that the same sacrifice can on occasion be asked of all.   Hence what life asks of us is what is most difficult and at the same time most satisfying since it requires more exercise of the gifts of the spirit and less rule-of-thumb than all the codes together. We are to be ready to endure or to enjoy, to forbear or to strike, to rule or to serve, to let work be prayer and prayer work: and to feel that individuality may be the fine instrument of service to others—taught by our best link with them, sympathy—this is the best.

Since the essential meaning of the process of organic life is adaptation, the phenomenon of a double source

Different gifts and necessity

Quality of life

of action in living beings—self-regarding and extra-regarding—does not suggest the principle of antagonism that man has everywhere taught himself to expect. The real antagonism is between action from appetite and action from sympathy. It is the distinction between these two types of action which lies behind the dualism that has haunted moral thought for nearly three thousand years from the Ahriman and Ormuzd of Persia to the god and devil of christianity: and this sense of dualism is to be sought for in primal biological facts. Everywhere in our history the sentiment has predominated that it is appetite which governs action; and this sentiment which accounts for all ethical dualism is a distinctively male as distinguished from a femel phenomenon. The mother who creates soul and flesh within her has any sense of conflict indefinitely modified; but the psychophysical harmonies are less real to the male and he tends to accept violent antitheses and to believe in a perpetual dualism of spirit and flesh. The woman left to herself does not recognize this hostility, since in her both have been made one and she feels their unity in a sense inaccessible to the wer. The root of the difference is that in her the links between the two—between spirit and flesh—are links of sympathy, while in the male the relation is appetitive—in place of links, greeds and discords; the flesh ravens, whereas in the femel the flesh loves. The sympathetic nature—the maternal—is always conscious that sins towards others are not righted by torments to self; and it is naturally intolerant of the unreal, of what effects nothing. Hence the strong instinct of an opposition between spirit and body, the unreality which would meet fault with an incommensurate penance, are, like the clinging to authority, male phenomena. It is the drag and strain of appetite which causes the good wer to regard his flesh with hostility; it is the appeal of sympathy which causes the mother-sex to look upon flesh and spirit as a harmony, as intimately and in their essence capable of being oned. This is plainly a moral fact which nevertheless has entirely escaped our ethicists.

It has been urged that what man rightly moves towards is a kosmic consciousness, that he ought to lose the importunities of self-consciousness in the realizations of the group consciousness: the self-absorption of the personal is to yield place to the satisfactions of the social communion, a *sacrum convivium* which will save man from himself and the group for man. Let us apply this principle to love. In the doctrine of the Mantinean the love of one person was to lead to the love of the beautiful and good in itself; the personal and subjective might so be transmuted into the objective and social, and our love would grow from its place in the personal consciousness and become universal love. Its fevers and pains and powers were not meant, it may be said, to advantage one or two and to absorb energies with perhaps no advantage at all—these were destined to form the great heart of humanity. On one side the splendour of love with its limitations, its egoism with two—and on the other the path away from man's self-consciousness, the power of learning happiness by mergement in the group ——

Is all personal love but a milestone along the path of development which is to be taken by human emotion and idealism? I think rather that such love is the firm anchorage of our ideal nature. This ubiquitous sacrament of self and other-self is in fact the essential sacrament of life; it alone comprehends the mystery of one and all, of individual and species. By love—that intimately maternal emotion—the bridge is crossed, the discords harmonized, the mystery intelligized. We cannot part with this bedrock emotion and hope to grapple securely a universal love. The best things pass beyond the personal, but they cannot slip their moorings.

[margin note: Self-consciousness and group consciousness]

II. TRUTH

What's this then which proves good yet seems untrue?

BROWNING

Truth and accuracy have a disconcerting habit of not being identical.   *The Times* newspaper, 3rd 'leader', December 10, 1936

And I the truer
So to be false

Cymbeline

WHAT is truth? The question Pilate addressed to Jesus received no answer. No answer was expected. "Is there truth?" was the question he meant Jesus to share with him; and since a love of truth is as rare as the pursuit of justice men do in fact seldom possess it. What do men mean by truth and what should they mean by it? When Jesus said to Pilate, "Everyone that is of the truth hears my voice" it signified that there were spiritual and moral verities which could heal the world. What the truth is, in metaphysic, in kosmogony, in theology, each teacher has undertaken to reveal to us. We are still without the answers. The substance of truth has always been unknown; but it is not so with its form; and it is our attitude towards the form of truth which we must completely change if we would reach that substance which is within our grasp—ethical truth.

Mankind from the very nature of his intelligence as immature, groping, inadequately informed, values what is already known and understood, values prejudice and conventionalized knowledge, rather than that ideal form which alone can bring us from light to light. This ideal form is the love and pursuit of intellectual truth, not merely for its own sake, indeed, but nevertheless with the sole intention of following where it leads. Races differ in their capacity for following truth and facing its naked lineaments, but even among those peoples whose perception of intellectual truth is greatest the nature of the

124

human intelligence still raises the most potent barrier to its apprehension. The ultimate fact about our apprehension of truth is this which I have called its form, namely the perception and love of intellectual truth. No one who is without this is truthful. What lies behind truthfulness is sincerity—a moral quality—and the power of appreciating mental facts, which is an intellectual quality. It is to this mental truthfulness and sincerity that the word truth can alone be properly applied. For the most august objective truths of the world are facts rather than truths; and of the same kind are a host of indifferent things about which we apply the criterion of 'truthful'. The apprehension of truth, then, depends on qualities both mental and moral, and for us truth itself consists in possessing them: neither the existence of god nor the strictest verbal veracity have the same claim to be called truth that is due to the apprehensions of intellectual sincerity. For truth is in the mind not in the object.[1]

When we look on the world of perceptions we recognize that there is an objective truth and not-truth corresponding with facts physical moral and mental; and that there is besides a mental-moral quality—mental truthfulness—which is altogether distinct from the possession of such objective truth. Is there also a verbal truthfulness having a moral value *ex opere operato*, a truth which belongs to all speech inasmuch as it corresponds with facts as we know them? Since there are truths of fact every means of expression clearly gives us the capacity for discovering a fact or concealing it. We can warn a man from a danger

Is there a moral value to mere verbal truthfulness?

---

[1] Arist. *Metaphysica*, truth is in the mind; not in what is but in our signifying of what is. Hence the possibility of truth has nothing to do with the impossibility of knowing things as they are in themselves—man has truth in himself and with his neighbour when he represents an object of knowledge as he knows it. Our consciousness of truth therefore is both formal and material, like our consciousness of right and wrong. But with truth the first moral duty is sincerity, while with conscience it is self-instruction. (See Conscience, p. 38.).

125

or tempt him into it; we can simulate liking or simulate dislike; we can assume a disinterestedness we do not feel or conceal the disinterestedness which really moves us. Every living thing can do the same; the hen clucks to tell her chicken that the fox is approaching; the peewit limps along the ground to withdraw her enemy's attention from the neighbouring nest. Speech is one, and only one, of our powers of expression and it has and can have no merit attached to its use which does not attach to every other. I can act a lie as well as tell it, and it does not matter whether I write a fact with a pen or signal it with a flag. Every means of expression with which living beings are endowed—and speech is the most highly developed of these—serves two equally important functions, one of which is to advise other living things of a fact and the other of which is to conceal it from them. There are indeed facts of a moral and intellectual order as to which we cannot or should not be indifferent; but in themselves all facts are indifferent. There is no moral meaning in my having seen one rabbit or two rabbits or none at all, in my having met a black haired man or a brown haired. The facts of the world—that they are so rather than otherwise—their colours, their shapes, their sequence—all this is indifferent—in itself and indifferent morally. So that in their simple relation to our power of describing them facts have no moral value; it is always some other fact which gives a moral quality to our statements about them. The most important relation of language to truth therefore is this: that statements about facts have no moral significance in themselves; facts have this significance when the accompanying circumstances have it and not because we can wag our tongues about them and describe them correctly or incorrectly.

The noble faculty of speech has however suggested to men that truth may consist in fitting a word to a fact. This notion confuses, as we see, two things which are

All facts as facts are morally indifferent.

Truth and actuality

radically unlike, truth and actuality. Verbal veracity is
not truth but it is readily accepted as a substitute for
truth, and the acceptance thrusts truth still farther from
us. Racial qualities intervene here: the Latin does not
understand the distinction made by the Anglo-saxon between lying and telling a lie, a moral snare which is spread
before us by the cult of verbal truth: we say *a*, which is
verbally accurate, knowing our interlocutor will understand *b*, we use a word which has two meanings, and the
equation of verbal truth is satisfied. But truth is here not
served at all; even actuality is outraged; what you are
doing is to preserve a pseudo self-respect at the expense
of the respect due to others; what you have gained by
using words to convey one meaning which you know will
in fact convey the other has been gained by precisely
that use of speech to conceal thought which the verbal
truth-speaker condemns as lying. Those who uphold the
principle of consistent verbal veracity suppose that if you
do not wish it to be known that you are going to Exeter
you have only to say "I am going to Bristol", and since
you pass Bristol station on your way to Exeter station
this is "not a lie". Now what is the value of such truth-
speaking as this? The only value seems to be that if you
are found out you can say: "I did pass Bristol." But then
your deceit has the singular meanness of throwing the
onus on the person to whom you are telling this kind of
'truth'. If you are found out he is to recognize your false
coin as true. This sort of equivocation is not morally
superior to saying your destination was Southampton.
For when we say one thing meaning another to be understood we are not truthful but untruthful, and there is even
a definite tendency to act lies where the wish to tell them
is habitually suppressed. If by our actions we deceive
others as to our fortune, our private interests, our hopes
and plans, we are just as untruthful as when we say *a*
when it should be *b*; and perhaps while the Italian is

Verbal veracity versus truthfulness

engaged in telling lies the Englishman is engaged in acting them.

The claims made for the sanctity of verbal truth

Whether there is any sort of merit in verbal truth *per se* or any such thing as value-in-itself attaching to verbal veracity is however a different matter from the strange claims which have been made for the sanctity of verbal truth. According to some, you should not 'tell a lie' even to save a life, though everyone agrees that you may kill a man in self-defence. To 'tell a lie' has therefore something in it of the wickedness of sin against the holy ghost; you have more right to kill a man than to tell a lie to him and it is more virtuous to let another man be killed than to say what is not true to his would-be murderer. When Cardinal Newman was asked what could be done in these circumstances he said one could knock the man down. But what poor sophistry is this! I may not have the strength to knock him down, I may have only one arm, or he may knock me down. Is the man's life to depend on the results of this altercation when he may be saved if I direct his pursuer on the wrong road? If the life of my loved one is sought by the tyrant, subterfuge not violence is my remedy. But if the lie which misleads—whether we act or speak it—is never allowable, then no one need try to escape death at the hands of a tyrant or elaborate a hiding place for those he wishes to protect, since the secret which is always at the mercy of the very persons from whom I wish to keep it can have no right of sanctuary, and I only mock by the elaboration of my acts that which can always be undone by the remissiveness of my tongue.   But some people qualify this position by saying that we have a right to protect our "moral rights" by a lie. So I have a right to lie to protect my life. In that case I presume I have a right to protect the moral rights of another man by telling a lie to save his life? A man, too, has a moral right to guard the anonymity of his work. I am not obliged to let it be known that I am the writer of such and such a book or the painter of such and such a picture. But will anyone maintain that while the author of the Waverley novels was justified in taking the elaborate steps necessary to preserve his anonymity he was not justified in saying "No" when Mr. Busybody asked him if he had written the books? The view ordinarily taken by those who see virtue in verbal veracity as such would be: Do all you can to protect your moral right, but if you are asked a direct question you must not lie. The reason seems to be that you are put in a false position if you are found out; that your moral personality is eclipsed or at least suffers diminution by the lie. But the belief that verbal veracity must be maintained on all occasions, at all costs, is as gross a superstition as that a man cherishes his moral personality by using the verbal subterfuges we call truth: in the case of the murderous pursuer you may cherish your soul by saying "the man you want ran round to the right" though you well know he afterwards retraced his steps. What sort of gnome in the sky is waiting to record this subterfuge to your credit and would have damned you had you said: "he did not run to the left"? We value our souls too little by such provisions for their safety.[1] Verbal untruths do not in themselves dishonour us or wound our intimate self-respect. Mere verbal **No moral** veracity not being in and by itself virtuous no such theo-**wound** retical title to virtue exists, and the real disadvantage of legitimate verbal untruthfulness is the practical disadvantage of being found out. The catastrophe accrues if you are found out. This would be a curious result if all failure to tell the truth affected our intimate moral character. Moreover the effect on ourselves of being found out is out of all proportion to the importance of the falsehood we have told. Clearly there is here an element

---

[1] Suppose the murderer threatened, "If you have not told me the truth I will come back and do for you also"? The absurdity of our confusion of truth and fact is evident here.

which is not due to any sense of inherent wrong or right but simply to social shame; the falsehood comes home to roost not in our consciences but in our discomfiture at the judgment of our neighbours. A falsehood is not intended to be found out, and when it is the shamefacedness is the same as if we were discovered performing our toilets; the shamefacedness of the small child or the dog found doing what it always hears it is not expected to do. The feeling is one entirely in relation to the judgment of others, not to self-judgment. The worst part of a useful lie is that it offers so many points of vantage to the enemy. "Lies have no legs", and facts outpace them not because they have more inherent virtue but because they have a more independent existence. They stand on their own legs not on the legs our fancy has fashioned for them. Yet it is equally reasonable to tell falsehoods and to be mortified if they do not succeed. They are meant to succeed, just as when I shoot at a mark; and if they fail it is not my want of skill it is the being found in undress, my moral garments stripped from me, the walls of my chamber thrown down, which brings me suffering. I had a perfect right to my walls, a perfect right to keep people from my chamber: in any case my discomfiture is likely to be as great whether I had a right or not, whether my falsehood was expedient or inexpedient, whether it was a real moral lapse in important circumstances or a venial error in difficult ones. But discomfiture is not self-judgment.

The ethical error   The ethical error has been to accord the same or at least a similar moral value to the verbal veracity of statements which all morality cries aloud should be made truthfully —because our interlocutor has a right to the truth—and to statements about which no such obligation can exist; to pretend to hold the false statement in equal horror in either case. It is because no obligation in morality can possibly be higher than the obligation of truth that we fritter it away and belittle it by expending its values upon mere verbal veracity. The real lie is a moral perjury, and there is no difference at all between taking away a person's character by a falsehood and making a true statement to convey what is false about him.

We have all then an indefeasible right to say what is not true, and it is as necessary to be able to say the thing that is not as to be able to say the thing that is. So much is this the case that if the gift of speech bound man to consistent verbal truth he would be of all creatures the most unhappy. The contention that verbal truth is what we owe to each other, what therefore we owe to the impudent and malicious question, is nothing less than a moral enormity. We owe nothing to the impertinent inquirer; we owe nothing at all to the inquirer as such; there is nothing morally constraining in the fact of his inquiry nor any obligation upon us to reply truthfully. We do not and we cannot owe it to our fellow men never to conceal what we know feel and think: may we conceal these things then in a cupboard, or by our silence, or by our acts, but not with our tongues? In human life with its complexity, its inalienable personal privacies, its suffering tragedy and shame, its wantonness and malice by the side of its sympathies and affections—the diplomacy which reserves the truth, the power to act a lie, to deny outwit and to conceal, are things strictly necessary. Is a man bound to ruin his ward's life by blurting out some secret which has been kept from him, only because an injudicious or inquisitive person asks him a direct question about it in the younger man's presence? Is it possible that speech —and speech alone—provides no means of protecting another in the face of impertinence and malice? Or is there something sacrosanct in the capacity to ask questions which places us all at the mercy of the inquisitive person, so that we owe him the sacrifice even of honour and peace of mind? For it is futile to say: we need not answer, or we can give some 'non-committal' answer. We

The power to ask a question in no way constrains the questioned

all know well enough that silence or hesitation or the phrase "I cannot tell you" generally betray what we had to conceal. The faculty of speech then carries with it an inalienable moral right—we cannot be obliged to tell what should be kept secret. This intimate sentiment of the right of concealment is found, as we have seen, like the sentiment of property, in all living things. The protective ruses of animals are the lie by which they defend their moral right to life; and the right of all the nobler animals to moral life is not less emphatic. "Do not ask any questions and you will not get any false answers" sums the actual position of questioner and questioned, and only our insincerity of mind hides the truth from us.

For the truth of course is that we all tell untruths. It is an absurd assumption that the world generally is truthful, or our own country in particular, or that elect body of persons who assure us they never "tell an untruth". Is it not a world, to begin with, in which idle gossip is the staple of conversation; is not the machinery of the press expressly employed to engineer the obscuring of truth and the presentment of lies—are not newspapers pastmasters of the lying art which creates opinion by assuming that "everyone" is saying what no one has yet said at all, and which disarms criticism by suppressing the only material facts? Even when we swear that statements are true we wade in falsehoods: "all lies", a solicitor said, pointing to his table piled with affidavits. And it must not be supposed that national snobbishness and the exigencies of 'propriety' and respectability—of which examples are afforded us in Great Britain and America and in the plays of Ibsen—do not demand constant recourse to verbal prevarication, to speech and acts intended to mislead and falsify: and lies again are the staple commodity in the various respectable frauds by which wealth is transferred from the unskilled hands of the needy to the skilled hands of those who have more than they want. All through the interests and methods of men we find subterfuge, equivocation, the *suppressio veri* and the *suggestio falsi*. How is it that man thus "fearfully and wonderfully made" as a channel of fraud should have come to lay stress upon the duty of verbal veracity? It is because verbal veracity is much easier than truthfulness, as faith is easier than works for which it has invariably been substituted.

If verbal untruthfulness does not harm the moral personality, is there any ground for supposing that it destroys moral security; that we have a right to feel that the person who tells untruths is untrustworthy? The answer is, No; there is no real ground for these popular beliefs. We have seen that no one lives without employing equivocal speech, and that equivocation does not differ from falsehood; and it involves a real moral perversion to assume that if a man has kept a tragic home secret from all comers he would be incapable of exact statement to the right person. And this example is good for all cases.

What we should aim at, then, is a state of society in A NEW AIM which prevarication is accepted for what it is, a strictly necessary form of defence, a right inseparable from the power of speech. Prevarication and verbal untruthfulness should no longer be looked upon as bastards of speech but as its legitimate children; children under their own name not masquerading as little cherubs of veracity. It should be understood that a man keeps to himself what he should not tell; understood that he should say: 'I have no knowledge of the matter'—no knowledge for you. There is no moral equation between lying to a person about his own affairs and lying to him about our own. In speaking or writing I should expect a person to make the excuse that seemed good to him, where the excuse is the sole object and no facts are owed or required.[1]

---

[1] An excuse—that is a reason given which is not the reason—is evidently not the truth whether it be a literal truth or not. Hence the excuse we

A falsehood may clearly be the happiest of expedients;[1] it may be as wrong to tell the truth as to tell a wicked untruth, it may be as iniquitous to tell all the facts in one case as it would be in another to withhold them. The phrase "At least I only told the truth" may cover heinous wrong, and in any case discloses no virtue. For truth-speaking may be as noxious as any lie, and there is nothing to choose between a wanton lie and a wanton truth. The one is altogether as detestable as the other. A falsehood may be a simple case of duty, and it is a strictly moral duty so to tell the lie which ought to be told that no one should know it for other than the truth. A man should be ashamed to risk his friend's peace of mind or the betrayal of his trust; and such a man's capacity for a high form of truth is more worthy of our confidence than is your verbal truth-speaker's. His lie on your behalf is easily found out, for he is supercareful to protect the verbal fetich; but nothing in his mental outlook suggests that we could count on him for an appreciation at all costs of any of the higher estimates of veracity. When we are careful to lie without 'telling a lie' we make the assumption that the 'point of honour', by some strange law of morality, always binds the person of whom a question is asked and never the person who asks it. The exact contrary is the fact and should be accepted as such.

A common type of un-truth

During the war of 1914–18 some wagons carrying the equipment of the scottish women's medical expedition in Serbia got tacked on to a train going elsewhere. Two

give is in itself morally indifferent; and hence the futility of all the conundrums set before us: "ought I to say this or that in those circumstances?" the only question of any moment being, Had I the right to mislead in that case? If so, I can say whatever is necessary to mislead—if not, not.

[1] And the most moral: conduct falsehoods—as distinguished from intellectual falsehood—may be lovelier than any verbal truthfulness

Magnanima menzogna, or quand' è 'l vero
Si bello, che si possa a te preporre
(Tasso, Gerusalemme Liberata, canto 2°.)

members of the party boarded the wagons and by dint of character and the invention of a 'General Popovitch' who would be wroth if the wagons were carried off, got them released. What shall be said of this falsehood? First, that it plainly is typical of a great number of falsehoods both legitimate (as here) and illegitimate. Since the pleading of privilege is seldom fair and special patronage is seldom just, the 'General' serves as often as not to buttress the wrong act and prevent the right one. But 'General Popovitch' sets straight some crooked things. In this guise is he in any sense a less worthy figure than his solidly veracious counterpart who is daily invoked by those in least need of protection? Not alone the material necessity of men but both courtesy and charity call for a measure of untruthfulness. I mislike those who *Social* tell us that truth and sincerity consist, *inter alia*, in the *veracity* exact verbal expression of our likes and dislikes and even of our passing moods. So we are not to say "I am glad to see you" when at the moment we are sorry, or that a visit has been a pleasure when there was no actual pleasure. But life, surely, should express the permanent not only the temporary, and in manners that nobility which is in graciousness should be preferred before an accurate diagnosis of our psychical condition. It is not insincere for language to register this permanent self, the self with which sympathy and education have endowed you.

It is often alleged that commerce is built upon verbal *Com-* truth. But what commerce depends upon is integrity and *mercial* the keeping of faith, and to be a 'man of your word' in *veracity* your dealings is not the same thing as a care for verbal veracity. An attempt to buttress this fetich is made by pointing out that lower natures do not appreciate truth, that the savage who is found out in a lie laughs. It is *The savage* true that social shame is not developed with the savage on *has no idea* this point as it is with us. But as we have seen such shame *of veracity?* is no measure of intrinsic right and wrong. The primitive man feels the same intense shame for breaches of superstitious caste rules on which the safety of the community is held to depend that highly civilized man feels if detected in some gross breach of table manners. But what diplomatist is dismayed when his diplomatic falsehoods are recognized? Truth has special difficulties for the undeveloped intelligence and if the savage does not appreciate verbal veracity it is equally true that he has no notion at all of truth of idea. The immature and untutored human intelligence has small appreciation of any value in verbal truthfulness, partly because this value is largely a growth of complicated social conditions and partly because the line between imagery and fact is not clearly

Truths of fancy and of fact

drawn. A child is not disconcerted when its fairy tale is exposed, just because it is itself unconscious of any difference between a truth of fancy and a truth of fact— as the infant is unconscious that the moon is not as well within its grasp as the ball. Nevertheless untruths told by young folk should not go unchallenged. It should not be taken for granted that any untruth was a necessary one: 'could you not have told him the fact in that case?' 'But what you said is not what happened?' are questions in place during the whole of adolescence, and the more the notion of accurate statement of fact replaces the repetition of the word 'truth' the deeper and better will the notion

Worldly lies

of truth be developed. If children see their parents are worldly and resort to what a child calls 'acting' they too will act and tell falsehoods for the same ends. No young person should be brought up to tell untruths for this reason. As to adults the plain fact is that the state of society presents legitimate grounds for some worldly lies, without which we should deprive ourselves and those we protect of what is properly due to us. Definite teaching and example however do not count for as much as the mental capacities and moral bent of a child; and one with quick perceptions, diplomatic instinct, tact and criticism,

will and must take notice by speech and act of what passes
unnoticed by the simpler and ingenuous nature. Social
frauds, the tissue of boasting lies, are by no means discouraged in home and school life; but while we cannot
think of a better use of speech than that which sends a
would-be murderer on the wrong track, our prevention
nevertheless is so strong, at least in a country like England,
in favour of verbal truthfulness that many people would
suppose a child who hesitated to put forward this solution
would be more likely to prove a trustworthy character
than the child who thought of it at once. The higher
appreciations of truth will remain out of reach till we
purge our minds of such inanities as this. The qualities
of an essentially truthful nature will always shame the
standards of truthfulness of the average man. No child,
of course, perceives the nobility of the higher forms of
truth, but every child must be taught to appreciate truthfulness, even in the smallest things—sincerity, honesty
with itself, accuracy of statement; yes, and the habit of
strict verbal truth-speaking. But any proper education of
intelligence and imagination will prepare it to understand
that this cannot be regarded as the equivalent of truth
in its nobler forms.

As soon as we begin to consider the role of truthful Truthful-
speech we realize at once that it depends in the last resort ness depends upon
upon character and even upon temperament. A truthful character
character is first and foremost a sincere character. The
sincere person is the only really truthful person, and the
strong character is more truthful than the weak. Falsehoods due to cowardice are wholly blameworthy, but the
dependent or servile disposition will always find it hard
to resist them. And it is evident also that our passions
and other qualities and defects of character may obscure
and misrepresent truth far more than the verbally untruthful person can ever obscure it. Some children and
some adults are truthful because they are blunt and

callous, callous of the feelings of others and with no sensitiveness for themselves. Others are untruthful because they are sensitive and imaginative, or again because they lack self-confidence. As a faculty the child's imagination is identical with that of the imaginative thinker. The poet imagines sentiments he has never felt and the child scenes and emotions it has never experienced. "I saw a little squirrel and it sat up and ate nuts out of my hand" is a good instance of a child's imaginative falsehood. To mortify the child for such imaginations in the interests of literalism and to force it not indeed into understanding and appreciating but simply into acquiring literalness as a fundamental factor in its mental equipment, is not education in any sense at all.   The great bulwark of a certain character force is a lack of imagination, which is at the same time fatal to intellectual and moral fineness. The unimaginative person is literal, therefore he is verbally truthful. But he may not be intimately truthful for in the finer things of the spirit imagination is all-important. If you have no imagination you have not the temptation to see things from other points of view; to imagine or to wish them otherwise. The Irishman it is said tells a falsehood because it is more interesting than the fact, because the truth is dull,[1] and the untruthfulness of the uneducated Italian is due, there can be no doubt, to his imagining the pleasant things that would fit the circumstances, eschewing by temperament the hard unpleasant ones. The teutonic characteristic of "truthfulness without candour" can be observed in Yorkshire and among the lowland Scotch; there is a great deal of want of candour among some latin peoples but it does not profess to be

(margin notes) Truthfulness and the imagination

(margin notes) Truthfulness without candour

---

[1] "He hardly knew what a statement was, and could rarely get one believed for the simple reason that in the very act of making one his imagination would suggest—'and if the contrary were true?'" hence a "wavering in his eye and the loss of conviction in his tone." This is profoundly true. A vivid or a fine imagination *must* influence our outlook upon fact, upon 'mere actuality'.

truthful, and it is highly undesirable that such a type of truthfulness should be fostered in children. Why should lip service of truth make us more satisfied with ourselves or with our relation to the person we deceive? Why is it more honourable to have used a tortuous phrase which he might accept as in some sort akin to the facts? or how can these ingeniously turned untruthful truths be a support to the ideal of truth when they are simply methods of circumventing it? I have found that natures which stickle most for verbal veracity are often capable of a singular falsity; a regard for this low form of honesty being compatible with an essentially lying disposition. That egyptian "truth-speaker"—what was he like? I picture him as nothing but an epitaph "a kind husband and indulgent father": no one was the happier for his truth-speaking and he does not suggest a care for intellectual truth. What the world wants is not a truth-speaker so much as a truth-seeker. For the paraphernalia of mere verbal truthfulness we should substitute a love of abstract truth, truth of sentiment, truth for its own sake. It was said in Esdras *magna est veritas et praevalet*; but such counterfeit coin as verbal veracity has nothing in common with the truth which is great and prevails; there is nothing to prevail, there is no truth. The truth which is great and will prevail is moral truth, the truth of justice and right. And all great truth prevails; despite our intolerance, our prejudice, our insincerity, great truth once born does not die. It is highly disadvantageous that only a negligible minority of men should be taught to care for intellectual truth. For the great role in human affairs belongs to mental and moral sincerity. These things are not natural to the people who love twilights, who do not wish to see and have no desire that ideas should be clear; they are the people who evade facts and find it easier to impose on themselves a habit of verbal veracity than to discover in themselves the mental vigour required to face ideas. Hence the

The role of intellectual truth

distinction which has been made between english (and german) love of duty and french hatred of lies. The Englishman does not hate lies; he has a general abhorrence of untruthful relations with his neighbour, and those who know both nations find a greater habit of truth-speaking among english people as compared with the french. Yet it is only the thought and sincerity behind speech which can fix right names to things and right meaning to words, and without these speech is merely dealing with counters.

Truth is, often, an effort, a difficult hard thing we owe; how can we confound this with our conventional relations Truth and to indifferent people? The truth I owe my neighbour sincerity may be loyalty or honesty, and then the merit of verbal truth is that it serves this ethical end; or I may have to pay this debt of truth by telling untruths. What is verbal truth without an object? But essential truth is an end in itself, it is sincerity. This is where it parts company with Social value verbal veracity as a servant of moral ends. There is an of truth obvious social value in truth-speaking, and if facts are in themselves no better than fancies the habit of telling truths is very much better than the habit of telling untruths. A habit of useless lying is noxious to character and to our fellow beings. Sense of relation, the basis and connexion of fact, are lost with the liar—and by the liar I do not now mean one who uses speech for malicious and treacherous ends but simply the person habitually untruthful and undependable. Behind the truth-speaking habit there is propriety both of reason and relation: the use of any of the means of expression merely for disguise or merely to represent what is personal to yourself alone plainly fails to correspond either with reason or with those social relations which are implied in the very means of expression. Small unimportant falsehoods can give no information, whereas veracity in small matters, as in great and important, is itself capable of forming the basis of what may prove useful truth. The lying inmate of a house is such an abuser of speech; it is an outrage on social interdependence that we should be made the butt of wanton deceits and baseless statements—those cheating lies which seem to be of two kinds, the servile lie of the man who fears you too much and the ignoble lie of the man who respects you too little. Speech must always serve the general ends of knowledge, confidence, and social intercourse.

Since the apprehension of intellectual truth (like the truthful nature itself) is a matter of mental and moral capacity the truth as it is realized by *A* is by no means always communicable to *B*, and hence mental reservations are essential in human intercourse. At a different level of education truth for the intelligence cannot be reached, but ethical and spiritual comprehension between two people need not be lost, and this is both more precious and closer to truth. Why should it be any stranger that intellectual closeness (man to man) is not always possible than that emotional closeness should so often be impossible? Shall I, ought I, to explain to a less instructed person how I believe, how little, how differently to himself? No, for there is no common language, and words which fail, and which must fail, to convey to your hearer what they convey to you do not enlighten his intelligence though they may put to flight his sympathy. This sympathy is a common language, the language of shared sentiment, and it cannot be a moral error, on the contrary it is a moral duty, to preserve it.

In the götterdämmerung which shrouds man's life he may prefer to temper the intellectual light he has and to grasp at shadows; but truth of sentiment and all truths of the moral order need no such twilight; all the light shed here can only make for our happiness and bring us nearer to a harmonious view of conduct. This light indeed does not show a man what he shall be but it will

Mental reservation

reveal to him what he is: and the moral conduct of life perhaps must always be approached in the spirit which said

> "Now we are sons of god
> And it has not been made manifest
> What we shall be."

III. LUST

Lust is the physical and psychophysical desire which attends the stimulation of the nerve centres and glands habitually associated with the functions of sex. Whether or not the stimulation of these ganglia of emotional sensation be exclusively a sexual phenomenon is matter for inquiry. In any case it is the normal incentive to the physical act and its normal accompaniment. What we are going to distinguish is a normal from an abnormal phenomenon of lust.[1] Normal lust is that which accompanies the sex act, the first years of puberty, and a psychophysical attraction and sympathy which most people identify with love and which is the feeder of passion. Abnormal lust is an excess and by-product of the sensual attractions, predatory and violating in its sexual aspect and in its self-regarding aspect a consuming lecherousness. So defined, lustfulness is as common in marriage as out of it, as prevalent in normal sensual relations as in the most abnormal.

When we look round on the sexual conditions existing on the earth we see clearly that sexuality is in excess both of what is necessary and what is desirable. If we omit those domesticated animals which are kept for no purpose but the service of femels, and whose lust like their size is artificially induced, it is still apparently true that there are some oversexualized animals in a wild state. This could result automatically from the exercise of functions which are, subjectively, merely functions of self-gratification, pursued irresponsibly with no prevision of the ends they serve and no possibility of appreciating the further momentous functions confided to the supreme parent.

---

[1] Lust—etymologically *desire*; and this is its constant character—desire, it may be, which is psychophysically normal and natural, or a desire which is pathological.

This egoism and this ignorance combined would lead just to the kind of excess in the seeker and non-bearer sex which is actually observable, and together they explain the phenomena of sexualism as we see it in male animals. The paramount cause of oversexualism and lustfulness, however, must be looked for not in natural ignorance of ends nor even in appetite but in an excessive use and abuse of the sexual act and the sexual incitements, a phenomenon which is overwhelmingly greater in man than in any other animal. We start then with an excess and an abuse—an excess of stimulation and the abuse of a natural function. How ought the various manifestations of lust to be regarded? We are accustomed, in the first

'Natural' and 'un-natural' vice

place, to distinguish 'natural excess' from 'unnatural vice'. It has been assumed that every abuse and every vagary of the act of coition possesses some sort of validity before the moral conscience as a phenomenon of normal nature. This has been a colossal ethical blunder. No approach to a moral opinion of lust acts as a whole can be arrived at until it is understood that abuse is not a function of use, but antagonizes it: drunkenness and gluttony have not the sanction which attaches to the acts of alimentation; and in the phenomena of sensuous pleasure and excitement every kind of lascivious lust must be permanently separated from the normal stimulations of the sex act, and from the sensuous delight which accompanies, or may accompany, the love attraction of man to man. In my view there is no natural or unnatural lust, if these words are intended to connote a moral quality in the one which is absent in the other. Acts of lasciviousness are the same wherever perpetrated, and lascivious abuse in marriage is no more to be justified and no more moral in its character than lascivious abuse anywhere else. No sort of moral sanction attaches to these things because they are associated with sexual intercourse. Wherever they occur they are to be judged as essentially the same.

All such lust is one—there is no other moral position than this.

In one of the biblical stories there are set forth the three modes of lust to which current ethics give the name of 'unnatural' 'natural' and 'incestuous'. The whole difference between a moral attitude to sexual matters and one which must always be essentially immoral depends upon our reaction to the problems there introduced. There came two messengers to a town given up to sodomy. That the visitors were angels does not affect the problem which is solely engaged with their quality as guests and the correlative duties of hospitality. The rarity of angels' visits depends, no doubt, on the infrequency with which an unknown stranger is hailed delightedly as a potential friend rather than put on his defence as a natural enemy. In Lot's household these visitors were received as angels; but the wers of Sodom when they heard of the arrival besieged the door of his dwelling just as soldiers in the european war besieged the doors of provided houses in the towns where they were billeted, only the wers of Sodom were not supplied with tickets. Lot, however, had his remedy. What the besiegers wanted was 'unnatural'; he therefore implored them to desist from their wicked design and to be content with his daughters who, he told them, were virgins and whom he would deliver over to them so that they might abuse them and wreak all their will upon them. That is how the problem of 'unnatural' desire is treated in the narrative, throwing light upon the natural affection of fathers and the primitive theory of family rights: and it will be recognized that the habit of 'giving away' women to prostitution or marriage coupled with a guarantee of virginity is an inveterate one.

The angels had come to destroy Sodom by fire and deliver Lot who was the only pious person to be found in the city; and the sequel to the story is that he and his two daughters reach a mountain where there is no other human being and both of them begot issue through their drunken father. But their ideas of morality had been learned at home. There they had discovered that it was a fitting thing that their bodies should be cast to the lecherous wolves of the city in order to screen two young males. Perhaps no more repulsively immoral story exists in literature than this and similar biblical anecdotes; but the writer is completely unaware of it. He metes out reproof and punishment to none but the wers of Sodom and to the wife of Lot who because she looks back at the city from which Lot himself had hesitated to flee[1] is changed into a pillar of salt, unworthy to be saved with this stout champion of natural vice. For to the primitive mind of humanity—the primitive male mind—nothing is unclean which may be referred to the sexual instinct; cruel coarse and lascivious its gesta may prove to be, but they always remain in a sense limpidly moral, dividing their perpetrator from the dogs without by an impassable barrier. Let us look at some of the episodes of 'natural lust' among what may be called the males within. The records of a 'white slave' brothel in America in the first decade of the xx[th] century showed that the victims were used over twenty and even over forty times a day; while among the violences employed to force the victims of this traffic to whoredom we have it recorded that other means having failed a girl was locked in a room for a day and night with two chinamen. Three thousand years earlier a Jew of the tribe of Dan arriving with his concubine at a place given up to sodomist practices thrusts her out at the door as his substitute that she may slake the lust of the town. After being abused all night she returns to his doorstep to die. Certainly it is better to be with the dogs. The Jew of the tribe of Dan, no doubt, had no mind to suffer non-sexual abuse since he was always well

[1] Gen. xix. 16.

146

provided with the means of sexual abuse; he would not, of course, like to be the butt of a lascivious onslaught at other people's pleasure, not his own, such as was suffered by the women in the Chicago brothel, and he no doubt explained the infamy of his act by his pious resistance to the notion that he should himself be subjected to any such violence. The course he took is common to all patriarchal societies, the constant feature of which is consideration for the comfort and convenience of wers at the expense of women: a fact which puts us at once on the track of this method of morals.

How indeed can every 'human' quality or trait be outraged, as in these cases, and yet leave a moral residue to justify them—something subserving a moral end? What *is* this moral residue? In the commonplace idea it is compounded partly of what is 'natural' and partly of what is theological. Sexual conduct has not only been closely connected with theology it has also everywhere combined subjection of the one sex with complete licence for the other. Such a conduct scheme might have suggested— but has never yet done so—that it was unnecessary to go so far afield as the creator of heaven and earth in search of the 'moral law' which underlies it. Did Jahveh tolerate the abominations described in the bible because they were the sad consequences of original sin? And if so, why was sodomy alone intolerable? Let us bear in mind that when wers have abstained from irregular sensual pleasures no merit has attached to the abstinence, because they have always, since the matriarchal era, been purveyors to themselves and procurers of women, whom they have in the process reduced in every age to the position of easy victims of their lust. It has never been dispassionately realized that what they have done is to place their own sexual demands in a kind of honour, to be regarded as the subject of inalienable rights; and so it has come to pass that god is not permitted to classify male excess but only

A moral residue to 'natural vice'?

147

non-sexual excess as sin: god may not even consider it an unnatural thing that women should be abused to death in soveran disregard of the natural goal of motherhood. The wer condemns wholeheartedly none but non-sexual sensuality: in primitive ages it did not and it does not now seem unnatural in his eyes that women should suffer every kind of physical and moral injury, or die, in the service of the male appetite. No just views about lust and the natural and unnatural can be framed until such notions as these are ousted. And this sex pathology joined to theology results in a monstrous and grotesque travesty

Impunity of male lust

of morals.   The two fetiches have been the impunity of male lust and a supposed obligation to reproduce the species no matter under what circumstances. They combine ill in practice. The brothel is the logical homage to the first, and the brothel has never been seriously restrained by christian governments or christian churches: but to redress the misbalance caused by the obvious fact that it flouts the natural ends of copulation married women are told that it is sinful not to bear every child that is or might be conceived. Excessive procreation for some women is to counterbalance the unnatural sterilization of others. Always the woman emerges as the victim, and chiefly the married woman who is made the repository of the supposed sanctity of both fetiches. A male may do with a woman what is 'unnatural' as well as what is 'natural'; a french harlot is examined not only for the natural use but for an unnatural; and it is because the male has never regarded his sensuality as unnatural that the habitual use of harlots and the wearing of what are called french or american 'letters'—which involve strictly sterile processes—rouse no comment. The significant point here is that while no complaint is uttered when males bring about sterility in order to gratify their desire —or as a result of syphilis—the sterility becomes morally abominable when married women frustrate conception.

But why do we call the act of coition 'natural?' Not because males have strong appetites but simply because it is the prerequisite to procreation. Whether sexual connexion is natural apart from this goal is a further consideration;[1] but meanwhile we cannot have it both ways— and either the sexual act is to be regarded as per excellency the natural act on the ground that it is the channel of reproduction, and then it is not natural when this consequence is defied, or it is to be regarded as natural because it is a sensual appetite, and then other acts must rank with it in naturalness. To suppose the excesses and outrages of male sexuality are essentially different from all other sensual acts is to counterfeit the moral coinage and to cut at the root of moral judgment. All lust is equally lustful, and a lascivious act is not more virtuous because it is done with the opposite sex than with your own. All lust is one

If this conclusion is a startling one it is so in virtue of our ready acceptance in the past of false moral coin for true. The truth is, as is shown by the old literatures of the world and by present day phenomena which pass unnoticed and unrebuked, that patriarchal humanity has always been purblind to the cruelties and distortions of sex lust and that in framing the moral code no branch of mankind has been influenced by the spectacle of its ravages and ruthlessness.

Sexual lust is then in many of its aspects definitely pathological and unnatural. But if we consider the sensual phenomena connected with the strong psycho-physical desire aroused by the presence of other animals of your species, by mental images and associations, by physiological processes which are purely subjective, we shall also see that these overpass the boundaries of sex; that the reproductive appetites and stimulations do not (and can not) exist without involving various sensual pheno- Constant sensual phenomena

[1] See Marriage, p. 263.

149

mena quite as natural to organic beings as the normal sensual phenomena of conjugation. For example, the young dog horse and cow appear not to distinguish at first between sex personalities. Their sensuous instinct is aroused with individuals of the same sex as everyone who has watched young animals together can ascertain for himself. The same is no doubt true in the relations of young persons of one sex in our species: in spite of the excessive sexual bias given by human education and suggestion to girls and boys the evidence of school life shows that the homogenic phenomenon is stronger.[1] Much of this is simply licentious and due to the highly over-sexualized stimulations in mankind, but some of it is not lustful at all. The sympathies and love passions of young people at the age of puberty are not a lust manifestation and should not be dealt with as such. Imagination and romance, the spirit of adventure and the craving for experience, are the elements at work. And the caution that is required here is because the sensual motions are an incalculable force—closely intimate in their character, whose sources we bear about with us, always potentially present—and that these motions are little understood or restrained by the adolescent; they may therefore play the same sort of havoc in a life which the habit of drink or any other sensual indulgence would play. The remedy is early adequate preparation and knowledge, and the formation of habits of pudic self-reverence and self-restraint. But some sensuous accompaniment of warm sympathy and affinity on the part of youths of both sexes in the early years of puberty must be regarded as perfectly natural and normal, with its roots in the arcana of organic being. Young people then at the age of puberty

[1] It might indeed be said that at the age of puberty the passions are not necessarily or normally directed to the other sex. The social suggestion is always that way, but it is still true that usually the passions of the young could take another direction (as younger to older persons, and homogenic attachment).

have not high sexual specialization and the finer the nature the more true this will be. On the other hand they do possess high emotionalism and a strong sensual and physical vitality which in the best young natures is joined to idealism and susceptibility. The outcome of such a combination is an experience of great intensity, psychophysical in its character, the motor of which however is ideal not sensual.

The disgust shown by gross sensualists, and especially perhaps by male sensualists, at all homogenic manifestations should serve to open our eyes to much of the championship of 'nature'. It is abundantly evident that those who work every kind of devilishness on women and children are loudest in denouncing homogenic attachments, and their dislike also extends to all intrasexual sympathy. Physical satiety in the oversexualized human type is a monopolist, and ousts the psychical side of human relations. It is sex satiation which makes extra sexual phenomena repulsive to the sex sensualist. This is a psychophysical phenomenon of wide application; and we should not fail to notice the moral squalor of the surroundings in which men are warned against sodomy in the bible (Gen. xix; Judges xix). In all the cases worse than sodomy was already there. *The sex sensualist's dislike of these phenomena*

Another sensual phenomenon is of course autoerotism. The sex sensualist obsecrates this as he obsecrates homogenic manifestations. But how should the good man regard it? As an involuntary natural phenomenon ethics has no concern with it at all. Pursued as a gross sensualism it deserves the obloquy due to all lechery; but in no case can self-use merit the moral reproach due to misuse of another creature, no matter of what sex or of what species. The moral obliquity which can palliate such disgusting lasciviousness as the abuse of immature girl children, the violation of women, or the over use of one sex by the other, on the ground that these acts do not *Self-use Auto-erotism* involve either self-use or homosexual uses would always have made any decent ethical code unattainable, and has done so. It is very possible that autoerotism may have become natural to dioecious species. At least there is no evidence to the contrary, and we should ignore the opinion of sexualists who were willing to fill the earth with venereal disease and of the male physicians who during the xix[th] century prescribed "a woman" as they would have prescribed a drug. The example of other animals—especially of young animals—the involuntary and automatic nature of autoerotism, and the fact that none of the evils denounced by the sexualists accompany it, suggest that we are in fact in presence of a natural phenomenon.[1] We need further confirmation from animal life, for autostimulation may be traceable to over-sexualization, or, on the other hand, may, as said, be a common result of dioecious organization in the higher mammals with the primates and man. It is likely, then, that autoerotism, or self-use, under right conditions is as natural as it is harmless; that the condition underlying it is part and parcel of our physical make-up; and that the assumption that sexual congress is the only regular outlet is on the whole gratuitous. If this were true no one should be without a person of the other sex at hand, which is, in fact, the principle of the brothel; but among women hundreds of thousands are so placed that sexual congress in their case has been regarded as an impossible and vicious thing. Meanwhile the growth of psycho-physical reticence and fastidiousness certainly tends to make the claim that we should be supplied with the body of another person as an outlet for our physical sensations crude and distasteful.

[1] Compare the complacent assumption of the over-sexed that non-sexual sensuality bred insanity—an assumption which has been proved medically to be without any sort of foundation—with the actual toll of sex insanity in lunatic asylums.

There is a degenerate sexual practice known as sadism Sadism
—sex pleasure induced or increased by the cruelties practised on the femel. It is a feature in brothels and in
married life, and is a disgusting phenomenon for which
ages of sex domination are responsible; it is the sensual
expression of a psychical abortion, the secular pleasure
taken by the male in disgracing women. Viewed in the light
of ethics a sadistic sexual act is more blasting to the soul
than the irregular sensual acts which we always denounce.

As to congress outside the species. It is not easy philo-
sophically to say where the horror of it lies, but ethically it
is not difficult. If it were without the bounds of natural
desire it would not take place, but it has existed at all
times and the Jewish deity issues a command against it
as against adultery or fornication. Its heinousness depends on two things which our inhumanity and our lustfulness have made us blind to. The first is the despicable
misuse of the creature who is not of our species, and the
other is that all such desire is and always has been human
'beastliness', the same word which applies to so much of
man's congress with man.

Sensual acts which involve homogenic sympathies have Herma-
been flayed by mankind under the supposed aegis of god phrodism
the creator. But how could a creating god who loathed
paiderasty have suffered the existence of hermaphrodites?
What is the hermaphrodite to do; especially in view of
the fact that the sex to which he more properly belongs
may be a matter of doubt and is often settled by the way
he was dressed in childhood? The phenomenon of hermaphrodism was apparently understood in Greece but has
been ignored by later civilizations.[1] Indeed it is not
possible to bring such a fact as hermaphrodism within the

---

[1] Besides the rarer case of complete physiological hermaphrodism
there are instances of actual though incomplete sex-crosses, to which
Havelock Ellis has drawn attention. And it is evident that psychological
hermaphrodism (see p. 296) presents similar obstacles to the sexual
view of life.

ethical purview, as in the case of the excesses we have been considering. In the middle ages a cock who laid an egg was burnt alive by persons who while incapable of appreciating the wonder hid for science in this poor fowl were capable of believing that the obscene cruelty of Lot enjoyed divine patronage. When there is right moral opinion we shall understand that there is no viler resource of lust than the abuse of a woman by the male; and that traffic in women in order to violate them is not morally preferable to irregular lust by consent. Both are sterile, they cannot be referred for their sanction to nature's law of reproduction. As we see, there has always been a specious disregard of this natural goal on the tacit assumption that all the rights are and must be with the overstimulated male; and the one universally privileged thing in a male-arranged world has not been the mother's role but the male's appetite. So it has come about that the violent and unnatural acts which spring from this appetite pass unchallenged, while at the same time private acts are reprobated which may be sensual but are not cruel, which do no unnatural injury to a mother and cause no irrevocable misery to defenceless girls. "The individual" said J. S. Mill "is not accountable to society for his actions, in so far as these concern the interests of no person but himself."[1] If no community should exercise control over self-regarding actions no community should fail to control the predatory antisocial phenomena of the sensual appetite. In this respect sexual violence and rape assault on the young and the sodomy of Sodom and Gomorrah are equivalent lusts.

[1] Or the interests of other adults equally capable of consent. The example Mill cites is polygamy.

IV. WHAT IS LOVE?

Τί τῶν καλῶν ἐστὶν ὁ Ἔρως, ὦ Σώκρατές τε καὶ Διοτίμα;
"How is love beautiful, O Sokrates and Diotima?"

THERE was a doctrine taught about love in Greece more than two thousand three hundred years ago; there was a gospel of love whose apostle was the John loved of Jesus; there is the appetite which our human civilization hitherto has taught us to identify with love; and there are the actual various manifestations of love among organic beings and in human history. Here we have to do only with the sympathy and attraction the attachment and the passion which are the staple manifestations of love between living creatures. Love is indeed the psychical phenomenon of greatest moment in life, so that nothing influences its happiness as does love, which in and by itself can make the glory and worthwhileness of life. Yet it has been the subject of doctrines which are wholly false. For contrary to what the whole world has believed love and sexual attraction have nothing in common. The radical false doctrine which has pursued love is that its type is primarily and chiefly or more especially an affection due to distinctions of sex; and this is belied by the whole history of sexuality. Indeed if it were really understood what love is it would be perceived that nothing in the entire gamut of feeling has less kin with love than sexual effusion. Sexual desire is not love, and at no time and in no species has the sexual satisfaction depended upon love. Lupanaria are the standing attestation of this fact among mankind. Conjugation for the savage like conjugation for present-day 'civilized' man, who pays and receives pay for the act of lust, like conjugation for most other animals, is not only not a 'love-act' but does not necessarily imply even a movement of sympathy. There is no basis of psychical fact whatever to justify the phrase

Love has nothing to do with the attraction of sex

'love-act' for the act of sexual coition. Our literature is flooded with descriptions of the sex sensualism in the human animal which for french writers is always "amour". Balzac who regarded himself as an ethical sociologist fills his 'love' pages with the play of instincts and sentimentalisms which never move from the welter of sensual desire. The confusion, there can be no doubt, is the result of male preoccupation with sex which has succeeded in obscuring the vision of love; this and the character of male desire itself which is an appetite rather than a sympathy, in contrast with femel desire where the reverse is true. The male conception of love, as male, has then always been defective. At the same time it alone has been articulate; our notions of love have not been derived from a comparison of the femel conception of it with the male but from perceptions and experience which are characteristically male.

The passion which has as its basis physical desire may no doubt accompany love, but we have clearly to recognize that this is no part of its connotation but is adventitious and accidental; it belongs to young love and at no age is it ever to be found at the heart of love. Passion which wears away, so that we can say concerning it "the love had died", is not love, it is not a love experience for it is 'Falling in love' a self-referring experience. But it will be thought that the phenomenon we call 'falling in love' belies these assertions, and appears to be love itself in spontaneous directness and reality? When what is meant by 'falling in love' is simply the ephemeral sexual attraction and not also psychical attraction—that sympathy and passion which is necessarily both a psychological and a physiological phenomenon—then we must say of it exactly what has been said of all sexual passion—it is not love and does and adolescence not tell us what love is. As young lovers we envisage the love object with qualities drawn from our own flaming imaginations, and our first love is not in fact a person in whom the qualities we are in love with inhere but a simulacrum clothed with what our imagination demands and our romance lends to it. The young person feels all the imperativeness of this passion; it is there, he supposes, that happiness lies and nothing but tragedy and immeasurable loss can follow the attempt to part him and the beloved object. But men do not look back to such a first love and believe that the loss was immeasurable. The psycho-physical conditions here make every such experience both exclusive and infinite in its suggestion. A similar criticism can be applied to 'falling in love' at a later age. For the 'susceptible' as we call them the experience has not the sign manual of love, not its constant attachment, not its unchangeable sympathy. For the sensual the experience remains a sensual one. Only when the permanent psychical love passions are present can 'falling in love' tell us something of what love is.   Love is a passion of sympathy, of intimate attraction and constant attachment. This is true of human love and of our love of spiritual beauty in man and in god. A new word is needed to distinguish it from the feeling excited by sexual desire and fed by physical beauty. Youths—young The girls and lads—are not in love with each other, they are amatory 'taken with each other' (*épris*). Sex attraction and its callow and shallow sympathies are described by such words as 'enamoured' and 'amativeness' which might well be restricted to this use, with 'amours' as their noun, while 'love' would express the higher and totally different emotion; and we should then speak of being 'in love' with virtue, 'in love' with holy poverty, 'in love' with beauty, with the loved friend, the loved spouse, the loved little life. All sex amours are of an entirely uncertain nature—a sympathy with no sympathy, signifying nothing for the future, not even a tie of any sort. Liking and attraction, the desire to win or possess, do not constitute love for persons any more than for things.[1] The sex emotion in fact as passion for a person is not as ancient an emotion as love. It had no existence until sensual desire was concentrated upon one object.

We shall find the types of love in the love of the mother for the little child, of the little child for the mother, and in the love of man for man, individual for individual, which we call the love of friends. The total perfection of love is revealed in these. And this truth always lay within our grasp. There is nothing more radical in nature than zoological sympathy and antipathy: this sympathy tells between species and species and occurs sporadically between the most dissimilar and mutually hostile species, as it tells between individuals in any race or species, entirely regardless of sex or of any other circumstance.[2] This is the universal fact subtending the love force. If there were no such fact the most perfect reaches of love and life would be impossible. For in all perfect love relations there is this profound and unerring zoological affinity; which subtends the love force though it does not exhaust it. And it is a psychophysical fact. Its nature as such needs not to be sought in the sensuous-sexual, where indeed it is not to be found, since its obvious example is not sexual but maternal; the organic attraction which we call zoological sympathy being founded in the senses and founded in the spirit, but not in the sex relation. Its character is sympathetic not appetitive. Just as there could have been organized life without the phenomena of strong reciprocal attraction and aversion, so there might have been gregarious sympathy without such a pheno-menon as the love sympathy. I think the alchemy which

Zoological sympathy

[1] Clearly love is one of the *likes* and hence the two constant meanings of the Greek *phileo* and Latin *amare* and French *aimer*—to be wont to do because you like to do. *Phileo* in contrast with *agapeo* connotes not only the love and closeness between living things, but the liking of things. If you love you like, though you can like and not love.

[2] See Individual and Species and The Other Animals, pp. 112; 193, 194 and *n.*[2].

brought love into life is to be sought for in the facts of maternal reproduction, and certainly the phenomenon of zoological sympathy must have its roots there also. Love therefore is founded in affinities as deep as the life process; and though in the result it is by no means bounded by an exercise of the life processes, yet here it was first learnt, for I think there would have been no love just of this kind had it not been for the facts of maternal reproduction. With all love there is physical liking which is Love is not necessarily present in affection. There is no love in psycho-
sensuous the sense I have described without physical sympathy and potential if not actual bodily intimacy. This is just as true for lovers as for love between mother and child. That is not love—though it may be friendship—where there is no physical sympathy, and conversely where there is physical antipathy there cannot be this love. And here someone will object that there can be nothing physical, nothing of the senses, in love of god, in the love which The love of
'god' makes martyrs for an idea. Love between organic beings is founded as has just been said in zoological affinity, but it is something besides, it is not exhausted in this sympathy; and while it remains permanently true that physical sympathy must accompany all such love, in the love of god, of goodness and spiritual beauty, nothing bodily is present. As was said at the beginning, the love of which we here speak is love between psychophysically organized beings and all such love is psychophysical.

From Diotima Sokrates learnt that the pursuit of the Diotima lower Aphroditê is not love but appetite, and has no point of contact with the fine and sentimental things we are accustomed to say about it. Diotima having asked him what he thought of 'love'[1] Sokrates had chanted the customary paean to the passion of Erōs and Aphroditê which is excited by sensual desire and fed by sensual

[1] Erōs.

beauty. And it is through her we are recalled[1] to the truth that these are not love figures at all: and this Aphroditê is not the ideal woman she is the ideal of woman created by the male in his image. About this image cling the selfish and sensual passions but not love and not beauty. This is the lesson that Sokrates learnt. But we have not learnt it. It has remained one of the great unlearnt lessons of the world. In those wonderful conversations a woman lifted from the wer the shackles which had bound him to the senses and taught him that the love which is beautiful takes its rise in the higher appreciations of the soul, and passes on, mayhap, to the ideal love of the beautiful and the good. But in the twenty-three centuries which have intervened the type of human civilization has not changed; the same obsessions hold us, so that we cannot see what Sokrates saw; and in spite of occasional saint and seer it is still believed that in normal man love is the same thing as sex emotionalism. Diotima, indeed, accepted none of the dualism which satisfies the speakers at the symposium: in its place she sets stepping-stones from earth to heaven—like the steps which lead in her woman's experience from undeveloped to developed life: she sets before us the two instruments which the femel has fashioned in dealing with the physical—a choice, and education by discipleship.[2] But it is clear that the ground for a discussion of what love is is so encumbered with the confusion between love and lust which is paramountly a male phenomenon that no speaker at the symposium is really free of it.[3]

---

[1] Recalled—because the original Erōs was the kosmic *logos,* the cause which brought harmony out of the primeval chaos through the reconciling power of love. The later Erōs is simply the god of sensual desire.

[2] Individual and Species, pp. 119, 122–3.

[3] Sensual desire and attraction to mental pleasures are both regularly confused in the *Symposium* with love. Benecke (*Women in Greek Poetry*) continues to call stories of sex desire 'love-stories' and marks them off from the "romantic love" between the sexes of a later epoch (pp. 146–7). But

But is love always of the beautiful? I think not. Many Love always of the beautiful? good men have loved evil ones and love is often the golden woof in the evil lives of two people. It is with human love as with the love of god, some love the good some not: and love is not determined by goodness, it does not go as a prize to the most virtuous. Zoological affinity and natural sympathy lie behind all other qualities, and some of the love-virtues—the things which make us loveable—are independent of the 'moralities'. But if we love the high qualities in our lover we love them with the same appreciations in ourselves with which 'god' is loved. Love then is no emotional activity called into being by spiritual and moral qualities, and man, like the dog, sometimes loves those who kick him and who return his fidelity with vileness.   But must love be itself beautiful? If one man Love always itself beautiful? loves what is good because it is good why should not another in the same manner love what is evil, and then his love would not be a beautiful thing. The answer is that at the core of all love there is that which forbids love of evil because it is evil; the evil man takes pleasure in cruelty but he does not love it, what we call love of evil is not love but hate: love cannot exist without sentiment, and there can be no sentiment about evil, there can be passion but there is not sentiment. Love has tenderness but evil evokes no tenderness, and hate annihilates it.

he cites Menander in Plutarch, Love is an affection of the soul not of the body, with which it has only an accidental connexion—and he reminds us that the same had been said by Enclides the Stoic.

In the *Symposium* Pausanias is made to declare that the love of the "common Aphroditê" is what meaner men feel "and is of bodies rather than of souls". In a remarkable passage in the *Carthaginian* Plautus makes the slave say: And you tell me you are able to love her whom you never touch? And his master replies: I love and fear the gods yet I do not put my hands upon them. That 'love' can be fed on anything but sexual congress appeared ludicrous to the Middle Comedy; but when we come to Terence we hear that sensual desire is not the ground of the love of Pamphilus and his wife. And Benecke notes that in the later comedy the characters who speak slightingly of 'platonic' love are always slaves, it is "never a person of refinement" (*loc. cit.*, p. 185).

Love asks for sacrifice, and the evil man's sacrifices are offered to himself. Love then is not only an incommunicable gift, not to be bought except with its own coin, it is a unique faculty of the soul, its noblest instrument.

Love comes as the most complete in itself of all things, the one immense riches of organic life. Its glory of response, which is the great glory of the lover, may be felt by the mother even in her unconscious babe—the sense that you are not alone but that what you pour out flows back into your own bosom, love being not only a gift but a great creator of gifts, the bridge between life and life, the one certain annealment of the soul's intimate isolation among its kind. It is in this sense that love precedes all other things—as the reconciler, making two things one and that which is without as that which is within; it is the self-conscious finding itself in other-consciousness, for nothing understands like love. Here desire and sacrifice, the fulfilment of self and the good of the other-self are oned, and human nature reaches as it were the kosmic point where to spend self for another is not sacrifice and to lose yourself is to find yourself. The measure of love indeed is always what you will give up for the beloved. This is the character of all love, for the little being, the dear comrade, the beautiful and ideal, for god. Hence we find John Chrysostom saying that though the lover make ten thousand protestations of love if he do not pursue what is profitable to the beloved he is more hostile than an enemy.

Two ways of Love But love has no necessary dependence even on love responses. In its intimate nature love reveals itself to us with two faculties, a faculty which seems to be independent of reciprocal love and the faculty for profound reciprocal attraction. So the youngest lover may learn the fulness of love though what he love be only his own image of beauty: he is a lover without having found love. And the soul may pass through life ever clothing from within the love object, being a perfect lover, with the perfect fruition of love, both lover and love. No one then can understand the mystery of love who does not understand these 2 things: that love can subsist on what it gives away, and that the equal love-passion is that which is prepared in the mysterious laboratory of life from fundamental inexplicable sympathies.

But though there are two faculties in love there is only one quality. In the *de imitatione Christi* we read:

The description in the *De imitatione*

> Love makes all heavy things light and all bitter things sweet, for it carries a burden which is no burden. Though weary it is not tired, though pressed not straitened, though alarmed it is unmoved. He that loves flies, runs, and rejoices; he gives all for all and has all in all; for he regards not the gift but turns himself above all gifts to the giver.

He who wrote those words knew love. They are true of no other love but the love I have described. There is an immediateness in love so that there is nothing else you want to do but that which satisfies its urgent claim, and you do not know whether the task be light or hard. When we act for a friend this immediateness may be absent—love has no need to remember, but for my friend I remember. A man for his appetite, also, will despise obstacles and leap and fly like a lover, but there is no other resemblance in his enterprise. We are told that the male man "loves and rides away", that "love is of his life a thing apart, 'tis woman's sole possession". It is apart because it is not love; what is apart from our life is not love.

Since we have allowed physical desire to figure as love we have regarded its ugly progeny as the camp followers of love. But if the description in the *Imitatio* be true to love then the lusts and cruelties we are so ready to call love-dramas have no part in it. What can be imagined more evil and cruel than to kill a person because he will not gratify your lust or cannot return your passion, and how can such things be set beside the thoughts and deeds of love? They have no more likeness to a love-act than the murder of a man who has refused you his purse. For love is not a greed but a sympathy. It feeds upon the claims made upon it not, as lust, upon the claims it makes. And no love is lewd. The perfectly harmonious love, no doubt, born of zoological sympathies and of the spirit, is the complete love of psychê and body —but there is no lewdness. The soul and body basis to love is not akin to the sexuality which is normally indifferent to love but to the maternal which is normally accompanied by it.

Love is man's chief moral asset, the first reconciler, the great teacher. It is one in its nature not because it proceeds by stepping-stones from the sensual to the spiritual but because it has always been spiritual and can never have had to learn what it has always had power to teach.

V. FRIENDSHIP

Sokrates: Anything more? That prayer, I think, is enough for me.

Phaedrus: Ask the same for me, κοινὰ γὰρ τὰ τῶν φίλων.

FRIENDSHIP has always been described with such truth and beauty that none of us is in doubt as to its character—we all know what is meant by a friend. What is necessary is to show its proper place in human existence and the conditions which should surround it in a social organization. Barriers have been set to our understanding of its place in life and its noble reaches of sentiment in favour of relations which were incapable of nobility; not only in the novel but in the real life of men even the callow sexual passions of youth in its teens have been allowed to divert our attention from it; and the notion that sex ties are the only serious ties to be sought and that all sorts of friendship are a second best or a substitute has acted as a great belittler of human nature and a real obstacle to human betterment. The love of friends takes its place with the loveliest affections of the human spirit; without it the love of lovers has no fineness: it is possible to love without mutual mental sympathy but where friendship is this sympathy must be,[1] though it may be independent of all personal affinity. For friendship is not necessarily planted in affinity and love, it is pre-excellently the relation of comradeship, of faith and trust between men, of affectionate service; and it is a companionship of the mind. So it remains a chief fount of happiness among all living beings high enough in the scale to entertain it. It has never been organized, as the family has been organized, on a wrong basis tyrannical and antisocial in character, therefore its

---

[1] This is true of reciprocal friendship, not of pity and assistance friendship, which is a different quality with a different virtue. In any case natural roots in sympathy of mind and personality are necessary to the *fruition* of friendship.

features are those of happiness and self-fulfilment. And in its nature it is higher than the companionship of kin, it requires more virtue and higher individuality. When you make a friend you manifest quite other qualities to those which suffice to keep you your place among kindred: you must have value for yourself, not group value; a call is made on you to stand out as an individual and cease to be the echo of a group or family circle. Among latin peoples with whom the family group is *societas in parvo* and society itself nothing but an agglomeration of these groups, friendship is made to appear excentric and unnatural. And perhaps it has always been as excentric as originality individuality and spirituality are excentric. But where it exists it is a higher thing than either kinship or marital relations in themselves. Its basis is not materialistic, it recognizes spirituality of outlook, it has no envy, is not greedy, and it sets before itself the advancement of each as individuals.

The moment we realize that comradeship and love are moral phenomena—matters of liking, sympathy, psychical appreciations—we know that they cannot be determined or bounded by relationships of sex or kin; and love can no more be a sexual phenomenon than friendship. Affinity it is obvious is a rare experience, but as obviously it has nothing to do with the sexual tie. Where kinsmen are friends they enjoy that equality and freedom from group interests which all friendship demands. The husband and wife who are friends have between them something more than the marriage tie, are something more than husband and wife, something which was not involved in that relation at all. It is certain that the legal marriage relation may exist between lovers, lusters, friends, or may imply no tie whatever. This is not possible in friendship. Here the knot is self-tied, and friendship, like love, is in all cases its own warranty—where they exist a tie exists. It cannot be as marriage can be a tie

166

solely on account of its legal and social sanctions.   It
is the weakness of marital and blood ties that in themselves
they lack the spiritual intimacy of friendship. Friendship
is the most disinterested of all relations; no glory or praise
accrues to you if your friend is great—only the glory and
happiness of John's rejoicing in the bridegroom. But
your relatives who have spurned you or put every obstacle
in your way adopt your triumph as their own.

Since friendship and love are actually life ties of this
mental and spiritual quality societies should accord them
civil rights. If it is asked: why should civil rights be
conceded in the case of voluntary ties which are their own
sanction and their own warranty? the answer is that
human relationships however individual and self-sufficing
touch the social organization at various points and should
therefore command the necessary social advantages. We
sanction any sort of marriage between the sexes whether
it is entered upon for comradeship, material interest, or
lust, as well as those which have as their definite end and
skope the rearing of young. Relatives who live together
—even distant relatives—are accorded certain rights in
case of illness absence or insanity, and possess rights of
inheritance. But the most devoted friend or lover who
in the joy and sorrow of life was our nearest and dearest,
who for us meant life itself, has no rights whatever—no
rights accorded automatically by society or by law; and
may be dispossessed—morally and materially—by a
distant unknown kinsman or by the near blood relative
who has cursed your life. No convenience of states and
no superstitions about a blood tie can justify such *lèse-
humanité* as this. A woman of some 20 years and a male
youth a few years later are old enough to discharge every
claim of friendship, and should have the independence
necessary for their fulfilment. At 24 in the case of a
woman and a few years later in the case of a wer it should
be competent for everyone to declare A or B his next

*The Rights
of Friend-
ship*

Next
Friend friend with complete powers to act for him in any way he desired.[1] Few such choices would be disavowed later if there was not mental weakness or immaturity and levity of character—and in these cases the marriage tie would be quite as disastrous. Faithfulness in friendship is equal to that of any wedded partnership, and the tie between friends as I have said is both more real and more effectual than that which binds in the sex relation.

HISTORY OF
FRIENDSHIP The natural relation of friends is more beautiful, more generous, and less tyrannous than the adult family relation. There has been none of the stultification due to the economic dependence which underlies adult family life: τὰ τῶν φιλῶν κοινά, the Greeks said—the common things of friends. Greece is indeed the classic land of friendship. There the blood tie held the second place— a conventionalized one; patriarchalism remained undeveloped, and the notion that civilization proceeds *pari passu* with legalism was never present.[2] The greek was the individualistic race, and friendship in its genesis and in its genius belongs to individualism. It was greek individualism which taught them that friendship and love were not sex phenomena. After the Greeks friendship in Europe appears to have had its home among those peoples who come from the asiatic borders; it is amongst these to this day that are to be found the phratries—the brotherhood clans—organized friendship and relationships closer than blood brotherhood. When we come westward where two other racial elements have play, the mediterranean and the northern or teutonic, there is a notable difference to record: the blood tie is strong among mediterranean people, who have greater dependence of character, and the Teuton owes his higher gifts for friend-

[1] As we admit that marriage ties can be so dear still earlier, so it should be possible to be declared 'next friend' before these ages on the recommendation of two older people.

[2] In all 3 respects differing widely from the fundamentals of latin civilization.

ship to the greater role which character plays in his life. As a matter of fact and history we get in the latin peoples intellectual clarity (as with the french), intellectual independence (as with the italian), but dependence of character. And strength of character, of course, involves more marked individualism. It is strange indeed to realize, whether we view mankind from the angle of philosophy or as a social being, that (the greek and slav examples apart) friendship has never yet emerged as a paramount factor in human affairs.[1] The real reason is the slow growth of our higher emotional and mental nature. Blood ties came first because psychologically they were more primitive, they were less awakened and less aware, less mentalized. Because they implied no selection they made less demand. Our first efforts towards a systematized group life were based on those mere kin ties which substituted rule-of-thumb obligations for any higher obligations of sympathy. With the weakening of the blood tie and the equalization of women and wers in this and other respects the place of friendship in the social life of humanity must take on fresh aspects: and one of the things to which we shall look in the future to redress the oversexualization that has marked the course of human development is an increase of love and friendship between persons of the same sex. The immense overemphasis all through the historic period on real and conventionalized sex psychology has militated against friendship. It has also concealed the existence of intermediate types. Friendship will grow with the disappearance of the sexual bondage and of the furrow made in human character as its result: it was in fact amongst a non-sexual people that friendship flourished most clearly. In the great age of Greece one of its forms was paiderasty which as organ- The Greek ized in Sparta and elsewhere was a paidagogic moral and paiderasts

[1] Note however the Samurai relation in Japan from the xii[th] century of our era to modern times. See also *infra*, love amongst women, p. 171.

military apprenticeship of young men to older men for the sake of acquiring their military science and learning the arts of life. The word has for us a significance almost entirely sensual; but it is possible that this element formed no part at all of original paiderasty:[1] it is also possible that the greater sex emotionalism of wers modified the character of homogenic love and that paiderasty among them always tended to become what it was in name the sensual passion of a grown man for a youth's beauty.[2] That paiderastic relations had a genuine educational skope does not render this the less likely.

There are, as is recognized in the *Symposium*, always women who love women and wers who love wers, and who do not desire sexual congress. Romantic love, for the Greek, concerned solely these human relations, relations where sex did not enter: no romance attached to sexual intercourse, and it is evident that the type of love and of romantic passion was woman's love for woman and wer's love for wer, because to the greek mind the impulses towards it were not sensual but psychical or

---

[1] Benecke (*Women in Greek Poetry*, pp. 76–86), who maintains this to be an amply proved fact, adds: The fragrance of its early purity and beauty was never quite lost, as long as the classical world remained. In well-nigh all the poetry dealing with it there is a tone of dignity and chivalry to which the poetry addressed to women never, perhaps, wholly attained.

[2] To the present writer it seems more probable that at first Greek male love-affection (not lust-affection) was centred on their own sex, nothing but sexual congress being reserved for this relation with women. It has been suggested that a current base view of women was the original cause of this. But it is more likely that homogenic attachment arose between women after the brutal *exordia* of male rule, of male self-aggrandizement at their expense; and that this homogenic attachment of women brought about male paiderasty. This receives some confirmation from the early date of Sappho's story and the fact that it is the earliest definite tradition of homogenic love. In both cases the relation was tenderer—finer—than any marriage had been.   It could, of course, be said that the reverse is true, that the wer was the first to desire homogenic love and that women followed suit; but this seems improbable (see *infra*, Women's love for women, p. 171, and male jealousy, pp. 280–1 and *n*.). It is remarkable that the centres of this love were among the short-headed races. (Cf. Amazons, p. 215.)

moral. It was not a love founded in physical relations and it was alien to all lasciviousness. Maximus Tyrius[1] notes that Sappho's type of love was the same as that of Sokrates and one is in the finest company with Sappho and Sokrates. This type of male love was put forward by the Greek the Slav and the Japanese: but friend love is common among women with whom it has been a love of comradeship and mutual insurance; and we may be certain that the friendships of the harêm in non-christian countries and the friendships of the cloister in christian have never failed to make the lives of women a sweet and noble thing in comparison with the life of the wers around them. The male Greek recognized the love of women for women and also that love—since it cannot be tied by sex —was possible between a woman and a wer where no sexual tie existed. He brought his own homogenic love into poetry and drama, but never woman's homogenic love: yet the greater Greeks—Sokrates, the platonic school, Euripides—distinctly realized women's freedom from sex and their trend in this direction, but no male could help assuming in his literature that though he could not love his wife she must necessarily love him, and in noting the affections of woman he misread sexual sympathy into femel affectionateness. The remarkable fact nevertheless remains that Greek women come down to us in the greek tradition, in women's poetry, and in drama, in three great love characters—none of which is· concerned with sex—the maternal, the homogenic, and as lovers of their brothers. This last I take to be a dramatist's expedient for bringing before us a love which greek taste was assured must exist, the unsexual love of woman and wer;[2] and how was the Greek woman to meet wers

Love amongst women

Platonic love

---

[1] Max. Tyr. xxiv. 9.

[2] Is it possible it might have been an expedient for bringing woman's love into drama while escaping what for the male was the Scylla of her homogenic love and the Charybdis—the obvious fact that women had not conjugal love?

unless they were her comrade brothers? Love and friendship between a woman and a wer are as certainly possible without sexual liking as they are possible within the marriage tie though not belonging to it. And a standard example of 'platonic' love is this which the Greeks chose—love between sister and brother.

The greek love mind Once more, the virtue of non-sexual love relationship lay as we see in this, that it could be spiritual-motived while the sexual relation had a carnal motive; this was a love of bodies, that of souls; the background of the one was a physical demand which need never be the case in the other. We cannot understand the greek romantic mind unless we appreciate this cardinal point of sentiment: and the distinction between personal relations which could be satisfied by the lupanaria and those which formed the glory of the Akademy because they are created by the souls of men was well fitted to express the mind of a people who more than any other realized a communion in things of the soul.[1]   It is asserted that the male Greek

Male Greeks attitude to the wife-inferior could not feel romantic sentiment for his wife because he could not associate sentiment and romance with sexual congress. But the Greek was able to associate sensual congress with paiderasty, and no difficulty was encountered in loving the cultivated hetaira in the greek sense of love which was radically unsexual—loves of soul and sense to which the impulse was moral not sensuous. The reason why the Greek felt no love for his wife—nor she for her husband—was first because, as we see, sexual congress and love are not original congeners, and then because the Athenian wife was in no sense her husband's comrade —both for love and for comradeship he looked elsewhere, to his own sex and later to the hetaira. He was incapable of associating romance with a domestic inferior, with the

[1] Benecke points out that whatever may be said of the paiderasty love of the Greeks they "were the first to teach that the mission of love was to make men better".

'slave-nature' that was so great a reality to the Greek and to which form was given in the position actually meted to the wife—a slave condition for slave uses.   The belief that coition is an unclean thing (though it is not so unnatural as the jewish male's belief that gestation was unclean) is a legacy of doctrines which are artificial and of excesses which are real. At the same time it must not be ignored that women frequently—wers infrequently—feel repulsion to it, and that as civilization advances a sentiment of its grossness may arise: and it is here that it is essential to remember that the natural sexual relation is *not* a love one and has only become so adventitiously.[1] The true point about marriage and romance is not that the physical relation spoils love—and the Greeks would have been the first, not the last, to admit this—but that the sex relation itself is not the natural and essential type of love. Where there is love the physical relation does not make it gross. The Greek mentalized love, set it forth as an affection of the soul, not because he was afraid of the senses but because in his mind the sensuous was far removed from all sensuality—the senses and the soul created together the kalokagathos, the greek ideal of loveliness.

The type intermediate between femel and male has been called 'uranian', supersexual. If the conditions of society allowed, many more persons would be found to be of this type than is now apparent; and indeed when this was regarded as a distinctly higher type the conditions of the greek age allow us to recognize that it was then to be found among a much larger number than the one in twenty said to be the proportion now.[2] Extreme sexualiza-

Uranian type of humanity

[1] See Marriage, pp. 267–8.

[2] The ninety-five per cent. which remains is not made up of 'normal' monogamists nor of 'normal' sexualists. Many men have no passion, while the larger percentage of males is polygynous and the larger number of women put child before sex.

tion has been the keynote of what has been called normal human psychology, and, as a corollary, no countenance has been given to the intermediate type. The reasons for believing that the less sexualized types of humanity are the higher are not only to be found in the oversexualization of mankind which makes it already sexually degenerate but in the fact that a large number of the very greatest men, of both sexes, could be shown to have had this temperament. There was never anything in nature to suggest that the higher human ties should be sought on sex lines, and the universal prevention that sex currents are moral currents and non-sexual immoral is seen to be still more false when the actual history of human sexuality has been realized.[1] Up to now—except in the aspirations of saints and idealists—the only normal type has been held to be the sexual type: but among men and among other highly organized animals there are myriads which do not conform to it. It is natural to be unsexual as well as natural to be sexual, and it would be still more usual were it not for the dead-set made in human education to foment sexuality.[2] There is then always a naturally large percentage of men of both sexes whose love and friendship is homogenic; the sexual type is always zoologically antipathetic to the non-sexual, whether of the same or the other sex, and no friendship is possible between them.

A false psychology　　There are 2 types of human friendship, that which would and does subsist between the less sexual among us and that which subsists between intermediate sex types.

---

[1] See Lust, pp. 143 seqq. and Oversexualization, pp. 250–1. Oversexualized human beings who ply for exclusive recognition as 'ordinary humanity' are not normal wers and women but abnormal.

The biological line of argument would be that maternal currents are moral currents; but it is evident that this moral current has been everywhere subordinated to the crudest sexualism.

[2] Note that the intermediate never fails to meet his compeer in a uranian or semi-uranian type.

It must be taken as a universal premiss that the existence of a conventional sex psychology has modified all human relations. There is in fact in every spontaneous relation between organic beings a complementary relation, and as far as may be a complementary temperament. But it is not true that the self-assertive active strong and protection-giving qualities are 'masculine' and the confiding passive retiring and protection-seeking qualities 'feminine'. These characters are human not sexual and though it is perfectly true that some of them inhere oftenest in women and others in wers yet the popular allocation of them is due to the male only, and hence the psychology of the situation is at fault. Biologically the male easily desires to dominate, but it is certain that numbers of femels detest this quality in him; and similarly there are numbers of males for whom what have been called the specifically 'feminine' qualities are not what they prize in a wife. In my view what goes to form affectional relations between adults is primarily a character and temperament difference, and not primarily a sex difference at all. Take one of the most emphatic of these differences—the nervous man will always desire the companionship of a calm one. Our characters and temperaments differ; strong, clinging, self-reliant, diffident, calm, nervous, courageous, timid—it does not at all matter which sex is the possessor of one of these opposites, he or she will be likely to desire that his companion should have the other, and only male fictions and the subordination of women have concealed how frequently wers are devoid of the boasted 'masculine' qualities and women possessed of them.   Difference of temperament is a source of happiness, and certain qualities of temperament very generally follow sex lines.[1] But this difference has not approved itself as a 'natural' introduction to com-

---

[1] When this difference of temperament is completely or partially absent we have the uranian or semi-uranian type.

panionship between the sexes, and in this role it has no long history behind it. If a fixed sex psychology had determined our affectional relations then these relations would never have failed to arise between the sexes at all times[1]—among savage tribes as in the Greece of Perikles. But it has not been so. The psychological relation, then, which we call that of 'wife and husband' is *not* a sex phenomenon but a moral one, and the popular idea that their traditional position is founded in radical distinctions of sex psychology is not based on any primary facts of psychology at all.[2] Nature presents the elements for these relations sporadically rather than normally or naturally; and if we took away the support which customs and the social organization lend to the masculine idea of its own character this would be evident. It is evident that married intercourse takes place largely without any tie of loving dependence on one side and loving protection on the other, such as we have assumed to be proper to the relations between the sexes. And if the idea of marriage were unencumbered of the male spurious psychology thrust into it it would be seen how closely married companionship follows the other types of friendship.[3]

Friendship in the future
    Of the two sexes the femel is the more affectionate, and close intimacy without lust is a mother trait; it is this which should be given skope in the life of the affections: affections should be developed at the expense of appetites. Where affection is greater, appetite is less. This is no doubt a law. Non-sexual friendship and love are to be placed among the greatest and most inspiring of human passions. To believe that friend love is emotionless and

---

[1] Just as the seeking quality of the sex and the protective quality of the mother have told universally.

[2] Take 'protection' as an instance. How often in marriage is not the purely surface protection done by the male and the real momentous protection by the wife?

[3] Incapacity for friendship for its own sake between persons of the same sex is a feature of our oversexualization.

passionless is the stupid common error of the sexualist: all mental passion, on the contrary, is concentrated on this type of love, as it is in maternal love—and all tenderness. These are not new ideas they are old truths. In the bible as in the other old literatures of the world love and friendship must be sought outside the conjugal tie and the ties of kin—the love of two women, Ruth and Naomi; the love of two wers, Jonathan and David: and though we have Jacob's love for his sons Joseph and Benjamin (Rachael's children) and David's passion for his son Absalom, this love is a poor offset to the fratricidal elements in these same histories. Of something like conjugal love there are at most three instances—the love of Isaac for Rebekah, of Jacob for Rachael, and of Elkanah for Hannah (the only essay at a delightful conjugal relation in the Hebrew Scripture—and he had two wives at a time)[1]; but in no case it would seem is there love on the wife's side. As illustrating what sexual 'love' normally means in the bible, we are told that Amnon "loved" Tamar (his sister), that is he ravished her by force, then hates more than he had desired her, and casts her away; and that Rehoboam "loved" Maachah above all his wives and concubines, "for he took eighteen wives and sixty concubines". In the Old Testament "love" for any woman in the position of a wife is indistinguishable from physical desire, and is on a par with Isaac's "love" for his son Esau because he prepared savoury venison.

The modern world not less sexual but less sincere than the old has conceded every right to that comparatively. modern thing romantic passion between the sexes, and no right at all to romantic love of friend for friend. Yet no rights in the world can be as strong. And it should not be possible for those who follow the spiritual teaching of the past to regard relations outside the blood tie as less worthy of human reverence, since we know that all the

[1] I Samuel, i.

ties consecrated by the story of Jesus were of this character: this is also true of Buddha; neither Master concerns himself with the blood tie or with the family, and the same fact emerges when we interrogate the philosopher-moralists of Greece.[1] The indian sentiment is the same. "He is no relation, but my friend, and friendship is a much stronger tie than mere relationship." When it was retorted that blood is "thicker" than water, the subtilty of the indian reply was, I think, lost upon the hearer: "Ah! that may be, but friendship is a much more ethereal thing." The great drama of the world, its great figures, give the lie to the notion that there is nothing better than family affection.

Friendship appeals as no other tie appeals to the awakening individuality of our youth and the treasures of our maturity; it is founded, as no other tie is founded, in reciprocal understanding; and the time will come when the cant which alleges that sympathy naturally accompanies the blood tie will no longer be customary. It will not then be any part of human mentality to see in none but sex and kin relations that which is important beautiful and permanent.

[1] Diotima in the *Symposium* 209: "They have a far nearer and closer friendship than those who beget children."

VI. THE OTHER ANIMALS

Man, in his development, has been but little influenced
by the best in nature and he has easily deceived
himself regarding his relation to the other animals. His
worst and characteristic vices he has described as animal
vices, labelling certain human conduct 'brutal' and
'bestial', whereas most of these bestial things are not done
by the beasts at all. For human bestiality is a phenomenon
peculiar to man, who has added something to animal
virtue but still more to animal vice; and the habit which
he has indulged for some thousands of years of thus
classifying his vices has made him blind to the phenomenon that explains his 'bestiality'—the phenomenon of
savagery. Savagery began with man's cerebral functions, Savagery
with the activities of the beast with brains; but it is not
confined to a past stage or to the lower stages of human
development: the elements of savagery are cruelty, lusts,
and superstition, they are the things for which man stands
and which distinguish him from the other animals.[1]

There came a time when man began to regulate his
relation to the animals by his theology. Two competing
doctrines then held sway; the one that the destruction of
life is wrong since all life is inter-related (India), and the
(later semitic) doctrine that the animals were expressly
made for man who might freely exploit and destroy them.
Long before man formed conceptions of divine beings,
however, he had formed relations with the other animals;
and primeval man's attitude to the life surrounding him
was one of comradeship, and sometimes of fear. If he
lived among the domesticable species he hardly distinguished them from himself; their needs, their pains and
joys, their weakness and their strength, their wildness and

---

[1] He has indeed gained as little by attributing his vices to his 'animality'
as by attributing them to the devil.

their tameability—he shared them all, they were his things too.[1] It has indeed been pointed out that in the pastoral stage of society the children and the flocks made one group—the importance of the young animals being certainly not less than that of the human young. Ancient literature and legend bear witness to this sense of near-ness—a nearness of circumstance, of feeling, of destiny. The book of Genesis, contradicting all modern theological bias, records that a covenant was made by the divine being not with man only but with all the animals: the 'covenant' remained both for Hebrew and christian among the most sacred and mysterious of religious con-ceptions, but it was made "with every living creature that is with you, with every beast of the earth".[2] The Song of the Three Children, a document of the ii[nd] century B.C. no doubt of persian affinity, which calls upon all things— the fish, the birds, the beasts, the cattle, and Israel, to praise god, was an outcome of this earliest sentiment and belief; but by the time Francis of Assisi came to write his Song of Creatures it was a sentiment which had long ceased to echo in christendom. The early matriarchal gods were depicted accompanied by lions, and Indra by the elephant; the cow was held sacred not only in Africa but in Asia, and theriomorphism, like anthropomorphism, had deep theogonic roots.[3]

---

[1] See the marvellous paintings of animals in the aurignacian caves. In indian tales "no sharp distinction is drawn between the animal and the human personages" notes Frazer. To this day the tibetan Dalai Lama prays always for "blessings on all human beings and the whole animal world".

[2] Cf. Hosea (750 B.C.) ii. 18.

[3] One of the 4 great precepts of persian zoroastrianism is the care of the cow; Gēush Urvan "the genius and defender of animals" is among the "immortal holy ones" attending on god; and "the protection of the dog" is one of the zoroastrian duties. The persian delight in the dog is also shown in the book of Tobit (350 B.C.) v. 16, xi. 4, and in the charming variant in the Vulgate xi. 9 "Then the dog which had been with them on the journey ran in front and advancing as a messenger showed its joy by

To primitive sympathy and affection—to interest and wonder—there succeeded theological neglect. Behind this neglect lay the barbarous notion that the doctrine of human immortality could be reinforced by treating other animals as things.[1] A few centuries of christianity and a little scholastic philosophy had taken all the nature out of our relation to other sentient beings and thereafter and right through the xix[th] century all but the strongest and tenderest men excused themselves for their pity and dishonoured decent sentiment by explaining how they came by it. Those saints who from the iii[rd] century to the xvi[th] were distinguished for 'humanity' had no influence whatever on the official christian position, though they comprised the most revered of all names.[2]

The first modern efforts to restore respect for these fellow-creatures of man were hence made with no assistance from the accredited teachers and masters in christendom.[3] When we consider religion and our moral

wagging its tail". Tobias' companions on his journey are an angel and a dog.

Cf. the lamb and the dove emblems in christianity, and the lion ox and eagle of the evangelists.

[1] While these 'supernatural' ethics were being developed in Europe chinese thought evolved the ethic of man and the other animals based on our relationship to them and on natural sympathy.

[2] Antony 'the great monk', Chrysostom, Martin of Tours, Brigid, Benedict, Gregory of Tours, Columba (the irish apostle of Scotland), Gregory of Rome, Isidore of Seville, Cuthbert of Lindisfarne, Werburgh of Chester, Guthlac of Crowland, and Bede; between 1100 and 1300, Anselm (who says of the hunted animal "but this unhappy little one does not laugh, for it there is no merriment"), Bernard of Clairvaux, Hugh of Lincoln, Francis of Assisi, Bonaventure, Aquinas, and the learned Saxon Gertrude of Helfta. The same tenderness to animals was preached by Colette the reformer of the Franciscans in the xv[th] and by Philip Neri, apostle of Rome in the xvi[th] century. And a story related of Francis de Sales places him in the line of the fine thinkers of all time. Many of these were apostles of the faith and doctors of the church, and the large number of scholars among them is noticeable. No catholic country, except Germany, has however taught that cruelty to animals was reprehensible, much less sinful.

[3] No pope after the time of Gregory the Great till that of Paul II (Barbo) in the xv[th] century lifted up his voice to protect animals. Paul V

progress by means of those gentler passions which it is presumed to inculcate, we habitually ignore the clue to the course which religious history has actually taken: this course has been almost entirely directed by considerations drawn from the principle of authority and from the desire for power—priesthoods everywhere have wished to represent an omnipotent rather than a holy deity. But originally the higher religious efforts of the race gave to the other animals their place in religion; they formed part of it through an aspiration after gentleness, and have disappeared from it with the exigencies of priestcraft. Three lovely anecdotes of Buddha underlie the buddhist teaching on this subject, and two such anecdotes indicate the mind of Muhammad: thus on one occasion he said: "Truly there are rewards for our doing good to dumb animals, and giving them water to drink. An adultress was forgiven who passed by a dog at a well; for the dog was holding out his tongue from thirst, which was near killing him; and the woman took off her boot and tied it to the end of her garment and drew water for the dog, and gave him to drink; and she was forgiven for that act." The same spiritual instinct and insight is prominent among the contemplatives, who found or nourished their spiritual life in solitude of soul, alone with nature. The sympathy of saintly hermits with all living things, their instinct for the soul of creatures who presented none of the soul-destroying characters of 'rational'

Hermits
and
solitaries

in the xvi[th] prohibited bull fights on account of the cruelty to animals, but in the xix[th] century a pope declared that a society to protect them could not be tolerated in Rome, and catholic books of moral theology (unrebuked by ecclesiastical authority) taught that animals had no more rights than "stocks and stones". The fact that the 3 popes who succeeded this one all applauded efforts to obtain right treatment for animals as a work "altamente umana e cristiana" is evidence of a change not in the theological thesis but in the world around them.

The connexion of a fundamental belief in survival as the destiny of all mankind and of neglect of the other animals is first seen in Paul's cruel question: "Doth god care for oxen?"

182

life, is an experience which we cannot set aside. What was its secret? On the one hand there was spiritual listening, for sounds dulled by our worldliness; on the other hand the clamour of barbarous human passion was still. Many of the solitaries became nothing less than missioners of a new religious spirit, they had relived the primitive life of man with the other animals and brought back to our relations with them the holy passions ousted by human sophistry. This sentiment of the life with nature is set before us even in the story of Jesus—with its fast in the wilderness from the companionship of human passions, its solitude with the animals and with the angels. The experience of the solitaries is related in almost the same—in identical—terms; they made themselves a refuge for chased animals, they pleaded for their lives, they released captives, they tended the hunted and harmed, on occasion they restored the dead to life. And in the same way, lion or bear or tiger, all animals help them, none harms them; they are fed by animals, warned by them, visited by them, buried by them. They gentilize each other; the wild animal becoming tame, the saint receiving still greater *intelletto d'amore*: there was the understanding which always waits upon sympathy, and which resists every other approach. It had been, indeed, ignorance not knowledge, it was not religion but theology, which robbed the animals of their due and us of our heritage. For man's life is based upon the life of the other animals. They came before him and made his development possible. If he uses nature well he is their brother, but if ill he is a usurper. And the right treatment of animals has in fact always been upheld by men of mind and imagination from the time of the pythagoreans who attributed to Pythagoras examples of the tenderest humanity, and whose teaching on this point was extolled by Clement of Alexandria.[1] After them came Empedokles,

[1] *Stromata*, lib. ii. See *infra*, pp. 198-9, Plato.

Lucretius, Vergil, Ovid, the elder Pliny, Plutarch, Arrian, Celsus, Porphyry, Maimonides the great rabbi, Leonardo da Vinci, Luther, Voltaire, Condorcet, Schopenhauer, Wesley, Mazzini. In xiv[th]-century England Chaucer describes the prioress as weeping over dead and wounded animals, and in the xvi[th] Shakespeare describes Jaques sobbing with the sobbing stag, and he makes his contempt for the cruel as evident as is Thomas More's in the Utopia.[1] Both address themselves to an active people who get along from hand to mouth without much reflection. It is the same with Chaucer who shows his own appreciation for the prioress's ruth by contrasting with it his next two characters, the sporting monk—whom he introduces as the 'manly man'—and the conscienceless friar. When we compare these instances of european humanity with the pity of the Buddha we discern on the one side the active standards of conduct and on the other a civilization of spirit not 'gothic' but drawn from the regions of the soul—from an inner life both peaceful and anxious. But east or west it was understood that through our treatment of animals we learn more concerning gentleness and goodness; that the right use of them is in fact the complete reverse of the theological teaching which makes their lives a foil and contrast to ours; and the greatest christians vied with the eastern mystic in this understanding of their place in our hearts and conscience. S. Francis, writes Bonaventure, when he considered the first beginning of all things was filled with the more abundant pity and called all creatures his little brothers and sisters since he knew they and he had the same [divine] original (*unum secum habere principium*).[2]

[1] *As you like it,* Act II, sc. (1), and Act IV, sc. (2). The english are a nation of sportsmen but the national poet was no sportsman.

[2] Bishop Butler uses the same language (*Sermons,* vol. ii, p. 128). The belief that we are all creatures of the same good god should have had the same result as the knowledge that we have all developed from the same previous forms; but it has not been so.

Something passed over Europe which froze the blood Cruelty in this direction, something which had taken the name of nature and of god in vain. That is a very degrading form of religion which asserts that care for animals is an obstacle to mercy towards men; and the attempts to gear up this type of morality to the standard of ordinary humanity have not been less futile and depraved. According to the theologian the claims of nature, the nervous system which the animals share with us, mean nothing and teach nothing. The desire for our own improvement or a vicarious lesson in the kind treatment of each other is to be the incentive to kindness towards the animals. But where did men learn about sensitiveness to pain if not from the nature which they share with us? Once a foolish italian marchese speaking of cruelty to horses said to me: "Non ammetto che sentono." Theology required of this man, who knew well that there is no more highly nervous animal than the horse, this ridiculous profession of faith—ridiculous on the human side but tragic on the animal's, since the cruel man belies the creed each time he assaults his beast, which he would find no pleasure in doing if the doctrine were true. We have then to realize that a blight lies upon european moral teaching in this direction. The animal "who does not feel" is a 'thing': if on our way to that public worship which is represented as a spiritual duty we see a poor dog hanging and cut him down, we perform a work of supererogation; if we check the boy who was torturing him there was no moral necessity to do so; and 'the christian' can only exhort a boy to desist from cruelties because they might tempt him to hurt his fellow man not because they hurt the animal.[1] With such principles no gentilization of the

---

[1] "Shame on such a morality!" cried Schopenhauer: "so we are only to have compassion on animals for the sake of practice"; we are to use them as stalking horses "on which to train our sympathy for men!" It is worth noting that Kant who rested morality upon the sentiment of duty acquiesced

evil-minded is possible; they represent a coarse casuistry which masquerades before us as divinity and humanity. Wordsworth was a man of the tenderest humanity and he gave us a very lovely description of his dog "Music". Thou must lie "without a record of thy worth", he writes, for "*this* man gives to man". They wept when she was dead not only for a thousand thoughts in which she had her share

"But for some precious boons vouchsafed to thee"

found scarcely elsewhere in a like degree. And then this bathos:

"Hence if we wept it was not done in shame"!

which demeans the man of sentiment and belittles the imagination of the poet. Simplicity passion and confidence are the birthright of honest feeling, which needs no teacher but itself.

Jewish anthropocentricism inherited by the christian and emphasized à outrance by the schoolmen destroys the conception of *oneness* in creation. Nevertheless it is this conception alone which is adequate to explain both what is and our relation to it. If in modern times it has been assumed that there is a natural and proper distinction between the conduct man owes to man and his conduct towards other sentient beings, the assumption has mistaken human nature and the history of human conduct. For man's original cruelty is to his simile, he can get at him much more easily and hurt him far more effectively. In primitive times it is improbable that even fierce savages tortured animals for torture's sake as has always been the way of man with man. The fiendish methods of disembowelment and slaughter found among some

Cruelty began at home

in the doctrine that animals are of the number of 'things'. When Schopenhauer brushes aside these 'duties' of the moralists he propounds in their place the "two cardinal virtues of justice and loving-kindness".

tribes are practised upon human beings; and we remember
that Ajax only massacred cattle because he hoped he was
slaughtering men. It is later that the animal is substituted
for the human victim; that the scapegoat is driven into
the wilderness bearing the sins of the children of Israel.
The same god who is represented by his makers as requiring the sentient beings he has created to be slain
and 'sacrificed' in his honour commended Abram for his
readiness to slay his son for the same purpose; and the
slaughter of animals which was a daily, nay hourly,
spectacle for the inhabitants of Jerusalem has a still more
hideous parallel in the atrocities which Jahveh is represented as inflicting upon men. Later, in the heydey of
the 'ages of faith'—nearer to our own time than to
Abraham's—men were still the chief objects of cruelty,
and pity for their bodies was regarded as a theological
offence if the 'soul' could be saved by burning them:[1]
with this object in view no cruelty hurt the cruel man's
soul, as no cruelty to animals hurts his soul if he intends
thereby to make an *auto-da-fé* in honour of 'his place in
creation'. When our theories had run away with
our facts and we were assured by the moral and religious
teachers that we could treat men well and at the same
time ill-treat the other animals, the suggestion that children needed protection from the cruelty of their parents
raised a certain outcry. The result has shown that nature
set no essential distinction between ourselves and the
animals, for the societies for the protection of animals and
of children have precisely similar work to do.

There can be no reason why man's present greater
humanity to his fellow should have a counterblast in
greater inhumanity towards other sentient beings. Men

Experi-
ments and
the tor-
ment of
animals

[1] Aquinas, *Summa* (pars ii Quaestio xi, art. iii) "If coiners (*falsarii
pecuniae*) and other malefactors are justly handed over to death forthwith
by secular princes, much more may those convicted of heresy not only be
forthwith excommunicated but rightly put to death" (*juste occidi*).

have ceased to disembowel their fellow man to 'save his soul' but the man of the same western civilization which ideated this kind of religion now appears to see a compensating piety in vivisecting the other animals: the two are complementary, both being done as a homage to men's essential value—the one superstitious and cruel the other scientific and cruel. The strange thing is that the believer in a divine creator can possibly think it a right or good 'use' of the other living creatures of a god of love to cut them open alive so as to find out what he had not told us. That makes the notion, so dear to theology, that animals were 'made for our use' altogether too ugly for acceptance.[1] It cannot but be essentially base to ill-treat animals on the ground that you not they have heaven before you; and how can the believer who "has the forever" deem it good and right to torture finite animals in order to delay his own natural death. This aberration is due to the assumption which is invariably made in western civilization that human life of what quality soever possesses an essential value in comparison with the life of any animal, and that man's immortal destiny makes it fitting that finite lives should be exploited for his benefit: these finite lives cannot help him to save his incorruptible soul but they can be required to keep going his corruptible body—that is, to postpone the hour when he will be required to enter on eternal delights. But why postpone it? Is the right answer that it is in order to prolong his chance of saving his soul? But what religious man can suppose that god would have denied him this chance if the idea of vivisecting animals had not occurred to us? If this were the position it would certainly be the most tragic pity that the chances of human salvation have already been imperilled through the aeons of time before vivisection was thought of. For

[1] Animals were not "made for man", for they existed many millions of years before we did.

the religious man, then, only one issue is possible; he must think of some way of extending his life on earth and perhaps thus increasing his chances of heaven which does not require him to outrage the other creatures of a god of love who has said "Not a sparrow falls to the ground without your Father".

What is the 'essential value' of man? Does it consist in (*a*) his having a different destiny to that of the other animals or (*b*) in the possession of far higher endowments, intellectual and spiritual or (*c*) in the fact that he is here in order to obtain a happy eternity. If it be (*a*) or (*c*) god, who has contemplated the hurling of millions of souls into hell, must discount this value of souls, if man does not. But if man's superiority be founded upon (*b*) his value must depend entirely on whether he uses these higher endowments—nay, on whether he possesses them; for it is obvious the larger number of men have not high endowments. Man has no natural right to live which animals have not also. On what ground would you torture your beloved dog to save the suffering of a cannibal man? Since it is the fact of vital not merely of human suffering which matters, no one's pain should under any circumstances be alleviated at the cost of the same degree of suffering to an animal: it is not a spiritual privilege of the higher to make the lower suffer for him. The scheme which requires animals to suffer to alleviate man's bodily ills many of which are brought about by his own vicious indulgence or that of his species is a peculiarly disgraceful form of exploitation, as it seems also to be a singularly vile kind of cowardice to assault the more helpless because of your own dread of suffering. Mankind is too apt to assume that it has rights over animals because it has power to coerce them. Nothing can undo the disgrace involved in vivisecting domesticated animals which are more easily and safely handled *because* they trust us so completely and love us; and the person incapable of

The essential value of man

feeling the shame of such a betrayal and the abdication of the moral perceptions involved in it is a profoundly unethical person.   To save human beings pain or to prolong their lives is held to be the great reason for vivisecting animals. But there is a second reason, namely the attainment of knowledge. On this earth the prime requisite can never be knowledge. If the attainment of knowledge be the ethical sanction for experimenting on living animals "then the animal which ought to be chosen for experiment is, undoubtedly, man":[1] the result of experiment on man would be the attainment of more real knowledge. But men, who vivisect animals, do in fact experiment also on the living human subject—they experiment *in corpore vili* or *in corpore paupero*. It is a phenomenon common in hospitals all over Europe. If we proposed to purchase valuable human lives at the cost of the worthless and futile, to increase human well-being by the sacrifice of the worst and most useless examples of our species, it would not be less but more praiseworthy than to make the other animals suffer for man—for there can be no ideal reason for the existence of human worthlessness. It is just that in the superior which would make him refuse to sacrifice the inferior man that ought to make it impossible for any of us to exploit the animals. The notion indeed that it is a finer thing to provide for those most like yourself —(and so for your relatives rather than your friends, for men rather than for other animals)—has no ethical sanction whatever.

But even if, in theory, we were abundantly justified in finding remedies for our diseases through the torture of animals and also in torturing animals or men to obtain knowledge for its own sake, we cannot trust our human nature when such theories are put into commission. There are things which, whatever the theory, it is vile

[1] Sir George Birdwood, in 1914.

for man to put his hand to. One of the best known modern objections to capital and other punishment is that it must necessarily degrade those who inflict it: whether this is applicable or not to our dealings with the evil-doer, it must in any case apply to the practice of vivi-secting innocent offenceless animals. The truth is that the materialistically-minded man places the material ad-vantage of the 'spiritual' animal (himself) higher than Man as a the psychical and physical advantage of all other sentient 'spiritual' beings. He metes out his right to material benefits with being the measure of man's alleged spirituality. Such spiritu-ality, which is the possession of only a small remnant of humanity, is brought forward to cover large materialistic transactions; this is a common phenomenon with the ruck of men but conspicuous by its absence in the spiritually-minded. Measured by any measure but that of man's material gain the liberty bought for pit ponies by a strike of coal miners is well bought; their freedom and happiness is a·better value than a great industrial advantage to the community at large. But in a strike some years ago the miners prevented some decent human beings from saving the ponies who had been left below: in this case the life of the ponies would have been far preferable to the life of such men. One cannot cloke every infamy merely by reiterating that we are a spiritual species.

Of all the absurdities which have been cherished by men's superstition and egoism none is more astonishing The char-than the denial of animal mentality and the assumption acter and reason of that the other animals do not lead a 'psychical life' as we animals do although they neither solve theorems nor pray for their eternal salvation. But now we are born into a new heritage, a consciousness of the oneness of organic life, bringing with it sympathies, potential understanding, an explanation of ourselves to nature and of nature to our-selves, which are elements of a new happiness—a make-weight to the inanities and the pettiness which are the larger feature of human existence. Men and animals have lived side by side for many hundreds of thousands of years. What has man—especially civilized man—done to understand them, to establish communication with them, to learn of them. Nevertheless in them is to be found every mental quality we find in ourselves—none excepted. Such truths were recognized by man primitively, for the distinctions which a mere development of his external resources placed between their life and his did not exist, and the ignorance added by a barbaric superstitious intelligence had not come into play: these two episodes in human history brought about what would have appeared to be an impossible thing, that these creatures—men and the other animals—should have lived side by side for so long a period of time each with the use of intelligence, sympathy, inventiveness, imitativeness, and with power of initiation and adaptation, without establishing a common language. How very few of us know even the little that is known about these fellow beings. Is this the reason of their 'silence' which is only broken in response to understanding? To the great beasts we no doubt appear as so many chattering monkeys. Is this a judgment much at fault? The thoughts of the animals would certainly be as interesting and more instructive than the habitual thoughts of most men, they would give us more real information than the thoughts of the savage, knowledge that is older than our knowledge, not obstructed by fallacious reasoning, experience that is more secure, profound instincts and subtleties of the senses of whose nature and skope men have as yet no idea.   Animals have not only their sorrows and joys, parallel to ours, they have the same distractions and helps —a genuine sense of humour, a universal spirit of play; they teach games to the young, they have sham contests, they dance.[1] They educate their young for the events of

[1] There have been several attempts to adopt a zoomorphical descrip-

life as they know it. Wild and domestic animals maintain *tabus*, a code of honour and a standard of right. Their gratitude for kindness and their memory of pain are as long as any man's, and in species as far apart as an elephant and a bird or a snake. Less articulate than we they have a more permanent dignity, they have preserved a greater natural beauty, and with the great-hearted beast words never do duty, as with shallow man, for deeds. Nor do the gross and selfish appetites, it would seem, interfere with the amity of animals as much as they do with ours; and in spite of their having no access to libraries recording the nobler thoughts of mankind they show themselves more capable of transcending family, tribe, and country, than we do. I have in mind the remarkable instance of an alligator, 70 years old, whose friend the trainer fell into the tank and was at once attacked by a new comer; the old alligator rushed to save her and a fierce battle insued. This is an astounding example of a reptile ready to destroy its own kind in defence of a friend of another species—surely the highest of all organic instincts, and a proof of the inherent domesticability and sociability of living things. As I record this case a male animal trainer while tending sick cubs was savagely attacked by a forest bred lion. Thereupon it was attacked by a femel lion who tore open its flanks and compelled it to release her friend the trainer who was caring for her cubs. It is amongst the animals also that mated love is best understood, for it has been pointed out that the only perfect ideal of marriage is found among birds. And they understand death: How can it be otherwise when they realize what it is to kill—when they fight for life and mourn death?[1]

tion of man which should differentiate him from all other animals—the 'pointing animal' or the 'tool-using animal'; but a letter to the press in 1926 informs us that what distinguishes man from the other animals is the playing of games; which is as accurate as it is to say that man, as such, is distinguished by being a spiritual animal.

[1] The feigning of death, resorted to by many birds and by the fox and

o

But indeed the false assumption that animals have not reasoning power and the arbitrary distinction made between their processes of reason and ours have been recognized in our time.[1] It is clear that an intelligent elephant for example has more mind than an unintelligent man. And if reason and love are strong, so are the other main attributes of character: There is no stronger mark of individuality in a biological sense than the power of forming attachments outside the group. This is displayed in every animal species.[2] Every strangeness which comes within our experience as organic beings also comes within theirs—except such as are the fruits of our vice; abnormalities and freaks of nature visit them as they visit us.[3] And within a species there is the same difference of individual character—the gamut of psychical qualities—

wolf is another example. Yet another is the killing of the maimed and sick. Animals who worry the old or sick to death would no doubt do it in a better way if their resources permitted. But the killing of those whose life is of no further use to themselves or others is an instinct not false in itself.

[1] A philosophic work published at the beginning of the present century asserted that the reach of canine intelligence is so small that a dog will not realize there are 2 ways of getting into a house. As I was reading the philosopher my little dog had just ascertained for herself at our lodgings in Guernsey all the ways of getting in and out and round the strange premises.

[2] A hunted rabbit was protected by a weasel to whom it ran in its terror. A dog protects a canary against a cat. A cat saves a squirrel. A male bull-terrier cherishes newly-born jackals found in a lair, keeping them safe and warm like a mother. Another terrier appoints itself the protector of newly-hatched chicks. The inseparable friendship of monkey and pet cat, of horse and kid, donkey and cat, cat and sparrow, cow and hens. These are often examples of immediate zoological sympathy, despite the difference of species. (See What is Love, p. 158.) In a recent instance of a dog and horse friendship the dog had to be accepted by the purchaser of the valuable race horse; the same thing had to be stipulated in the case of the friendship of a French horse and a chicken. A Persian kitten who used to eat mice became the fast friend of a white mouse which when brought to him in the usual way showed no fear. The mouse would nestle against the cat—which was entirely carnivorous—and used to be tenderly carried in its mouth. Cf. Individual and Species, p. 112.

[3] Such as a ewe with 4 lambs, or an individual of one species with the number of *mammae* of another species.

weak or strong, sweet tempered or sour, resourceful or
stupid, just as with man.

With a difference. For the basis of character in some The dog
species is not the same as in ours. An italian zoologist
described the difference by saying, "Il mio cane mi
insegna la filosofia: i cani non sono come noi, la loro base
non è l'egoismo." "My dog teaches me philosophy: dogs
are not as we are—their basis is not egoism." This is an
ethical distinction second to no other in capital importance. The dog's moral basis is naturally non-egoist,
whereas the evolution of man has proceeded along egoistic
lines. The dog does not put forward his own needs and
feelings first; the affections and instincts which engage
him to others are the springs of conduct. A singular
instance of this is that if he is hurt, even by a stranger, his
instinct is to assure them it is all right and that it really
has not hurt him much. Whereas man is naturally resent-
ful of those who cause him physical pain, however in-
voluntarily. Indeed many men have no spark of the
delicacy of feeling of the dog they misuse. Naturally, he
has not had man's social evolution and with it his skope
for vulgar egoisms; and one of his charms is that in
flagrant contrast to ourselves we receive from him nothing
but good manners. The lesson of his friendliness also
should be laid to heart; for though this is among the most
important of social habits it is only to be found in a very
few tribes of men. What the dog teaches us is that the
basis of action and choice need not be hedonist, need not
be personal at all. Man who prides himself upon his
superiority has never yet shown himself capable of the
dog's self-control universal faithfulness and vigilant protectiveness; and, of course, the remarkable thing is that
the dog has elected to exercise these qualities for man.
The dog's congeners[1] in their relations with each other

[1] The nearest congeners of the dog, zoologically and psychically, are
the wolf and fox. The wolf at least is everywhere both gregarious and

and dogs also in their relation with man combine independence of action with a trustful reliance on co-operation such as we men have not made possible for ourselves. The modern European—faced with the truth of the physical continuity of living beings—still clings to his hypothesis of psychical discontinuity; human megalomania has succeeded in blinding him even to such a psychological wonder as the dog's love; and with that wonder before him he has described the moral qualities as the proprium of man. In any case the dog has taken man to his heart and man has taken the dog to his. We may imagine how the love began—the dog's ancestors had the friendliness we see in him now, and the serviableness; he came up to man's lair, or her wigwam, and made proposals of amity and mutual protection—perhaps a dog mother brought her young to the man-mother. That vigilance which is the dog's wonderful natural endowment is complemented by the strong moral instinct to guard and protect: with swiftness, tenacious strength, and an extraordinary scent these qualities used in the service of man would evidently become a factor in the process of human domestication. It was perhaps the fact that man had at his side a fellow being with this intuition of approaching danger, this faculty of mounting guard, and this strong instinct to warn and protect, which made possible the upgrowth of the first human societies—the dog who came to the man's shelter made it her castle.[1]

domestic; parental cares, which are shared, are followed by a life in the strictly interdependent society of their kind. Is it this dowry of sociability and intimacy which makes the dog so delightful?

[1] "Perhaps these qualities in the dog were necessary to the establishment of society." P. Chalmers Mitchell, *Encycl. Britannica*. This suggestion receives some confirmation in the stories of man's creation told among the Khasis of Assam, the Kumis of Eastern India, the Korkus tribe in the Central Provinces, and the Mundas: each time the creating deity made a man the man was destroyed by an evil spirit. Thereupon the god made a dog first and afterwards a man, who owed his safety to the dog's watchfulness; in the Kumis story the evil spirit is a great snake, which is

So the dog—in his intelligence, in his helpfulness, in his love—is the first friend of man, his only self-constituted partner. He alone has entered into these relations with us, and the reason, no doubt, is that they were at his own initiative. And his place—unlike the case with other animals and with man himself—can never be filled by machinery. The machine can do what the man's hand does and the horse's hoof, but no machine can bring what the dog has brought us any more than machinery can replace the human spirit.

There is in an intelligent and sensitive dog the whole psychical gamut of feeling and reticences.[1] The dog lives with you as you live with her or him, as lover and comrade lives, and keeps for you the intimacies of companionship. When we think of what love for the little child is, of the passionate sentiment felt for a little being whose mind is not as ours, just because it is not as ours, we must realize that the dog's love at the man's side brings something that even the child does not bring, for no child remains a child to us for 14, 16, 18 years as our dog does. And then the dog lives with us the life of a man with himself— no one else does this; in the complexities and calls of human life it is not possible that anyone would or should: but when I lose my dog I lose this extraordinary precious

frightened away by the dog's bark. (Frazer, *Folklore in the Old Testament*, ch. i, p. 18.) In Europe the cult of the dog is indigenous in Sicily, where he is the escort of the god Adranus, and the trusted companion of a pastoral people.

Cf. also the title of Anubis 'opener of the ways'. Anubis is a beneficent deity who is regarded as custodian and messenger of the gods. It is noticeable that the hieroglyphs preserve the 2 aspects of the dog—as gentle and domestic (the seated Anubis) and in the rigid standing attitude of fierce protectiveness (Ophois). The Egyptians pictured the star whose appearance presaged that rising of the Nile on which the well-being and safety of their land depended, as a faithful dog watching over man—and called it the dog star.

[1] A horse will show this too—one who was accustomed to kiss his owner resented being asked by him to salute a stranger in the same way.

thing, my momently life with myself shared and accompanied by love. For in this relation love is everything, there is nothing to dispute it. The dog suffers a love tragedy; you cannot part him from his man and wound nothing but sympathy. The gregarious animal's longing for its companion is a pain of thwarted instinct, it is not a love tragedy. But with dogs love is uppermost, it is stronger than sympathies, it towers above gregarious instinct, and shares with man even the maternal love.[1] Dogs are among the great lovers of history. Human hearts and canine hearts break, and a dog and a man may each die of joy: nor is there any difference at all in the kind of pain we suffer over the loss of the one or the other.

There is another most delightful moral quality in dogs to set beside their non-egoism. Their lovely qualities are found in the same degree in the male as in the femel. Though the femel is the more companionable and has generally more intelligence and affection there is no such difference in psychological type as is usually to be found between sexes, in men as in monkeys in most of the hoofed animals and in many of the carnivores; the same faithfulness, the same watchful foresight, the same abnegation, the same assiduous love is shown by both—the male bestowing on man that mothering of which he has no other experience. In our own life we regard the action of mind on body as a wonderful thing—the dog's mind acts on his body in the same ways. A dog wrestling with his foe is insensible to the blows rained upon him, as the high-spirited man would be. There have been only a few men with the philosophic powers of Plato, and he did not hesitate to find philosophy in the dog, while our mediocrities have denied him even intelligence. And Plato discovered more than philosophy. "Where shall we find gentle nature which has also a great spirit, things

[1] The mother with newborn pups will snatch time after a day or so to go to her loved one.

198

that seem to be inconsistent with one another? and yet no man can be a good guardian of the public interest unless he combines them." But natures so gifted are to be found—"for example, in our friend the dog".[1] The dog has a strong sense of fun, he understands make-believe, he shares our absurd sense of self-importance; and no man ever made has a stronger sense of responsibility than he. Someone said, "Plus je connais les hommes, plus j'admire les chiens":[2] and I think the best testimonial to the character of man is that the dog loves him.

'Our friend the dog'

The conclusion is that there can be no safe basis for ethical life unless we are capable of feeling the sense of duty towards the other animals; just as in our relations with each other there has been and there can be no sound ethical life in face of the secular injustices—of which men are part conscious and part unconscious. Sophistries and megalomania far from exalting man demean his soul, and undermine the supports of sweet ethical sentiment. Why a fine man treats animals finely is simply because it has been the general low level of justice and generosity to our kind and not any inherent distinction between ourselves and the other animals which is accountable for our neglectful treatment of these.[3] How are we to treat the other animals? With the same criteria

---

[1] *Republic*, ii. 375 and 376. ("Surely the nature of the dog is very charming?")

The ancient mourning custom of shaving the head (recorded both by Sappho and Sokrates) was observed in Egypt by all those in a house where a dog died, as Herodotus reports.

[2] The words are attributed to several people, and were certainly paraphrased in 1850 by Lamartine.

[3] It is recorded of Mazzini and a friend that in one of their conspirator conferences for the liberation of Italy both men put out their cigars which were causing distress to the dog with them. The members of Scott's expedition to the South Pole put the tired and sick draught-dogs on the sleigh and drew it themselves.

as we use or should use with each other—our duties to them are as definite as between man and man. The false moral trail which has guided people in this matter has led to the inquiry whether a man should risk his life for a dog.[1] The answer probably, as in all similar cases, depends on the affections. It is said to be a 'duty' to save a human being, but I think there is no duty to save a human being at the cost or even at the risk of your own life. Clearly a positive duty to risk your life requires you to be ready to give it. Actions of this kind however are settled by sympathy by honour courage and the social virtues—there are things which a man thinks due to these though they are not positive duties of human life. We are far removed from all real moral sentiment if we assert that it is every man's duty to risk his own life to save a baby, and 'wrong' for any man to risk it to save his beloved dog. There can be no call whatever to risk your life to save a baby, except the call of the affections or of sympathy. If you save the baby or save the dog the act is equally an example of humanity.[2]

"It is not good for man to be alone." We do not realize, living as we do in the midst of dense masses of men, what we owe to animal life, or what human life would be without it; what joy comes from its beauty and what we should lose if the earth were silent save for the noise men make in it. The race would lose nothing if there were far fewer men; but the loss of the animals could never be

---

[1] At the same time men everywhere risk their lives for utterly futile motives.

[2] The falsity of sentiment has gone so far that it has been deemed worthy of record that a man saved a dog from a cart-wheel at the cost of injuring his own hand: this sentiment perhaps is a homage to the fantastic notion that man is god to the dog. Man might however, without losing catse, show towards the dog no less self-forgetfulness than the dog displays. There was a story in one of the magazines some 30 years ago of a man who returned to a sinking ship to die with his dog; and one refused, in the wreck of the *Titanic* in 1912, to get into the boats without her dog. They were found drowned, the dog clasped in the man's arms.

repaired. Man makes the world ugly and himself ugly; human sights and sounds and smells develop and degenerate as hideous things: this is partly counteracted by natural beauty—the beauties of tree and soil and horizon; but animal beauty is the great foil to human ugliness —the grace the freedom the naturalness the dignity of the "great and sane and simple race" of beasts.[1] And the living sounds proper to them,—to man's best servants the cow and horse, to bird and insect,—are as it were a permanent harmony in a world made up of human discords. Man not only makes the world about him ugly, he is the enemy of the life round him,[2] and his own enemy. It is not allowable in moral life that we should treat animals as bad men treat their fellows. It must have a highly deteriorating and hateful effect upon human character to live among sensitive animals whom you never care for, for whose comfort and happiness you never make provision—as the Italian lives with the mules donkeys and horses who serve him; and while this is so it will not be understood that to live in sympathy with the animals is one of the elements of happiness. Men have been shameless usurers in the toll they take from animals for the little they give them. And if the world makes moral progress the barbaric horror of the slaughter-house and the episode of vivisection in any account of our relation to the animals will appear as the monstrosities they surely are.

[1] In contrast with our spiritual squalor the dignity of their life and death is seized by the poet: the hunted wolf dies, closing his great eyes, and without uttering a cry

> "Et sans daigner savoir comment il a péri."
> "Comment on doit quitter la vie et tous ses maux
> C'est vous qui le savez, sublimes animaux."
> (ALFRED DE VIGNY, *La Mort du Loup.*)

[2] "Whenever man has come up with them I should suppose they have seldom escaped from experiencing a certain proportion of misery." Waterton.

When we flout the instinct which tells us that those who cannot plead for themselves need our help most we flout that which is best in human nature: the lust of domination for its own sake has been a corroder of the heart, and mankind has lived too long with the opinion that men exist to be exploited, which has served him so well in the ill-treatment of animals also. But by the side of the animals is that army of wers whose birthright is tenderness and compassion, a tenderness not exceeded by woman's. Our views will one day come into honour; at present we are looked upon as freaks if we are wers and fools if we are women. Meanwhile it is right to remember that so large a number of men do not exhibit the qualities which raise them above the other animals, and that superiority does not and cannot consist in using a far more highly evolved instrument in the pursuit of ends infinitely mean. The 'glory of human life', then, as distinguished from animal life, has not belonged to the vast numbers of mankind at all. There is a remarkable 'logion' which declares that "those that draw us to the kingdom of heaven are the fowls of the air, all the beasts upon the earth, and the fishes of the sea";[1] and there is only one sense in which the animals have been "delivered into our hand"—they are placed in our moral hands, that heart of man which having come upon a greater maturity is able to embrace and comprehend their need.

[1] *New Sayings of Jesus*, Grenfell and Hunt, 1904.

VII. WOMAN AND WERMAN*

All animals, male and femel, which consort together, have a virtue of their species which all are able to pursue in common.
PLATO, *Kritias*, 110.

W HAT relations would be established between woman and werman was always matter fundamentally important for the history of conduct. That the biological qualities of the two sexes involve essential ethical matter we have already seen; and these qualities determined the natural relation between them. But when we come to trace the actual historical relations of woman and wer we shall find that they have been dominated by a phenomenon which has troubled and changed not only their relations as mother and mate but the psychological character of both.

When primeval woman and wer first speculated about their differences and fixed an idea, and a name, to their impressions, they had none of the material before them which has sufficed for their descendants. It would not have occurred to the primeval mind that women lacked physical strength or lay under physical disabilities. There was no established distinction between a hirsute face for the one and a smooth face for the other, and none between long hair and short. Primevally, as now among savages, femel beauty did not exist, and neither height nor size, strength or vocal timbre were the sex marks we now consider them to be.[1] Women and wers were naked, and

* See pp. 234–6.
[1] The australian woman even today gives birth on trek and continues the march with the tribe. Savage tribes are often hairless; and it is probable that, as among numbers of vertebrates and most invertebrates, the wer was smaller than the woman. In Neanderthal man the sexes were similar in appearance; the same was true in ancient Crete and Egypt—in Knossos and Egypt the sexes were indistinguishable. The 'majestic stature' of the women in ancient India was recorded, and the statues make no difference

the obvious distinctions between them were the external physical differences, the salient psychological differences, and in the third place the presence or absence of the great biological powers. The external differences were the breasts of the woman—the source of child nourishment—and her bigness during gestation: in the male it was the sex organ. It is certain that in the woman's case the name mankind fixed upon her referred to the reproductive powers represented by these differences—gūnê, fē (from *fuo*, *feo*, I make or bring forth, I become).[1] And it is possible that the intromittent sex organ provided a name for the male.[2] If not, the male adjective ἀρρηνής connotes what is rude and untameable. As with the physical so it must have been with the psychological characters, they were differently appraised in primeval human communi-

in the height of the sexes. Tacitus states that the german woman was equal in strength and size to the wer; and the roman women were the taller in the age of Claudius. Indeed this was noticeable in Rome in the late xix[th] century before the city developed into the national capital: the roman woman was often of the admired 'Juno' type, her voice deep and strong, contrasting with the smaller male and his high thinner voice. The dignity of figures of women and wers together, the sexes equally tall, can be noticed in the vase room of the museum at Palermo, and at Agrigentum a vth century B.C. vase represents Alcaeus as shorter than Sappho. Greek sculpture recognized the beauty of groups in which the young male figure is placed in juxtaposition with a finer woman.

The N. American indians today resemble each other closely, 2 out of 3 wers, at least, are of feminal type; and a recent writer (R. Wyndham) describes nilotic negro tribes where the sexes are indistinguishable in appearance: in the Nuer tribe the women have narrow hips, and the wers are not broad-shouldered; these look "effeminate", "But they will fight a lion single-handed".

[1] Both come from the common root *gan*, sanskrit *jani*, to produce. *Gūnê* the Greek word for a woman, from this root, is the same as the icelandic, scandinavian, and old high german word for a woman; and as *queen*, anglo-saxon. [*gān*, to produce (from which *genus*); sanskrit *jani*; greek *gūnê*; scandinavian *kona*, *kune*; icelandic *kvan*, *kona*; anglo-saxon *cwén*; o.h. german *quena*.]

[2] Cf. Greek ἄρσην (ἄρσις) for ἄρρην.
Cf. the word for the femel sex θῆλυς (τὸ θῆλυ) from θηλή the breast or teat; breast-giving, fruitful, rich and abundant (θάλλω). The cornucopia was originally a femel symbol.

ties and in those succeeding ages of barbarism and semi-civilization on the fringe of which we still live. What is it that would have struck a woman and a wer as regards themselves and each other? I think it would have been the difference not in bodily but in psychological activities. She would note in the male discontinuous irresponsible aggressive action, and in the place of obvious biological powers she would be aware of his sex urge. He would note in her together with the life powers—reproduction and nurture—domesticating faculties matching with these life faculties: it is to her not to himself he would look as the house-maker, endowed with the discernments and perceptions adapted to her place in the life scheme. He would know that she, not he, was the helpful fore-seeing one in all the events which have to do with the care of life. Hence the names they gave each other signified life-bestowing man and rough-man.

It was then the presence of great powers not of great disabilities in the woman which first impressed mankind; the fact that of the woman came life, that she, and she only, had the reproductive power, was creator, propagator, source of growth. That this was in fact mankind's earliest realization and underlay the types of conduct which he first developed, and afterwards determined his religion, is to be gathered from every hint which the remote past has preserved for us. All ideas of mystery sacredness and power centred in one sex—the mother. The woman not the wer was held to be inspired and indued with the gifts of magic and healing; she was the natural prophet of the race. So the eleusinian mysteries, the paramount mystical and spiritual experience of early religion, are mysteries of Demeter the Great Mother; a woman inspires the delphic oracle; and the tradition of the Sibylline Books—of which women alone are authors—bears witness to ancient facts long since lost sight of by mankind. These conditions persisted through

The mystery of the reproductive power

thousands of years of human history, and were so inrooted that they may still be found among indigenous races all over the globe. In the nigerian Egbo tribe of West Africa there are today more wise women than wizards, and knowledge is passed on from mother to daughter: when the worst calamities come upon the people recourse is had to the age-long memory of matriarchal power; then the shibboleths of the male magicians are impotent and none but an elder woman of the ancient governing races can save. Behind the present male god of this tribe is his mother, "She-who-dwells-alone" and "is not as the others", arbiter of life and death. The name of Io the supreme mother deity of the Maoris must not be pronounced even by the chief male hierarchs; and no wer might listen when the great italic mother Maia, *Bona Dea*, was named. This mysterious silence about the name of the Great Mother who had been supplanted by the male god was transferred by the later semitic peoples to 'Jehovah' (Jahveh), where no reason for the silence existed. Only a few statuettes of the prehistoric period have come down to us, but among them images of women with symbols of power and fulness in their hands predominate, as do sitting figures of steatopygous women. Prehistoric Egypt was remarkable for the absence of male statuettes,[1] and all the statuettes and sculptured figures of palaeolithic Europe (aurignacian age) were femel. Recent palestinian excavation showed that "femel deities abounded" and numerous plaques portrayed 'the great mother'. Every clue from the past is evidence that for primeval man the life power was the great mystery.

Matriarchy   We find then that the earliest of all social systems was

[1] Petrie notes that sculptures in the round were of women, the male head being occasionally represented by scratchings on tusks &c. In Crete and Cyprus the images were also preponderantly femel; and the outstanding finds in recent mesopotamian excavations were cult figurines of the mother god type. Similar cult figurines of clay are found in the Indus civilization, 3000 B.C.

matriarchal. Matriarchy means that it was the fact of motherhood which determined the type of the human community: the earliest organization of society was founded on the paramountcy of maternal functions; the sexual role of the male was controlled by the mother requirements, and there were no paternal rights. In these communities the mother and her relatives ruled, a sister's children ranked before a brother's, and the wer kinsmen of the mother acted as the woman's delegates. The mate came to the mother's house and served the family as Jacob served for Rachael. To this day a young wer among the Mrus serves three years for his wife in her parents' house; the Banyaia husband (on the Zambesi river) may not sit in the presence of his wife's mother and he must assume a crouching attitude so that his feet are not turned towards her. The husband serves and obeys the wife's parents whom he takes as his own; but he may not eat with them nor call them by their names. In some tribes husbands live in idleness, having neither work nor power; but in most they are set to incessant toil and to the lowest tasks, and even then if a husband should not please he is obliged by the laws of the tribe to go away; he can take no property of any kind with him and has no claim whatever to the children that have been born. There is no evidence that it was paternal instinct which played any part in modifying this state of things: the human male was not obviously endowed with the nurturing faculties which are conspicuous in many birds and in some mammals, and it was not a share in these which he coveted. What eventually brought about the substitution of a male ruled society for one guided by the woman was a distortion of the sex instinct. The distortion was both physical and moral, showing itself in unbridled sexuality and in a craving to dominate the femel. Male reflexion upon his share in the reproductive powers of the mother—sometime in the millenniums before our era—led to the absurd biology which is put in the mouth of Apollo by Aeschylus[1] and which has ruled, against all probability and all evidence, until this present century.[2] But mother-right was not dependent on primitive ignorance of the mutual dependence of the sexes; on the contrary it is always found associated with a system of mating and with some test of the male's fitness. Matriarchal matrimony and care in the choice of the male parent had been preceded by an original ignorance of his share in the reproduction of a child;[3] but the matriarchal systems of society, as we now know, were to be found at each of the great centres of human civilization—Crete, Babylon, Egypt—civilizations which were far more advanced and of much greater antiquity than we dreamed of even a few decades ago. There is evidence that the male realization of his share in reproduction brought about cataclysmic changes among savages, resulting there as elsewhere in a swollen notion of its importance and in the megalomania upon which all patriarchal institutions are based. For the wer was not

[1] *Eumenides*, 628–36.

[2] The theory maintained throughout the xviii[th] and popularly credited during most of the xix[th] century of our era was not only the ancient absurdity that the male gave the 'life' and the 'soul' but that each 'spermatozoon' was a tiny human being which had entered the womb as a mannikin complete in all its parts, and had only to be developed there. [The male (pollen) cells inaptly called 'spermatozoa' were discovered in 1690; the actual human ovum was not detected till 1827.]

[3] There can be no reason to presume more knowledge on the part of archaic man than exists among other animals. Nothing suggested a connexion between childbirth and the act which had occurred nine months before it. There was promiscuity of intercourse, and in a society of this sort or even in one where marriage arrangements existed the occasional sterility of women would be far more prominently in evidence than the fact that a woman who had somehow escaped mating was childless. Sterility, the fear of which haunted and haunts primitive communities, was seen to be obviously independent of sexual conjugation. The most primitive survivors of mankind are still ignorant of the relation between copulation and gestation, an ignorance expressed recently by the writers of *Savage Life in Central Australia* in the words: "that the father has anything to do with conception is an idea wholly alien to the native mind."

satisfied with asserting an equality with the creating mother, he invented for himself the exclusive role of creating father. The natural mysteries which formed the occult knowledge of women in the matriarchal age were now exploited in a wer's club; such clubs still exist among a large number of indigenous tribes, and they are maintained by a superstitious terrorizing of the women.[1] The two weapons everywhere employed were evidently violence and make-believe, and no clue in anthropology is more instructive than that furnished by the most powerful of these clubs in West Africa, which was originally a woman's society. The wers first won its secrets and then killed the women and forbade any woman thenceforth under penalty of death to share in the rites. The secrets so exploited, we are told, had been brought "by a divine woman" who came down "to teach them to her sisters".[2]

The next stage in the history of woman and wer is the sexual stage, dominated by a changed idea of that male share in procreation which had played so insignificant a part in the earliest history of mankind. Natural restraints had brought about matriarchy but this new notion worked in a welter of selfish ignorance; it roused the male imagination and stirred the natural ruthlessness of the seeker-sex, it touched his vanity and turned his head. The secrets of life wrested from the custody of the mother became in the process no longer birth interests

The change to patriarchy

[1] On the way to the wer's club the bull-roarer (the australian *tundun* and *witarna*) makes its terrifying noise to scare the women from approaching. Sometimes they are invited to regard it as the god's voice, or the divinity itself; a nice study in god-making.

[2] The fact that this had been in origin a woman's secret society was told, only a few years ago, with great hesitation as the "unexpected explanation" of the wers being obliged to resort to a woman of the tribe when the Egbo spirit took flight. She can recall it, no wer could do so (see p. 206). To raise the sum required for entrance to the higher grades of this Egbo society the wer will sell his wife, or her children; but he cannot keep the Egbo spirit in the mystery house he robbed her of without her help. He becomes in part the woman's exploiter and in part her suppliant.

but sex interests, and the substitution of the wer's house of mystery for the woman's relegated her to the position which had been his: by the time of the greek drama her biological inferiority figures as one of the themes. Thereafter human history has been marked by the femel taking as her principal role that of sex mate to the male; this has led to the belief that sex has supreme rights and to a curtailment of life for the mother-half of the species which has made the human femel a biological anomaly.[1] The

The absurd
biology delusion has prevailed that the male alone is the full member of every species and the femel throughout nature a submember.[2] All the assumptions and beliefs about women, as Legouvé saw,[3] repose on this false natural history, and all their disabilities derive from it. The importance of wers has since been supported upon property and civil privilege and upon an education in life and letters from which the woman has been excluded— which made it easy enough to speak of her as ignorant or even uneducable—but its real pedigree is to be traced to phenomena analogous to the savage 'wer's house' and his bull-roarer and thence through male gods and phallic cults to the complete subordination of the mother man in the interests of the sex man. It is obvious that in this lineage there was no room for the 'wisdom' of humanity to have intervened in order that 'nature' might come by its own and rational laws and customs be deduced from some striking superiority of wer over woman: among savage men and semi-barbarous men no moral or mental advantage in the wer could have been discerned, and the pedigree therefore takes us back not to an evident natural superiority of the one man over the other, but simply to the fictitious biological superiority claimed by the male

---

[1] See *infra*, pp. 223 *n*. and 274 and *n*.

[2] Refer *supra*, Biological Sources, pp. 55–8—the reverse is truer.

[3] Legouvé, *Hist. Morale de la Femme*, Bk. iv, ch. i, pp. 247, 249–50 (7th ed.).

for himself. Nothing has been too magnificent for the wer to predicate of himself, too mean and vile to allege about women. The reason is of course pathological; an uncurbed licence has been permitted to domineering sex instincts. Thenceforward an onslaught on the human rights and on the property of women became the rule, and vituperation of the femel sex one of the common-places of literature.[1] A Paul saw nothing extravagant in supposing that the wer had been created in the image of the supreme being and was the glory of god while woman was only the glory of the wer. In Japan she is taught to bow down before her husband as he enters the house; in Bosnia and Croatia she kisses the hands of all the males as she serves them at table—even grandmothers are to kiss the hands of their grandsons; and a woman is not expected to cross the road when a male is passing along it: in all parts of Europe the lowest specimen of humanity has held it right and natural that he should control the life of some good woman, force her to do his bidding and to accept in silence any ill-treatment he meted out to her. Of what quality were the theories and views which led to such relations between the sexes as these? They point to a sex pathology which has coloured all the strands of the wer's life and of the woman's and prevented him seeing facts or interpreting them. The queen-bee because she was the principal personage in her surroundings was supposed to be a king-bee; a little hymenopteron fossor because it was observed to store caterpillars from which in time an insect like itself appeared to emerge, was called by the chinese wers *jiga*—"mimic me": our human *jigas* assumed that these wonderful operations could only be accomplished by the male insect; a male however does not lay eggs so the *jiga* was supposed to continue the

[1] See *Medea*, ed. Verrall, lines 420–30, and footnote to lines 421–3 where *Odyss.* xi. 456, Hesiod *Theog.* 591 foll. and *Op.* 375 are also cited. Cf. *infra*, p. 213 *n.*

species by means of a charm addressed to the caterpillars it was burying: "mimic me". But of course the '*jiga*' is a femel and she lays her eggs by the food she is storing for the progeny she will never see.[1] When it was recently discovered that some gametes contain ten chromosomes and others only nine it was at once announced that when there were ten the cell was a male one; but it turned out that when there were ten the cell was femel. The leader of the wolf pack was reported to be always a fine male, when it was known that it was generally an old femel she no doubt ceased to present an imposing figure.[2] And the wer cannot be trusted to make sound scientific experiments when these come athwart sex prejudice.[3]

[1] This droll piece of natural history is as old as Confucius and perhaps older. It may be recalled that the Jewish rabbis strove to prove that the Queen of Sheba was a king. The Brahmă-brahmā legend was the conscious fraud which started brahmanism: Brahmă is the great being without attributes. To get the non-existent male principle, the 'brahman', "a male" called Brahmā is created out of Brahmă. Moreover Sarasvati, god of speech and learning, becomes the 'wife' of this goblin. (As Māha-Divī—"the great god"—becomes the 'consort' of Siva, and Ishtar of Marduk; see p. 233 *n*.)

[2] Darwin notes that it is the cow-seal who acts as sentinel of the herd (*Descent*, p. 153). The elephant herd is led by an elder cow-elephant; and the femel rhinoceros leads her family, followed by her young one, and then the bull. The reports of male observers as to 'harems' of animals are also certainly prejudiced by the same jiga-making mentality.

[3] When the frontal region of the skull was supposed to be the seat of the intellectual faculties male observers invariably 'found' that this region was more highly developed in their own sex. But when it was ascertained that the frontal skull in apes is larger than the parietal their observations showed that the femel skull approximated to the simian. The facts are that there is "greater height and length" in the occipital skull of women "with equal breadth" (Manouvrier and Weisbach), and Topinard pointed out that "a very markedly greater breadth of the posterior region", to be observed in the femel skull, is a feature of superior races. (See Havelock Ellis, *Man and Woman*, The Brain.) If there is a difference in the 2 skulls it appears to be that the line of brain development is with the woman, whose skull has not undergone what is noted by Havelock Ellis as an approach to the "savage, simian, and senile" in the male skull. Perhaps Bacon had one of the ablest and most scientific minds of all time, yet his

This megalomania led to the spurious hermaphrodism in which the sex arrogates to itself every capacity and function of the species, and acts as though the world could get on very well without women at all, except for natural child-bearing. The wer has posed for his portrait as complete man, and presents himself to us decked out not only in plumage borrowed from the woman but with a catholic psychology, only the weak and dependent traits being absent, for these are left in block to her. That there have been rational and sentimental estimates of the part women play in sustaining society does not affect the secular patriarchal assumption that the wer is sufficient to himself and by himself, nor the fact that child-bearing and subordinated service or servitude have been the only activities everywhere ungrudgingly reserved to her. In all patriarchal religions and in every part of the globe we may trace the doctrines that woman is not altogether man in the sense that the wer is, that he alone is endowed with an 'immortal soul' while she is soulless like the other animals; that she is unclean and wanton, the first author of evil, and peculiarly subject to diabolical possession.[1]

account in *The New Atlantis* of 'a feast of the family' is an exhibition for all time of nonsense and sex megalomania.

[1] This becomes a common dogma of the orthodox faiths: however much they may vilify one another's gods they have a common religious tenet in the sinfulness of woman; here, all are righteous and have their feet set in the strait way. They may distrust each other's power to save the human race but they meet on the common ground of the difficulty of saving women. (*Laws of Manu, The Damathat*, ix: "Women are as impure as falsehood itself. That is a fixed rule": Paul in 1 Corinthians xi. 3, 6–10, xiv. 34–6, Ephesians v. 22–25; 1 Timothy ii. 11–15: Muhammad "O assembly of women give alms—for verily ye are mostly of hell on the day of resurrection".)

It is highly necessary to realize the canker in the relation of the sexes which has been brought about by such atrocious doctrines, and which are a pathological phenomenon inimical to human progress. Schopenhauer says that the woman is a kind of intermediate thing between the child and the wer, who is the only proper human being. Weininger wrote that the wer, only, has a soul; woman is soulless. And Canon Edward Lyttelton,

The gods
change

Not only did the wers become gods but the gods became wers. Matriarchal gods had been mother gods. All the gods of the pantheon have behind them the great divine mother. Behind every god-the-father in Asia, in Africa, in America, in Europe, there is an older mother divinity. The great male deities make their appearance but with uncertain credentials; sometimes the god is son, sometimes brother, and sometimes husband of the primitive divinity, and the paradoxical title 'mother of god'— for a deity set apart in a shadowy background as a majestic memory—sufficiently betrays the origin of these male gods.[1]   All the earliest literatures of the world —the babylonian and the hebrew, the indian Rig-Vedas and Homer—though they record a patriarchal constitution of society more or less complete retain obvious traces of matriarchy and of a stage transitional to patriarchy. The curious prevention that the ascent from savagery coincided historically with the advent of patriarchy—with the recognition of father-right in place of mother-right—is due to two simple historical mistakes: for first, the greatest

successively headmaster of 2 colleges for boys, Haileybury and Eton, put forward as an argument: "It is pretty clear that St. Paul regarded man as standing nearer to God than woman and as being the more immediate recipient of divine truth." Is it also "pretty clear" that it is nice for schoolboys to learn they are "nearer to god" than mamma?

[1] Among the west african Ibibios the mysterious *Eka Abassi* is 'mother of god'; and the greek Zeus had been born of 'the great mother of the gods'. There is no term for a male divinity in hebrew; the numen is neuter; Astarte is *eloah*, and the english version of the scriptures translates the same word as 'goddess' and 'god'. The large preponderance of femel over male gods in the greek pantheon and that they always incarnated the powers of nature is confirmation of the truth that what mankind saw represented in women was power and powers. The attributes of creator, sky-lord, thunderer, were transferred in block to the new male god; the very name of Zeus having the same root as that of the pre-babylonian great mother of the gods; while the 'I am' of Jahveh has its origin in the femel god Hāyāh (hebr. Hawa or Havvah) whose name means 'to be'. And we may cross from Asia Europe and Africa to find the original tribes of Polynesia boasting their descent from the great mother Vari and chanting in their song of creation: "We have no father at all, Vari alone made us."

civilizations of the world were based upon mother-right in those far off ages which we had supposed were ages of savagery; and next, the mixing of the long-headed people with the short heads no doubt initiated the first notable expansion of human powers. It brought the first tremendous impulse to the historical development of humanity, a development side-tracked almost from the first by the establishment of patriarchy and the regime of physical force which dominated the Iron Age. The principle of father-right was the affirmation of sex whereas mother-right was the affirmation of principles less fundamentally appetitive, more sympathetic, less aggressive. Therefore on the one hand we have at the opening of the modern period those widening mental powers which were to give us in the course of centuries the philosophy, the literature, and the art of Greece and the measured order of Rome, and on the other side there was a definite ethical stultification. These two facts, this *plus* and this *minus*, have characterized all subsequent human history.

In the legends of the amazons we have a far-off pre- ^{Amazon legends}hellenic echo of a great conflict, the conflict of the great mother with the sex man. It is traditional and invaluable testimony to a catastrophic episode of sex, to some immense resentment felt by women towards males. The amazons were perhaps preponderantly women of a short-headed race, which may suggest that patriarchal notions originated among the short-heads. But that it was these women who fought may be due to a special quality of brachycephalic races which I have pointed out elsewhere, and not to the fact that the detested notions originated among them. Or, again, it may have been that the amazon peoples were more advanced than others and more capable of feeling moral and intellectual resentment.[1]

[1] The amazons not only fought wers, they killed their own male offspring; they lived by themselves and would consent to no form of marriage, mating once a year and rearing the femel children. Cf. the argonautic

The extravagances we have been considering were due to nothing but an ignorant sex direction of human society and they were consolidated everywhere by fraud. When the mother god was changed into the male god myths which set woman in a good light were changed into myths where she was set in an ill light and the wer in the good. Thus a half-conscious process reshaped the mythology of the race and developed later into a fully conscious one. Every old literature of the world bears the marks of deliberate fraud in omitting the names of women, substituting the names of wers, altering the incidence of a story. In history as well as in literature what resounded to the praise of the woman slipped out of the page. Only wers were magnified. The wer has wanted the woman to believe herself inferior, to think little of her maternal powers and nothing of her mental capacity and to this end has practised upon her every kind of physical and moral deception. Her character has been defamed and her defences weakened—for example by asserting that women are natural rivals and that their jealousy of each

legend of the isle of Lemnos which was found to be inhabited by women only, who had put to death their fathers husbands and brothers. Note that all the earliest male 'heroes' fight with women: Hercules, Achilles, Bellerophon, Theseus; and Poseidon fights not only with Athenê but with Hera for the possession of their cities.   In irish myth the other-world is represented as an 'island of maidens'. Froissart has a delightful description of a matriarchal society: On the return journey from the embassy to Baja-zet for the ransom of the Comte de Nevers and other french prisoners, the french lords steered to the ionian *Cephalonia* where they were met by a large party of ladies and damsels who entertained them gaily. They told the french knights that they had generally no visitors but merchants. I may be asked, writes Froissart, if the island were solely inhabited by women. I answer, no; but women have the soveranty of it. The wers were employed in carrying the fine silk cloths made by the women to foreign markets. They honoured the women "for their work and because they have a sufficiency of wealth". None dare approach the island to commit any injury. The ladies lived in peace "without fear of anyone"; they were amiable and without pride "and certainly, when they please, converse with fairies and keep them company". The french visitors "were very happy there". (chap. xxv.)

216

other is a fact governing all their relations.[1] But the greatest deception consciously practised upon the woman consisted in feigning that she is not the natural protector of her young ones, that she does not and cannot defend herself and them, that she is no fighter but is nature's non-combatant. This as we have already seen is a piece of falsehood which outrages all nature—from the highest to the humblest animal. In this way women have been deprived not only of their natural weapons and prevented from employing the artificial ones but they have undergone from century to century the strongest possible pressure which has crushed out their self-confidence in every direction and caused them to distrust their character as women.

A good man may say: where is this hateful type of wer; and where (on the contrary) are the lovely relations between the sexes, the tender appreciation of woman by wer and the lives of mutual affection and honour? And the good man—wer or woman—must be recalled to the philosophy of history. It would not be worth while to set out any faults of the past with any hopes for the future

[1] Women have been taught to vilify each other; it has been part, as J. S. Mill saw, of their sycophancy to wers. Yet their solidarity was acutely realized in classical times, and is prominent in euripidean drama. [Cf. the entire structure of the *Medea*, and especially line 823 with "it is the natural thing that woman should befriend woman" in the *Helena* line 239; and also the *Iphigeneia in Tauris* (1061) "We are women, a race helpful to each other" etc. with the remark of Menelaus in the *Helena* (line 830) "for it is a woman's business to do kindness to a woman".] Epiphanius records that it was the women who had exalted Mary.   The delight of women everywhere and of italian women especially at the triumphs of the great mathematician Maria Gaetana Agnesi in the xviii[th] century is characteristic of the way women have ever greeted women's achievements. In the early xv[th] century the english soldier and the french priest burnt Joan of Arc, but Christine de Pisan wrote the *Poème de la Pucelle*.

In the story of the classic conflict between Athenê and Poseidon over the naming of the city which was to be Athens it was the women who supported Athenê, and were thereupon deprived of their civic rights by Poseidon enraged at his defeat by a woman. They have never lost their rights for any better reason anywhere. [Cf. *infra*, pp. 280–2, and Aspasia, *infra*, p. 239.]

if lovely things like those did not exist at all; they exist, but they do not and never have prevailed, and the customs laws literature and common opinion of humanity are the permanent record of the ugly relations I have described.[1]

And as the wer has, consciously and unconsciously, denied to women the qualities he wished to monopolize, so too he has mirrored his least seemly features in her; his foibles and vices have seemed to him to be hers. *L'homme se reflète dans la femme*; *l'uomo si rispecchia nella donna*:[2] he is vain, he calls her the vain sex; he is the more jealous, he cries out upon her perennial jealousy; he is sensual and he makes her the type of sensuality; inconstant and he derides her inconstancy; he is the irresponsible sex but he mirrors her to himself as so: he cannot see her moral strengths in his haste to cover her with the tatters of his own moral weaknesses. Above all, because his sensual life is strong—because with him the appetitive dominates the sympathetic—he thinks this is *her* life, he sees sex everywhere, and sees it till his picture blots out the mother. She is the worker, but he regards himself as the sole 'worker'. He is more hidebound than she and

"The wer mirrors himself in the woman"

[1] If this could be seriously questioned it must be possible to show that in the history of our species the reverse process has been at work—a process of encouragment of women to exercise their faculties, to value themselves, to criticize wers, to share the pursuits open to mankind, to place their maternal instincts on higher ground than their sexual, and especially in this matter to share together with wers a racial effort on the side of restraint. It would have to be shown that the maxims of mankind represent women as worthy of confidence and of trust, capable as the mothers of the race to help it not hinder it—as bringing riches to the general store and therefore held in universal honour. But no! The wer who wished to thrust her into the position in which she has found herself could not afford to make such maxims current; and it remains the historical truth that woman's character has been consistently bedraggled by the weight of custom law literature and common opinion.

[2] A farcical instance of this was pointed out to me by Dr. Maria Montessori: urinals for wers have always been ubiquitous in Rome and the consequent indecencies of street life flagrant; but the Roman male calls the Roman woman "*pisciona*". (Urinals were never considered necessary for women.)

218

he figures her as clinging to conventions: perhaps too
we may say that while his instinct for what is authoritative
makes him a hero-worshipper, he supposes the woman
is always looking out for a hero—himself.

These things have led in their turn to sex antagonism, Sex
to male hostility to women. For sex antagonism is a male antagonism
phenomenon. It is not woman the defrauded it is wer
the defrauder who is jealous of the rivalry of the other
sex and has nourished an age-long literature of scorn for
it, and whose current coin of small talk concerning it is
belittling or lewd. The periodic uprisings of women
against the injustices suffered and the antagonism of
some fine women in all ages to the prevailing type of
male have been distinctively moral episodes, but wers
have never justified the base opinion of women they have
made current, while the 'vices' they have proclaimed are
also those by which they profit. Hence there has been
a twofold display of antagonism to women—hostility to
their sharing the common activities of the species and
hostility to everything which puts sex in the background:
the unlimited tolerance for the woman who is pretty
sexual or debauched has been countered by an unap-
peasable hostility to those who are not willing to put the
sexual interests of humanity in the forefront.   If one
sex, at a moment of special enlightenment of the race Wers pro-
which has never existed, had undertaken to restrain the tecting
other so that the ends of nature might be inforced, of nature
which he alone had a noble perception, against which she
alone was recalcitrant, the method and temper would no
doubt have been different. If one only of the two sexes
had instinctive knowledge of what nature required of the
other, the fate reserved to it by the high gods would have
been a tragic one—to keep the prison for half the human
race so that it could never exercise the faculties it possessed
nor fulfil vocations often ardently desired. In the discharge of this high hateful office the good wer would

have cried out against his lot not overwhelmed its victims with his disdain. For there could be no explanation of such a relation of the sexes except a 'divine' will or a decree of nature against which for some inscrutable reason the woman alone had ever wished to rebel, and we should have to imagine the wer passing his years on this planet as the apostle of our highest interests—of nature and of God. It is not however possible to regard the relations of the sexes for the past millenniums of years as determined by the wisdom of the wer in search for the clue to the well-being of mankind; neither is it possible to give credence to the thesis that it has been constantly necessary to restrain woman from "flying in the face of nature" or flouting the gods. This restraint has only been necessary to keep her from disputing the wisdom of the wer.

Wers 'protecting' women

After digesting the fable that the mother of the race is always trying to "fly in the face of nature" we are invited to assimilate another of the same kind. The wer, we have been told, has compensated woman for her incapacities and disabilities by affording her his constant protection. Apparently, at least in 'civilized' times, he has always arranged that this protection should depend on her consenting to live in the state of moral nonage. He has made it appear that she needs his protection, and she might well picture to herself a monster which he is placed at the portals of the world to withstand, some constant lurking menace to all women from which the wers' prowess alone could rescue them. But what the woman has to fear from human society as it has existed up to now is sexual and other violence, and both are supplied by the wer himself.[1]

[1] In the Wyf of Bathe's tale Chaucer imagines a similar situation with the exorcizing friar (lymytour) as the hero:

—"there as wont was to walken an elf
There walketh noon but the lymytour himself,
Wommen may now go saufly up and down;
In every busch, and under every tre,
Ther is non other incubus but he."

A further incongruous tradition is proper to patri- Woman's
archalism, known as 'the woman's place': this does not place, and
wer's place
mean where women ought to be but where the wer does
not want to be himself. Woman is said to have a 'mission',
a mission of service, of virtue, and of moral influence;
and as her 'place' is so confined her 'mission' bulks
correspondingly large. Women must be good in order
to have a good influence on the wer; they must put up
with bad and irreligious husbands in the hope of con-
verting them. Woman is required to be gentle, patient,
forgiving, serviceable, self-effacing, self-sacrificing—she
must find in herself all the christian virtues. So we have
the wer protecting women—from wers, and the woman
protecting the wer from himself. If these have been their
relations it is not surprising that the notion of the mission
grew up. But if it was the character of the dominating
sex to be in part a menace to the woman and in part her
pupil, it is clear that the mission must always have been
exercised, as we see it has in fact been exercised, in a strait
waistcoat. Shackled hand and foot, the only mission she
was called upon to explicate was one to please not one
to save. It is these aspects of patriarchal religion which
have resulted in havoc for the moral standard of the race.[1]

The wer's achievements throughout history have been Male
put forward as justifying the predominant place he has achieve-
ments
occupied. It is nevertheless certain that this predominant largely at
place was largely due to factors altogether independent the expense
of women
of sex merit. Obviously one of these factors has been the
control of all the means and opportunities; so that when
activities from building a house to building up a code of
law are laid to the credit of a sex it should be remembered
that only one sex has been in the position to perform
them. The next factor is the direct and indirect assistance

---

[1] The idea of the 'mission' of a subject sex appears in Paul's epistles,
but it had already figured in the laws of Manu where its original biological
significance was completely lost in the male lust to dominate.

received from women: without their work their courage and their personal sacrifices a very large part indeed of what the male has accomplished would have remained in the womb of time. The greatest of wers have owed their leisure to be what they were to the co-operation of their wives. The indirect aid of women, the direct learning and technical ability which was a woman's share of the achievement but was credited to him alone, and the mass of her independent work which is never put forward in any synthesis of human achievement—these things may be left out of history and the common memory but must be reckoned with in any fair apportionment of the work of the world.   There is besides all this a primitive fact of heredity—male geniuses have owed their greatness primarily to their mothers. From saint to sage, from artist to hero, this has always been true.[1] The last factor is the biological factor due to sex—shall we say it has accounted for one-tenth or two-tenths of male achievement: the male is the leisured sex, he has no biological responsibilities, and his loose-end energy and roving instinct both stimulate certain intellectual and imaginative (but not moral) activities.

The aes- thetic imagina- tion   It may be that these energies and leisures of the wer make him pre-eminent in the aesthetic imagination: great literature, great sculpture, great painting, great building, great music, great poetry—the wer has shown all these to be his powers. But one is hardly justified perhaps in venturing the conclusion that he is endowed to a greater extent than the woman with powers of the intellectual

---

[1] (Cf. The Family, p. 327.) The inheritance of famous wers from their fathers could in the main be represented by Napoleon's saying that the only thing he owed to his father was a weak stomach. Whether notable women owe their greatness chiefly to their fathers the custom of count- ing inheritance only through the male and the constant suppression of femel talent have obscured the means of judging. Possibly it may prove that great women are the offspring of two able parents, notable wers being usually the offspring of one able parent, the mother.

imagination as an offset to activities for which I think she disposes of higher powers—namely those of the moral imagination. Such a conclusion is not yet justified because although artistic powers and genius can and do at times burst through the trammels of circumstance the circumstances of wers' lives have been propitious and the circumstances of women's lives highly unpropitious for developing that individualism, that liberty of expression and sincerity of thought, the bold self-reliance and initiative which are the essentials of all intellectual creation. The woman of the nations has had about as much share of these essential things as has the slave among freemen; and if the race could boast but one Dante, one Shakespeare, one Michelangelo, all the odds would favour that one being of the sex which held the stakes. Nothing has been proven up to now but that in the case of women there has been defect of every psychological circumstance which goes to make the artist, however miserable his position. In other paths of human activity the achievement of the wer has been extraordinarily poor and slow. The statecraft of the world has proved to be Government on the most modest scale provoking us to echo the words of the Swedish chancellor: "See with how little wisdom the world is governed!"[1] It may be placed to the account

---

[1] The assumption—the puerile assumption—that only the wer can rule and that the nations would come to ruin if women intervened was met and scouted by Plato in the *Republic*, Bk. v. 450–6: Woman and wer, he says, do not differ in any respect which affects the administration of the state, and we have never considered what we mean by 'difference of nature'; there is an opposition in nature between bald and hairy wers—if bald wers be cobblers why not forbid the hairy to be cobblers? But such differences do not affect the educable nature of man, and whether it be a wer or a woman who has the soul of a physician they are essentially the same; whereas the physician and carpenter are different. We see that one has natural gifts and another has not; and what this should mean—since the gifts of nature are equally diffused in both sexes—is that neither woman as woman nor wer as wer has a special function in the state; the pursuits of the one are the pursuits of the other.

Plato it is evident puts forth a persistent keen purposiveness into the

Medicine of the middle ages that we had to wait so long for the discovery of the circulation of the blood, but the fact remains that the general standard of treatment of sick people until quite recently was not much above the wizards' magic or the quaint medical guesses of 2,000 years ago.[1] Modern surgery was made possible by anaesthetics and skilled nursing, and the second of these is due entirely to women. If it were not the fact that in many desperate illnesses the nurse is more important than the physician the death roll would be far larger; and the woman has been the nurse. Therapy medicine obstetrics and sanitation, certainly, are among those things which have suffered a definite setback from the exclusion of women.[2]

Immemorially, then, the wer has placed all the oppor-

argument of Book v that he may get his thought seized and acted upon; but 23 centuries later the male world had not moved an inch towards realizing the apparently elementary truth that the qualities and capacities which make good and bad women rulers are also those which through history make bad and good male ones. That wers ruin states without women's intervention. [Cf. also *Laws*, vii. 805–6, 814.]

[1] Cf. the surmises of the elder Pliny with some of those of Thomas Browne 1500 years later.

[2] Not the wer but the woman has the sanitary faculty; it is she, not he, who has *mysophobia*—horror of filth. When Florence Nightingale was going out to the army hospitals in the Crimea, a major wrote, in scorn of women's knowledge of hospital work, that 200 scrubbing brushes were the first thing she had ordered. The hygienic care of the sick begun by Fabiola in Rome in the iv[th] century and practised by the great Hildegard in the xii[th] contrasts strangely with the filthy hospitals still in use in the xviii[th] and xix[th] centuries without light or air where dying persons would share a bed with 5 or 6 others and even as late as the middle of last century the death-rate of the patients was 50 or 60 per cent. It was a woman, Suzanne Necker-Curchod, who showed what a hospital could be when she founded her own in Paris in 1778. Miraculous, indeed, must have seemed in old days the cures effected by the nuns who gave the sick light and air and cleanliness. The woman has, then, been excluded from bringing progress but not from bearing the brunt of disease: the inforced deflection of life round sickness and disease is a suffering (and an obstacle) which has been mainly the woman's—who has made no fortunes out of them; and, quite apart from the professional nurse, of either sex, the alleviation of suffering has been almost wholly women's work.

224

tunities in his own hands, and immemorially he has minimized and forgotten to record the help he received from women; yet on these two things his apparent gifts to society have chiefly depended. But the secular refusal of all education and intellectual training to women which has characterized patriarchal history was sufficient in itself to account for most of the output of the sex which received education.[1]

The refusal of educa-tion

[1] Apparently the first males in history to deny education to women were the athenian who refused it to their wives. In the 200 years from the middle of the xvii[th] to the middle of the xix[th] century the lowest depth was reached, and a "Projet d'une loi portant défense d'Apprendre à Lire aux Femmes" was published in Brussels by a french wer in 1847. In the reign of Anne, Mary Astell designed a college for women which the queen would have approved; it was stopped by bishop Burnet. And when public educa-tion was introduced the ruling sex discriminated everywhere against women. Lady Mary Wortley Montagu wrote in the xviii[th] century: "My sex is usually forbid studies of this nature and folly reckoned so much our proper sphere that we are sooner pardoned any excesses of that than the least pretensions to reading or good sense. We are permitted no books but such as tend to the weakening or effeminating of the mind. Our natural defects are in every way indulged, and it is looked upon as in a degree criminal to improve our reason or fancy we have any. . . . There is hardly a creature in the world more despicable or more liable to universal ridicule than . . . a learned woman: these words imply, according to the received sense, a tattling, impertinent, vain and conceited creature." But in the previous century 2 excellent books had been published, one in Holland and the other in England: Anna van Schurman's *Dissertatio de Ingenii muliebris ad Doctrinam*, etc. and her *Epistolae ejusdem argumenti*, in which she replies to the teaching of her day—"that the study of letters should not be allowed (*non convenit*) to christian women, except to those only who are divinely inspired thereto". (Her works were edited, by a woman, at Leipzig in 1749. In the edition of 1641 the *Gynaicologia* of Lotichius (1630) was included.) At the same time "Sophia, a Person of Quality"'s book appeared: *Woman not inferior to Man*, a short vindication of the natural right of the fair sex to a perfect equality of power, dignity, and esteem with men.   Steele, writing in 1710, suggests that parents "imagine their daughters will be accomplished enough if nothing interrupts their growth or their shape. . . . I could name you 20 families where all the girls hear of in this life is that it is time to rise and come to dinner; as if they were so insignificant as to be wholly provided for when they are fed and clothed."   Mary Queen of Scots cited Sappho and Erinna Deborah and Cassandra as examples of learning and authority in her correspondence with Elizabeth of France; and had maintained in a public oration before

Nevertheless it is women not wers who are to be credited with the earliest progresses of our species. It is they who are the chief founders of civilization as it is the wer who (as the sole ruler during the historic period) is chiefly responsible for its failure.

There is no history of this earliest progress. But when men began to delve into the past of the race it was impossible not to discern that the higher conduct functions, the higher social agency, had belonged to the woman who bore and matured life and not to the wer who hunted lusted and scalped his neighbour. This moral presumption is so strong that if there were no evidence for it it would yet require formidable evidence to rebut it. None but a patriarchal society could have passed over these moral considerations and planted upon us—as the sole moral agencies—the wer priest the wer legislator and wer judge; the wer counsellors and physicians of souls. Confirmation of the woman's part in the first civilization of our species reaches us through the legends and traditions of mankind. The development of the cave into the hut is not the work of the hunter but of the mother:[1] round

Henry II and Catherine de Medici in the great hall of the Louvre that women should be skilful in the liberal arts and sciences.

Women have endowed education to an extent entirely disproportionate to their opportunities and means, but the wer has never failed to deprive them of their own share of it: when Mary Astell wrote, in 1696, arithmetic was unknown as part of a girl's education in England (but not in Holland); public education was introduced within 20 years of the landing of the Pilgrims at Plymouth Rock, but the women waited for it 150 years, while the schools at Boston, established in 1642, were kept from girls till 1789 when they were magnificently opened to them for *half the year* that they might learn to read, spell, and compose in English. (Mozans, *Women in Science*, p. 99.) Yet of xv[th] century Bohemia Aeneas Sylvius (Pius II) could say that the women of the people there knew the scriptures better than an italian priest. See also *infra* (pp. 230–1) Christine Pisana in the xv[th] century; p. 245 *n.*, Fénelon in the xvii[th] century; and p. 238, Pope Pius IX in the xix[th] century.

[1] All ancient legend makes the woman the inventor and first builder of the house. Cf. Hestia.

about the woman were the fire she first kindled, the animals she first domesticated; the magic of her ingenuity gave the corn and the oil, the milk eggs and honey, the fruit tree and the medicinal herbs.[1] It gave us garments —for the babe and the wer and the woman—it gave us succour in wounds and sickness, the agricultural and domestic implements, and the first art of speech—the greater range of her activities and the need to reach the mind of the child first gave names to things. The legends of the remote past all record that the arts and crafts of life were due to women; agriculture is attributed to them both in Egypt and Greece, and Isis certainly, Pallas probably, were in origin the human saviours of the race who brought the great gifts to men. Diodorus Siculus says that such men were placed among the gods (under patriarchal auspices, as we know, it was the heroes of combats who were deified) and an example comes from the far east perhaps 3000 years before our era when the empress Se-ling was deified in China because she first taught the spinning of silk. By the Greeks the invention of bridge and canal is attributed to the babylonian Semiramis[2]; and there is no older tradition than that of Athenê bringer of all the useful arts.[3] When the woman

---

[1] The tradition of the woman as the first physician is universal. Brigit (Brigindo, Brigantia) the great tribal mother, in Gaul Ireland and Britain, was herself known as 'the Physician'; and among the Kurds the hereditary physicians are still women. (Mrs.) Bird, *Persia and Kurdistan*.

The details of the story of *Agnodikê*, like so many others, do not depend for their accusatory and revealing character on their authenticity.

[2] Herodotus ascribes the triple circuit round the Euphrates to Nitocris. But though he ascribes the great monuments of Central Asia to her and Semiramis the inscriptions attribute them to wers.

[3] She gave the plough, the sail, the wheel, the olive (Vergil, *Georg.* i. 18–19, *Oleaequae Minerva inventrix*); she first taught us to yoke oxen, to build a ship, and is the first to tame and harness the horse. The Egyptian legend of Hathor is that she came from the far south on the coast of the Red Sea, and brought with her a company of metal workers. Brigit also is called 'Brigit the Smith'. And the Khasi tribe of the Synteng (N.E. India) say that their tribal mother taught them to smelt iron.

is represented in archaic images with the horn of plenty and power or the key-of-life in her hand it is not only because the woman represents fertility it is also because she signified for man the copious activities and the directing power of the one who had the care of life: she is source of fulness—the Demêter woman; the founder of the hearth—the Vesta woman; the house of bread —the Isis, woman; the first craftsman—the Athenê woman.

And she is the first legislator. Prevision of necessities, intuitive wisdom, natural self-restraints and sympathies suggested *to her first* the elements of a conduct of life. She taught these to the wer at the hearth she had founded, as she taught them to her children. The domestication of mankind, the elements of social conduct, and the arts and crafts of life were the works she undoubtedly put forth. She had not more leisure than wers, but she had more time—for she had no dissipated time. It was not only a mother principle which guided human society, it was a woman principle, a gynekosophy, in which this spirit underlay the civilizing of the race, was the fount of right conduct, the urbane virtues, and religion: it was the core of these things, personified in none but women gods and represented by none but women priests.[1] Such founda-

Women and gentilization

---

[1] That the first male priests acted in virtue of their wives is suggested by the fact that the Flamen Dialis had to resign his office when his wife (who was a priest) died. And it was the wife of the Pontifex Maximus who led the worship of the *Bona Dea*. That male priests were usurpers is also indicated by the custom of dressing themselves as women practised by the priests of Dionysius and of the *Dea Syria* (Atargatis).

The two divine ideas in the social philosophy founded on womanhood are the Magna Mater with unbounded power over the natural world, and the feminal principle, represented in Hebe Hestia Vesta Artemis Athenê, which had power over all our human society and brought all succour to it. Thus Rhea represents mother power for the creation of life, the daughter Hestia mother power for its protection—herself no mother but simply the feminal principle which creates the moral order. The great cities of antiquity all claimed to have women founders, who were their guardians; the headdress of Rhea, Cybele, and Artemis is the mural crown, or city-

tional virtues as *Themis, Dikê, Fides, Hospitalitas,* are guarded by women;[1] of the divine trinity invoked by Plato in the *Laws* (Hestia, Zeus, Athenê) it is Hestia we are to call upon to defend justice and the oath in courts of law. The Erinyes, again, represent this feminal principle which protects the civilized instincts of mankind, requiting transgressions of social right and order; and despite later male representations of them as furies they are the 'Venerable Ones'—the *Semnai*—of an earlier civilization, those early propitious gods (*Eumenides*) whose names might not be pronounced in the male age. Indeed whenever women appear as evil beings we may scent a travesty due to patriarchal antagonism.[2] The

tower (cf. *Artemis Soteria, Athenê polias,* and *Athenê promachos*). Within the city the just spirit of Themis rules, whose daughters are Justice, Good Order, and Peace; while in Peitho persuasion and eloquence are discerned for the woman whose influence is towards encouraging the phratries and other larger confederations of men. That every great early civilization yields proofs of such a matriarchy and gynarchy cannot fail to suggest an explanation of that 'golden age' to which mankind looked back from one where aggression, violence, cruelty, and rivalry ruled. (Cf. the *Tâo-Teh-King* and the change to a later "depravity", cap. i.) With the advent of the iron age a 'god of war' and destruction has a chief place in every city, yet even in Sparta the prizes for victory in the games continued to be those iron sickles which were kept in the temple of Artemis. The ubiquitous male god of war never possessed the good character of the mother gods. [Note the opposition of the 2 ideas of rough man and gentle man as soon as the iron age and war supplanted a 'golden age': the title of Artemis ἡμεράσια means the cultivated, the gentilizer, a tamer of wild things; and Athenê is contrasted with Ares Thērītas, 'the savage one'. Cf. also the 2 sea deities Aphroditê who is the god of calm seas, and Poseidon the disturber.]

[1] Dikê (Justice) is identified with Astraea (the star-woman) who lived among mankind in the golden age and was the last of the gods to quit the earth in the bronze age for the constellation of *Virgo* where she dwells. Her emblems are the scales and a crown of stars.   A title of Ceres was *Thesmophora*, 'bringer of the law'.

[2] Cf. the Sun-god of the matriarchal age in Babylonia who becomes the 'dragon' of the patriarchal age (Tihamtu, Tiāmat). The word denoting good spirits denoted, after the advent of the patriarchal epoch, bad spirits. Cf. indo-european *deva* (spirits of light) with iranian *div*; or the 'daēva' of the *Avesta* in contrast with the original meaning of daēvas in the Gathas.

great matriarchal gods come down to us full of fair fame:
Magna Mater (Cybele or Rhea) all-nurturer and 'mother
of the blest', is not only glorious but the pure and beautiful
god—the earliest symbol, indeed, of the *kalokagathos*:[1]
Hathor, on the banks of the Nile and in Nubia, is known
as god of light of beauty and of love; and in Italy Bona
Dea (*Maia Majestas*) is the ancient 'good god' of mankind,
and the source of sex cleanness; so is Isis in Egypt; in the
classical pantheon Athenê is the only god who "presides
over the moral and intellectual life of man", and nowhere
in the egyptian pantheon does moral quality so clearly
emerge as in Maāt, divine symbol of moral order, truth,
and unalterable rightness—"she who knew no lord
or master".   These divine women founders and
guardians of human society existed in every part of the
world—Atargatis in Syria is not only the source of generation and fertility but the founder of social and religious
life; in Tibet it is *Samantabhadra Bodhisvatta* 'the genius
of goodness'; in Japan it is the great sun-god Amaterasu
personifying wisdom gentleness and courage. Juno's
titles in the west are *Sospita* and *Moneta* (helper and
admonisher); Themis, protector of the oppressed, bears
the civic title 'saviour' as Artemis ('the Upright') did in
Achaia: and the fire on Hestia's and on Vesta's hearth
is the centre of religious life in Greece and the centre
of religious life in Rome. The woman deity, then, is
urbane, a gentilizer; the male god is only powerful and
capricious.

        In 1407 Christine de Pisan wrote in the *Cité des*

Women
and
learning *Dames*: "I say to thee again, and doubt never the contrary,
that if it were the custom to put the little maidens to the

So the 'wise woman' of antiquity, beneficent to mankind, became the
execrable 'witch' of the later Jewish and especially of the christian age.

[1] Cf. the surname of Artemis—*Kallistê*, and the cretan Britomartis
('sweet maiden') who dispensed happiness on earth. Cf. also the name of the
woman ancestor of the N.E. indian Khasis—*Kyngas hounig*, 'the sweet
one'.

school, and they were made to learn the sciences as they do to the wer children, that they should learn as perfectly, and that they should be as well entered into the subtleties of all the arts and sciences as wers be. And peradventure there should be more of them, for I have teached heretofore that by how much women have the body more soft than the wers have, and less able to do divers things, by so much they have the understanding more sharp there as they apply it." What she said would be true had been true, it recapitulates, no doubt, the earliest chapter in mental history. This mental history began in women's minds; they wrote its first pages. The same disposition which made them the earliest gentilizers, the first civilizers, discriminated in their favour against the male hunter in what concerned mental development and cultivation. There is plenty of evidence of this pre-historic phenomenon; in Vedic times the literary ability of women was conspicuous, and it was women who preserved the ancient Berber and Libyan scriptures; and while the traditions of the dawn of human society tell us of women founding towns, defending order, building bridges and irrigating, composing scriptures and perfecting speech, the biographical subjects depicted in the tombs of male pharaohs are chiefly to do with warfare and the slaying of large wild animals. It has frequently happened even in the historical period that women were the cultivated half of the race, it was so in Japan from the end of the viii[th] to the end of the xii[th] century,[1] and in the commercial civilization of America a similar condition exists now. But in every case when any group of women were given the opportunity of intellectual training they have taken to it like fish to water.　　There is another element which would have counted in the beginnings of social life—the earlier mental maturity of the woman. If she had at 18 the maturity which is not attained by the wer till he is

[1] Cf. Muslim women, pp. 240–1.

25 she would, in free conditions, always have led in mental matters.[1]

Literary frauds

Confronted with such facts as the substitution of male for femel personalities, the suppression of feminal names, and the wholesale masculinization of mythological legend, it is impossible to assert that any ancient scripture is the work of the writer whose male name is now attached to it. 'Moses' Miriam and Aaron appear in Exodus as a trinity of early socializers and hierarchs, but this woman with a brother (Exod. xv. 20) suggests the matriarchal family, and while the story of Moses (and of Aaron) in its present form is riddled with difficulties and suggests an altogether different tradition, the personality of Miriam loomed large in a tradition which has disappeared from the present biblical version.[2] The suggestion that Moses wrote the first 5 books of the Hebrew scriptures was only made by Philo at the dawn of the christian era. The *Iliad*

[1] Erinna died at 19; Joan of Arc had done her work at 17; M. Gaetana Agnesi whom de Brosses called "*una cosa più stupenda del duomo*" was a universal genius before she was 20 (she was 21 when he met her at Milan). Fulvia Olympia Morati was invited by the university of Ferrara to lecture on the philosophical problems of Cicero's *Paradoxes* before she was 16 years old, and was offered the chair of Greek in the university of Heidelberg.

[2] Renan, *Le Peuple d'Israël*, t. i, 167, cites Micah vi. 4. The so-called 'Song of Moses' (Exod. xv) which is said to have been originally complete with the first verse is *Miriam's* song in verses 20, 21. Voltaire in the *Dictionnaire Philosophique*, and other places, denies the existence of Moses. See also *Peuple d'Israël*, t. i, 159–60. One of the few remaining fragments of an earlier bible than the one we have is that conspicuously matriarchal utterance, the Song of Deborah in Judges v. It is obvious that the last 21 verses of the book of Proverbs which preserve the fine teaching 'Lemuel' received from his mother records a completely different position of the householder woman and her relation to her husband to that which is presupposed elsewhere in the bible. The Vedas of India were similarly 'edited' perhaps 1000 years B.C., and with them the ancient Laws of Manu were of course edited to coincide with the establishment of male brahmanism.

In our own day a woman collaborated in a famous book, but her name did not appear on its title-page, and even an acknowledgment in the preface was withheld.

again is the complete recast of a story in which Achilles was probably the protagonist of a different conflict.[1]

Why should wisdom learning and letters everywhere, and in primitive religions which embody the mental achievements of man, be personified in women, so that wisdom is as distinctively a feminine attribute as war is a masculine one. If these things had never been discerned in women it would be incredible they should figure in mythology as possessing them; it is incredible they should be represented as exercising powers which they had never dis-

---

[1] Cf. the myth of the heel of Achilles and the "thou shalt lie in wait for its heel" of Genesis iii. 15. The drama of a conflict between the sexes emerges in every ancient literature—in Babylon the conflict of Ishtar and Izdhubar and the war of the male Merodach with the sun-god Tihamtu and her followers; in Greece of Athenê and Poseidon; of the 50 daughters of Danaus and the 50 sons of Aegyptus; in Palestine Cain and Abel, Jacob and Esau, Miriam and 'Moses' (book of Numbers xii); and very probably Jonah and the whale; in Rome Romulus and Remus; in Egypt the Two Brothers; in India the Two Princes ("revolt of Irochon"). (See amazons, p. 215 and *n*.)

With the brahmanic desire to prove that brahman authority was anterior to that of the divine mother vedic traditions underwent a complete masculinization; note such sayings as "woman is brahmin and wer is brahmin too" (where the new teaching is that wer is brahmin). Dual divinities and trinities discover a whole history of such conflict changes. The divine mother and the daughter (representing the feminal principle by the side of the maternal, as we saw) is changed into a mother and son (Hathor and Osiris) and finally into a father and son. The trinities derive, I suspect, entirely from causes which led eventually to the substitution of father right for mother right: the first trinities are composed of two femels and one male—Leto Artemis and Apollo, Hestia Zeus and Athenê—then we have two wers and one woman—mother, father, and son—and finally 3 wers. The post-Khammurabi triad of Babylon did not however succeed in displacing Ishtar as paramount deity. Later she is 'associated' with her enemy Marduk! We have in the story of Zeus's jealousy of his wife and his creation of Athenê after swallowing Metis, an excellent parable of the transition period of the sex conflict—the civilizing feminal principle is made to spring not from a mother but from a father.

A ludicrous instance of the male obsession to masculinize is the turning of the 3 femel legs which appear in a shield of Athenê 600 years B.C. into 3 male legs, with an appropriate martial fable to 'explain' the blazonry of the Isle of Man. (*The Three Legs of Man*, W. R. Hall Caine, 1925.)

played. If they had been subordinate and the wer had led in the arts and crafts of civilization as he has during the patriarchal age the existence of women gods of power and skill is not conceivable.[1] Why should Vāch or Sarasvati be the divinity of speech and learning, the inventor of the Devanagari letters, and 'mother of the *Vedas*'. Why should Vergil attribute the fruits of the earth to *sancta Pales* and why should it be Isis not Osiris who makes corn to grow? There is only one answer. The first great civilizations in pre-babylonian Assyria in Crete and in Egypt were the work of a matriarchal age, the work of women. They were the result of the preference of Hestia to Zeus, Isis to Osiris, Pales to Pan.

Language   The psychology of language has itself been shaped by the exclusive male direction of human affairs; a false sex psychology, like the false sex biology, is incrusted in the words we use. It is seen in the monopoly by the wer of the name for the species, in the use of feminine terms to express what is mentally morally and physically effete; while women who speak the Romance languages are obliged to refer to their sex on every occasion by adding a sex tag to the words they employ. Male pronouns may be indifferent, their use does not necessarily and always involve that sex reference which is never absent in femel pronouns: if we say, "Ask any man" we have no thought of sex; but if the only men we could have asked happened to be femel men we drag in sex at once. It is the fact that the male had become the only actòr on the stage of life[2] which is recorded in the restricted use of *man*, *homme*, *uomo* for the male man, a use which, quite apart from its mischievousness, is a source of flagrant ambiguity in

[1] They afford the same evidence of the domination of the femel idea that Jahveh and Allah afford of the male idea.

[2] Cf. θεοί τε καὶ ἄνδρες and πατὴρ θεῶν τε καὶ ἀνδρῶν. Cf. also the common restriction of 'youth' in the singular to a male youth, and of 'fellow' to a male fellow.

literature.[1]   Language was not required to supply an adjunctive feminine to words until the rise of patriarchy. The *dignior* of Latin was not in origin masculine at all, it was simply the original form of a word. We have many evidences that primitive language carried with it no sex tags; for example in the neutrality of plural pronouns, which persisted in certain cases even in Greek. Wecklein comments that in these cases it was realized that the special significance of sex is not suited to generality of expression: and the way to achieve the end he so describes is for the relative pronoun *he* to become common in gender, and for gender to be expressed only in those (few) cases where it is wanted. If several women can in our present speech be correctly referred to as "themselves" why not one woman as 'himself';[2] evidently the gender relative is no more required in the one case than in the other. As an habitual element in language gender should be discarded altogether. In any case those languages which like French and Italian oblige you and your interlocutor to refer to yourselves as sexes in every sentence will never become the common speech of mankind.

The change undergone by the words male and fe- 'female' male in English to make them verbal parallels to 'man' and wo-man, so that the femel appears as a cadet to the male,

[1] *Man* connotes the human race in Anglo-Saxon, *wifman, wimman,* the femel person which changed into *woman* no doubt because of the difficulty of pronouncing *a wimman*: we might with propriety hark back to the forms *weman* and *wimmen*—Caxton prints *wymmen*. The male person was *wer, were, weor,* and *werman, wearman,* with plurals *weres* and *wearas.* The Spaniard (as well as the scandinavian and germanic races) has preserved a term for the wer—*varon* (formed I think on the gothic *vair,* which is the lat. *vir* and A-S. *wer?*) Cf. italian *donnone, uomone*; and medieval lat. 'baron and feme'. In *donna* (*domina, domna*) the italian preserves for women an equivalent to spanish *varon* for the wer—domina, the lordman; varon, great or important man. The term *donna* has of course lost this meaning.

[2] Or one wer as 'herself'—*she* and *herself* are used in Scotland as male pronouns. [Among the Khasis in N.E. India there is not only a great preponderance of femel nouns but there is only one form of the plural pronoun, and it is feminine.]

is instructive. The word femel has of course no etymo-
logical kinship with the word male; they have no community of origin in any language. *Femella* is the diminu-
tive of *femina* as *masculus* of *mas*; Chaucer spells it femel
(1388) and Ben Jonson femall (adjectively) in 1601:
male—which is now the same word as in modern French
—was spelt *mascle* in both languages and is still spelt
masle by Thomas Browne in the xvii[th] century.[1]

English which has preserved so much has lost the
word for the male man. The use in this volume of the
now obsolete term *wer* and the spelling *femel* will be justified, I hope, by the greater clearness and accuracy they
bring to english speech.[2]

[1] Patriarchal trails in speech are seen in the later semitic meaning of
'father' for source or origin; and in the apparent genders 'horse' and 'mare'
'fox' and 'vixen'. In Chaucer's time a wer could still be a 'shrew', and a
woman could still be an heir, not an heiress.

[2] The classical instance in our language of the ambiguity of using 'man'
for wer is the translation of John i. 13, "nor of the will of man", when the
Greek and Latin signify "nor by the will of the wer". Or take the absurdity
of translating ἀρσενῶν γέννα (*Medea* 429) "the race of man".
"Can man be free and woman be a slave?" Shelley asks: and here 'man'
takes some of the connotation of *homo*. Indeed, which did Shelley mean?
If he had turned the lines into latin would he have written *homo* or *vir*?
When you say "she was a woman of intelligence" what does it mean—intelligent for a woman? If it means an intelligent human being speech
should express this netly, as when people say of a wer 'he was a man of
parts'. "She was one of the best of men"; if you say "of women" you
weaken it. As language now is, woman and wer cannot say to one another
"you are a better man than I".

Since women became voters a ridiculous redundancy is very noticeable;
politicians and others have been tumbling over each other to drag in the
word 'woman'. They have discovered that when it rains 'men' and women
both get wet, and that the 'men' and women of this country like their meat
fresh. A scientist recently spoke of "populations of flies and men"; our
politicians would certainly have respectfully added "and women", and
they could be relied on to amend the well-known major premiss in
Barbara to: "all men and women are mortal".
It was found out in the war, said sir Alfred Mond (lord Melchett),
in the House of Commons, that the world "is not divided" into women
and men.

It was a curious accompaniment of the servitude of woman that her shackles were set forth by the wer as golden ornaments. This began with the early christian suggestion that it was the woman's 'glory' to be subject to wers as it was the wer's glory to take his orders from the supreme being. Greece and Rome were not so hypocritical; the Greek wer thoroughly realized that he only consulted himself in the position he left to women: the Roman created their disabilities by law and both Latin and Greek thereafter assumed that women could not do what they might not do. The muslim like the christian code for women had its threefold basis in their 'natural incapacity', the 'advantage' accruing to them through the restrictions imposed, and a liberal recognition that what the wer wants is what ought to be.   It has been claimed, however, that christianity "raised women". It would appear more historically exact to say, with Maine, that "no society which preserves any tincture of christian institutions is likely to restore to married women the personal liberty conferred upon them by the Middle Roman law".[1] For the first adoucement of their position, after those epochs of civilized history where matriarchal institutions lingered longest, came from classical Rome: the women of lineage freed themselves completely from marital control, and the best Roman jurists thereupon gladly invoked the *jus gentium*—a law of nature before all law—which would restore to the woman what the law had taken away. A deadlock of social relations followed upon the subject position of the athenian wife and was met in the great age of Greece by the freedom of the hetaira; but in our era the horrible position of the christian whore and that traffic in women which has been recognized as a growth of christian ages have to be set against the roseate picture it is desired to paint of the position of women under christianity. The gospel of Jesus had at

Women and Christianity

[1] *Ancient Law.*

237

once placed them in a noble light, but this gospel was rapidly transformed into the christianity which received official approval; and the strictly male type of the theology of jews christians and muslims with their male sacerdocy and exclusive male ministry in *spiritualia* has effectively buttressed the natural sex bias in ruling out a noble view of woman: so that the utmost that any patriarchal communities can claim to have set before themselves at any time is a decent view of her.[1]   Two restricted and class movements improved the status of european women: the

Feudal status

exigencies of the life of the feudal castle where the lords lived together in a stronghold surrounded by the villeinage resulted in a dignity and equality for the feudal lady by the side of the feudal lord which has been preserved, more or less, at first as a status and property equality and in recent centuries as a merely social one, ever since.[2]

Chivalry

Chivalry was an outcome of this feudal dignity and was the nobler in conception. Its tendency certainly was to raise the idea of womanhood but it demanded the spirit and the social quality of knight errantry and could not withstand the prevalent sentiments of the wer about women

Monasticism

and the arrival of the burgher tradesman. There was one feature of christianity which should have permanently dignified the woman's position—this was the life of the abbey: but despite the learning the power the holiness and the usefulness which accompanied that life from the vii[th] to the xv[th] centuries—in France England and Germany especially—not a trace of advantage has remained. Growing theories of the importance of the male priesthood and the xvi[th] century catholic reaction against the reformers turned the wer's mind steadily away from every freedom for women. Even as recently as the Rome of Pius IX they were not taught to write, and a woman was

---

[1] The views of the sainted doctors of the christian church, however, do not provide even this modest residue.

[2] See Guizot, *Histoire de la Civilisation en Europe*, iv.

publicly shouted at and rebuked in the Corso by a priest because she was reading in her carriage. The case was not different in puritan England. Things which favoured women had never any chance of taking root, it was the things which disadvantaged them which had all the chances. The idea of womanhood was low at Athens when the wife was nothing but the breeder of legitimate children.[1] It was high when the wer had to treat with the free roman matron. It would not need stating that the opinion the wer held of women was high when their position was high were it not that he has always supposed that the case of the woman was different from every other case in this particular, and has put forward the extravagant doctrine that the woman excites sentiments of chivalry and honour in the male only when she has no position but that of an appanage to himself.

Every reawakening of the human spirit has presaged a reawakening for women. In the great age of Greece Sokrates was the disciple of two women,[2] Plato was very largely influenced by Aspasia and his own lectures were attended by women, some of them dressing as wers in order to do so; while Aspasia herself could be heard regularly instructing the wives of Athens that a woman's life was not comprised in housekeeping. In the great age of Rome, as we have seen, the women of the historic roman houses declined the subordinate position of the legal roman wife; a movement which bore fruit 200 years later in the spiritual awakening that accompanied the first preaching of the gospel. When the european renascence began in Italy it was so intimately connected with renascent womanhood that it was possible to describe it in the words: "l'humanismo si sposa alla gentilezza feminile."[3] There is no history of mankind's great spiri-

Epochs of enlightenment

(At the renascence)

(Epochs of religious awakening)

[1] See p. 257 *n.*
[2] Plato, *Symposium.* Xenophon, *Memorabilia*, ii. c. vi. 36.
[3] Sabbadini, *Vita di Guarino Guarini.*

tual realizations—it certainly is not recorded in the falsified scriptures and in the names which have come down to us. But in the case of every religion it can be shown that the spiritual ingerence of women at the dawn was succeeded by their spiritual subjection, without it being possible to show that the great faiths profited thereby. On the contrary we shall with assurance assign part of the immense spiritual failure of all such revivals to the rejection of the woman's quota.[1] Indian religion and philosophy, as the great sayings of the earliest vedic scriptures show, were not founded amidst the subordination and seclusion of women. Purdah and 'suttee' belong historically to much later epochs, and even now the ruling position held in chinese and indian households by the elder matrons is a survival of matriarchal status. Muhammad lived in more evil times and among a less disciplined people but even he did not exclude women from education and liberty, and he places the mother higher than the father.[2] Until the 10th caliphate, indeed, muslim women continued to enjoy a real freedom.[3] In the great epoch

(In Asia)

---

[1] The origin of such prehistoric religions as the zoroastrian, semitic, taoistic, and buddhist cannot, as we say, be learnt from the later traditions about them; but Zarathustra's daughter, who alone among the members of his family bears "a name that has connotations of religion", must be regarded as his co-operator in the creation of the parsee religion; and Lâo-Tsze, founder of original taoism, could find no perfection till he reached the ages when there was knowledge of the "Great Universal Mother". Cf. p. 229 n. Muhammad's spiritual life was fostered and nourished by his wife and elder Kadijà; and though in the event he proved unable to slough the patriarchal notions which had been in possession of the world for so long none of his successors attained the spirituality of his daughter Fatima, 'our lady of light', who preached the religion of Islâm in Muhammad's time, and through whom the line of the prophet is preserved.

[2] "O messenger of god what relation is most worthy of doing good to?" He said: "your mother", this he repeated thrice; "and after her your father."

[3] The seclusion of Muslim women at the close of the xth century (A.C. 991) was an outcome of the profligacy of caliph Walid II, who introduced servile classes of women as dancers and entertainers. Syed Ameer Ali notes that this caliph did more to stop the progress of the muslim world than any one else.

of Harun-al-Raschid and Mamûn their culture equalled that of wers and the names of distinguished daughters were assumed by their fathers as surnames. The irony of the position in later Islâm is shown in the exclusion of women from the pilgrimage to Mecca the aqueduct of which was built by the empress Zobaida when on her own pilgrimage there in Raschid's time.   But the impossibility of maintaining through the centuries the highly artificial conditions imposed on the minds and hearts of women resulted in sporadic examples of femel eminence and learning even in the darkest ages; and a better position was occasionally enjoyed by small groups of women amongst the most backward patriarchal peoples and was connived at by the other sex. In the case of (The Gospel) christianity the fact that the gospel had its origin in a singularly feminal atmosphere could not be entirely missed during those first few hundred years in which the story was freely read.[1] And had there been impartial observers when the hidden history inscribed in the roman catacombs was revealed we should not still be awaiting that unwritten chapter which will set before us the overwhelming evidence that the founding of christianity as a great world religion was due to the women of Rome: it was due to the fact that the roman matrons, who were the first to receive it, were free and powerful at the centre of world empire.[2]

[1] Jerome in his Epistles makes use of it, and it enters into the tradition of the conversion of Gaul. Cornelius Agrippa, in the xvi[th] century, again bases his argument upon it. That it played no part when the bible became general reading, after the reformation, was due, no doubt, partly to the reformers' preference for the Hebrew scriptures over the 4 gospels, and partly to the hostility shown by them to the claims of women. It is interesting to find the jewish christian Edersheim writing: "Here", i.e. in the gospels, "our attention is directed to the spiritual influence of mothers rather than of fathers."

[2] Rome was not evangelized by Paul (see Rom. i. 8–16) nor even by the earlier visit of Peter. That Christ took possession of the soul of man at the centre of the known world was due to the fact that he was met there by the *matrona,* in whom all the elements of a permanent moral and spiritual progress were present.

The last civil and political upheaval which influenced Europe before the end of the xix[th] century was the french revolution at the end of the xviii[th]. And women once more claimed their rights. The fact that the answer they received was the Code Napoléon[1] affords the clue to our aborted progress all through the patriarchal age. For the great uprisings of the human spirit have been followed by a singular intellectual abjection. This was specially observable after the renascence, when it was not unconnected with the religious movements of the time definitely hostile as these were to freedom:[2] the catholic reaction and puritanism both exploited women. In fact the intellectual abjection among the males following upon an intellectual revival is rigidly related to their low views of the other sex. The sequence is remarkable in England where the lowest depth in the relation of woman and wer was reached after the english renascence had been succeeded by the puritanic movement. It was in the xviii[th] and first half of the xix[th] centuries that coarseness in the sex relations was for the first time joined with hypocrisy, callousness and brutality being cloked by sexual sentimentalism. The final disfranchisement of women which now spread over Europe had been prepared in the 2 centuries preceding: through the period of the renascence —in the burgher cities of Italy or in England—gilds and crafts had been open to both sexes and women held a position in the industrial world; for still longer they held a notable position in monastic life; this ceased at the reformation to exist in protestant countries while in catholic countries its freedoms were taken away. So that from the beginning of the xviii[th] century no free position existed anywhere for women either in the civil or in the

(Political revolution)

Followed by intellectual abjection

[1] See *infra*, p. 291.

[2] Take 2 examples in Italy: in the xvi[th] century the *cappella papale* held in the Sistine chapel was so "holy" that women could not assist at it; and in the xvii[th] century pope Alexander VII prohibited a translation of the latin liturgy into the vernacular and called the translator a "madman from hell".

religious world; the sole careers open to them were marriage and prostitution.[1] It was in this immoral period that you were 'womanly' only if you did what no wer ever did or wanted to do: if he rode a horse he wore short comfortable clothes, therefore a woman rode in a garment which swept the ground; if the wer liked a walking stick it was 'unwomanly' to want one, if he enjoyed smoking tobacco the 'womanly' woman must "dislike" it "for herself". If the wer liked stretching his limbs in victorian drawing-rooms, every lady must regard it as womanly to sit upright on the uncomfortable seats. Not only his self-accorded privileges but the pleasures and amenities of his life were always matter for laughter if they were enjoyed by women. Artificiality in her circumstances, insincerity in dealings with her—these were the keynotes. What was everywhere reserved to women—what was all she had—was the mediocre. No standard of work was proper for her which rose above mediocrity. In earlier times women's home life had meant the skilled exercise of crafts—baking, brewing, midwifery, the compounding of medicinal herbs and simples—but the victorian woman was a 'lady' only on condition that she never attempted to do anything a wer could do except eat and sleep, or if she 'emulated' him[2] and painted a picture, painted a bad one. The keynote of her life was inefficiency and help-lessness. The victorian 'lady' neither swore at the driver

The 'Lady'

---

[1] In the first quarter of the xvii[th] century the Yorkshireman Mary Ward formed her Institute of Mary to combat the perils of ignorance for girls. 90 years before, the Council of Trent had decreed that every community of women should be strictly inclosed. Urban VIII issued a bull condemning the Institute on the ground that the members had "undertaken a task beyond the strength and resources of their sex". Mary Ward was imprisoned. The father of the catholic faithful—with the centuries which had seen the great women abbesses stretching behind him—could not understand an order governed by a woman or any woman being free of male domination.

[2] "To want to be like" a wer was the cant phrase for wishing to have human facilities.

who tipped her over (as the xviii[th] century lady had done) nor interrupted 'the gentlemen' talking. Her damning feature was that she retained no power to help any other sort of woman; hence she was the essentially unwomanly woman.[1]

But the speculative and scientific activities of the second half of the xix[th] century had been more prolific of results than any other period of the world's history, and they were steadily accompanied by a woman's movement, which became militant in the 8 years preceding the war of 1914. The militant movement had shocked english wers into realizing another sort of woman, and immediately war broke out the effect was seen in the tasks expected of her. The war did not make it found a revolution which had been accomplished in the minds and sentiments of women themselves. During and after the war women received the political representation which they had never possessed (except in parts of the United States) since the rise of modern constitutional governments.   The xix[th] century was the real *foyer* of the revolt from patriarchalism; never during the thousands of years it endured—not even in imperial Rome or during the learned age in Italy—had women as such entered the arena for liberty, a liberty which every discovery of the xix[th] century converged to restore to them—in biology, anthropology, archaeology, and through that critical

---

[1] Philippa of Hainault had come from leading an army against the Scots when she made that great page of history her appeal for the burghers of Calais; and during the Scottish invasion of England the following year she harangued the troops, writes Froissart, at the battle of Neville's Cross. The victorian age would have denounced her as unsexed. The victorian lady was armed *cap-à-pie* in one direction only—as a wooer, for which role nature had not fitted her.

Syed Ameer Ali has pointed out the barbaric element in the idea of the secluded lady—that the uncultured mind regards walls and warders as more effective protections than nobility and purity of sentiment: and for the european male of the xviii[th]–xix[th] century femel ignorance and ineffectiveness were assumed to be badges of innocence and virtue.

scholarship which undermined patriarchal theology. Up to the xx[th] century the flowering of the spiritual and intellectual movements of the race had died down without forming any moral fruit. There had been uprisings of peoples against injustice and tyranny, which have left their traces in the minds and customs of Europe; there have been in some ages aspirations after cleanness of life and holiness: but none of these movements cleared the moral atmosphere, for all suffered from one and the same defect, none had released the moral forces of women.

Nevertheless the secular ill-treatment of women disturbed the mind and heart of the finest wers for over 2,000 years[1]—Plato, the first, and Euripides, the Jesus of the gospels, Bernardin the saintly preacher of Siena, Cornelius Agrippa secretary to Maximilian and friend of Erasmus, Condorcet whom the revolution left standing as the noblest figure in France; and the great men who cared for education and who have beaten the air in this direction, from Plato, Plutarch, Musonius Rufus, and even the christian father Clement of Alexandria, to the spanish Vives, Thomas More, and the english schoolmaster Richard Mulcaster, in the Tudor age, Thomas Fuller in the time of the Stuarts, and the great french prelate Fénelon; in the xviii[th] century, Talleyrand who promoted *l'école unique*, and in the early xix[th] Alexandre Vinet in Switzerland—all of whom claimed education for both sexes.[2] We are accustomed to hail Sokrates as the wisest of men, Jesus as the most holy, but Plato makes Sokrates require that woman and wer should co-operate in the government of states and asks this question which still remains un-

Great wers and the freedom of women

---

[1] See p. 249 at the end of this subsection.

[2] Fénelon (1651–1715) had to ask that girls should learn how to form and join together letters correctly or at least to keep a straight line in writing, to spell, and to pronounce words properly when reading. Dupanloup and he had both argued for the essential need of education for women and for its special value for them in a convent life. The popes returned the answer. (See pp. 238–9.)

answered: "Do we think that femel watch dogs ought to guard the flock with the males and hunt with them and share in all their other duties; or that the femels ought to stay at home because they are disabled by having to bear and rear young?" "We expect them to share in whatever is to be done." "Then we must train the women in the same way as the wers."[1] The gospel took up the parable for the case of sex morality, but christians have completely ignored the teaching. The male had always judged woman; Jesus comes judging no woman, and it is not the Galilean who has conquered.[2] We quote the wisdom of great and good men but if they advocated women's liberties it is passed over unnoticed. Condorcet's enlightenment and Victor Hugo's genius are praised but the fact that they passionately advocated the equality of woman and wer is not mentioned.[3] Thomas More who was raised to the altars of the church as saint and martyr placed women and wer priests side by side in his ideal community, Utopia.[4]

"Why call ye me lord, lord, and do not the things that I say?"

These men were the predecessors of that series of wers in America, France, Italy, and England, born in the first decade of the xix[th] century who became champions of the woman's cause. Others who had remained silent

---

[1] *Republic*, Bk. v. 451.

[2] Luke vii. 44 seqq. John viii. 1–11.

[3] Victor Hugo, letter to Léon Richer June 8, 1872. "Depuis quarante ans je plaide la grande cause sociale à laquelle vous vous dévouez noblement. Il est douloureux de le dire: dans la civilisation actuelle, il y a une esclave. La loi a des euphémismes; ce que j'appelle une esclave elle l'appelle une mineure; cette mineure selon la loi, cette esclave selon la réalité, c'est la femme. L'homme a chargé inégalement les deux plateaux du Code, dont l'équilibre importe à la conscience humaine: l'homme a fait verser tous les droits de son côté et tous les devoirs du côté de la femme. Dans notre législation telle qu'elle est, la femme ne possède pas, elle n'est pas en justice, elle ne vote pas, elle ne compte pas, elle n'est pas. Il y a des citoyens, il n'y a pas des citoyennes. C'est là un état violent, if faut qu'il cesse."

[4] *Utopia*, Bk. ii, chap. ix.

had nevertheless, by an impulse of genius, been aware of the truth: the reader of the last stanza of Faust or of the early fragment *Über die Natur* will realize that Goethe had always been aware of it, and even Renan had something of the same vision on the Akropolis at Athens.

There is no ground for justifying our past civilization as a genuine attempt to secure great ethical ends; its peculiar injustices are without this excuse: nothing but sex licence explains the relation of exploiter and exploited which has persisted between the sexes, and it is the sufficient explanation.

How did it become possible for this relation to grow up between woman and wer? I think there is one adequate psychological answer. Women have undergone and with so little resentment their loss of powers rights and interests because of the maternal exigencies; because they alone of the two sexes are moved by an imperative altruistic need. In pursuit of the things necessary for life— shelter safety and peace—the femel throughout nature must deploy acuteness and skill in evading the obstacles which nearly always menace and in seizing what often seems the unobtainable from hostile surroundings: and I consider that when the woman found she had to deploy similar ruses to combat the male scheme of life the proceeding did not appear to her very different in character from that which she habitually employed in obtaining those necessary things. Since the femel, unlike the male, *must* obtain shelter and some peaceful surroundings for her little ones, she has been accustomed to obtain these by hook or by crook; and when patriarchalism brought with it an outcrop of violence and destructiveness these must have seemed a necessary evil to the mother-sex, like the cataclysms of nature, and she set herself to circumvent and nullify them as far as her charges were

Why the woman suffered these things

247

concerned.   It was a comparatively easy thing for the egoistic member of the species to seize and keep what belonged to both or to the mother alone, since the altruistic sex has always in her view the things which must be accomplished for wholly dependent little lives. To know them safe and sheltered was dearer to her than her appetites and when she could give these gifts she easily forgot her other interests as a member of the race. Here is the great and abiding danger for the femel of the human species—that she may find it all-sufficient to be able to give those mother gifts which she shares with every other mother in nature. But in allowing all other human interests to be torn from her she parted not only with things exalted and desirable for every member of the race but also with her rights and interests as these affect the rights and interests of her children. It is clear that the male has exploited the affection of the woman in order to wean her from the larger racial interests: in himself he has recognized a complete freedom from hampering reproductive processes and from the psychological cares—the sympathy anxiety prevision—which attend them. And having made his *coup* and once established these early historical relations, they were maintained through the centuries by superstition false science and brute force. When you are treating of the human species where there is no marked natural instinct of paternal interest and care, so that you have from the first —in a matter of fundamental importance to each—selfish appetite and ruthless desires confronted with the unselfish maternal and sympathetic desires, you have all the elements for the evil civilization mankind has established. The ruthless and selfish uppermost, the sympathetic and unselfish subordinate.

As a result of the woman's character she plays for her own hand less than the wer. This fact was far more than a handicap in any struggle when what the rule of the wer established was the rule of brute force. Warfare swiftly became the chief human industry, and the moral rights of women were smothered. Indeed moral considerations as such ceased to exist; right had been might, now might became right. Male supremacy is based on this perversity.

Reference to pages 245–6.] See pages 245–6 *supra*, Plato; and page 217 *n*. Euripides, *Medea*. Gospel, Mk. xiv. 4–6 "Let her alone, why trouble ye her?" "Why trouble ye the woman?" Luke xxiii. 27–31; and the frequent comparison of women to the detriment of wers. Bernardino of Siena (1380–1444), "Wherefore, as thou seest thy wife endureth travail on every side . . . thou O! husband be sure thou helpest her . . . Let all help her whereinsoever they may . . . All this travail, seest thou, is of the woman only, and the wer goeth singing on his way. Once a baron's lady said to me: "Methinks the dear lord our master doth as he seeth good, and I am content to say that he doth well. But the woman alone beareth the pain of the children in many things . . . and all this oftentimes with grievous travail. If only God had given some share to the wer—if only God had given him the child-bearing!" And I answered: "Methinks there is much reason on thy side." Heinrich Cornelius Agrippa (1486–1535), "Liberty and privilege which were given to women are restrained by the laws of wers (whose tyranny usurps the laws of god and nature) abolished by use and custom, and extinguished by the manner of their education". Condorcet, *Esquisse d'un tableau historique*, p. 367: "Parmi les progrès de l'esprit humain les plus importans pour le bonheur général nous devons compter l'entière destruction des préjugés qui ont établi entre les deux sexes une inégalité des droits funeste à celui même qu'elle favorise. On chercherait en vain des motifs de la justifier."

Turgot said that "inequality between the sexes springs direct from barbarism". Finally, that greatest known genius of his age, Goethe, wrote: "It cannot be doubted that in all civilized nations women must gain predominance. . . . The saying, 'he shall be thy master' is the formula of a barbarous age long since past. Wers cannot reach the highest degree of cultivation without conceding the same rights to women" (and cf. Goethe, *infra*, pp. 284–5).

OVERSEXUALIZATION

THE strength and self-negation of the maternal character may constitute a menace to the progress and development of the human mother, but a still greater menace to the race lurks in the strength and self-assertion of sex character in the wer. The human male is oversexed; sex plays an inordinate part in his life, and through him mankind as a whole is oversexualized.

The femel in other species is defended against an excess of sex life because there are seasons of the year when no male approaches her, and her breeding and nurturing periods are respected by the males. But among mankind these safeguards have not been allowed to stand. The human femel, wife or harlot, has never enjoyed all through recorded history freedom from the male nor the control of her own sex function; she has been the victim of excessive sexuality, mankind being the sole species where the femel is prostituted and where the mother-mate knows no repose from the male. The truth that has always been lost sight of is that every woman is by nature more than sex and that no wer is by nature more than sex. Sex is what is cut-off from the reproductive organism— *scissus* (*sectus*)—its end is itself and it is always self-referring. The system then which causes women to regard the sex relation as of higher moment than the maternal and forces them to be mate first and mother afterwards displaces nature's system—it makes the femel look towards the male whereas nature makes the male look towards the femel. We cannot get behind the primal data which give us a male dependent on the femel for his own gratification and a femel looking towards her dependent young. Patriarchal mankind failed to reproduce the natural-moral safeguards and made it impossible to bring to our assistance the thoughts and tendencies which are nature's counterweight to the self-seeking of the male. The social system which failed at this point must have brought with it oversexualization; and man is oversexualized. There is an example of oversexualization outside man in the stickleback whose sex excitation ends in a disease produced by the pressure of its enlarged gonads. The human stickleback fills his hospitals with blind and diseased babies; he is the only animal with whom the immature femel is not safe, who assaults the femel infant for lust, and rapes maims and kills the femel adult. To describe such phenomena as 'nature' or to speak as though no ethical improvement upon them were possible is to dishonour and degrade the wer still further. When we remember that the 'civilized' wer brings extermination to indigenous tribes by importing venereal disease[1] we recognize that there can be no mitigation of the sex evil under the patriarchal type of society, which simply changes its methods without civilizing them: the modern world traffics in women, buying and selling them for lust without shame, enslaving them without pity. If we except some matriarchal system of ages gone by and the examples of systematized polygynous or polyandrous marriage, no regularized normal sex life has in fact ever yet existed. The exigencies of sex have always included acts which are irregular, abnormal, lascivious, and revolting both to the spiritual and the bodily senses: it is to this lechery that the world has allowed every licence and has even regarded it as immoral to count the cost.

The wer is less continent than the woman; he is the seeker-sex and appetite in him is stronger than in her. That this should be contested is amazing. We cannot oust from femel nature the mother instinct and having this instinct at the very root of her being the sexual in her is not

---

[1] Ten or twelve thousand years ago there was no syphilis, as there is none in the other animals. None is found in any human remains earlier than "those from medieval cemeteries". It has been calculated that in the United States the cost of prostitution and brothels is 12 times as much as what is spent on 'church work'. The extent to which monogamy in christian countries is based on fornication is shown in these and other statistics: thus 'white slaves' and public prostitutes in the United States number 1,300,000; one sixth of the public harlots die each year, the average life of these and 'white slaves' being 5 years.

sufficiently strong to act by itself.[1] Lust then is paramountly a male phenomenon and nowhere in nature is it normally so strong in the mother.

Every age of mankind has recognized the greater strength of the sex appetite in the wer. Lucretius pictures the primeval wer coaxing and bribing the woman to cohabit by bringing her berries and fruits.[2] Tertullian complains that it would be more becoming to honour male continency than femel seeing that for the male it involves harder toil.[3] And Darwin in commenting on the strength of the sex instinct throughout nature notes the little progress towards continence yet made by the human male.[4] Patriarchal polygamy (with a cloistered woman) owes its persistence to the fact that the wer has always been afraid of 'free trade' in this matter. For the tradition of woman's virginity is as old as the records of the human race. The chinese legend of creation represents the first woman as refusing to sacrifice it even for the sake of peopling the world and the gods therefore allow her to become the virgin parent of mankind: and this instinct to preserve their inviolability is shrined in legend and story everywhere.

No religion of the world became such a complete mirror of male appetite as the religion of Greece; but the Greek never forgot that women felt differently,[5] and Hestia the daughter of the Great Mother Rhea—when wooed

---

[1] Biological Sources of Ethics, pp. 67–8. That the desire of the woman is not as great as that of the wer is assumed in polygamous marriage: the husband is to give 5 days to the 'great wife', 4 days to the next, 3 to the third—which makes his share about 4 times hers.

[2] De rerum natura, Bk. v, lines 963–5.

[3] De virginibus velandis, cap. x.

[4] Descent of man, Pt. I, ch. iv, p. 182 (ed. 1913). "The sex instinct has escaped all training" wrote a Russian at the beginning of the war in 1914.

[5] The Great Mothers had unmated daughters, the original italic god Bona Dea was herself one of the virgin mother gods, like the sumerian Innini, and like the egyptian Great Mother, Neith, whose priests were women virgins. Nothing but a virgin instinct in women can explain such traditions.

by Poseidon and Apollo—swears by the head of Zeus
that she will ever remain a maiden. Scientific observers
have frequently asserted that women are on the whole
sexually indifferent or merely passive, or even that they
are insensitive and have little sexual feeling of any kind,
the maternal desire with them always taking precedence.
Some such fact must represent, at least, a normal condition otherwise it would have been meaningless for wers
to record their conviction that male libido is in fact shared
by the woman.[1] Homer had described the lives of women
and wers as they had been lived nearly 1,200 years before
our era or 400 years before the foundation of Rome. The
wer in the homeric poems is always represented as requiring everywhere and under all circumstances the satisfaction
of sex desire just as of food desire, while the women are
capable of virginity and continent widowhood. Twelve
only out of the 50 young women servants constantly
exposed to temptation from Penelope's suitors lose their
virginity;[2] and while Odysseus has a wife in every port
Penelope cannot be persuaded to change her condition.
Human sensuality, it may indeed be said, is not as evident
in the homeric age as in ours. Penelope is completely
free of all sexual proposals on the part of the wooers, and

---

[1] Lucr. *de Rer. Nat.* iv. 1192, 1207. The same sex, however, is more
frequently found asserting that women adopt harlotry for none but a
libidinous reason. The incoherence of the views formed by a patriarchal
education obstructs the reform of sex relations, which suffer greatly from the
ignorance women have been kept in. Our societies offer the extremes of
disbelief in male vice and of disbelief in the possibility of male virtue. As
no form of male continence has ever prevailed, S. Philip Neri, in the xvi[th]
century, acknowledged with tears to his confessor that he was a virgin: even
in the perfervour of the first christian age no ecclesiastical order ceased so
soon as that of "the Virgins of both sexes". Since then, there has never
been any pretence among christians that virginity can be expected of the
wer; celibacy for the priest and chastity for the monk take its place.
Virginity nevertheless is confidently expected of all unmated women (outside of the unnatural class of whores) as well as of the hundreds of thousands
of women in religion, cloistered or otherwise.

[2] *Odyssey*, Bk. xxii. 420–9.

there is much less sexual coarseness in the poem than belongs to the christian age.

But the secret kept at the heart of nature is that sex is not the stem root of organic life; it is not the fundamental relation of *our* life. In all organic existence there is a fact more fundamental. No process of nature indeed has proved so unstable as the sex process and in no species is this process the primary interest of the femel. It is not the root, and should not determine our human relations. Of the two differentiating factors within a species, reproduction and sex, the moral passions cluster round the first, the lusts attaching to the second. For

sex, as we saw, is *scissure*, it is directed back to the femel organism by appetite, and nothing can prevent its primary predatory aspect; what can be prevented is the free action of the maternal character. This is what has happened; and in claiming for the sex function the importance which matriarchy discerned for the maternal sacrifices have been wrung from the woman in lieu of her natural gifts. The obverse of excessive sacrifice on the part of the woman is male licence, and the obverse of her free gifts is male restraint. The position of sex in their lives is illustrated by the external organs of femel and male respectively. The femel has no sex organ, and while the sex organ of the male signifies dependence upon others the breasts of the femel signify dependence of others upon her.

As things now are, each generation of wers deceives and misguides the young generation as to the male's place in nature. In turn, each wer grows up to abet the false system because it is traditionally allied with privilege and power: but before this stage arrives the male child and the male youth are the prey and sport of falsity no less than the woman. Their ethical character—like hers—is exploited by the sexual tradition. The difference lies in this that while he comes to profit by the system she has always suffered from it.

Oversexualization creates one of the great human problems. Those same men who vaunt the triumphs of civilization, the triumphs of man over the animal, and of man's 'higher nature', exhibit from millennium to millennium the great sexual abjection which is always with us, the slavery of the male to his sex. The wer allows himself to be dominated by his sex and only of women does he expect something better. But mankind's better things cannot be realized until the wer tackles this problem; to tackle and to solve it is the great gift to the race which he holds in his hand. He must henceforth be the first— not the last—to recognize that nothing is achieved till he achieves sexual self-control and does away with the present moral abjection. Mankind as an ideal union of forces and powers cannot subsist with one filthy partner.

I call it moral abjection when the wer creates the current sex theology which makes it appear that god places the male organ under his special protection, as though the one end the creator desires to secure is its unstinted gratification. For example: A woman asked the arch-priest of a sabine parish whether she need satisfy the constant demands of her husband; the answer was, "Si, a qualunque ora di notte o di giorno, anche se i maccheroni fumano sulla tavola". An irish dominican in Rome at the same time said to an Englishwoman who had been told she would die if she had another child, that if she died in childbed as the result of the sexual congress desired by her husband she would "go straight to heaven". Could moral abjection go further than in the creation of such a type of morality?

Another disgusting example of sex pathology was seen in the treatment of the Englishwomen who claimed the political vote. In 1910, on November 18th, 22nd, and 23rd, they were "frequently handled with gross indecency by the police", and every sexual affront was offered, such as arresting one of the agitators as a "prostitute", "and making her walk several yards while the police held her skirts over her head". A memorandum with the evidence was sent by members of all parties in the House of Commons to the then Home Secretary. This memorandum was also published. See

Woman and Werman, p. 292.   The horrible results of the *Brahmanic Law of Marriage* are evidence of the excessive sexuality brought about by male dominance in sexual matters. Among Hindus there is an unmitigated form of that alliance between lust and religion which is a common feature of patriarchal societies.

MARRIAGE

IN the first part of this subsection we traced the historical relations of woman and wer. But the history of woman for the past 3 or 4 thousand years is a marriage history.

The state of marriage is based upon a civil sanction to the congress of the sexes; the only definition which covers all forms of marriage is that it is a recognized sexual union. But throughout the modern era mariage (as the word imports) has implied also a subordinate condition for the woman—it has meant that a *maritus* attached to himself a femel; the old latin word *matrimonium* recorded a far earlier state of things. What the earliest sex relations were is matter of controversy. It is difficult, I think, to escape the conclusion that there was a primitive promiscuity, but this may have synchronized everywhere, or at least among some races of mankind, with the monogamous instinct which has been selected as the type of matrimony over a large part of the globe: among the simians, the nearest mammalia to ourselves, promiscuous and monogamous relations coexist.   The first organization of matrimony was certainly matriarchal; the mate, that is, served the woman as her agent in reproduction receiving in exchange the gratification of the sex instinct which from the first was a larger factor in his life than in hers. This type of matrimony comported both (successive) polyandry and polygyny, for the mate in a matriarchal household could be changed. Primitive patriarchal marriage when it supervened on this was entirely polygynous. It was brought about through the war conditions of the early Iron Age which favoured capture-marriage, and partly by perhaps a still earlier type of exogamous and purchase marriage, for while matrimony remained inter-tribal the husband never possessed any rights over the wife's person. Patriarchal marriage was succeeded, in its turn, by monogamy which for the first time had a mixed sexual system as its basis—marriage and fornication together.

Everywhere, whether in polygamous or monogamous societies, marriage has represented and summed disabilities for woman. The contempt for the *mulier*, the wife-woman—for woman as wife or potential wife—has been its invariable accompaniment. It has nevertheless been the universal assumption of modern civilization that marriage assures to her security and dignity and is the true basis of civilized society; that it is also the happiest condition for both sexes, certainly for the woman whom it lifts from the degradation of promiscuous lust. It is clear, however, that under the mixed sexual system of monogamy only one class of women can be so protected, and that if the civilized woman were not economically dependent there would be no motive for her to barter her sex in any relation. But it is said that marriage protects the woman by tying the male. The male no doubt is more or less sexually promiscuous; what is it then which attracts him to marriage. There is the greek motive[1] and this is certainly the prevalent one—the male monogamist seeks a home-maker. In contrast with this the two incentives to the woman are that she has been educated to regard marriage as women's sole career and that she desires a home of her own; both of which have ultimately an economic basis. The fundamental attraction of marriage remains therefore on the side of the male—he is not so fitted as she to obtain one form of permanent comfort, an ordered home. What remains then as its

---

[1] "We marry that we may have legitimate offspring and a woman to keep the house" (contemporary oration which has been attributed to Demosthenes).

S

gift to the woman when we have eliminated what is adventitious? The external things of home, wealth, or social status can evidently be secured by holy matrimony without anything holy about it; and if its gift to her be a permanent home for the children, at whatever cost to the parents, this too can be secured by the legal tie. When woman is perfectly free she will still in a very large number of instances desire to tie the husband to conjugal fidelity and, failing this, to a permanent legal relation. At least I feel sure both these things would continue to be desired until women had had time to realize the completeness of their economic freedom and to appreciate the truth that no one can vow to love another and that the right of one person to another for the payment of a carnal debt is a barbarism. For though some, or even many, marriages may be kept inviolate in honour of the contract, in an exceedingly large number of cases the conjugal relation would be better maintained on a basis of freedom; it would cease to exist when its continuance was no longer desired, it would be maintained in no other way than by the will of the parties.   The christian argues, however, that but for the marriage tie the husband would break up her children's home and outrage the conjugal union. Marriage insures that he cannot legally do the first, and that the covert outrage need not be an overt one—the home will remain intact. The first of these benefits is, again, economic, it would not accrue but for the economic dependence of women; the second cannot be regarded as an ethical though it is a social asset.

The price which the woman pays not only as mother but as mate is one of the considerations which must eventually determine our view of the marriage tie. A good mother or a good father could keep together a home that is morally a better one than the home of unfaithful partners and divided wills—the tie in these instances may be an obstacle not a protection to the children's interests.

There remain the interests of the partners to marriage themselves. And here by common consent we appear to have left the object of marriage obscure. This object is not the breeding of children, for sterility in no wise alters the relation, and its sacredness and sanction when it is regarded as a religious rite are not derived from the conception of the family as the human unit—since the sex couple is regarded as this unit in the absence of children. Patriarchal marriage must therefore be defined as the relation of a sex couple in a religious or civil union which has for its object (neither the procreation of young nor a partnership of minds and interests but) the subordination of a femel mate to a male. If marriage were conceived of as not essentially the subordination of a woman to a wer but as essentially for the rearing of young then there could be no marriage where there were no children and the adultery of the childless woman could not be regarded as a greater offence than the adultery of the wer.[1] Repudiation of women for barrenness or because they were not sexually desired has been a common feature of patriarchal marriage and was the ground of the energetic reaction to current jewish notions which is made in the Gospel.[2] Adultery, now called a sin, began as a crime; it was *lèse-majesté* against the male. Obviously it could have no other aspect when perpetrated by the wife of a polygamist; and after monogamy became the rule (as in Greece and Rome) adultery still meant femel infidelity.[3]

Definition

Adultery

[1] Nevertheless it has been visited everywhere with atrocious penalties. Cf. also the crime of 'petty treason' in english common law which prescribed burning for the wife who killed her husband. How could killing a husband be a worse thing than killing a wife—a crime which is rampant in all countries.

All patriarchal marriage, polygamous or monogamous, has meant the single principle of subservience of women to one male.

[2] Matt. v. 31–2.

[3] The adultery of the male consisted in the wrong done to another male. As the jewish male phrased it: a wife violates her own marriage, and a husband violates only that of another. This view of it was held to by the

It was two sentences put in the mouth of Jesus which changed the theory thenceforth accepted by all christian populations without however effecting the least change in the secular sex standpoint of wers who continued to regard the adulterous wife as a peculiar monster of iniquity, whereas even up to the year 1923 in such a country as England the adultery of the husband entailed no penalty whatever.[1] Such a type of marriage as this has no title to existence. It is based on nothing but one-sided sexual rights.   We see that it has proved difficult to stabilize marriage on a procreation basis; as a merely sex union it is not less so. It has been assumed that every ratified union between two persons of different sex is sacred. But in what does the sacredness consist? The mere consummation of the sex act or even mutual fidelity to it are not sacred things. What reasons are there for tying together in a perpetual or a dissoluble union these two persons? The *pudor* of the monogamous woman is alleged as the striking reason, but this is because we have never yet considered the outrage possible in marriage itself.[2] Another reason is no doubt the modern european

canon law of the christian church: adultery is *violatio alieni tori*, and "the husband is not an adulterer if his accomplice is a free woman", and if she is not free "the husband's adultery does not consist in the fact that he has left his wife, but in the fact that he has corrupted the wife of another". The *Codex Justinianus* however repeats the verdict of Antoninus Pius: "It would clearly be iniquitous that a husband should exact a chastity from his wife which he himself does not exhibit." (*Digest* xlviii. 5–13. And Augustine, *De conj. adulterio*, ii. 19.) The opinion of Seneca, of Plutarch, and even of the comic dramatist Plautus, agrees with that of Aristotle and is greatly in advance of what has prevailed in christendom.

[1] It merits notice that the presumed responsibility 'before his god' is not in the case of the sex accompanied by any social pains; whereas in the case of the woman all her theological responsibilities are reflected in civil penalties.

[2] It is one of the modesty fetishes spread before women in which the idol does duty for the spirit. In handfasting it is clear that no such modesty safeguard exists, and the ex-lord chancellor of England in a letter to the public press published March 1, 1923, on the matter of divorce, wrote: "There are marriages today, from which there is no release, where the

custom of regarding two persons of different sex as the social unit; and a third reason is an underlying belief that a tie of this sort is a preservative of male morality.

That mankind should run in sex couples is a very late expedient in the history of human society, and it is perhaps not a natural one. We have already seen that matriarchal marriage, greek monogamy, and the patriarchal marriage which prevails out of Europe knew and knows no such custom.[1] No one will pretend that the entry of couples "like the animals into the ark" promotes the social interests of educated people. Sex couples as such do *not* form the social unit; they signify nothing sacred nor by itself estimable, nor do they connote the immaterial interests of mankind. But are they a material safeguard of society's immaterial interests? Is the european monogamist right in holding that the everyday recognition of sex couples is a strong factor in the maintenance of sex morality; and is marriage itself a principal element in the education of the wer, not needed by the woman who has the education of maternity. There is no reason to suppose that the type of marriage we have had has proved an education for the wer, and the price paid for it by women would in any case be too high. When we consider the history of the world we cannot say that the happiness of wives has ever been a social end, but it would be perfectly true to say that their service of husbands has been a social end. Under right conditions, however, the wer's tie to the woman would rank as educative: marriage should be for him, what motherhood is for her, the touchstone of unselfishness. At present a

The 2 sexes as the social unit

Marriage as education of the male

beauty of a woman's life is being churned in the mud under the hoofs of a beast."

[1] It is a custom, nevertheless, which in our past societies where women have possessed no separate status in the polity has in fact created 'society'. There is no 'society' in polygamous countries. The Athenian male's social life was like a club life; he did not live in the society of women till the hetaira made her salon in Athens. Cf. Sect. iii (the french salon), p. 408 *n.*

male's selfishness is accentuated by it. The existence of an overt relation, again, is a support to the greater sex frailty which has hitherto been a cardinal fact of the wer's life. But in return for these things the wife should be compensated not subjected to fresh disabilities; especially should she expect from her mate some self-discipline on the lines of femel unselfishness. Monogamy and a marriage tie in any case cost more to her than to him, for where there is no legal bond he must remain his wife's wooer. It may indeed be assumed that the wife's custom of bestowing a handmaid on her husband solved one of the problems of monogamous unions: it is not at all certain that if women were free to choose they would always prefer the position of the monogamous wife; and in many an imperfect marriage irksome sex relations will appear the easiest to devolve. Harêm polygamy is always an abomination because in this system women exist primarily as sex adjuncts to a wer; but the 'chief wife' and the handmaids of primitive societies still are superior expedients to the monogamy plus whoredom of more civilized ones.[1]

Polygyny

Polygamy

Since the barbaric belief has prevailed that it is an obvious duty to populate and even to increase the population, the male is held to be fulfilling a sacred duty while gratifying his passions, and the woman has suffered the loss of every right human and maternal in obedience to the ubiquitous necessity of child-bearing. When this fetish is banished, and the right of the male to his uncurbed appetite joins it, marriage will be set upon other foundations. That the sex rights of woman and wer are morally equal is involved in the very terms of the sex act. A femel has, indeed, more natural right to motherhood

Only one sex standard

[1] Polygyny was certainly suggested by the wife herself—who escaped by it the dual burden of male excess and excessive childbirth. It was initiated by the biblical offer of the 'handmaid', as Sara offered Hagar to her husband, the greek wife the *pallakis*, and the roman the concubine. Cf. femel jealousy, pp. 280–2 and *n*.

than a male has to free sex gratification, to secure which the whoredom of childless women has nevertheless been commonly invoked.

Should sexual congress be used only for the one end of procreation, any other use being considered as playing   The upon a means without regard for the end? To resolve   conjugal   act this we should have to gather up data lying in two different directions. Is, then, the appetite involved an exclusively reproductive phenomenon? Is it simply an accessory of coition or would unisexual creatures have possessed it? If it is exclusively sexual has a set of co-ordinate phenomena been produced by its exercise which as by-products of the procreative appetite are at least as legitimate as the by-product of mere sexual gratification.[1] The sensuous appetite, however, may be derivatively and not primarily sexual, in which case it has a natural history apart from procreation and has no exclusive rights as a sex phenomenon. Then there are data in a second direction: the sequence of cause and effect is not as certain among men as among animals—this may be due to domestication (and irretrievable) or to the excess of human lechery (and retrievable). But the fact remains that conjugal relations may continue for a very long time without procreation insuing. If 'married' people are always free to unite, if, as at least one christian church has conceded (in agreement with Paul?)[2] they may unite *ob concupiscentiam sedandam*, then why may these particular sex couples do so and no others? Clearly if there is here a universal requirement which has to be provided for and if 'mariage' is the sole legitimate provision for it, then marriage should be universal. But universal monogamous mating will never take place in any conditions of human life.

[1] See Section ii, Lust, p. 149. These by-products are now universal. Their existence may alter our view of the sex use, or we may regard them all (but equally with sexual excess itself) as illegitimate excesses of that use.
[2] I Cor. vii. 9.

Among all living creatures the motor to coition is always—at least in the male—a physical appetite and nothing else, it is not the intention to procreate. If sex congress is to be delimited strictly by procreation then the thesis must be that as soon as reason supervenes—as it does in man—it becomes man's duty completely to moralize and rationalize the relation, making it at all times consciously subservient to its natural end. In practice this thesis would do away with all mere gratification in marriage and all congress out of it, not on the ground that this sensuous appetite is everywhere wrong but on the ground that where congress between the sexes is concerned its only legitimate end is pregnancy. Taking together the universal facts of animal congress, which is sought in unconsciousness of the end, the universality in mankind of the sensuous appetite especially as related to sex congress, and the impracticability of limiting conjugal relations by the hope of offspring which may never be fulfilled, this thesis would appear to overshoot the mark. It is clear that in nature mere desire and the fact that its satisfaction affords physical pleasure are the sole incentives to the sex act. Are we to say that this act becomes a 'natural' one in man only when it is consciously related to its end? A parallel case is the appetite of nutrition. To like food is the complementary instinct to the necessity for taking it. I do not think a man is more moral because he says he eats only in order to live.

The problem of all monogamous sex unions   We are left with the fact that the actual problem in all sex unions is never openly faced: it is that desire is stronger in one sex than in the other, and there can be no moralizing of the relation while the male, by employing checks, may decide that the woman should not be a mother, or while his sexual excesses cause in her excessive pregnancy. Marriage as at present conceived must entail mere sex exploitation of the less sensual partner or the onus of frequent undesired gestation; both are an obvious abuse of the woman. The remedies are, first and fore-most, the observance of a strict restraint; for the marriage tie must always rank as an inferior state while it is regarded as an uncurbed outlet for the sex instinct and legalizes the exploitation of another human being bound to render you sex service. Then there should be some form of check where the woman does not desire children.[1] Neither of these remedies can be moral without the other. The wer should not be allowed complete licence for the appetites and place upon the woman the responsibility for averting the normal result to herself. In the unequal Safeguards
necessary problem of sex relations safeguards are a necessity— safeguards of the nature of the close time among other animals, and of oestrum or periodical stimulus in both sexes, which might prove to be producible in our spe-cies through selection and regulated self-restraint. The woman must be the sole arbiter of procreation. Any system which makes it impossible or difficult (as mono-gamous marriage has done) for the woman to control the sex act must result in sex degeneracy. The mere fact of her exercise of this control over the male appetite is a moral fact; which makes as much for his dignity as for hers. During gestation there should be abstinence from congress. For marriage should be felt to be primarily "a life-long partnership in all divine and human rights",[2] and in such a partnership the sex element is the least.

Is there a marriage 'debt'? Or is all violation of Is there a
marriage
'debt'? the personality to be resented? It cannot be said that a sex partner owes no sort of sex service. If all affectionate relations fail, the alternative is for each to resume his physical freedom, with or without a continuance of their civil relation. But distasteful sex congress is not the only

[1] There should be no question of women being prohibited from control-ling births while there is no question of sexual control for the male. And it is possible that a wer of better nature may choose rather physical 'infidelity' to his wife than physical brutality.

[2] Modestinus.

violation of personality; uncongenial work is so too, and a very large number of persons in monogamous countries marry for other motives than personal affinity and are ready to pay the price of distasteful relations. No lifelong affection or friendship can be established by contract, and therefore in my view a lifelong partnership of the sexes can bear its seeds only within itself.[1]

Wooing

Nature turns the sex desire of the male into a school of gentility—the male woos the femel;[2] and it is certain that whenever in the history of human relations the male has desired a femel (who was not in his power) he has courted her. Wooing is advantageous to the sex relation; it prescribes a code of sex manners, and these manners are an assistance to the sex which is usually the less ready, and are the response to this less readiness. Wooing is nature's method of gentilizing the sex instinct; it is a compensation for the gentilities of maternity, just as there should be a male chivalry as some compensation for the lifelong chivalry of woman to the helpless. Wooing is not in its origin an other-regarding quality, but it is ethical derivatively in the attitude it encourages and the consideration it ingenders. The fact that the femel approves it makes it desirable. Sex manners are in fact matter of general importance to happiness. We have to recollect that the femel is endowed by nature with gentility of manner, but biology has not so favoured the male, or, rather, he depends upon his relation to the woman while she has learnt from her relation to life.[3] Women

Sex
manners

---

[1] If we desire to salvage less perfect but still agreeable unions it is again human character which will decide; they do not persist because of the legal contract, which as we know does not prevent the large number of desertions and divorces. But the legal contract may make incompatibility and cruelty permanent for those who are too timid or scrupulous to defy the law.

[2] See Wooing, pp. 65–6.

[3] If the woman never wanted help the services of the male would not receive the necessary encouragement. Hence her need of help helps him to give, and makes his life more complete. The woman when with child

do not like male truculence; and those women who it is said like it only exemplify the serfdom which has made their attitude possible. The marriage bond and the custom of prostitution have both put women in a position where wooing is unnecessary. The perversion of human manners has made the woman (in monogamous lands) both wooer and exploited, and the wer the exploiter and wooed.[1]

The conditions which led to the 'love marriages' and marriage comradeships of monogamous nations are very recent events in human history. When we look at the long story of the races of mankind we find that love has had less to do with marriage than with any other human relation.[2] The wooing we have been considering was not and is not love, though it is often sympathy. Neither was it the nucleus of romantic sex relations: these seem to have followed upon a psychological development— they could not be realized until one wer and one woman was desired to the exclusion of all others.[3] But it has not yet been recognized that romantic 'love'—which is primarily a romantic relation to the woman[4]—makes its appearance as the first idealization of woman after the matriarchal era, and had definitely in view not so much individual 'love affairs' as a new universal sentiment imbodied in woman—a Beatrice, a Laura.[5] As I have said

'Romantic Love'

'Romantic' courting

needs help and it is a husband's business to give it. With our present civilization she gets little of this.

[1] Ray Lankester, the biologist, asserted with approval that the scheme of nature which made the male the wooer had been changed by the human male into the system which makes the femel the wooer. That is how 'nature' is sustained in a 'civilization' based upon male sexuality.

[2] Cf. Love, pp. 155–6; *supra*, p. 257 *n*.

[3] It occurs in polygamous conditions also, but always on the condition that for the time one only is desired.

[4] On the woman's side there has always been more human affectionateness and her friendship for the other sex has not failed.

[5] This too has been spoiled by the wer, whose romantic 'love' has robbed

elsewhere[1] the halo placed round ancient and modern monogamous courting seems to be an exaggeration and a materialism. For the true romance of marriage is its comradeship, and this aspect of its romance has no necessary connexion with the romantic amour—for it is not love—which initiates many of our monogamous unions. But romantic marriage, once conceived of, came to stay. It came to stay in a sense which makes 'romantic love' no misnomer: at the stage of the world's history which we have now reached we may be sure that unions of this kind will never cease to exist, whether they be private or social contracts—unions of extreme tenderness, noble lifelong comradeships, strong as death. All love is romantic, but this love waited longest to be developed.[2]

Mariage de convenance Marriage, however, must still continue to be of the pre-romantic pattern, it is nothing less than an absurdity to presume love could be as common as marriage. As this is so, an obviously exaggerated licence is conceded to physical attraction and the sex passion, which are privileged as no other appetite is privileged and given the right to fruition *ruat coelum*. This absurdity which in some other countries is only an irregular sex phenomenon is in a country like England accorded all the rights of respectability and looked upon as the mainstay of matrimonial

woman of her mother strength, her mother rights, and made these a holocaust to a subsidiary sentimental relation to the husband. For it was not possible that the male apart from her should act with wisdom in such matters. This sex emotionalism in the male is the origin of male sentimentalism, i.e. his 'romantic' amour. He has laid undue emphasis on this emotionalism, forcing it on the woman also, to whom it is not so natural. A 'romanticism' towards the male sex appears in the viii[th] c. writings of a Japanese; but romance on the femel side is largely a product of her subservience to the wer. She is a semi-serf, idealizing the privileged sex.

[1] Love, p. 157, and see *infra*, p. 269.
[2] It will be recognized that it is its development which must make sex unions at times, like all other love unions of friends, independent of the desire of children. They are unions sacred by the same title as these other unions, and by no other.

projects. But in Latin countries propriety of circumstance is regarded as the right introduction to marriage; it is held that suitability of temperament education and position is a surer guide to married happiness than passion.

That woman's physical beauty should be the basis of the wer's choice is the condemnation of our present marriage system. It is to be expected that it should be so in polygamous unions because here, as we have said, women are overtly regarded in a sensual light and no other; but one of the surprises in a world of surprises is that we have not seen (or not chosen to see) that such a basis for marriage casts into the melting-pot all claims for the 'holy state' and for 'christian marriage' as the serious introduction to a lifelong union. There can be no poorer compliment to both parties than marriage for the pretty face; yet our old-fashioned prudes smiled upon this blatant sensualism side by side with the prurient.[1] If women are chosen for their looks why should they be judged by their virtues? Male sexual selection is however itself a purely artificial thing, and it is not astonishing to find that women's physical beauty has not played the large part in life which is assigned to it in novels and common parlance. It is the quality called charm and not looks which makes one human being permanently pleasing to another; its role in a country of sentiment and refined perception like France has been completely predominant; and to have persuaded women that physical beauty was their chief charm and proper weapon has been but another fraud upon them. We know that nowhere in nature does the femel deck herself out for the male, he decks himself out for her. We see that the ugliest men marry, of both sexes; and the natural thing is for the wer to see beauty

Femel beauty

The 'pretty face'

[1] Not only sensual but anti-social; why should the male be licensed to select the poorest types as procreators? The standard for the wife and the harlot are thus the same; and bathos is reached when the wer is astonished at himself—or at the superlative quality of the woman's genius—if he finds he can prefer some other qualities in a woman to her looks!

where he has desire—the desired is the beautiful.[1] There can be few statements more convincing than that enough sex incitement exists without this one; and the sexual demand for femel beauty must go. What end of nature does the pretty face serve?[2]   The very idea which we have formed of the feminine is largely the result of spurious sexual selection—one direction of femel development, one likely line of femel psychology, singled out and emphasized to the exclusion of others as important, to represent femity in general—because the wer wanted woman to be like that.[3] A cow or a goat with 'a feminine head' is said to be a good milker, but to be a good milker is not the same thing as to be a good mother and is probably of no service to the young: such criteria in fact point out no essential femel qualities, they are in mankind merely the outcome of one-sided choice, the 'unfeminine' being only what does not serve to incite or encourage the male.[4] What the wer dubs 'unfeminine' is also what is simply human—without trace of sex—self-protective, self-assertive, independent and equal. The wer has made a new virtue for the woman—admiration of himself; and its exercise is the real meaning of 'feminine'. It is certainly hard on woman that she should have the task not only of bearing the whole race but of pleasing all the males in it.

The 'feminine'

[1] *Desire* is not beautiful, but *the desired* is. Lucretius (Bk. iv, line 1278) recognizes that the woman's face neither creates nor deflects desire.

[2] That women are sensible of male beauty is a fact commonly overlooked.

[3] For example, calling a woman 'feminine' who has the type of charm preferred by the wer; or 'feminine' when she is retiring and timid or self-sacrificing but not resourceful.   This connotation of 'feminine' as a male-pleasing character to which it is the highest interest of women to live up ("nothing attracts a wer in a woman so much as ——") synchronizes with romantic amour in the wer. It has been noted that the women in greek drama could only be known to be women by their clothes. When romantic love supervened it created the spurious womanly.

[4] This combining of femity as the male would have it with the possession of the femel biological qualities is also unsound: a bull-faced cow was said by a farmer to be one of his best milkers, and a laying hen with male characters has been known to be a very good layer.

Not long ago in a dispute between parents an english The male as father magistrate gave his judgment on the ground that the wish of the father was most likely to be what was good for the child. More recently a judge in the United States organized a campaign against separating the children of the poor from their mothers, declaring, *inter alia*, that in a majority of cases the mother could rear her children better without the father than with him. The instinct of fatherhood has been acquired, and it is not deeply seated. What the mother does for the child is definite, natural, and necessary; *per contra* the father's services are contingent, he only comes to share the parental life through his relation to the mother.[1] It is only through this absolute law of our nature that the position of the father can be understood. The femel's will to associate Monogamy and paternity the male with her life is the only determinant of such services as his,[2] and among men it is the femel will to monogamy which must constitute the sole permanent sanction of the male will to paternity. Pure paternal instinct therefore is not a potent force in life: in western lands a wer desires an 'heir', in China he wants a son to perform those rites which insure felicity to his ghost; reasons which would not count for much with a mother, who is less ready than a father to exploit the child for ends extraneous to its own well-being. The character of fatherhood can be discerned in that tyrannous relation which male parents have devised between themselves and their children, and by the fairly common experience that the advent of a child makes the first breach in a young couple's happiness.   Side by side with the poverty of the paternal instinct we have had the predominance of the sexual. The result in misery to wives has been met from Misery of wives

[1] Except in the examples of natural double parenthood in some species of birds.

[2] The alternatives are simply imposing monogamous unions or harêm polygamous unions by force.

time to time by their banding together to rid themselves of their husbands. There have been coteries of husband poisoners, and to this day in Henry VII's chapel at Westminster there is an image of a woman saint who was invoked by married women as late as the xvi[th] century. For a peck of oats she would get rid of the male cumberer and was hence known as S. Uncumber.[1] That there was a solidarity among women born of this antagonism was clearly recognized by Euripides;[2] and both the malignancy of the revenge taken upon women who murdered husbands and the fact that divorce was either forbidden to wives or made extremely difficult shows that the strength of the wife's desire to be quit of the husband was commonly feared. Why forbid divorce if she seldom craved it? The lot of the wife—the lot of the drudge—is as bad amongst the working poor in polygamist countries as elsewhere in like conditions; but in the households of richer people maternity must be very generally exercized with more liberty and less friction than in those monogamist european households where the wife not only sees herself outraged but her children's rights sacrificed with their mother's.[3] Marriage and paternity, then, have both been spoiled by their circumstances. As we know them, they are examples of that sheer waste of the biological and ethical reservoir which human blunders and malice combined has made possible. Pure paternal instinct is an infinite enhancer of the beauty of human life; it endows the male with that sense of responsibility denied him by nature and ranges him with the mother

[1] Sir Thomas More recounts the story.
[2] *Medea*, 410–30.
[3] Patriarchal polygamy, though it places sex exigencies in the centre, was never an attack on the freedom of mothers in regard to their young, whereas patriarchal monogamy places the young mother under the tutelage of her mate. Patriarchal polygamy, however, *because* it is a male system gives no more freedom to the mother in the later and higher relation to the adolescent child than does patriarchal monogamy. (Cf. *infra*, p. 294.)

as a fount of self-sacrificing energy. It was the parallel subjection of the mother which spoiled this fair picture, bringing fantastic privileges for him, fantastic burdens for her. The true objective of matrimony is to make the wer—who is the recessive factor in generation—the overt partner and sharer in the production and nurture of progeny. Patriarchal marriage aborts nature by making the male dominant; but the primeval types of matriarchy had given paternity no skope and had placed the entire stress on the merely sex aspect of the male mate. He had no role psychical or parental, no claim was made upon him for the higher gifts. The best type of matrimony the world has yet seen was the matronal which the women of Rome had created for themselves. It was not yet a perfect type because the world around them was patriarchal, but it upset for the first time the unnatural conceit that 'a woman's first duty' was to the mate, that it was his to rule and possess and hers to bear children and minister. The first duty of the materfamilias is to her children, and the first duty of the mate is to his wife. These are inviolable laws of nature, and the customs which run counter to them run counter to the ethical interests of mankind. At the present level of sex civilization the monogamous relation offers so many occasions to violence and coarse brutality that nothing but the most complete freedom personal social and legal for the wife can meet the case. That inherent femel requirement—liberty of choice in all her biological relations—has been made impossible in the case of mankind by the tabus and other superstitions of the past; but matriarchal institutions in certain directions suffered from this inappreciation of the role of personal psychical liberty as much as did patriarchal, and new relations between the sexes will now mean also greater skope for human personality.[1]

(marginal note:) The best type of matrimony

[1] See Family, p. 317.

CHARACTER OF WOMAN AND WER

WE want to arrive at a real notion of the social contribution of woman and wer—their ultimate social character, undefaced by the many artificialities of the past.[1]

It was a particularly striking discovery that while we expect the same set of generic qualities in horse dog or monkey irrespective of sex, this genial expectation altogether fails with the appearance of 'rational' man.[2] There was however no truth in it. The truth was to be found in the natural data, where a difference is unfolded in the specific character of the two sexes. But in all the higher animals generic character is the same: women and wers are divided by specific character and meet on one and the same ground in generic; and it is the generic character which is inalienable.[3] Specific qualities though they yield us a positive basis for character are not the property of all the individuals, and if there is one natural path along which it is better that mankind should travel, both are called upon to take it. The difference then that it was sought to establish in the past was that women and wers have not the same general powers; whereas truth lay in the proposition that they have not the same specific character.

A difficulty meets us at the outset, since the only classification bequeathed us by the wer is one in which he attributed all the best qualities to himself. It is a false classification which has been responsible for obscuring the salient fact of human solidarity and responsible at the

[1] "Standing on the ground of common sense and the constitution of the human mind, I deny that anyone knows, or can know, the nature of the two sexes, as long as they have only been seen in their present relation to one another." John Stuart Mill, *Subjection of Women*, ch.i. 38 (ed. 1869).

[2] Man thus appeared to be the only animal where the two members of the species did not belong by their qualities to the same genus.

[3] You say the individual *a* or *b* presents (or does not present) all the specific characters; but generic characters are always present—vertebrate or invertebrate, solitary or social, &c.

same time for our blindness to the meaning of original natural distinctions. It led us to suppose that the wer was the common reservoir of the virtues, a small feminine pitcher being occasionally filled from it when it belonged to an 'exceptional woman'. To take a very important quality and an unimportant: the attribution to the wer, not to the woman, of generosity; not on the ground of a magnanimous record in the treatment of women but because his judgment is indulgent and women's hard in cases of feminine incontinence. But indulgence to those whose faults minister to your vices is not to be confused with generosity. Adam's excuse for all that goes wrong is still to be heard in his mouth, not in Eve's.[1] Or take talkativeness; woman and wer are both talkative, and he enjoys an extra incentive to malicious gossip since he has always had a greater desire to defame women than women have had to defame him. Wers and women both talk when they should be working, reveal secrets that have been confided to them, and are untruthful to each other, each of them as a means of self-defence.[2] Certain radical qualities are, nevertheless, founded in the deepest psychological distinctions to which we have been so blind: vanity is such a quality and it throws out branches such as boasting and cruelty which are much more apparent in one sex than in the other. On the same natural plane we come upon the prevailing defect of women, which is their fatally facile adoption of a narrowed outlook. Women brought up by wers often have

(margin notes: Talkativeness; Vanity)

[1] A very ludicrous instance of this came within my knowledge after the war broke out in 1914—when a wer informed a group of women that the cause of this greatest conflict in history was "women's extravagant expenditure".

[2] In her *Woman not inferior to Man* "Sophia a Person of Quality" writes (1640) àpropos of Cato's view of women, that "to oblige men to prove all that they advance by reason would be imposing silence upon them; a grievance to which they are perhaps full as unequal as they pretend we are".

the balance redressed because they are then able to share that contact with the outer world which has always been of singular importance to them on this account. At present the wer's method of approaching a subject and the woman's are different; but it is not possible to foresee how much is here due to the very different conditions of their lives and how much to differences in mental and moral quality. The one intellectual distinction I find between wer and woman is that her intellect is synthetic, his analytic.[1] All through life her mind is quicker; and her intellectual eagerness is not inferior to his. Mankind foolishly let go the sense that 'women are wise', leaving this useful truth to be recognized only by the individual wer in his personal career. Compared with women most wers are elementary and crude: for the wer does not grow up; she becomes a woman, but he retains something of the boy.   It has not been suggested in the past that women are more cruel but it has been suggested that they are more insensitive. This probably represents the truth that women are less emotional in the presence of horrors where practical services to living things are required. Nietzsche boldly stated "Those who know how to discriminate . . . will perceive that women have intelligence and wers emotion and passion". And the woman appears prosaic by the side of the sentimental male: in liking for sentimental verse, in sentimentalism in his relations with the other sex, the wer outpaces the woman. Sentimentality is the by-product of sentiment, and it is women who have the larger gifts of feeling. But the wer possesses a most delightful quality in the strength of his emotional reactions; he can be much more easily moved by an emotional appeal than a woman, and he carries feeling into action with none of the hesitations that assail her.

Side notes: ntellectual character · Insensitiveness · Sentimentalism · Emotion

[1] Women have a greater power of synthetic judgment than the wer: it is called "intuition" because the steps are not discerned. It is not the result of analysis.

It is emotion not ideality which is at work, and the part played by emotion in his life has been too long overlooked. Wers easily let things slip; whereas women have marked tenacity. The wer is more content with the formal and conventional; and all history reveals that he has more truculence but less independence than she. I think another distinction is that women have more reverence for ideas and less for persons; and it belongs with this that their moral courage is greater. The wer is much more susceptible to derision; women are constitutionally capable of neglecting the fear of mockery: this is not because they all have independent minds and no vanity, but because the presence of a far stronger motive sweeps away everything else. The wer indeed has never yet understood that there is a difference in her vanity and his. He is *led* by vanity, but woman is not. And he has hitherto been subjected to an education which makes the most of his poor qualities and the worst of his rich ones. Education has done nothing to redress the natural handicaps of the sexes.

Women have greater moral and spiritual ideality; but the finer types of wer have great aesthetic sensibility, otherwise sensibility is rather femel than male. It has been noted that there are in very fine types of women a great liberty serenity sanity and proportion; a free-spirited understanding of life and its happiness, and a special quality of giving much in return for what has been received: these qualities which should have a large role in human life have hitherto been tucked away in small domestic corners. Again, in very fine types of wer there is unlimited spiritual ideality. But when we come to human fineness all sex character becomes unimportant; wer and woman meet then on one ground, as they do at the basest level: the finer wer indeed has the woman's fineness; and it has been noticed that then feeling is more like hers and finds similar expression. Irritability,

Tenacity
Convention
Truculence
Independence

Derision

Moral and spiritual ideality

Character fineness and sex

277

swift psychical reactions and extremes of mood, with a receptive sensitiveness to external impressions, are temperamental in men of genius of both sexes. But our customs have done all that is possible to prevent the production of this highest kind of genius, that which sublimates sex.

Is the
Nietz-
schean type
of maleness
a social
require-
ment? Some women and a few wers suffer from an excess of tenderness. Is absence of tenderness and is hardness a social asset? Clearly there is a kind of hardness which is part of all personal and social discipline. I think most women would be as ready as any wer to operate to save a life or to cauterize with a red-hot poker when no anaesthetic was to hand, though, it may be, at more cost to themselves. And there is no sort of reason why the wer, who as a rule has considerably less natural tenderness, should not kill a frog[1] for the woman medical student: if this ought not to be expected then we ought to expect the wer to return to nurse the baby, and women should be content to employ a wer in the sick room of either sex.[2] When the delicacy of wers is equal to such tasks it will be time to call upon an insensitiveness in women to be equal to the others. Callousness to suffering has in my opinion no role at all in life; none of the things it alone is capable of doing are things that ought to be done. Firmness oppugnancy self-assertion tenacity and strength of mind and nerve for necessary services are always wanted. But wers are not better equipped with any of these things than women. It is the distinctively masculine brand of hardness which is a compound of insensitiveness and truculence for which I see no use. There is less use for these than for hypersensitiveness, and less is to be learnt

---

[1] Or the rat in the house. Captain Scott thanked his companions for sparing him the dreadful task of killing the dogs on his polar expedition.

[2] Where is the difference, and where is the inferiority? If a woman weeps over a dog the average wer is amused; but when he shouts himself hoarse over a football hero he thinks he is doing a fine thing.

from them. The saying "boys will be boys" is made to do duty for much of the rubbish we bandy concerning 'masculine' and 'feminine'. It has come to mean that boys should be what they want to be and girls what others want them to be. Trenchant things have been said from time to time about boys.[1] But boys are not un-governable they are ungoverned, and this is a defect which must obviously be shared between nature and nurture. Hardness (like stubbornness), itself for itself, has no citizen rights; it has no real strength: and no hard-ness is called for but that which is assumed *ad hoc* by men whose sensitiveness is balanced by their self-control.[2]

Women are the aristokratic sex. They are not so fond of associating with their inferiors in conduct and educa- Aristo-tion as wers, and the wer more easily than she 'reverts to kratism barbarism' in the absence of a restraining civilization. But women's aristokratism is not of the feudal or ceremonial type, it has rather the latin quality with no dependence on the external, and it expresses a principle of natural authority. Women are as little likely to have been the authors of the feudal system as of the ritual minutiae of the Pentateuch.　　　Each sex has its own boldness and its own timidity which spring from different roots: her Boldness timidity is an expedient of the protective instinct and his and timidity betrays dependence on authority and convention.[3] Bold-ness in the wer has a physical source, and is a valuable social asset in dealing with many matters of external

---

[1] Plato, *Laws*, vii. 808.

[2] Cf. Human Character, p. 393 *n.*

[3] The femel cowers, but it is not for herself. It is an actual fact that the wer is more afraid of responsibility than the woman: Bismarck said of the german soldier, "He goes to meet certain death with the simple words 'At your orders', but if he has to act on his own responsibility dreads the criti-cism of his superior officer or of the world more than death, to the extent of allowing his energy and his correct judgment to be weakened by fear of blame and reproof". A physician in this country a year before the war of 1914–18 recorded many cases of wers breaking down under responsibility and from nervous anxiety on promotion.

interest: wers fill their canvas with brush work, the woman's picture is stencilled. But if she has less of this breadth she has more boldness for its roots are in the spirit. Woman, it has been said, "*works* with her spirit"; she is more painstaking, more anxious-minded, more kindly, more affectionate; she puts her personal troubles less forward but is in certain directions less placable than the wer. Women 'nag', it is their short-coming; the wer

False sentiment

bullies. And we see he has indulged in an orgy of false sentiment based upon his relations to women: all the exaggerations we have noted and all the foolish and cruel disabilities that have been imposed owe something to this unwholesome sentimentality.[1] To take but one instance of the false criterion set up for the woman—in her case 'honour' has been restricted to preserving a state of physical chastity.

Jealousy

We blundered into the notion that women are the more jealous. No doubt we should have revised our beliefs on this subject sooner had harêms consisted of wers huddled together as rival paramours: for the harêm has been possible just *because* women are not jealous, or not nearly so jealous as the wer. The only romance of the harêm is the love-friendship between polygamous wives.[2]

[1] See *supra*, pp. 242 and 267–8 *n*.

[2] El Jabartee (in vol. i of the Memoir of his father, Obituary year 1188 of the Hegirah) records the story of his father's chief wife and Zeelakhà a slave he had purchased in the year 1156 Heg. The first wife freed her, paying her husband the price from her own purse so that she should not be resold, and gave her to him by marriage contract. When Zeelakhà was sick unto death the first wife sickened also: Zeelakhà then made her prayer, 'Make my day to be before her day!' And died that same night. "No life remaineth to me after her!" exclaimed the first wife, and having seen the body carried out before her, she fell into the travail of death and died at the close of day.   The number of murders committed by women bear a very small proportion to the number done by wers, yet they include all those that may be caused by sex revenge. It is remarkable that although the ideas and customs of the harêm (for ex., taking wives in turn) have assumed and done the utmost to provoke sex jealousy between women, in practice it does not 'come off'.   Nature shows us similar instances elsewhere:

It is in sooth forgotten that the woman has not as much skope for this sort of jealousy; motherhood disputes it with her. We find Rachael and Leah sharing Jacob on the flimsiest maternal pretext. The maternal feelings, it is true, may themselves arouse jealousy, but not to the extent that professional jealousies daily devour the wer. They make him—these jealousies of his fellow wer and of woman—into a permanent competitor in the community, preventing co-operation everywhere.[1] For it is

the males of eiderduck fight at the breeding season, but the nest is occupied by 2 femels "who live together in perfect concord". Two swan mothers have been known to share the same nest alternately, *each hatching all the eggs*. Compare with this the northern nigerian tribe of *Munshi* where a woman will give one or two of her children to a less fortunate mother. When rival males have fought, leaving one on the field, the femels are quite content to herd with the remaining bull, and show no jealous desire for him. Compare the behaviour of cows in a field or a group of hens with that of a couple of their bulls or a couple of their cocks.   In our species male professional jealousy is a ceaseless problem: nowhere is vanity greater than among dramatic artists, yet Sarah Bernhardt says in her memoirs that she was beset by the jealousy of wers more than by that of women actors; and it has been noted that while fathers are generally jealous of actor sons, women actors train and encourage their daughters in their profession. What is true in every profession is as true in every office where wers work together.
But there are, as suggested, indications that this wer jealousy has been fomented into existence. We remember that under matriarchal conditions no wer was assured his place as husband (see *supra*, p. 207), polyandry—which ignores the thesis of male jealousy—has always existed in Tibet, on the Malabar Coast, and, till 1860, in Ceylon; Strabo notes its existence in Arabia Felix—[Among the Malabar Naïrs it is a survival of matriarchal matrimony—the males live in their maternal home but are the mates of women in other homes, the woman selecting the mates she prefers]—and it would seem that greed and many other passions are capable of controlling this otherwise uncontrolled passion. Thus the xxiv[th] chap. of the Qu'ran speaks of wers requiring their concubines to pay them a tax which was to be earned by prostitution; and living on the sex gains of wives and other women is a form of livelihood rife in all countries. Take away, indeed, the incentives to jealousy due to his own vanity and hectoring, and almost any passion suffices to cut the cock's comb.
    [1] Hence women have greater powers of combination than wers. Woman, the all-worker, *can* combine as the wer cannot. This capacity to combine is not the same thing as military discipline or even as team-work. See *infra*, p. 285 and *n.*[2].

evident that there is no inherent mother-rivalry to match his sex rivalry. Two sex rivals each want the same thing; and there is in man and many other species a truculence ready to support the desire which is not at all common in the femel. It is nevertheless probable that male jealousy is not a fundamental instinct but has thriven on the over-emphasis of one side of life and the spirit of domination of sex over sex. If polyandry in women checked sex desire in wers women-prostitutes would not exist.

Contrary to the generally received opinion neuroticism and the severer forms of hysteria are more common in wers than women. At puberty disturbing mental changes assail the boy which leave the girl unperturbed. Such disturbances at the femel climacteric must be as rare as the similar phenomenon at childbirth; but whether there be or not a definite male climacteric when the wer is less reliable than at other times in his life, he most certainly suffers a disturbing factor which may operate at every age. This produces the phenomenon, peculiar to the wer, of 'running amok', like bullocks, or like Ajax. Ajax, as he sets forth, is the classical type of those who run amok, and he was satisfied when he surveyed the shambles around him.   The characteristic of this form of mania is that it is wreaked in all the intimate relations of life— the wer assails or slays his wife, his children, his mother, an aged relative or the infant at the breast, the woman he is going to marry or the woman he cannot marry. He is most dangerous in the home and the nursery; but occasionally he runs amok in the village, on the high seas, in the midst of a pleasure party—a type of dementia which is certainly responsible for many of his assaults on the other animals. If duly recorded it would be found to account for a large part of all the crime in the world. This rampant form of mania could not have been dissembled had it not been for the age-long fable that

Puberty and climacteric

hysteria is a woman's ailment. Yet the facts had been known as early as 1618 when Charles Lepois, Henry II's physician, "trusting, as he said, to experience and reason, overthrew at one stroke the doctrine of hysteria that had ruled almost unquestioned for 2,000 years, and showed that the malady occurred at all ages and in both sexes, that its seat was not in the womb but in the brain, and that it must be considered a nervous disease".[1] *'Hysteria' and the male amok*

The belief that the wer was the stronger sex would not have held its ground in the past but for the assumption that greater weight size and muscular strength meant greater mental and moral strength. This is not, of course, a thesis borne out elsewhere in nature, but where would be the use of a 'separate creation' for man if it did not permit at least the male half of it to flout the creator's other works? The woman excels in vitality, longevity, endurance and in strength of moral character; her judgment is less impulsive and more farseeing, she has greater self-control, greater power of conscientious work, and is less affected by sexual disturbance or sudden mania.[2] *The stronger sex*

We made another blunder when vanity in dress was held to be a monopoly of women; indeed it is quite as great *Dress: fashions versus uniforms*

[1] This "so revolutionary" doctrine was confirmed by Willis, and we owe to the genius of Sydenham in 1681 a picture of hysteria, lucid precise and comprehensive. (Havelock Ellis.) 'Hysteria' is then an improper term; but women do not suffer from the male mania of running amok, for which a proper term would be *arsēnia*. See footnote at end of this section, pp. 286–8.

[2] Wers are more liable to faint in emergencies or from excitement than women—as Fox fainted after one of his great speeches in the House of Commons; and it was a wer who fainted as the first number was announced at a recent irish sweepstake; and a wer who fainted when the news of his win was brought, the male messenger of good news fainting with him. In 1910 an ex-police constable who was taking honey from a hive cried out, "I am stung" and died. No trace of a bee-sting could be found. An italian soldier whose party was ambushed at the Benedeguina Pass in January 1936 was found dead "untouched" clasping the picture of his fiancée; the poor young fellow had died of fright, as a Londoner aged 53 recently died of excitement at a cup-tie. In 1927, 12 wers died while listening to the broadcast description of a boxing match in Chicago. 7 of these died when one of the boxers was floored in the 7th round.

a blunder to call this vanity 'unmanly'. Most forms of vanity are consistent with enterprise and courage. It has not been understood that the changes of fashions and hue in women's dress are only a compensation for the fact that gay official dresses and decorations have been an exclusively male delectation. It is only of very recent date that elaborate habiliments according to social class have been discarded; and dressing chiefly for convenience is not only quite a recent custom but was confined to one sex: as this convenience counted far more in the life of the wer it was speedily set against the earlier vanities; but such convenience only began to count in the xxth century in the lives of the same classes of women. Women's dress has certainly been to a considerable extent affected by the artificial sexual selection of males, but fashion in its essence is followed almost as much for our peers in sex as for our peers in class—women dress for women, the wer dresses for the wer, and a woman or a wer living among none but the opposite sex each becomes dowdy.

Woman's disinterestedness I do not think that the natural character of femel and male suggests that he would be the more acquisitive— it suggests rather that the mother sex would be both altruistic and acquisitive. But the lop-sided education of humanity has made the wer the acquisitive sex; *l'appétit vient en mangeant*, and while history shows us that the wer parts with nothing it shows us that in the infime proportion in which women have had control of the world's goods the proportion of their sacrifices has been immense.[1]

Slancio Goethe asserted that when a woman's other advantages are increased by a sufficient energy "the result is a being

[1] There is one french village whose taxes were remitted "for ever"; it was the gift to herself chosen by Joan of Arc. The £50,000 awarded by the government of the day to Florence Nightingale she allocated to found the Nightingale Home for training nurses. A Toronto woman, in our time, was the only member of parliament to return her salary. But we waited for a contemporary Japanese general to bestow his emperor's gift on the men who had fought with him, instead of spending such gifts on self-aggrandizement.

than whom nothing more perfect can be imagined". But it is not energy that is wanting to woman, it is a katabolic element, that which the italians call *slancio*. This is obstructed by her anabolism which in its turn makes certain character achievements easier.[1] And it should not be forgotten when the social contribution of the sexes is weighed that the anabolic temperament seems to stabilize certain faculties which however much they are to be found occasionally in a splendid form in the wer are more widely distributed among women—aesthetic feeling and imagination are among these.

"Women work harder and longer" than wers "but have too much tact to tell them so" was said in 1910 in a speech at Cape Town. The wer of the future will have outgrown the need to be managed, flattered, pampered and kept in ignorance of troubles, in order that his temper may be kept sweet and his nose to the grindstone. No doubt women understand that wers are more easily discouraged than they are, but I think their aumbry should contain better remedies; and if there were a true equality these better remedies would be forthcoming. The woman has a natural educating power and governs by harmonizing tendencies rather than by imposing conditions. These qualities were perceived in the case of related religious houses between the vi[th] and the xvii[th] centuries, where it was always the abbess or prioress who ruled the two houses.[2] Nature shows us that she repre-

Wers treated as children

---

[1] Perhaps impatience accompanies '*slancio*'. The wer is impatient in the little things of life and patient of the great wrongs. Woman is patient over the daily life, and impatient over the great evils. Impatience in small events has in fact a useful role. It is in the great events that impatience has no role.

[2] The custom was based no doubt on the fact (which had operated in the original clan matriarchies) that a woman is a more successful leader and governor of both than a wer; that she employs and harmonizes elements in a mixed society as he cannot do. Talleyrand had realized that a woman in a great position can act as no wer can act: "Nothing is more efficacious than confidence; and it has its fullest force when it springs from the care

sents not simply a principle of nurture but a principle of discipline. What we have done is to invoke nature for femel duties and reject it for femel powers.

Self-criticism

I do not know whether it is as a result of all this that the male of our species has certainly less self-criticism than the femel. But he does not comprehend—small blame to him—the incongruous amalgam which woman became

Woman 'a mystery'

when the eating of that apple upset her natural status. If only the civilization of christendom had ever reached the point of proclaiming that the act of Mary undid the act of Eve we should all be living in a fairer world. As it is, what the wer can "never understand" is the strength of character with which nature endowed the woman crossed with the adventitious sex dependence imposed on her by himself.[1] This hotch-potch found naïf expression when a woman said to a militant suffragist: (*ipsissima verba*) "The 'men', you know, *are* better than we, and we ought to give them a good example."

As inspirer

Wers are inspired by women, not women by wers: how strange that this truth revealed through all history—that the wer has not inspired the woman—should have failed to be recognized.

THE MALE AMOK

The following cases are taken from a casual collection of newspaper cuttings I made between 1910–14—nearly all of them happened in two or three months of the year 1913:—

At Aquila a husband kills his wife, who is with child, and their

and attention of a great lady, around whom are gathered all ideas of power and protection." Woman works by combining, the wer by competing. Let it be said, indeed, that goodness has been easier to her, because the prevalent motor with her is sympathy. (See also *supra*, p. 281 *n.*[1].)

[1] "——but in the book of woman he is ignorant; this is not a saying of today, it has ever been so: our book has not been mastered, therefore to hide their ignorance they say in woman there is no wisdom." These words were said a thousand years ago by Sunjota to her husband when he asked her advice.

2 children. In Berlin a husband assails with fists and kicks his wife, who is with child, and then throws her and their 2 little girls out of the window. At Chertsey a husband kills his wife and 3 of their 18 children. A New York waiter, returning from work, fires 12 bullets into his Brooklyn flat which is found by the police reduced to shambles, with the wife and 4 children dead.

"Baby pulled a face" said a little sister of 8 in evidence; for being only 6 months old baby did not like the "cheese and beer" which the grown-up brother left in charge had "forced into its mouth". So he cut the baby's throat.

When an Italian killed his wife, in May 1913, the court presumed that "a sudden mental exaltation had affected his psychical faculties". A Salisbury stationer laid his little daughter of 9 years on a bed and cut her throat: "It was an awful sudden impulse" he wrote to his wife.

But it is not only the mania of violence it is also discouragement which causes these murderous attacks—the action of a London policeman who on his return from night duty took his motherless children out of bed and shut them in a room with the gas turned on, is typical of such cases.

Then there is running amok in public places, a village, a café, a ship, a school: in June 1913 a schoolmaster at Bremen invaded a school armed with 6 revolvers and fired continuously killing several scholars and teachers. A Swiss tailor had done the same thing in a café, and an American ship's officer also. In October a Liverpool carpenter ran amok among the congregation of his sect, armed with revolver, razor, and bludgeon. A large number of such cases were recorded in the year before the war, especially during September and October 1913. September opens with a German schoolmaster setting fire to his little town and shooting and wounding 18 people, having already stabbed his wife and the 4 children. At the Ferrara barracks a Roman lad with a field bayonet pursues the first 3 women he meets and tries to murder them and a passer by. On the 28th of the month a poor country girl in Rome who had repulsed the importunities of a youth was set upon by him and a lot of other blackguards, and sexually outraged "with unheard of violence" the italian paper says. And on the last day of the month a french farm lad of 15 wiped out an entire family of his employers. At Kettering, in October, a "well dressed" wer asked his way of some little girls— Nellie King, aged 9, offered to show him; he took her up on his carrier, told her to get down and feel the tyres, and drove a steel spike into the back of her skull.

In none of these cases was drink alleged as the cause. The cause is "sudden mania". Two other cases from before and after the war may be cited: in 1911 jealousy of his wife's wooden leg which procured her many visitors was the provocation for a Paris innkeeper's homicidal prowess; and in 1918 an english crippled ex-soldier, aged 22, after "singing some songs" went to kiss his grandmother "as usual", and stabbed her in the neck. "I wanted to do it", he explained.

IN CON-
CLUSION

The past
and the
future

BEHIND the problems connected with woman and wer there lies the fact that their relation in the past has been regulated by artificial arbitrary conventions;[1] the paramount effect of which has been the neglect of the woman's psychological contribution to the race. If nature had been interrogated it would have been impossible for the wer to take up a position as representative of the species for nature everywhere tends to create this sort of hermaphrodism in the femel.

It has been sometimes assumed that nothing but the domination of the wer has kept sex antagonism at bay, that this sleeps only while woman is subject. But sex antagonism has not slept, it has been a constant phenomenon of human life; and it demands, I think, but an elementary philosophy to perceive that the licence wers have accorded to their sex desires would have produced such a phenomenon. The past relations of woman and wer have not then eliminated sex antagonism and they have not obtained security for her in any other direction. Take the division of labour between the sexes as an instance. Under the system which has produced our present civilization the woman has never been freed from excessive labour, what has been kept from her are the

[1] Plutarch (*Lycurgus*) "That *acquired* womanishness which vain custom has added to the natural". Even Epictetus appears to have seen that male sensuousness creates a false femel type; women, he says, see that "there is nothing else for them but to serve the pleasure of wers", and so they are prized for nothing but this.

mental activities and moral government. Her greater
vitality has been exploited to the uttermost: the 'home-
keeping' which it is alleged is her share of the world's
labour has included in most lands tilling, ploughing,
sowing, beast of burden, the care of the house, the care
of the wer, and the care of the child. A natural division
of labour would certainly have established the rule that
since the woman carries the child the wer should carry
everything else. But what we find is that in most of the
countries of the world the wer leaves the porterage of
heavy loads to the woman, especially he leaves it to the
woman who is his wife.   But there is a psychological
division of labour also, and here the chivalry of the wer
should not have been unlike that of the woman. He
should be ready to give on his side as she gives on hers.
There should have been consideration for the gestating
woman and readiness to be burden bearer for her. You
say: All these things have I done from my youth up?
Where have you done them, and to whom? The condition
of peasant wives all the world over, of the working woman
in every town, and of the teeming millions of women
outside Europe, is sufficient evidence that no chivalry to
woman as woman is established as a principle in any part
of the globe. There can be no reason at all why the wer
should have complete rest when he comes back from a
short or a long day's work, while the woman (who has
to tend the child) works early and late for all of them. The
formula of married life is that he 'works' and she 'keeps Formula
the house'. The fact however is that whether the woman and fact
works outside the home or not her daily support of the
family is more than equal to his. In our times the increasing complexity of home and social life is making the
house-mother's burden too big for one person to carry;
and the wer, who is the leisured partner in reproduction,
must in future take his share of the domesticities. A higher
domestication is always to be found among a certain

number of wers, and this should be welcomed and appreciated not as at present ridiculed and discouraged until comradeship between the sexes and real mutual comprehension of interests cease to exist at all. Everywhere the woman has the mothering instinct towards the wer but on his side there is no natural socializing instinct to correspond with this. Greater domestication would however be entirely to his advantage and would I think in some sort make weight against that farouche element of sex, the sense of inachievement and dissatisfaction due to its biological incompleteness, which haunts the sex act for him. For it is probable that the wer has not been happier than the woman. He has less love, less spirit of service, he is less complete in himself and perhaps less interesting to himself. He has had immensely larger liberty and many more pleasures, he has enjoyed the happinesses of the heedless sex, freedoms psychologically impossible to the greater number of women—but not the profound joys which have fallen to these;[1] and his very licences have closed to him the sealed founts of the waters of life. Of the life of the wer—not of the great or the blessed but of the average mass—it may be said that he has loved his life to lose it. No wer would exchange his lot with a woman's; he would not forgo its dignities and freedoms and that prestige which he is well aware has been confined to his sex in our absurd civilization. But his choices have also been determined by the fact that, in the mass, he has never cared for some of the best things; and I think if the conditions of life were equal between the sexes women could increase the happiness of wers. He, too, must learn to give where he

[1] Nor the immense suffering: even the worst human conditions have not comported for him what they have for her, the outraging of the maternal, the violences and the slavery of sex, such long-drawn-out miseries as those of the indian child widow or of the wife and the sex slave in Japan and China. Again, for the wer have been those intellectual and artistic joys of which the woman has everywhere been thwarted.

takes and to take by giving. Up to now he has developed at the expense of the woman; and she has been the cheap sex. Under patriarchal rule her motherhood has been held cheaply, infant life held cheaply, the fruits of her labour have gone to enrich the wer, and she has in every possible direction cost the community less than he. Yet in nature, as we have seen, the femel is the precious and costly sex. The cheap sex

These elements in the relation of woman and wer point to an evil which is fundamental and not simply to the errors (necessary or unnecessary) due to human imperfection. Something has been wrong at the core of human life—we have been measuring our human relations with a sex measure; measuring all life with it. It has made indignities a part of femel life: in every age and under all religions for a very large class of wers woman has been nothing but an object of prey. Classical Athens subjected all women (together with minors) to police supervision.[1] France is regarded as one of the most highly civilized countries that has ever existed in the world, but french jurisprudence provided that the wife who left the conjugal roof might be brought back by the gens d'armes, and under the Third Republic the rite of civil marriage and the restrictions on the liberty of wives are made for slaves rather than for french women.[2] Our sexual relations have never been civilized. Typical of the attitude of the church is the bas-relief in an Auvergne château of the xvi[th] century which represents three angels forging the head of a wer while three demons forge that of a woman. These were not clerical pleasantries, they were the sex pabulum of a theology which brought about The sex measure

---

[1] "Of all the Greek prisons I visited the woman's prison—there is only one—impressed me most. The atmosphere mentally and morally was so much better in every way compared with the male prisons. A woman governor presides over it." Thomas Mott, American prison reformer, 1922.

[2] They degrade them to the condition of the Armenian christian wife.

the witch persecutions.[1] The indignities offered to women are the fruit of sex subjection. No really civilized society will tolerate the subjection of one sex to the other, but least of all when it is on behalf of sexual interests. The inherent injustice of thought which has accompanied this relation of wer to woman saps the roots of justice everywhere and suggests and excuses all the injustice of the world. There is an ubiquitous unjust mind which makes the flowering of justice impossible. A wretched inequality permits the wer to cast any scurrility at women and put forth any claim for himself however maniacal; but if a woman makes the least criticism of a wer or the most holy of protests she is treated as wanton and unsexed, and the cry is "Out, strumpet!"[2]

Creation of an unjust and of an immoral mind

Remedies

The first remedy is that the wer's oppugnancy to criticism should cease. Women's criticism is an integral part of human betterment.[3] Boy and man the wer has been badly bred; in a deep sense his spiritual and moral education has been inferior for thousands of years to that of women, for its direction has been towards licences to which he was prone and away from the spiritual forces which operate in the case of the femel. Apart from the sexual interests our badly brought up wers do not think of their lives in relation to women's lives.[4]   Pending the arrival of a new sex opinion women should possess very much better means of protection against lust, and that violence which will not disappear till there is less lust. History has shown that the male will not penalize himself to protect women.[5] If it were everywhere recog-

---

[1] Cf. the legend of Lustucru, and see *supra*, p. 219.

[2] This unnoticed phenomenon is clearly of the first ethical importance; and one which has degraded the human male. See Oversexualization, p. 255.

[3] Plutarch records how efficacious was the criticism by young women of young wers in Lacedaemonia (*Lycurgus*).

[4] Whereas nothing could prevent women caring for the life of both.

[5] The penalties for sexual assault are indecently inadequate and are of all penalties the most often quashed. Assault on infants and immature girls

nized that as things now are women run risk from the
wer as he now is, a step forward would have been made to
requiring better conditions. Society should regard violence to women as a definitely worse thing than violence
used from wer to wer.   Where the woman is subject
the male phenomenon of aggressive physical force is
not understood and has no perspective: the exercise of
muscular force creates the illusion that you are lord A
of a supreme activity—creates the mentality of the stag muscular
illusion
and the cock fighting their rivals. The combat has no
value, but it makes the protagonists unaware of any
values in the femel of the species; they suffer what is
(biologically and psychologically) a complete delusion.
But human civilization requires that there should be no
such delusion.[1]   Among external conditions which
have played a noxious part for centuries is the dress of
the sexes. The greater the distinction between the dress
of the two the greater the sexual suggestion: 'feminine' on her side spells sexual on his—that is the constant relation.   The instruction which was given in
greek temples perpetuated the matriarchal 'women's
house' and acted, I think, in favour of restraint: but it
did little to check a general oversexualization because
this temple instruction flourished throughout its history
under patriarchal conditions. Sex knowledge and what is
proper to self-defence and self-respect should be taught
in women's *scholae* under scientific women and physicians:

and all rape with violence should be requited by castration. We have
tolerated the sentencing of the girl mother to death for infanticide, and
there can be no comparison between the wrong she does and the horrors
suffered by children and women at the hands of the lecherous.
    The law, "save in the feeblest and most inefficient way", does not protect
the wife "from her husband's personal violence". (Anna Martin, *The
Mother and Social Reform*.)
    [1] With us jealous rivalry masquerades as protection of the femel; con-
flict ousts sympathy as a law of life; truculence is substituted for power:
see pp. 60; 72 *n.*[2]; 73; 77; ch. x. 352; 353; ch. xi (Force), 358–9; 362;
363 and *n.*[2]; and cf. p. 466 and *n.*[3].

and I make bold to assert that given the conditions displayed in human history the requisite in the sex relations is pride on the woman's part and modesty on the part of the male—its respect and its restraint.[1] But if all education should fail to decrease male lechery we have the two weapons of eugenics and the limitation of male progeny or their eunuchization.[2]

All patriarchal societies have sacrificed women to the doctrine that the value of the mother was measured by the value of children; a doctrine which has sacrificed the child with the mother. It has been remarked in the case of Indians, Turkish, and Chinese what characterless wers are born of such sacrificed mothers. Women have been overwhelmed with disabilities on the score of their duty to the child and to childbirth, though their mentor has done nothing to lessen the waste of infant and mother life. At the same time he has recognized no obligation to prove himself a suitable father, and offered no criterion of a suitable mother except that of being attractive to himself. Before the dawn of recorded history we

The place of the matri- potestas

took the wrong turning. Patripotestas once new is now old without being reverend. There is no other cure for the crude physical *potestas* practised by the wer, for the constant evil resort to social systems based upon force, except the return to matripotestas. The mother would not have been side-tracked by a sex pathology, she would not have misjudged the wer as he has misjudged the woman, she is mother of both halves of the race, whereas history shows us that this mother-psychosis has not ac-

[1] A good bishop was asked to give a rule for the guidance of girls and boys—"that the maidens be brave and the lads modest" he said. "You have surely mistaken and intended to say that the boys should be brave and the maids modest?" they answered. "I have made no mistake", said he, "nature has already done what you say".

[2] Perhaps this would evoke an outcry—from those persons who have always looked upon the existence of a class of sterile harlots with equanimity. See Killing, p. 343.

companied fatherhood. I do not know that women could have been more loving than they have been throughout their history, but the wer could with ease have been less lusting; and it was the subordination of so many other considerations to considerations of sex that made it easy to take that wrong turning which led to an immoral universe. Kindness has never failed in the general relations of woman to wer; there has always been a far vaster amount of it than of male kindness for women; and she understands him as he seldom understands her, she does not feel her son is an enigma (as he feels his sex-mate to be). It is this maternal element in woman's affection which is one of the permanent natural supports of human relations. So when the world comes to see that the sex emphasis was the wrong one it will find in matripotestas the only key that is both natural and ethical. Motherhood in fact endows man with the vision that sex withholds.

It is not necessary in order to make the world go that mankind should put up with violences on one hand and self-suppressions on the other—a licensed egoist and a subject offerer of holocausts. Any society of men in any part of the globe would yield roughly the proportion of seven unselfseeking women in ten, and perhaps three out of ten wers.[1] But even if this natural distinction did not exist, if the woman's moral instinct proved to be in the long run no better than his, her subjection would still demoralize the world. Always and everywhere the subjection of the maternal to the sexual is a radical immorality. In subordination woman deteriorates; and she is never seen to less advantage than under male leadership. Nature's shepherd-man is woman; and to have substituted the mailed fist for this has been the great usurpation.

The important truth is that woman's real contribution to the race and to human society is a psychological

---

[1] In a house it is not rare for all the women to be unselfish; it is rare for half the wers to be so.

contribution—the psychological coefficient of maternal activities, which belongs to her as woman apart from physical motherhood. It is commonly recognized when we resort to childless women for maternal care that physical motherhood is not necessary to arouse maternal tenderness: and this should be as much a truism among men as it is an obvious fact throughout nature, were it not that the wer has insisted that there is, in the case of women, a strict interdependence of character and exercise of function.[1]

Cross heredity in sex

There is a large body of evidence to support the belief that though the natural phenomenon of cross heredity is comparatively inactive in the physiological domain[2] it is a frequent and important phenomenon in the psychological domain. The facts that the woman gives rise within her own soma to both sexes and that either sex transmits gametes which possess the psychical and physical characters of their two parents suggest that sex differentiation is in its nature neither radical nor absolute; and the ambisexual must be regarded as one of the intermediate forms recording the long history of the development of sex. [It is one of those "intermediate forms which stretch from one ideal sexual condition to the other ideal sexual condition".[3]] Ancient mythologies and philosophies have each posited an androgynous origin for mankind;[4]

[1] Many women are morally unfitted to be mothers (wrote a woman who called attention to these matters in 1921) and may be entirely devoid of the physical maternal instincts as distinct from compassion for all helpless creatures: they are not 'unsexed', and the work they perform in the world scheme is of a finer and far more important kind than that not very uncommon sort of human motherhood which is indistinguishable from physical instinct.

A slight alteration in conditions may produce infertility and sterility even in the wild state; and A. R. Wallace notes that these animals are vigorous and long-lived. "It is not due to ill-health that they are infertile."

[2] The sex modifications being unimportant or rare (embryo gonads of one sex in the other; milk in male glands; beards on women; complete physical hermaphrodism).   [3] Weininger, *Geschlecht und Charakter.*

[4] *Symposium,* 189–91. The original Laws of Manu recite that among

and perhaps the psychologically 'ideal' man is not to be found in the physiologically 'ideal' sex separated by an opposite polarity from the other: perhaps no specialized sex type can represent the highest humanity. For it is certain that the emphasis on sex has deprived humanity of some of its birthright. Laô-Tsze said: "He who knows the masculine and at the same time keeps to the feminine will be the whole world's channel." Scotus Erigena said: "If you would be spiritually beautiful you must rise above the sexual contrast and express a combination of the nature of wer and woman." And Goethe declared that the inexorable tendency of civilization is for the wer to approximate to the woman type. The scheme of life which gave us 'the warrior' and 'the beautiful woman' has been exploited *ad nauseam*; and it has been the prevailing scheme.[1] But Chaucer describes his brave and worthy knight as "of his port as meek as is a mayde", while the squire of twenty years is "courteous, lowly, and serviceable". The friends of a royal academician who died in 1915 praised "the modesty of his genius, his sweetness and gentleness, the majesty of his self-conquest". These are not characters we are popularly allowed to associate with masculinity: Is it the example which is admirable here or has such a character only a *succès d'estime* like the sermon on the mount? It will not serve us to vaunt the greatness of mankind if we must eternally be ruled by the mentality of ordinary men; and it is these who lay most store by the ruck distinctions found or fomented in the sexes. We want a world based upon our common

the earliest men, "There is no sign of wer or woman, no development of the sexual organs amongst them. They are called generally 'beings'". [When men came to eat a coarser food ("thalay rice") "the male and the femel sexual organs were developed, and the male and femel sexes became evident to all".] There is a similar iranian legend. And the jewish mystics, also, asserted the original androgyny of mankind.

[1] Nietzsche makes Zarathustra say: "wer is made for war and woman for the diversion of the warrior".

humanity; and for this it is essential that there should not be two separate angles of vision. We should look to felicities of character and originality for the distinctions which enhance and beautify life, for these are not the gift of mere brute sex appositions. And neither biological fact can be allowed to arbitrate: in the beginning this arbiter was motherhood; since then it has been sex; but for the future man will crave rest from sex under the influence of a maternal consciousness sublimated, universalized. Along the present lines no further progress is possible. History shows us that there is no sacrifice which the wer has not been ready to accept and none which the woman has not been ready to give. Such conditions stifle moral development. We do not want in women nothing but the specialized maternal type where personality and individuality are merged in 'making things go right' and in complacencies; and we do not want the specialized masculine type. Both of us should recognize that we can do better than this. Woman in freedom will certainly develop on her androgynous side: the specialized wer type will wear away with the we hope inevitable progresses of the human spirit.[1] That is what Goethe saw. He saw the arrival of a power more potent than any force brought to bear by the wer. The happiness of wer and woman lies along lines of approximation. But man, that strange and ignorant occupier of the globe, has never had in himself or in his circumstances the elements of a perdurable happiness: poor humanity has always been groping with its strong passions and its weak powers of reasoning. Have we not all been blind together? Yes, and the same can be said of every slave state: but though

[1] Wers of 'uranian' type say that it is natural to them to treat women better. I think their attitude to her will be entirely good; and such a new non-sexual relation between them will be a new instrument of progress and harmony. That wers have 'desired' woman has not made them treat her well; neither has their love brought this about, nor has her universal serviceableness to them; and the son's love for the mother has not achieved it.

the slave and the man who enslaves him both sit in dark-ness it is not the same darkness. The exploitation of woman by wer has added to man's shame, as the cherish-ing of the race by woman has lessened it.

In man's disordered world one thing only has been untried—the equal ingerence of woman and wer in mental and moral life. That it remains to be tried is and has been the hope for both of them. For woman is the civilizer and educator as the femel is in nature (Is not the parental male her handiwork, her jiga-jiga?). And in his moments of vision and his hours of doubt the wer has instinctively turned to the thoughts that are hers.[1]

The male arbiter has placed nature in disarray; for a world dominated by the wer is a world dominated by sex. Some day it will be possible to write a book when sex has ceased to be thrust into the centre of the human picture, as though it were the proprium of humanity that it should be central there, and only there.

"*Toute notre civilisation est aphrodisiaque*", wrote Berg-son.[2]

---

[1] It is wers themselves who have uttered some of the loveliest of all sayings in comprehension of this problem. (For example, *A Praise of Women* attributed to Chaucer; Cornelius Agrippa's *de Nobilitate et Praeexcellentia Foeminei Sexus* (1532); the last lines of *Faust*; and Fiona Macleod's 'Song of the Celtic Women' in *Pharais*.

The phenomenon noticed by Field Marshal sir E. Wood among the Cape Coast fanti—"the women had most of the qualities lacking in the 'men' "—and by Borrow among the maragatos of Spain, and which is patent to all eyes among the burmese, will reveal itself widely east and west of the world when all adventitious sex prestige has ceased. It has, of course, its counterpart in animals as far separated as the elephant, lion, goat, falcon, bee, and orang, where force and goodness of character or utility as a species are found not in the male but in the femel. For instance, it is the elephant, only, which has the steadiness and courage to face the tiger; the she-camel which is 'the ship of the desert' (the male is too excite-able and quarrelsome and has no spunk if baulked); the femel falcon which has the qualities that characterize the species; and while an orang will come to the help of another in distress, a male orang will never do so.

[2] The words recently uttered by an ex-Prime Minister of Japan deserve

WOMAN THE TOILER

In spite of the fact that the wer calls woman the weaker sex he has never in any country had any misgiving in burdening her physically. The 'misgiving' has always sprung up when moral and mental powers would be called upon. Herbert Spencer and the 7th lord Shaftesbury both called attention to the overworking of women. Speaking on the guardianship of infants bill in the House of Lords in June 1925, lord Arran said: "A working-class woman works harder than a working-class 'man' . . . and if it were not for the part she takes in the domestic side of her establishment I do not think that the working 'man' would be able to earn the money which has gone to buy the property."

"In 9 families out of 10 the husband is fully as dependent on his wife's work as she is on his" (*The Mother and Social Reform*, Anna Martin). But wers exploit the theme of the 'weakness' or the 'disabilities' of women not in order to save them from hard work but in order to magnify their own value and importance. Wers, however, live a large part of their lives as drones at the expense of the woman in a sense in which no women have ever been naturally dependent on the wer. If she is ill someone has to be found to look after the children, to look after the wer, to nurse his wife. If he is ill, she adds nursing to all her other activities. If the wer is left alone nothing is done. If she is left alone all goes on as before. When temporarily disabled by motherhood it is not an 'able' wer who steps into the breach, it is another woman who looks after her and him: and these disabilities of his are accepted as permanent. This accepted helplessness of the male is obvious also in his professional life based as it is on women's work; and also in the division of labour in occupations where he receives all the remuneration and all the prestige—for example, the country clergyman, country postmaster, and country policeman. In the universal industry of farming her work usually counts for as much as his; and in the ancient occupation of lodging-house keeping it is she who is the wealth producer. Woman in fact is and always has been the great toiler; the one of the two who has toiled without recreation and without remuneration.

record: he said that the question of the relation of the sexes has never been seriously approached, that no "true solution" has been reached east or west; and that this proves that there has been no substantial advance in ethics. In this way has a subject which the history of the world shows to be second to none in ethical importance been treated by the world's philosophers and moralists. Cf. also p. 252 *n*.[4]

Lord Shaftesbury found women in the coal mines dragging trucks on all fours along the galleries, a chain between their legs. Such has been 'western civilization' with women in a subordinate position.

CRIMINALITY

The criminal statistics of every country demonstrate that crime of all kinds is so overwhelmingly a male phenomenon that if mankind consisted of women only it would not be a criminal species. In England in 1909 only 168 women were sentenced for larceny against 2,879 wers. 5 women were convicted of shop-breaking and 1,102 wers; and though the number of women servants is enormously larger than the number of male servants 1,365 wers were convicted of theft and only 284 women. As between girls and boys, 11 girls were tried in courts of summary jurisdiction and 293 boys—more than 26 boys to 1 girl. Even for begging 22,207 wers were brought up and only 1,225 women. And for cruelty to animals 3,057 wers were tried compared with 15 women.

For the year ending March 31st, 1922, there were 21 times as many males as femels in convict prisons. In no country in the world is the number of murders committed by women sufficient to constitute a menace to society.

Three
types of the
human
family

THERE are three types of the human family—the
matriarchal, the patriarchal, and the greek-roman
patriarchal in form but founded upon a monogamic union.
The prevailing type of the natural family is matriarchal,
which was certainly the original form of the human
family, since obviously it is the mother who reproduces
and maintains her species while the spectacle, always
before men, of a natural obedience given to the mother
and to no one else was the correlative of the natural
dependence upon her of progeny. This common phenomenon among mammalia was never observed between the
father and the young because he was—except in some
oviparous species—unable to do for them what was
necessary to life. Hence Montalembert rightly noticed
that the mother is the type of natural authority. When,
later on, children give obedience to the father it is given
in essentially the same way as to a nurse or any stranger,
the necessary obedience of the young to the authority of
the elder.

In the matriarchal family the incidence is on the relation of the mother with the children she creates.[1] The
patriarchal family, on the other hand, is artificial, its
method being both arbitrary and unnatural: here it is
neither maternity nor paternity which counts, but simple
male ascendancy, younger males succeeding to elder
males' rights. The salient feature of the patriarchal
system, therefore, is that parental rights are waived in
favour of those of the eldest male ascendant; a man owed
allegiance and obedience to his grandfather or great-
grandfather in the same way as his own father owed it.
The incidence of the patriarchal system is then simply
upon maleness, and as a system it is a primitive example

[1] See Matriarchy, pp. 206–7, and the male as father, p. 271.

of arbitrary or non-moral right; it creates a disciplinary system *à pro* of those who have seized the power. In the greek-roman type we have the first attempt at the legal family which depends neither on natural status, as matriarchy, nor upon customary power, as patriarchy, but upon a combination of this tyrannous power with legal right. In the greek type the incidence is on racial considerations. The male wishes to insure suitable descendants of his body and therefore enters the state of marriage.[1] In the roman type the incidence is on the *patria potestas*; the roman family system is a simple exposition of this father-right. The classical family was based upon marriage. In the matriarchal family there is no marriage or rather the marriage is of no importance. In patriarchy the case is the same, though with its conditions reversed, the mother is of no importance here and the male is of no importance there. In neither type therefore is marriage a central fact; motherhood is everything in the matriarchal family while male liberties are all-important in the patriarchal; the male for example never finds himself deprived of the power to contract as many concurrent unions as he may desire. With the advent of the classical family the case alters, for here the incidence upon racial considerations and upon property gives primary importance to the legal status of marriage, which is not however in any sense a safeguard either for the mother or for the children but only for the male and for property—it secures to males the control of all goods and chattels whether these be relatives, slaves, animals, houses or lands.

The family and marriage

I do not class the christian family as a fourth type because it follows strictly the greek or the roman pattern. The christian type appears to the European to possess per excellency divine and civilized sanctions. It consists in a strict legal monogamous union, the rule of

The christian family

[1] Marriage, p. 257 *n.*

the husband, and a common roof which shelters tne parents and the young of both sexes and later on the parents and unmarried femel adults. There are no incestuous unions. The family thus presents a lifelong hierarchy in which the mother exercises a subsidiary authority and male children take precedence of femel children. It will be seen at once that these characteristics while owing a great deal to the classical type and something to the jewish-patriarchal cannot be traced to the direct teaching of the gospel, Jesus never being represented as having by word or act assented to any of them with the exception of a strict monogamic relation. In the 'christian' system the male still rules by divine right but parental right supplants patriarchal. This is the type of the family sanctioned by Paul who is the real author of what is thought of as 'the divine institution of the family'. Our conception of the family is in fact based on the judeo-roman elements which we should expect from him: the roman *patria potestas* is combined with the jewish commandments concerning the honour due to parents—a lesser honour to the mother and a greater honour to the father; while a latent patriarchalism of sentiment pervades the various family relations. For Paul, the wer is "the head of the woman" and the monarchical ruler of mother and children (*patria potestas*); adult children owe patriarchal honour and obedience to their two parents (10 commandments) so that the parents now constitute a permanent hierarchical head, unmarried children remaining with them as lifelong minors. It was obviously not possible to adhere strictly to this system; the human species could not as a whole remain in perpetual tutelage in deference to the fact that it is born of parents; hence femel children, whose rights were already less under the greco-roman and jewish family systems, were rushed into the breach as the only actual upholders of the divine institution of the family. And as in the case

Paternalism replaces patriarchalism

Paul the author of the christian conception of the family

of the patriarchal and greco-roman types, so here also, Freedom of male liberties became quickly established as the real males nowhere so staple of the system; indeed these male liberties are great as in larger and wider under the pauline system than under the 'christian family' the patriarchal or the greek-roman, for in the european christian system young adult males are free of both parental and patriarchal control.

The one permanent universal and essential feature and condition of human family life is that sisters and brothers, who do indeed form the closest kinship in nature, not excluding even the maternal, live together in a sexless relation. Nevertheless this was obviously no part of the primitive design which the Hebrews assign to Jahveh, since the offspring of "the first" woman and wer must have intermarried. Although in the secondary myth of the formation of man 'Adam' regards the creation of Eve from his side as a pledge of monogamy, the actual poly- Monogamy gamy of the Jews and the frivolous ease with which male Jews divorced the wife[1] make it clear that this other condition of the 'institution of the family'—a sacred life-long union of one woman and one wer which the christian world teaches was ordained by the god of the Hebrews— has never yet been one of its essential features.[2] The direction which was given to the jewish tradition by the words ascribed to Jesus however (Gen. ii. 24 and Matt. xix. 5), took so firm a hold on the first generation

(margin notes: Essential feature of family life: brethren)

---

[1] Mishnah iii. 6.

[2] See Marriage, p. 259. The Jew was polygynous throughout his history, and the ordinance cited in the gospel is derived from an earlier matriarchal state of society. It is the gloss added by Jesus (Matt. v. 32 and xix. 9) which so startled the disciples, who said to him, If the case of the 'man' is so with his wife it is not good to marry? It is this clear unequivocal rule given by Jesus [which required: that the wife's house should be the 'domicile'—*ubi tu Caia, ego Caius*—the carnal fidelity of the husband (without which the monogamic "one flesh" is nonsense), and the denial of any right of a husband to dissolve the union which she does not also possess] that has been set aside in christian societies which have always preferred the patriarchal Paul to the matriarchal Jesus.

of christians that widowerhood and widowhood were preserved as inviolate as the marriage itself.[1] The unique and essential achievement of civilized family life then *ubique et ab omnibus* is the relation of sisters and brothers.

Three-fold basis of man's conception of the family There is of course in the case of human beings a moral as well as a natural basis for family life; the child remains for long years a moral fledgling. But there has been a third factor at work which is both artificial and tyrannical, and in this aspect the institution of the family was a stage in those systems of arbitrary right which have always demanded uncontrolled authority on the one side with unlimited subservience on the other. It has, that is, really existed for the advantage of a *tertium quid*, a third moral entity set apart from the ostensible terms of the relation— arbitrary male right. There have been epochs in human history when the male parent exercised the power of life and death over the child; when he could sell the children into slavery or the daughter into prostitution; marry them to whom he would and issue to them any arbitrary command that pleased him: until a few years back he could still neglect the bodies and souls of his children with no check from the laws, he could beat and maltreat them, cruelly overwork them, and keep all education and human opportunities from them. In recent christian epochs children served their parents hand and foot and knelt on cushions in their presence as a relief from standing.

What is the parent's claim in justice and nature? What claims can parents have to these and other rights and services? If nature be consulted it is evident that the family of human custom and authority runs clean counter to it—for in nature the young leave the nest or the burrow as soon as they can fend for themselves and no longer know it or are known of it: moreover the services rendered, the duties paid, are entirely and exclusively on the

---

[1] The bishop to be the husband of one wife and the woman elder to be the wife of one husband. And cf. Tertullian *Exhortatio ad castitatem*, and *Ad Uxorem*.

parents' side. The widely different system due to human custom and authority has been backed, as human custom and authority always have been backed, by theology. The theological ground is difficult to justify—your parents give you the precious boon of life and the rights of the father, whom patriarchal mythology represented as the bestower of the boon, are presumed in some recondite way to refer back to the divine paternity.[1] But this dual ground for the claims of fathers—human custom and authority supported by theology—is very far from approving itself. Life is very often no boon at all; and its gracelessness may be (and often is) greatly increased rather than diminished by the harsh and unjust action of parents. Parents perform a purely natural function in begetting children who come into the world without their own consent. They may be and constantly are nothing but the result of gratifying physical desire, this gratification and not the child being what is directly sought: neither is it right to suppose that in itself a desire to have children is noble or meritorious. Finally the fact of procreating is neither more nor less divine or laudable than the fact of being someone's child, and the only sacred part of parenthood is discovered in the good parents' consciously good acts towards the children after they are born; they may merit in regard to their children through those good kind and holy offices by which man merits of man.

The mother, it has been held, is good for the child even if she is a bad mother. The child thrives better with her than in the best conditions without her. The little life feels a sense of security and safety with the mother which it feels nowhere out of her presence and care. The maternal patience, the honied voice, the loving welcome well known sounds, the cosseting, the unfailing interest and the natural gift for individualizing the attentions she

The mother's relation to the child

[1] This again is a pauline conception.

307

prodigates—on these things the young of all species thrive; for the small creature suffers from nothing more acutely than its helplessness, nothing is so healing to its developing life as the warm tended sensation of safety. On the other hand the father's biological share in this little life has no ethical merit whatever, it is his subsequent good offices, to young or to adult children, which may be so great as to deserve a lifelong debt of gratitude.

How family life fails

These past bases of family life of course require to be brought to the touchstone of the growing moral sense of mankind. The moral grounds for family life are, it is obvious, open at all pores to control and revision. The protracted adolescence of the human young requires a continuance of family relations through difficult psychical periods, and the handling of these depends entirely on the virtue intelligence and capacity of the parents. As to the system of family life derived from the arbitrary demands of parents nothing less is wanted than its complete abolition. It serves no ethical end at all. A system which upholds the convenience and good pleasure of fathers through the exercise of tyrannous will over a mother and children has no beauty or fitness; the arbitrary family not only serves no ethical end but disserves the ethical requirements of the relation. It is this possibility of unlimited despotism which distinguishes the human family from every natural family. Of the purely human grounds for family life we may look upon the moral as the good human ground and the despotic as simply

Two purely human motives for family life—a good and an evil

evil. The good motive which makes men organize the family—the moral education of the child—is as we see always at the mercy of the personal character of parents, and the evil motive—parental despotism—undoes the proper ends of family life and blinds men of bad disposition to the paramount character of the childrens' natural and moral claims. The husband's tyranny over the wife with its consequence the supremacy of the male parent inhibits the natural role of the mother which is to moderate and gentilize. Nothing that could be said would exaggerate the harshness and selfishness of parental tyranny, which does not serve but flouts the ends of education; for if you must know how to obey if you would know how to rule subjection to tyranny makes a tyrant or a slave, not a ruler.

The position of the daughter in the human family is central; the theory of adult family life stands or falls with it. If the permanent subjection of children is due to a natural or to a divine law it applies to all children as children of the womb, not to daughters only. When it is perceived that none but femel children are required to submit to it, it is time to recognize that there is no duty at all. Daughters may have had no education, no occupation, their whole and sole career may have been the performance of small offices for the parents or the adornment of the domestic hearth, but to this they were as much chained as a serf. Their only exit was marriage; and while a bad and imprudent union with the meanest and most unworthy specimen of male kind cuts the gordian knot of daughterhood, not the finest claims that can be made upon human beings, not the noblest profession and career, have hitherto been held to justify a daughter's freedom or to supplant in importance the duty of fulfilling the pettiest whims of parents. Until the first three quarters of the xix[th] century this state of things was unquestioned. The change began with education in universities and the general movement for rights and liberties for the femel half of humanity. As one writes in the first quarter of the xx[th] century such a view of daughters' lives may almost be said to be already relegated to the *pagus*—where all customs and all mythologies end. But in the past, few sections of the human community can have suffered such curtailment of life and faculties as the daughter in the home. Under that unnatural regimen she has suffered an eclipse of all the rights of personality often resulting in nervous breakdown and even in loss of the starved mental powers. Her life has been as precious to her as the lives of the favoured members of the family, and as fleeting—she has watched the years roll past her, the opportunities go by, her talents and energies curbed and wasted, the originality shackled and despised. The parents have sat by the hearth pouring this adult human material into that family mould which it is their self-imposed task to create and maintain. The daughter must suffer the constant thwarting not only of personal desires but of her personal appreciations and convictions. And on the other side, nothing; no outlet, no worship, no large worthwhileness. Hundreds of thousands of daughters in every country after spending it may be even fifty and sixty years with the parents have been left unfit to cope with the world, crippled in health and means, friendless, solitary, and of no value to anyone. They have been used all their lives by others for self-regarding ends, and then thrown out upon the wretched dregs of life, with no pity, no respect. They are the burnt offering to the fetich of family life which has always spelled chiefly, and after adolescence exclusively, the subjection of daughters in the service of the home.　　　Who has not seen the haunting faces of women of dominant character fineness and power, who could have been this noble thing and done that great one; whose lives nevertheless have been passed in beating strong helpless wings against cage bars. That there are hundreds of thousands of happy homes and of daughters in them who would not change their state for all the gold of the Indies is of course no justification of such conditions. The mental abjection of many women in the home has been so great that, like slaves, they have never realized what they have missed in life, all they have been deprived of. It is as bad for the community as for the individual that such ignorant content should be

Family life is the subjection of daughters in the service of the home

fostered. There are of course the subaltern natures for whom nothing much better than a dependent life is possible; but while subaltern males receive all the aids that social conditions can give them subaltern women are simply thrust further down into the slough of despond. The life of the femel child has been held to be satisfied if she is the home drudge, or the drudge in some one else's home, their nurse, or the Cinderella for a sister's or brother's children. Yet with such a caste system in vogue among us we have allowed ourselves to be astonished at the indian child widow whose career was analogous to that of many of our daughters.

Between the iv^{th} and the xvi^{th} centuries every country *The con-* in Europe came to offer the example of a life for women *vent escape* based on their own choice, a choice which sanctioned the woman's spiritual freedom and her personal spiritual value—her soul, that is, and her right to some other destiny than that of marriage. This was the life of the convent. But so noble and spiritual an attempt to recognize her freedom failed because of the general low opinion held about women, who if they were not wanted, or if they did not marry or refused to make the marriage destined for them by parents, were forced into convents. Thus this outlet for her life became merely another means of exploiting her, and the immuring of scores of thousands of women against their will in every christian country did not differ in cruelty from the pre-christian exposure of femel babies.

The sufferings that children may endure at the hands of parents are no longer ignored. But family life tends to *Subtle dis-* perpetuate and accentuate group faults, and neither the *advantages of family* magnifying of a child's capacities nor the assumption that *life* it can possess no talent denied to those around it are a help to its proper development. The pregnant saying that no *"No man is* one is a prophet in his own country and among his own *a prophet in his own* people illustrates the second case—that contempt which *country"* is bred by familiarity in all inferior minds—and both cases prove that family life is weak in supplying the test and touchstone of merit which a man finds in the outside world. For the members of our family we never grow up, we never grow out of anything. Mill has noted somewhere that families are content that there should be six or seven little Y's all to the pattern of the parent Y's— an increase merely in quantity but not in quality, of numbers not capacities. And a false idea of worth and of right is easily produced by family life. It is inevitable and.it is even highly useful that the child should think its parents always right and suppose while it is growing up that they are excellent and infallible, but it is not inevitable or useful, it is simply monstrous, that parents should think themselves so, and a very real loss to truth of outlook that adult children should continue to think them so. Infallible right, of course, cannot belong to every family group; all institutions, school, and university, tend to produce such mock standards, in which human subalternism finds an excellent substitute for the business of seeking right ones; but no institution rivals the adult family in its power of imposing false criteria. Much has been said of the beauty and value of family affection, but not enough has been said of family fear, and adult family life, perpetuating the child life, provides a natural leverage for fear which buffets the strong as well as the weak and yielding.

The tie between the adult members of a family depends ultimately upon economic relations. That is its inherent weakness. However tyrannous the parents with £300 a year might be, absolute liberty would be accorded to and taken by the daughter with £5,000. It may be said that extraordinary circumstances do not abolish the rules good for all normal conditions; but circumstances do not alter cases which are really based upon natural and 'divine' laws. In such cases the difference between 5,000

The
economic
founda-
tions of
'family
life'

pounds and 300 would be altogether negligible. It is certain that a sum equal to five hundred a year, or the power of making it, would free the daughter no less than the son, and that ninety-nine out of every hundred daughters would at once cease to be sacrificed to the convenience of parents. Up to now the property of women has never been safe, that is why the lien on their services has never been otherwise.[1]

Morality requires us in the first place to recognize that the duties of parents to children are both more definite and more important than any duties of children to parents. There is only one obvious duty and it is that of the parent to the child. The first reform in the exercise of parental authority therefore would be that all exploitation of the child at the will or for the sake of the parent should be completely done away. The principle "Cannot a man whack his own nigger?" has held the field long enough, and wreaked itself on the best elements in the commonwealth of life as well as on the most dependent. There should be no exaction for personal convenience at the cost of some real good for a child, a small additional happiness for you should not be put in the balance with substantial advantage for him. I do not mean that services should be measured, still less commercialized; that the child or the parent should say: This would be a great

(marginal note: How the family should be amended and constituted)

[1] In the Old Testament it deserved record that Achsah asked for her portion and got it (Joshua xv. 18); in the Hindu law the horrid rites of suttee were the Brahminic expedient for appropriating the property of which a widow was tenant for life; in the iv[th] century Augustine of Hippo denounced as essentially iniquitous the law (the *lex voconiana*) which restricted the amount of property heritable by a woman. Yet after 1300 years the women of the french revolution had to ask (and in vain) that they "should not be so often deprived of their property". What the wer gives he can, like the Lord, take away, and he usually has taken it away. Why should the supreme sanctity of 'family feeling' be held up for our reverence even where its tendency is to injure the lives of children, when this sacred feeling has not proved strong enough to impress itself on the property laws devised by fathers of families?

pleasure for me and that is not so big a one for you and therefore my wish shall prevail. And I do not mean that sacrifice should not be offered and also accepted. But sacrifice should cease to connote constant loss to an unselfish—or an involuntary—giver on one side with parallel gains to a selfish recipient on the other, whose selfishness is upheld by law.   In the second place no obedience should be exacted from adult children. When maturity is reached the parents' writ, as it were, should cease to run; there should be no authoritative power to override their desires. The influence normally wielded by parents will always be sufficient and more than sufficient; where it is now insufficient it is obvious that legal and religious authorization have failed to make it otherwise. The source of the power of parents and the binding affection of children is to be found, of course, in intellective-emotional relations during the most impressionable period and continued over long years; resulting, in the case of the human family alone, in rela-

The claim tions which are lifelong. Lifelong claims and lifelong
of affection responsibility and lifelong services may result from family affection, but this is altogether different from claims and rights based upon the blood tie or the moral law. Everywhere and always the affections have supreme rights and inherent responsibilities; and these affections are created and maintained in family life just as elsewhere, perhaps more than elsewhere owing to the fact of constant proximity. On the other hand this proximity and the likeness in unlikeness of members of a family may and do have a contrary result. But the self-evident fact about family life is that that absolute sanction which exists in the case of the adolescent family fails as absolutely when it is transferred to the adult family: the kid is weaned, the birds leave the nest; there is no guarantee divine or human for the wise control by parents of adult sons and daughters. Since the family exists primarily for the

children and not the children for the family parents are rewarded for their labours by the natural intercourse between young and elders during adolescence; and the affection and occasional companionship of adult children should be regarded by parents as their perfectly sufficient recompense. If they were not it would not matter, for the natural rights of parents are themselves nothing but rights of service. And no one is obliged to have children.

Parents have no right to sacrifice children to their interests, nor have children come to years of discretion any claim to the sacrifice of parents. But there is the return of love and sacrifice due from children to parents in need—the *honorare* of the commandment—which is The *honorare* an obligation of the same kind as that owed to any one who performed those offices for us: honour your friend's deeds towards you, that is easy; but remember to honour the home you have left, the service of long years ago, the love, the vigils, the sacrifices—*honora matrem et patrem.* Not that that commandment was the most obviously moral; if both.can forget their duty it was far more important that the parent should not forget hers than that the child should not forget. "Can a woman forget the child of her womb?" so constant is her fidelity that the fidelity of god is proposed as its parallel. The obligation is on the child then, who can forget, to 'honour' that singular faithfulness and expenditure of love. But the love, the gifts, the anguish of maternal care are, like childbirth itself, first nature to the mother. She can hardly pretermit them; she does not perform them expecting a correlative pain and devotion, which indeed would in nowise be natural. She is recompensed by their performance, by their necessity which is her necessity. Nevertheless wherever fine things operate there can be no oblivion of what parents have done, what you in your turn will come to do and understand. But I would make

the commandment 'honour the good parent' for the un-
qualified commandment is void of moral meaning.

The patriarchal family in modern times is largely a
class relationship: where the child earns its own bread its
alleged theological duties have not the same force. If the
adult child ought to make its choices in complete freedom
—just as much freedom as though it were orphaned—
then it must not be the duty of parents to hoard for it.
The provision made for children is motived by affection,
expectation, and thirdly by dependence of some sort, such
as accrues from the deference of your own plans and
wishes to the wishes and plans of parents: parents, however, who have 'invested capital' in the child owe it no
further provision; and such an investment of capital in
a child, even at personal cost and self-denial, is a more
natural and more moral thing than requiring that young
children should work for their parents and be themselves
regarded as 'capital'. Nevertheless it is well known that
the children of the poor are often welcomed on this
ground, and they are put to earn as soon as they can be
made use of with no further consideration. In many cases
parents who have not even desired your existence or have
desired it for unworthy reasons and used you at their
own caprice and for their own pride—much that is done
for children and spent upon them ministers in the first
instance to parents' self-esteem—grip the purse till the
gods strike it from their hands. Their decease is the
desired release for the children who, while the parents
live, can enjoy no sort of natural liberty. It must in fact
be realized that the money which is left to elderly children
is a poor gift, and that it is a morally squalid thing to
leave what you can no longer use, after enjoying through
life the liberty it procured, to those whose life has been
spent, at your good pleasure, in waiting upon you for
it. There are only two kin relationships in which
a definite responsibility is incurred, that of parent to child

and that of husband and wife reciprocally—and between these alone, which I call responsible kinship in the first degree, should intestacy inheritance be legal. While states recognize a power of legacy it should not be competent to parents to will everything away from a child, nor for one parent to leave the whole inheritance absolutely to the other, however young the children may be; and the estate of married people with children should be made to resemble feudal estates, the property of both and inalienable without the consent of the other.[1]   There should be no expectation of inheritance between brethren. *Status of brethren* And it is not legitimate that nephews and nieces should look to aunts and uncles for money, still less that they should inherit by legal right from cousins. It is outrageous that brethren should be expected to dwell together, and that criticism should even pursue a woman who maintains a sister but does not wish to share her home with her. If a wer supports his brother but does not take him into his house he receives praise and no criticism. The difference is that the wer's freedom of choice is recognized. And this signalizes a secular injustice in human history. Why should a woman's life be made wretched and why should her powers of choice be crippled? A woman requires not less liberty of choice than a wer but more, even though she demands less liberty of movement.

We are apparently increasing human longevity; *The aged parent* parents who live to be eighty or ninety mean children whose years amount to 60 and 70; and there seems to be a natural rule that young parents give a finer chance to their children,[2] so that when early marriages are contracted parents' lives will nearly cover the span of life of their

---

[1] But divorce should separate estates.

[2] Our potential powers, mental and physical, not the powers we have exercized and the greatness we have achieved, being what is actually transmitted.

children, and will completely cover all the years of
vigorous health and mental maturity. In their turn—at
60 or 70—those whom the aged call 'children' will need
the assistance that the middle years demand. It cannot
be a natural thing that all that should then be open to
them is to take up the burden of the still older life. When
the 'children' of threescore years have themselves children
how do the duties lie, or is it possible that no scheme but
the patriarchal responds to the ethical necessities?

Does the second period of human helplessness call for
the same sacrifices as the first? If so, then the title to
these sacrifices is neither merit nor relationship but age,
and an old person who has children is no more intitled to
them than the old person who has none. The relationship of parent and child ought not indeed to be intruded
in the claims of old age; and we should remember that
while the care asked of children is frequently equivalent
to the sacrifice of life, the care that parents give to children
can seldom be so. The habitual way of looking at this
question has been to regard the natural services given
by human parents to their young as repayable by the
services of adult moral beings, conscious of what has been
done for them and acting on the spiritual principle that
makes sacrifice a religious debt and therefore not unnatural in the highest sense and not, in man's case, a
reversal of the natural sequences. On such reasoning as
this the child is more or less bound to care for and sacrifice
himself to the parent. Nevertheless this parcelling out
to adult children of the role of caretakers towards their
parents is neither natural nor ethical. If the sacrifice is
to be claimed *qua* parent then the worst parent can exact
it equally with the best. If daughters' lives may properly
be sacrificed then sons' also; then the parent has a lien
on the married child equally with the unmarried, and on
the adult who is doing the most important work in the
world equally with the do-nothing son he is maintaining

in the expectation of succeeding to his fortune. But it is an obvious fact that no parent can insure that his progeny shall remain with him, since their marriage or business may leave the parents alone. We cry out at the impiety of an adult child not devoting his life to his parents; but if the child had married we should say nothing. We pretend to think it right to sacrifice any child to any parent, but should we consent to the world's work being habitually postponed to the claims of old age? Is it then to be not the minister of state or the man of science, the magistrate or the artist who has made his reputation, but only the unmarried daughter, or perhaps the unmarried son, to whom all choice and freedom in life are denied? No moral or religious scheme of life could stand erect on such foundations. But let it be looked at from the side of the parent. Would a good and intelligent parent be content to think that her or his life must necessarily monopolize the life of a child. That for the child there would be no choice, no liberty, no duty, no call, but the parents' need. It is certain that the unworthy parent accepts the sacrifice with most assurance; that it is the nobler parent who realizes the power the old have of penalizing the lives of the generation in possession.

One remedy consists in simplifying life as we grow old. Solutions The Hindu ideal divides our life into three stages, the of the problem first two are growth and work and the third is retirement and contemplation. An obvious justification for the simplifying of life which this third stage implies is that the necessity for pomp and 'appearances' which are proper to office, to the days of vigour large stipends and representative or public life, can properly be eliminated from age; so that age and a simpler life should accord together. But if age requires less state it requires more comfort. Unlike infancy there is a moral and psychical need as well as a physical to satisfy; the habits—complicated mental demands as well as material—begotten of long mental activity, of choice and individual exigency, cannot be set aside without uncalled for sacrifice and suffering which may easily amount to cruelty. It should be possible to have greater social simplicity with the addition of luxuries that men in full work have not time and should not make time to indulge, as well as to spare the old the fatigues and rubs of the active life. Young life and aged life need much the same things—greater consideration than middle life and less 'show'. When we are old, when perhaps we toil not neither spin, what is expended on social ceremony should be less and what is spared of life's wear and tear should be greater. The state kept up by old people, its costly panoply, is, like their hold on the purse, a morally squalid thing.   In the Hindu system, however, it is reckoned that a man's working years are between the ages of 25 and 50; but in Europe 40 to 65 are the years most prolific of the higher forms of work. We are approaching a period when 'age' will barely count before threescore years and fifteen, and much of the higher work of the world has always been carried on by those of an age not to toil but to judge —that is the origin of gerarchies. Governors, administrators, commanders, and magistrates, throughout the world's history, have done their work between the ages of 45 and 75, and it has been the same with the great works of philosophers. The exceptions prove the rule. Had men retired at 50, Caesar would never have been dictator or Cromwell protector, nor would Trajan have consummated his noble reign. We should not have had the *Divina commedia* or *Faust*, some of the greatest work of Buonarotti or the finest of Titian. To the second half of life we owe the chief writings of Aristotle, the theory of Copernicus, the *Novum Organum* of Bacon, *L'Esprit des lois* of Montesquieu, the *Philosophie Zoologique* of Lamarck, and the Critics of Kant; and Victor Hugo (like Sophokles) produced masterpieces at four score years.

Hence as most of the world's thinking and nearly all its magistracy has been done in this second half of life—for neither the knowledge which comes to us from experience nor the wisdom which gives us judgment belong to the first half—the problem of later life does not alone concern the helplessness of old age but the relief required in later middle life for the higher forms of labour. The claims of late middle age are as exigent whether you be a 'child' or a parent, and the needs of extreme and helpless old age are as prominent whether you have had children or not. 'Children' therefore are not the natural or sociological provision for age. When notions of arbitrary power on one side and superstitious subjection on the other cease to influence in human affairs as they have done hitherto, it will not appear unreasonable that those who have exercized all the freedoms and choices to late middle age should be called upon for some sacrifice in order to free those who will otherwise miss these dues of life. It is more natural that parents of 60 or 70 should enjoy such happiness as watching the careers of their children than that they should share their lives; and when social custom has ceased to require that adult daughters should form the permanent society of parents, choice and affection will determine their living together as in the case of sons. If here, as elsewhere, strength or weakness of character will still prove the actual determinants then, at least, the absence of a compelling custom will lend countenance to weakness. Up to now what custom in England has required of the son and of the daughter represents very closely what nature requires and what nature repudiates. That marriage alone can free a child is simply a thesis of barbarism.

And as there can be no justification in nature, in reason, or in the natural sympathies, for treating the child as though it existed either physically or mentally for the service of those who begot it, so also parents who are doing the world's work cannot owe the sacrifice of their life and activities to adult progeny. It has never been believed that distinguished men owed such a duty, and when parents propose to themselves that their choices and activities should be limited by the alleged needs of their mature children it is evidence not of any call of nature but of the mediocrity of the parent. Not virtue but waste allows a mother to sacrifice herself to the exigencies of a worthless son for whom every provision has already been made. Per contra, young folk do not appreciate the parents' wish to live on their children's lives: the natural thing is for people with adult children to resume an independent life, and when they do so they can contribute far more to the younger life. It is not natural that adults should bound their interests by those of an adult child. Underlying these customs is the supposition that the family is the centripetal point towards which normal human obligation duty and moral activity converge; that it forms the moral 'unit' as well as the social.[1] All real religions, however, from Buddha's to Christ's and to catholicism have taught that divine vocation had higher claims upon us; and this is an admission which, like the distinction of kinds of happiness in utilitarianism, undermines the entire structure. Owing to theological and legal doctrine parents and the aged have on the whole been better cared for than children and the young; and the reverse should have been the case. And the reason why the predicament of the immature matters more than that of the old is not because population is important nor because they are themselves more valuable than the mature—they are less valuable—but simply because what is done for them when young may alter the whole course of their life and relations with other men; whereas with the old neglect and unskilfulness cannot have these consequences. There are tribes

[1] See *infra*, p. 326.

which kill their old people, and we look upon this as a great savagery: but there are european peoples who grudge every *sou* of the savings of toil spent on the aged, and where the parents eat their bread in bitterness and reproach; is the one more evil or more ugly than the other? Where there is no affection it cannot be galvanized into existence, and if such claims upon us are not met with a certain spontaneous sentiment the soup must be seasoned with gall; for it is sympathy not the sense of duty which renders services palatable. Neither can laws better such conditions. Imaginative sympathy or something of a nobler disinterestedness and self-control will alone procure that the general treatment of the unloved aged should be *douce*, and of the unamiable not harsh. The physically strong often despise the weak; yet they were themselves once very weak and should remember they were totally in the hands of the one who performed a mother's service towards them, as wers when they are old are helplessly in the hands and at the mercy of the mother element in human society.

There is a general human advance to differentiation of capacities and to individual choice of moral environment which must dissolve 'the family' as an adult institution, and will enlarge, we hope, not lessen, the field of human compassion.

The clan system[1] is essentially as barbarous as the patriarchal; neither presupposes any great diversity of needs or capacities, any real choice of surroundings, and moral environment. With advancing differentiation and

The 'blood-tie' and the clan system

---

[1] In the tribal family there is a great extension of the theory of blood kinship which in the patriarchal family only includes the descendants of one male ascendant. This consciousness of kinship to the third and fourth generation persisted in Europe among the Scots and Irish but not elsewhere: such clan agglomerations as appear in a latin 'participation' of a death stand alone; apart from these occasions the latin family is a close corporation with no real intimacy or mutual dependence between kin; among the illiterate and the small bourgeois 'the family' consists simply of the parents and children.

civilization both systems have deceased in Europe, leaving the later family as sole survivor and representative of a control exercized over adults by a hierarchy of kin. These systems in the past had not the same origin as

Ancestor worship and 'blood' kindred

ancestor worship, but they and it alike are products of a similar barbaric state of feeling. The notion of some mystic tie between persons who are popularly described as of 'the same blood' is probably a false one. In the kin

Unlikeness between close relatives

systems of the past there has been a complete failure to recognize that nowhere is such diversity to be found as between persons of the closest kin—sisters and brothers. This natural fact illustrates the power to 'breed true' to one part of the common heredity-material to the exclusion of other parts. The diversity thus produced between people of 'the same blood' is usually not the diversity which attracts but that which repels; and the incidental likeness of bearing, figure, voice, or appearance, and of failings which in yourself are just round the corner, banish sympathy instead of provoking it. Friendships among kin, then, are generally born of resemblance and differ in this from the normal alliances of friends and lovers outside the 'blood tie': for dissimilarity in the family does not breed sympathy—where A differs from B he has no gift for him. If the blood tie were indeed a real thing, the tie between brother and brother, brother and sister, and sister and sister, would be nearly constant instead of being—at any rate as to the first two pairs—a rare theme of poets; and the very condition of such attachments—that they imply a choice between persons equally closely related—suggests that their affinity is with friendship rather than with blood relationship. Between sister and brother (moreover) it is often not the blood tie which may decide the relation but the marked difference of opportunities and experience.[1] For it is

---

[1] They are in fact, like avuncular affection on women's part, examples of femel affectionateness, not of blood-tie intimacy.

obvious throughout history that brothers have not only exploited but shamelessly defrauded sisters; and though it is not at all uncommon for sisters to support brothers and pay their debts, it is rare for a brother to support a sister. When have we heard through the whole history of humanity of brothers protesting against the iniquitous conditions of life of these nearest of all kin, close by the memories of childhood and one in inheritance from the same womb? There have been no such protests, except from the rare individuals whose actions exemplify no law.

If blood kinship were a real tie then it would be commonly felt between cousins-german, whose blood relationship is almost as close as the blood relationship of parent and child. Aunts and uncles are, like your parents, of the half blood (as brethren are of the whole blood) but these relationships have not played a large part in human intimacy. Our aunts and uncles may be the joy or terror of our childhood; and as to cousins they can become among the best of relations: like our own brothers and sisters and the sisters and brothers of our parents they may be very like us or very unlike, but they afford, what the relation between brethren does not necessarily afford, a delightful relationship if it is desired with no inforced tie when it is undesired. They afford, then, what probably lies at the root of the privileges of kinship, a basis for approach and a common meeting ground, a relation which can be closer than our social ties and not as close as our ties with our chosen friends—at choice. A cousin can be much to us, or nothing—no effort is required to annex him, no introduction to him is necessary, only the qualities always demanded of us in other equal relationships, just that which it is often so hard to give to our brethren. *Cousins*

The fact has always deserved though it has not received notice that where the family life of adults is closest there crime is rifest. Crimes against the person in Italy are *The latin family* disproportionately crimes of violence between brethren and of sons to parents, and murders among the closest kindred easily spring from quarrels over a few halfpence. This is an old story in all close family corporations; blood-tie fidelity plays no part in Old Testament history which begins, like classical history, with a fratricide and is largely concerned with family hatreds and the clash of their interests.

The family as 'unit'   The laws of Europe suppose that the 'family' consisting of father mother and children constitutes the social unit: the relations of men to society and to the state are thus envisaged as group relations, the parents are regarded not only as women and wers but as mothers and fathers, and the actions of the children are supposed to include the parents. This notion of group action serves no useful purpose; and the only proper significance of the family-unit is that the training of children by their parents is in fact the best usual scheme. But by custom children are largely trained in residential schools and colleges, and it is therefore not the mental nor even the moral development of young people which the family unit actually stands for, but the relation of parents and young up to 10 or 12 years. Parents, equally with children, pass naturally out of the group unit when their function is accomplished; from a social point of view they do not in fact remain parents, neither can children remain children: the notion of them as a 'crown' to their parents is both selfish and unnatural. The primitive social unit was not the family but the tribe.[1] As we see, the family we now believe in is no longer the tribal or even the patriarchal, but is a family consisting of parents and children. And when this blood-tie fetich, in its turn, points out the brother or sister as the proper object of affection, and custom and proximity make these the easiest choices, we are kept from those which would be more congenial and more spiritually helpful.

[1] Nicolai, *Biology of War*, § 11.

326

Nothing is so infrequent as the transmission of great *The parent and heredity* powers or of genius from father to son. There is nothing a man can count upon less—be he mother or father— than to be represented by his child; spiritual procreation does not consist with physical. One way in which child- less people could help society and procure for themselves joys perhaps not less great than those of parenthood is by *Adoption* the practice of adopting children. Some of the greatest of mankind have known none but adoptive parents, and part of the glory of Aristotle and all the glory attaching to a Marcus Aurelius and a Trajan is due to this practice.

IX. MONEY AND PROPERTY

BARTER and exchange, the creation of material wealth,
and the pursuit of wealth for its own sake, have
characterized human existence since the barbarian
emerged from the savage. They have become the principal exports of european countries, far more obvious than
their exports of christianity and morals. For the root
motives of imperial ambition and colonial enterprise are
the expansion of commerce, the opening of new markets
and of fresh fields for "earning a living", and the search
for fresh profits, and it is these interests which now underlie diplomacy and war. Hence, in Europe at least, the
foundation of civilization is commercial and the staple
value money. But no real civilization is in the least compatible with such a foundation and such values. They are
a constant menace and hindrance to the temper of mind
which civilization really requires. The place taken by
this production of wealth, by the multiplying of goods,
the manufacture of things with no other end than to
create a need for them, and the magnifying of all this side
of human activity, has eaten into the civilization of the
United States and of most of the countries of Europe.
It is to be laid at the door of modern Europe—the
Europe which displaced the ages of discomfort and
popular ignorance, a political and religious system which
was international, and manual as distinguished from
mechanical industry—that it has raised the material
creations and the material rivalries of life to the position
of first importance. It has established nothing less than
civilization on an economic basis where life is paramountly a financial concern. There are races of the
asiatic continent which have never lost, as some sweet and
grave spots of Europe have never lost, the certainty that
life cannot be expressed in terms of commerce; but their

effect on the world is a minimum, and the self-confident impact of what is grosser vulgar and soulless in european civilization everywhere overrides and overwhelms the tenderer spirit, leaving its secret where they had failed to find it.

And the secret which retires at the touch of these gross things is life; the hours spent for their own sake and the spirit's sake, the accumulation of spiritual treasure, work because the work is good and integrates this spirit, not work which does nothing to ennoble in the doing and has done nothing but amass wealth at the end. To live just to accumulate spending power is degradation of life; and if the supreme prize of life is the ascertainment of ideal values then money is as great an obstacle to its attainment as brute force. The fine susceptibilities and awarenesses of the civilized mind require a certain definite simplicity; pomp, I think, and luxury also should be the appanage of the *respublica*, never of the private person.[1] Such a reform of our manners would be one of the clearest ways of reaching a real human equality without touching the inherent inequalities: whereas our present system not only conserves unreal inequalities but creates them. The hereditary fool in the seat of magistracy is on the whole less of a moral anomaly than the setting in a place of worship those who may owe their fortunes to ugly market frauds but whose pomp luxury and circumstance will only be bounded by their ability to pay for them. We are told that the incitement to the production of wealth and to individual effort would cease to exist if such prizes could not be secured; but what we want to know is whether the advantages of immense wealth are compatible with the higher forms of civilization. The appreciation of fine and beautiful things has nothing to do with increase of wealth, and we know that a cultivated society is not the same as that which welcomes luxury. Obviously, too, it

[1] Cf. Political Government, p. 375.

is not only on the one hand the display of wealth which is injurious it is on the other the sordid necessities of an economic civilization. In a civilization where "it is a crime to be poor" (as the Frenchman said of England) a large part of the best material is forced into conditions of anxiety and sordid distress. The theory is that amongst this best material there can be no temptation to get money by illegitimate means: our practice is to visit with legal penalties the dishonesties of the poor, with social ostracism any suspicion of the same thing among the educated, and to condone everywhere the profiteering of the rich. But we do not really believe that the outrageous inequalities of fortune are no temptation to educated people; we give our judges—if we wish them to turn a deaf ear to bribes—not only large salaries but large pensions; yet it is far less iniquitous for the poor person in anxiety to get some money illegitimately than for a man placed in the seat of judgment by his fellows and paid by them to do justice, to sell it. There are of course acts which a large number of men never do whatever the circumstances, for character is stronger than every circumstance; and there are completely disinterested people incapable at any time of feeling them. But this does not detract from the important fact that the sordidness of an economic civilization is a drain both upon life and upon character.

Money and tyranny   Money is used like other forms of power for tyrannous ends, and in aid of false moral sentiment and a false estimate of family and other duties. Our trading instincts are introduced everywhere until every relation of life appears to be subject to pecuniary sanction. In the age of Sokrates a man took his friend's purse as well as his own to help him to acquire knowledge, that he might be under a noted sophist, or take lessons from Phidias. In Friends and money the economic age you take a man's love, his heart's blood, ask him to share your anguish, strain all the fibres of his being: he may pass tormented nights for you,

330

nurse you in illness, be your moral bulwark with the world, but both you and he think it another matter that he should *pay money* for you. You must not owe to him what is purchased with coin, what represents his material goods. And this monstrosity, this stupid vulgarism, existed in a society where 'ladies' were expected to permit any chance male escort to pay for them as a matter of course. In a world where services, introductions, marriages, 'honours', are bought and sold we pretend that money must not be "accepted" at the hands of friends and lovers. But it was because the Greek took so much of moral value from his friend that he felt free to "drain his purse". They understood that when you have accepted moral gifts money gifts should have no separate value to your friend or to you. For money as a possession has not an independent value to which a different code is attached. Obviously a friend should use his lesser riches to procure your greater riches. We know our friend's circumstances, his needs, and we put ourselves to grave inconvenience to place him in a position "to earn his own living", "to keep himself", when a little of our spare money would enable him to do the work he is best fitted to do. *Why* do we think and feel like this? What does it mean? His 'pride' is not spared for it would be ignoble on my friend's part to feel himself freer if I have been put to great pains than if I had used my surplus coin to help him to do what was worth while, and above all what secures his moral liberty: an editor forbids a man who writes for young people to say what he knows to be true of life and true of morals, he "earns his living" regularly and regularly stultifies his power of setting forth what is good. Am I then to love my friend's soul yet be content to watch this mortification, this slow dying of the best he had to give—this abjection. Or what right has a man in such a position to ask respect for his calling?[1]

[1] We are repeatedly told that those who are free can act according to their

331

There is something mean in the mentality which would take a dead friend's money but not the living friend's; while not one person in a hundred thousand would refuse the money left him by a stranger, or the money paid into his bank by an unknown hand. Why we think such things is because we are dependent on the tradesman's opinion that money should not pass where there is no *quid pro quo*, and of his particular quiddity.

There is then no reason why we should think honourable what the Greek would have thought shameful; there is no sense in which coin should be regarded as the more inviolable part of our riches and the least communicable. These notions depend on the importance given to the tradesman view of life which gives such great prominence to money and justifies our vulgar respect for it. We ought to be sure that the true dishonour attaches when a friend, poor or rich, permits the consideration of money to decide anything between them. Two 'friends' set up house together and the poorer insists that the standard of comfort shall be that of the slenderer purse and that the richer 'friend' must therefore go without everything that the other cannot afford. There is no legitimate self-respect here, no 'dignified pride', and it is not friendship. Two old friends cannot meet because one of them cannot afford the journey: how shameful! Homage in these cases is done to nothing but the tradesman's outlook upon values, that ignoble development of an economic civilization which as we have said makes it shameful to use a man's purse and honourable to risk his dearer interests. The 'friend' in the first instance is required to sacrifice himself in order that the other may say: "We pay half and half." 'Junius' somewhere observes that "the first

convictions: What nobler use of money on one side or taking on the other than the money given to the priest threatened with excommunication for telling the truth or the man unable to do justice without exposing his family to want?

foundation of friendship is not the power of conferring benefits but the equality with which they are received and may be returned".

Why is it then supposed that the giving and taking of money will end in loss of mutual confidence and of self-respect? No such consequences follow between men capable of friendship. Money quarrels among kinsmen are of common occurrence, yet it is assumed that we may always take a kinsman's money and that this is never derogatory whatever sort of person he may be. All this line of argument is false; for proper taking and proper giving does not depend on kinship or status or fortune but on the spiritual relations between men. Indeed the only acceptable gifts should be those of friends and lovers, which include the lovers of ideas as well as the lovers of men.

But an industrial age has tried to make us believe that 'earning one's own living' is a bulwark of spiritual independence. It has even been argued that other animals in a dependent condition afford proof of this, that there is a difference between the animal who seeks his own food and the one who is fed by us. This is completely untrue— no one thinks of the cat as either tame or obliging, neither does a caged lioness become so. Parasitism is a quality of character and is entirely independent of economics. If the fact that he waited upon others for his food rendered a man dependent in spirit then the larger number of human beings has incurred this consequence. Most human beings since the age of savagery have lived in a state of parasitism. Very few people indeed since that time have hunted or grown their own food; and "independence" in this particular has therefore meant the exchange of counters for food, these counters having represented not only the purchaser's actual labour but also inherited wealth. Why should the passing of a counter secure the independence which would be enjoyed by actually procuring your

Earning one's own 'living' and independence

333

own food, as does the wild animal or the wild man? Why should a wer be "independent" who hands over a coin for his food, and the woman "dependent" who makes it edible?

Parasitism Parisitism then is a moral phenomenon not an economic. The son of a great house may be a born parasite, the wife in a harêm free of all taint of it. The parasite is the man who gives nothing back to man, and who is willing to squander moral freedom for material goods—Xenophon represents Sokrates as affirming that no slavery can be more disgraceful than this. No great man cares for money for its own sake nor has he 'a price'. But nothing is more completely certain than that the greatest works of the world would never have been done if those who did them had been earning their own 'living'. The spiritual teachers, the artists, reformers, seers—all the elect of the earth, Jesus and Buddha first—lived upon what an industrial age contemptuously calls 'charity', which in these instances can only mean that those who had material goods gave them to him who could bestow on his fellow men the true riches. The prophet is fed by a raven—that is the symbol of his material life. And the artist has been one with the prophet, he has depended upon patronage in material things—the lovers of ideas and of beauty have been his lovers and have made the achievements of his genius possible. From Confucius and Muhammad to Vives and Erasmus the tale is the same, for the greater the originality and the fineness of the message the less chance that it can be delivered if you must work for a livlihood. The great friars, of course, Aquinas and Catherine, Bacon and Scotus, were free of this necessity, but there is nothing so noble to be placed to the account of Can Grande as that he supplied the needs of Dante.

The right place for money is where it is wanted not where it is.

What kind of property is money? It is the kind of
property which may represent a gift like the gift of heart's
blood or it may be such that only by an effort can we
realize that it represents a personal gift at all. A man
who has amassed twenty million sterling 'giving' a
thousand to enable a scholar to publish his work; a man
with a thousand a year 'giving' twenty shillings to save
a Goethe from starving. What gifts are these? What
sort of right has the man to his twenty million that the
student has not to his studies? One man has a million
pounds and it is 'wrong' of the starving man to take a
shilling of it; the utmost you will concede is that he has
a right to take it to save his life. But why only to save
his life? There are moral and spiritual ends superior to
this one. The only answer given by our moralists and
theologians is that the moral law is one, that theft is
theft if it be only of a copper and that the wrong is done
whether the defrauded be rich or poor. But the moral
law is *not* one, it is the fault of the moral teachers that they
have neglected to point out the difference: the moral law
is not one while one man is permitted to starve and
another to possess abounding wealth. I will aver that if
any man with a serious need takes a hundred pounds from
another's million no moral law whatever is thereby
offended (except only if the taking be a breach of trust):
the law which is offended is a social one based on the
system of economics which protects the millions a man
may accumulate without any regard to the fact that other
men are starving or are unable to obtain knowledge or
health. Such a social system is at no point in contact
with ethics, and the shame felt by those who sin against
it is, like other forms of shame, a social not an ethical
phenomenon, it is no evidence of wickedness. The commission of these acts would not make the world a whit
the worse, they would, I think, by their implications,
make it the better. No moral purpose is served by

subsuming all classes of 'theft' under a single moral law. It is in this social system that we inflict great penalties on poor people who rob the rich and shake hands with rich people who have robbed the poor.

Its 'rights'   What is meant by inviolable rights of property? Are these simply the result of a legal convention, or is true property that which is earned by your own work, or is it what you have *got* no matter how? If a man hires you and you give him the work and he withholds the pay and you take what is owed you: if a large fortune has been acquired by stock exchange speculation or by peculation and a girl to clothe a baby or a boy to buy mechanical tools takes a pound or five pounds of it—In what sense are these acts immoral or evil or unjust? If they are wicked, why are they wicked? Is the sanction the universal sacredness of property? But property has and can have no such sanction. Perhaps however such acts mean dishonour? How they touch honour—unless playing the social game whatever the social game may be spells honour—is no more obvious than how they encroach on morality.[1]   Those views of life are materialistic, they weigh life itself in the scale

and vital   with material goods—life on one side, 'goods' on the
interests   other. As soon as the war of 1914–18 was over, property interests would procure you facilities for going abroad which mere affectional or ideal interests could not have obtained. The safety of a dear dog must not depend on its need or on your affection, you must say it is 'valuable'; if it is your baby it had better be heir to an estate: this constant coupling of the value of a thing with what it would 'fetch', which then commands protection and privileged treatment, stamps the social system that would be ready to throw 'civilized' nations into hideous war to procure some material utility.   Is property

---

[1] The legal dictum: "possession is nine-tenths of the law" is illuminating. Not justice, or right, or morality, but what has been grabbed and what can be held.

336

the best guarantee of social liberty? I think that property, which is one of the major instincts of organic life, is a bulwark of the individual's liberty; but our present system does not secure the ends of liberty because all gross disproportion in the allotment of wealth procures licence for one and to another a ban on his freedom. and social liberty

Is money or its equivalent the proper sanction for the performance of service? What is to guarantee a professional man devoting himself to your interest. I pay a physician or a lawyer and then I consider him bound to give me his time and talents. On my part the money I give may only mean my going without another thing in order to obtain this thing, or it may mean a great personal sacrifice, or it may mean no sacrifice whatever. What does this curious money transaction really secure? The physician may be called upon to sacrifice himself out of all proportion to the economic advantage which will thereby accrue to him; or it may be that the very fact of my great wealth may make him feel sure of his money and neglect to give me the care I need. The hospital physician is not paid; and is the soldier 'paid' to die, or the nurse to face disease and death? It would certainly mean a great change in our social habits if we were not able to buy services; but the poor have always been in this position. With all our payments we run the risk of being betrayed, defrauded, badly served. It is to the interest in his work of the scholar and scientific man, to man's natural spirit of emulation, his ambition, pride, even his vanity, his thirst for praise and admiration, his desire for success or achievement, that we must look for the normal sanctions, together with the finer moral sanctions and sympathies. The younger Pliny had considerable wealth but his eagerness to excel as a pleader rivalled that of any penniless advocate today. The love of applause and of office, like sympathy and duty, existed before the industrial age and will survive it. In any case Money as the sanction of service

it cannot be ethical to relate the sense of responsibility to the receipt or non-receipt of fees.   The truth is

that the hireling spirit is the enemy of the work spirit. The paid servant in the gospel is made to say: "I have done only what I was paid to do;" but for the Jesus of the gospels moral and spiritual work was not of this kind at all; no man should labour simply as a hireling.

This economic basis of life has led also to a licensed piracy in the exploitation of nature. We say the other animals must be restrained. But no animal needs restraint one tithe as much as man, as no animal is so capable as he of becoming noxious to his kind and to the whole living world. It appears to me that any final judgment about the conduct of life waits upon the recognition that the other animals have just as much right as we to the planet. We exploit land and water for our needs and our pleasures, and when we say that damage caused by rabbits, say, involves us in economic loss the statement does not take us far. Corn indeed would not be grown or fruit planted if we could not reckon on harvesting them, and we ought to have power to protect them by every means, short of cruelty. But mere economic rights or the pursuit of human pleasure, though they make the rabbits or the birds troublesome to us, create no right on our side which is greater than theirs. The self-restraint—the imposed restraint—to which man has been forced in other directions where he has been accustomed to subjugate and dominate his kind he will have to learn towards the other animals: the command to possess the earth and subdue it belongs to an age which was as yet unconscious of the elements of ethical life. It is then certain that in so far as man becomes a moral being and human society a civilized and not merely a complex phenomenon, economic interests will sink behind ideal interests and sympathy with life will take the place of greed for possessions.

In the hebrew belief that prosperity was god's reward for righteousness we europeans imbibed a doctrine, athwart christianity, which has no counterpart in other asiatic religions. Righteousness and money kissed each other. We do not find the professional moralists or the christian church bringing any charge against the ugly features of a civilization which is based on our pecuniary interests; everyone of them has been tolerated, and the franciscan himself was accepted as a symbol not as an example for imitation.

X. KILLING

OF the 4 or 5 motives for killing another man, which include the retaliatory and the punitive, there are 3 which may be regarded as organic with their bases in organic life. The first of these is defensive, and its type is to be found in maternal conduct; the second is the will to violent extermination as the result of the passions, of which the type is the combats of rival males; and the third is utilitarian killing which is exemplified in some of the habits of other animals, but is scarcely admitted as a principle among present day civilized human beings. Yet it is the first and third of these types which are in fact and in principle ethical, or at least not anethical, instincts. The first includes defence of the helpless, of oneself against aggression, and of moral rights when these are opposed by physical force. The third type is exemplified in the animals' instinct to destroy the dying and incapable member of the pack, the sickly young, and sometimes the newly born. The last has been a common human practice, and there has also been a species of euthanasia in primitive tribes where it has not been uncommon for the helpless aged to consider it a duty to end their lives. In the words of the Russian mujik, "I live other people's life. It is time to retire". But Infanticide infanticide has been very much more common; it was done in the great days of Greece and Rome, in Greece under the aegis of its noblest lawgivers and thinkers. The christian church set its face absolutely against this and the kindred practice of exposing the newly born; but exposure and the subsequent servitude of exposed children persisted in the christian west as long as slavery itself, and it was the common practice of abandoning children which led to S. Vincent de Paul's foundation of the first foundling hospital.[1] Infanticide is still common

[1] In 1640.

in christian countries and prevails in China in the case of girl children. A practice so common cannot be stigmatized as unnatural; but it is no longer tolerated as a natural thing, and the problem it was intended to solve must now no doubt be dealt with by control of pregnancy and sterilization. The modern view has been that infanticide is irreligious or uncivilized: the killing of a newborn infant is not only felt to be as wrong as the destruction of any other human life, but it does not satisfy the modern moral sense that a child should be brought into the world to gratify one set of instincts and then destroyed to satisfy another. Nevertheless the destruction of infants was a material necessity in ancient human groups and communities whether these were nomadic or dwellers in over-populated cities: and modern men have not solved their difficulty so long as they insist on the unregulated use of the means of procreation on one side with a scrupulous preservation of all the consequences on the other.[1]

At the other end of existence a fresh problem arises, Euthanasia which is not solved, though it is supposed to be solved, by the civilized and artificialized conditions of material life. That the case of the aged presents a real moral and social problem may be accepted on the authority of Thomas More—the great english jurist who has been canonized as a martyr for the catholic faith; he tells us that in his ideal state the incurably diseased and those who are unable "to do any duty of life" or who by "over-living their own death" are "noisome and irksome" to others and grievous to themselves, are recommended to

---

[1] Infant mortality is now combated by welfare institutes which will do much to counteract the diminishing population due to 'birth control'. Our immediate forebears accepted it as right and proper that married people should breed huge families of which a very large proportion died. This meant greater suffering in infant and little child life than infanticide. But (like pains in childbirth) these deaths were regarded as cruelties of the will of god.

341

put an end to their lives.[1]   The incapable aged "live others' lives" and even if those others were always willing so to sacrifice their own years of existence that is no reason at all why men who have had their life should Quality of accept the sacrifice. At the root of this problem we come life to the nature and character of life. Organic life, then, always implies not only certain conditions of life but a certain quality of life, and not merely the fact of existence. It is generally assumed and some people specifically assert that the keeping alive of hopelessly afflicted humanity is the characteristic mark of civilization. Two aphorisms 'the right to life' and the 'sacredness of life' cover the ground of their argument, and at the same time shut out all concern with the quality of life which they reduce to the materialistic term—the quantitative term—of mere existence, making the intangibility of life—mere life— not the fine flower but the fetich of civilization. The search for the murderer of a completely obscure human being, who in life was accounted as of no account, and who could never have gained the ear of society for the alleviation of his life needs, is impressive: suddenly, though he may have been starving to death from society's neglect of him when one of society's wastrels knocked him on the head, he becomes something which was too sacred to be touched. But how does this concern for his life sort with the common practice of warfare? The truth of course is that civilized man with his belligerence and his slum dwellers has shown no esteem either for quantity

[1] "He shall do like a godly and virtuous man"; his is "an honourable death". In the cases of repulsive and noxious illness, and of those who are facially or otherwise repulsive and intolerably afflicted, the afflicted man's desire to go should arbitrate. But if any one who loves chooses to segregate and care for him (with his consent) there should be means of carrying this out. There was human wreckage preserved from the late war which no really humane sentiment would have saved. The primitive Indian Channa- cocos (of Paraguayan Chaco) adopt a system of euthanasia of old males (not femels); weakly children are also killed.

or quality of life, and the subject has been riddled with anomalies.

There are violations and outrages inflicted upon men compared with which the painless putting out of life of a diseased or incapable man or one at the end of his life is neither horrible nor wicked. A great wrong done under the impulse of an evil passion is a very much more heinous thing than a very small wrong deliberately done from the neutral desire to put an end to what nature is ending. But we are as horrified at hastening the death of a person in unalleviable pain, or of a new-born deformed infant, as we should be at the most callous and abominable murder for money. Our sentiment is so falsified on these points that many people even confound murder and suicide. The same christian nations which have allowed a husband to slay his wife if he suspected her of adultery would condemn as sinners those who kill themselves for a good reason. You must not 'usher yourself' unbidden into the next world, but you may be despatched there by your husband in defence of his sexual rights over you.[1] What sense of right reigned in a world which inflicted the death penalty on the mother who kills her new-born child and permitted infants to be exposed and slain at the will of the father? What moral principle was at work when you killed a woman for unfaithfulness to a husband and gave husbands the right to kill the fruit of a mother's womb?[2]   If I were asked whether there are any natural rights I should say there are two—the right of a mother over the life of her new-born child and of all men over their own lives. But though their right over

---

[1] As recently as the autumn of 1928 the Spanish minister of justice broadcast some points in a new penal code, one of which runs: "A husband who murders his wife may no longer advance unfaithfulness as a plea of justification, even though he may have excellent proof of his suspicions." These, he says, are put forward as "more humane" laws.

[2] Let it be remembered that the father's 'right' to kill the child depended upon the biological fiction that the child was the *father's*.

their own lives has been strenuously denied men have always been told that they can be called upon to die at the wish of other people: at the call of country or party, however frivolous, you may be required to die but no one must put you out of life to save you sufferings, however horrible. During the european war of 1914–18 the watchers in a military hospital stayed up all night to prevent an insane soldier from killing himself, while outside the guns could be heard mowing down men who would never live to be insane. Soldiers were throwing hand grenades into each other's faces, but the maddened and mutilated would be sent back to be anxiously cared for in perpetual homage to the doctrine of the 'sacredness' of their existence.   When it is claimed, then, that the preservation of human life is the great achievement of civilized man it must be remembered that no animal has had anything approaching the disregard for life which man himself displays. All the mammalian life destroyed by other mammals would not equal the shambles men make of their own species;[1] and had modern man restricted himself to infanticide and euthanasia the sacrifice of human life—in quantity and quality—would have been immeasurably less than he has made it by his bellicose propensities.

Suicide   Suicide has been called the act of a brave man and the act of a coward, and it may be either or neither. It is a trumpery spirit which praises a gallant death in battle and refuses praise when a man takes his own life that he may insure the life or happiness of another. It is thought respectable to venture your life footballing mountaineering or ski-ing (the element of 'danger' is often the acknowledged lure in games of skill) but you must not deliberately take your life for any spiritual motive nor because you suffer extremes of mental or physical anguish. How

[1] See p. 348 and *n*. 2.

absurd! When a man has suffered what for him is the supreme loss no one should think he is obliged to go on suffering; the contribution he can make can in hardly any case balance the suffering to himself nor the moral destruction of his life. That there should be a social stigma attaching to the taking of one's own life is ludicrous, and so is the pretence that this is always done when the mind is unsound. If someone who has suffered long years of painful illness is deprived by an accident of speech or sight or movement and puts an end to his life, where is the insanity? It seems rather to be evidence of some mental unsoundness when men live on a burden to themselves and others.[1] And *why* should we try to keep anyone alive who wants to die? We came into the world by the will of other men but we can leave it by the will of the man whom it most concerns. Why should mere living-on be foisted into a place of moral eminence while considerations of love and honour and all the goods that may be so much more good than our continuing to cumber the earth must be set aside?[2] The will not-to-live from an ideal motive operates and should operate as the will-to-live from an ideal motive operates; and that we may and should cling to our own life at all costs with universal approval for doing so is a monstrous proposition in face of man's actual disregard of human life. Suicide

---

[1] "Suicide is an enterprise where you are regarded as insane if you succeed, but if you fail nobody says anything about the insanity. You are regarded as sane." Dr. Edwin Smith, Battersea coroner.

[2] Men in classical times especially have suggested that a mind imbued with piety towards the kosmos—of which we are and for which we are— would reject suicide. This conception of the kosmos cannot but be imaginative and there is small piety in deciding to live on when your life is noxious because of it. The suggestion that everything may be suffered by yourself and others, piety to the kosmos being only offended when we play a man's deliberative part, or that the kosmos is reverenced when we die a lingering death from disease or are hurled to death climbing Mont Blanc but outraged when we put an end to our life because it is spoiling another life, would seem to be itself a special kind of impiety.

was recently put forward by a commonplace medical practitioner as in itself proof of an unbalanced mind; but some of us would prefer to be unbalanced with Zeno and Epicurus, Lucretius and Seneca, Arria and the unknown woman of the Larian Lake, Paulina wife of Seneca, Pomponius Atticus and the Plinys, Longinus, Thomas More, Roland, and captain Oates. To go when you ought to stay and to stay when you ought to go is cowardice. "Above all things remember that the door is open," Arrian reports Epictetus as saying—"but if you stay, do not complain."[1]

There is therefore no law of ethics or of political morality to require that a life should be kept going whatever the circumstances, indeed some of the medical fetishes in this regard are so barbarous and gross that the very sufferings which the physician is there to avert are outrageously preserved for the helpless patient and those who love him, partly in impious homage to the alleged sacredness of human life and partly to protect the medical profession.[2] Meanwhile it would be hard to find a clearer and on the whole less baneful assertion of the sacrosanct character of human life than the custom of requiting murder by capital punishment.

Death penalty

It is evident that man living in society has not an obvious right to life at any cost, perhaps no more right than he has to property on the same terms; and *primâ facie* the theory that he who takes life should forfeit his own is more just than most legal theories: why should he take life and keep his own? The Italian nourishes a sentiment that it is wicked to take life as a punishment;

---

[1] The strong independence of the ancient Roman which made him unwilling to regard himself as the prey or sport of the miseries men might inflict on him is very unlike the christian duty of resignation, but does not appear to be less noble.

[2] Some part of the legal and medical preservation of worthless life is forced upon society as a safeguard against the attempts to get rid of people illegitimately.

yet nowhere are there more assassins to exemplify the infliction of this penalty on the innocent, and nowhere in Europe is murder so slightly punished. There is also a sentiment in Italy against taking your own life, not apparently for the theological reason which prevails in England but because life is so good a thing that the chance of its smiling upon you again should not be thrown away. No doubt it is this sentiment which moves the Italian in discarding capital punishment—life, sensuous life, the life of the sun and the senses, is so good, you think, that the murderer should not be deprived of it, and you become forgetful of the dead man whom he has deprived.

The fact that in taking life society takes away what it cannot give, is no sufficient reason for rejecting this penalty when it is balanced against the citizen's power to injure and destroy the society of which he forms part. The strong objections which are taken to capital punishment are of course in consideration not alone of its irreversibility but especially of its irreversibility in the case of an innocent sufferer, and of its alleged degrading effect on the hangman and others participating in judicial killing. Lastly, its deterrent effect is denied. These do not appear to be final arguments against the practice in view of other circumstances of man's life.[1] Where the point of ethics comes in is in the appreciation of degrees of murder. It is monstrous to assume that all homicide is equally culpable; no common moral term could serve to describe the iniquity of murdering a friend and

---

[1] Compare, for example, the disgusting atmosphere created by pauper lunatics, especially those 'watched' to prevent their committing suicide. They are described as of obscene speech, filthy habits . . . spitting into each other's plates, "the most damnable indictment and the most degrading example" of humane and scientific treatment; the attendants have to watch these things continually and to administer a "barbarous" and "brutalizing" discipline. It is not, of course, necessary that capital punishment should involve *any* degrading circumstance.

patient for the money in his wallet while you give him injections for his health, and the killing by blow or pistol a brutal mate or father who is offering you violence and menacing your life day and night. How false to say, "Both are taking life and this is the supreme fact in the two cases". What of spoiling and defacing life and trampling it under foot? Or should it be only those who menace you with death who have a supreme right to life? It is the fact that there are differences in degrees of murder amounting to difference in the kind of act committed which is chiefly important in the question of the rightness or wrongness of the death penalty. We say everyone has a right to kill in self-defence,[1] and if we did not say so we should have to tolerate it; we also say a woman has a right to protect herself by killing a male assailant, and there are certainly sorts of lynch law which are not only justifiable but inevitable: to give the death penalty in any of these cases would be outrageous. But while men perpetrate murder for vile ends I cannot suppose other men have no right to kill them.

War   War has been looked upon not only as a political but as a natural phenomenon: as a natural phenomenon, however, the warfare of two 'armies' of a vertebrate species has no place.[2] War has therefore to rest on its justifiability as a political manifestation. In this aspect national hostility can in no way be distinguished from other group hostilities; it has been shown times out of number that civil war is as fierce as national war; as nation A will accuse C with which it is in conflict of every imaginable iniquity and if its quondam ally B becomes its foe will repeat precisely the same accusations against

[1] And therefore, of course, to do the same acts in defence of others.
[2] No other mammal but man sets out to extinguish its species; and mankind's love of warfare is nothing but the running amok of that rivalry of sex which is so active among the males of many other animals.

it which served for C, so in internecine warfare the selfsame hatred and contumely is showered upon your fellow
countrymen as upon a hostile national group. Division
into nations does not therefore create the justification for
war, which is due to ebullitions of hate anger and greed,
passions which have always acted between family and
family, and more especially between members of the same
family.   This consideration helps to discount the
appeal to patriotic sentiment as a justification for war
but it does not do away with it, and the real reason for
rejecting the claims of patriotism as such is that no
definition of the notion can be framed which is not equally
valid for every case of resistance to aggression and injustice. Where these exist, physical resistance will always
be forthcoming, and when they do not exist no sentiment
about your 'country' can justify war.

But it is contended that war is necessary in order to *War and
over-
population*
keep down population: "Would there not be too many
people if it were not for war and pestilence?" But what
civilized or moral idea lurks in waiting upon war to check
your population? and what is the difference between
killing unwanted infants (which you think wicked) and
killing 5 or 10 million adults to make room for them?[1]
War however is, it appears, a workshop of many virtues *War a
displayer of
virtues*
which would never otherwise be displayed. It "opens
the most fruitful field to all virtues" said Frederick the
Great;[2] "nothing, in fact, (wrote Bernhardi the xix[th]
century prussian diplomatist and historian) is left but war
to secure to the true elements of progress the ascendancy
over the spirits of corruption and decay," "the brutal
incidents inseparable from every war vanish completely

[1] The chinese minister Li Hung Chang refused to allow the river
Hoangho to be canalized because its great floods "drown many tens of
thousands who would otherwise live on in misery and starvation". Such
are the devices which the vicious practice of over-population makes
necessary.

[2] Who yet despised war as his letter to Voltaire of Nov. 27, 1773, shows.

before the idealism of the main result".[1] But it is, of course, impossible to conceive a more parlous condition for virtue than that it should wait on the horrors of war. The immane savageries of war leave their scars on mankind from generation to generation and include every disgraceful passion of domineering injustice.[2] It has been earnestly asserted that there are things worse than war. But they are not the things men usually fight about. And so war remains an evil added to the other evils of the world. War is the supreme anti-social act of nations and it has been upheld by none but the crudest doctrines.

Success establishes who is in the right The notion that success is synonymous with right (which underlies the belief in the arbitrament of war) is more widespread than its merits would appear to make possible. It is said for example that "rebellion is only justifiable if it is successful"; so that success makes it right and it is might which makes it a success. Hence the victor in a war is believed (especially by himself) to deserve his victory. But war is not the same as a game of strength and skill; the winner in a match has really won the game, but unless war is, like a game, undertaken for its own sake no proof is offered that the victor ought to have won it.

War brings a righteous decision Bernhardi wrote: "war gives a biologically just decision, since its decisions rest on the very nature of things." This "very nature of things" is that a stronger biceps can

---

[1] If the alleged ideal splendour of this main result—domination by the biologically best—is to justify all violence against effete peoples then civilized communities must abandon for good their present theories about the rights of life; they must assume that communities which contain higher types of humanity (in greater proportion) possess an ideal right to trample on the virtues and power of suffering of communities where the reverse is the case; and finally they must stifle those instincts of humanity which pity and protect the weaker and the suffering and adopt the thesis that might may be right and a substitute for these virtues or instincts.

[2] The quality of its virtue is seen in the rule which requires an innocent invaded people to salute their devastators.

Mark Twain wrote a striking description of what men actually are asking god to bring about when they pray for a victory.

always crush a feebler one; and if, because it is of the very nature of things, this will show who is right in a quarrel it will also prove whether it was A or B who betrayed their friend C, and any other moral proposition.[1]

But war can prove nothing. That is its condemnation as an arbiter among civilized peoples. Every hope of civilization is based upon the conception that right is truly might. All the forces which war against the spirituality of civilization are founded upon the essentially unethical suggestion that might can ever be the same as right.

War proves nothing

To kill is a natural instinct. When animals strive with each other they try to kill—to deprive the other of life; as soon as the other is dead it is satisfied. But warfare as a principle is introduced by the human savage and combines for him the double zest of sport and the headhunt. These 2 motifs have proved so irresistibly strong that they have made going out to war the world's chief industry and human history a history of killing.   Wers like war:[2] with certain passions they have had it their own way throughout recorded history and therefore we rightly

The instinct to kill

[1] When men's own physical strength was used in war they might imagine their victory in terms of a sporting event; now, however, they are armed adventitiously, and it is not easy to discern where a sense that god protects the strong man as such can creep in at all, since factors like 'silver bullets' may determine the event.

It is not even true that right tends to enlist might on its side; this only happens in those organized societies where just laws are executed on the unruly through the command of adequate force.

[2] And the civilized like it for the same reason as the savage: "This is better than big game shooting" was a sentiment which the most important english newspaper deemed worthy of record in a letter "from the front" when the war of 1914 began. The military toast is "To bloody war, and plenty of it"; and their delight in these 2 activities suggests to the sex the absurd and childish aphorism that war protects women. An ex-viceroy of India when the Balkan war broke out in 1913 announced in the House of Lords: "Here is something with which women have nothing to do." Such were our seers. He had perhaps never read the *Troädes*.

No soldier and no civilian layman can be made to suffer as women suffer from war.

conclude that they have made warfare their staple activity because they liked it. If wers did not like it there would not be any war. War exists because wers have always been goaded to it by a restless energy and the love of destruction. War therefore is one of our problems: the problem is the fact that a very large proportion of wers like fighting for its own sake and also assume that most ends are in the long run obtained by fighting, that is by force and violence. On the other hand only a small proportion of women like fighting for its own sake; women as a whole will despise war, wers as a whole admire it. From savage times to now wers have hypnotized themselves into the belief that the deploying of muscular force is a soveran function, but it is in fact a subaltern one, a power, that is, to be used under control. Our histories catalogue military events as the chief landmarks of peoples, and this form of activity has been supposed by the fighters to be also a supreme exercise of responsibility. But in truth it never is so, and the idea which lay behind the very ancient division of ruling powers into femel authority exercised by male delegates was capable of establishing a higher social principle. Readiness to throw himself into offensive action, the easily roused activities of the male, may prove a factor for civilization; but it is clear it requires tempering, and this is to be found not in the male but in the femel. Male war with exclusive male control is the root of savagery in a state; the counter-balancing responsible and constructive elements of the femel are a biological fact which will compare favourably with the biology of the prussian diplomat. The war which broke out in 1914 was the catastrophe of a false principle.

But must there be something to take the place of war? Is war a natural passion which we must find some means of sublimating. Murder is a natural passion, but unless you conclude from this that occasional murders (that is,

retail killing) will always be necessary you cannot conclude that some outlet must be found for wholesale killing
in war. There is nothing to sublimate in war; you do
not sublimate murder. But you replace anti-social energies
by social ones, which is part of the necessary process of
civilization. In the future mankind must pull its weight
more evenly, and will do so. Its qualities and forces must
be re-estimated readjusted and balanced. Up to now we
have nourished wrong notions of authority and power.
The world we are emerging from was based on obedience Liberty
and physical force; Treitschke had said that obedience authority
is the fundamental requirement of a state, and deduced and war
from the "soveran power" of states the "absolute necessity
for war" since no international tribunal is thinkable.[1] It
is this kind of thinking in Europe which preceded the
war of 1914–18 and ignored all care for the liberties of
other nations and for those who would prove to be the
weaker in the tussle. It believed that true and acceptable
authority is that which is exercised by the physically
strong.[2] Now this implies a servile complex.[3] The men
who think these thoughts are ruled by fear, they are
always ready to fight ideas with fists and never ready to
understand the legitimate aspiration after freedom of
action and initiative: we have in fact only just arrived at
surmising that civilized states should have some better
resource than war, that the 'ordeal by battle' is as barbaric
as the ordeal by water and fire; but meanwhile whenever
war breaks out we are always told that it was 'inevitable'.
But some way out of inevitable war would certainly be
forthcoming if it were the rule that those who make war
from the armchairs in their cabinets should always be
the first to fight each other before the troops were called
upon. It would be the best of all proofs to their country-

[1] Treitschke, *Lectures on Politics*, and see *infra*, Internationalism.
[2] Today, by the most heavily 'mechanized'?
[3] See Force (ch. xi), p. 362.

men of sincerity.[1] War is the most wasteful the most cruel and the least rational mode of settling a dispute; and the demands made by nations would be both more just and less extravagant if they were to be settled not by fighting over them but by arguing their merits. Soldiers should exist only as an international police; to keep that peace between nations which we require within our own borders.[2]

Summary

The value of human life as such is a necessary fiction of civilization, the precise meaning of which is that it is necessary to protect men's lives against the murderous instincts of fellow-men.[3] What we shall look to is not the complete abolition of killing but a readjustment of our notions about it. There would be (a) some forms of euthanasia (b) infanticide of the hopelessly deformed and afflicted (c) recognition of the absolute right to take one's own life (d) the death penalty for taking life on vile impulses (which would include the sheer impulses of violence) and from vile motives, with real moral discrimination in all other cases of homicide (e) very exceptional instances of 'lynch'-killing due to the immediate

[1] This drastic means of disposing of our statesmen at a moment of stress would be more than compensated by the immunity from wars which it would normally secure.

[2] One would suppose from the advocates of war that all the best and most thoughtful of mankind had agreed with them. These men, however, did not agree that war was right: Lâo-Tsze, Cicero, Lucretius, Vergil, Seneca, Lucan, Plutarch, Epictetus, Erasmus, Thomas More ["War or battle as a thing very beastly, and yet to no kind of beasts in so much use as to man, they do detest and abhor"], Montaigne, Pascal, Fénelon, Shaftesbury, Voltaire, Frederick the Great, Condorcet, Herder, Schopenhauer, Lamartine, Victor Hugo—and indeed some of the finest soldiers also, including Garibaldi, who said that the first thing for Europe to do was to make war impossible. As to Goethe he shows in *Faust* (lines 6957-72, and elsewhere) his immense revulsion from war; and Leonardo da Vinci called it *"pazzia brutalissima"*.

[3] Even the superstition which maintains the 'sacredness of human life' has been active in flouting it—Luther advised the parents of a child whom he held to be "possessed" to drown it.

sense of moral outrage which cannot—and perhaps should not—abide some deferred tribunal[1] (*f*) the abolition of war.

[1] The loss of such impulses and actions, owing to the social habit of remitting all our emotions to the tribunal of our fellow-men, would be a real weakening of human moral quality. Cf. Force, pp. 359–60.

At present the unjust circumstances of men's lives, the example of war, the miserable standard of personal justice between man and man, and the tardiness of legal justice, all encourage acts of personal violence.

XI. FORCE

Where the princely man abides the left weak hand is in honour.
But he who uses weapons honours the stronger right. LAÔ-TSZE

Legislators never appear to have considered that although there
are 2 instruments to their hand—persuasion and force . . . one
only is used . . . force pure and simple.   PLATO, *Laws*

As force is always on the side of the governed, the governors have
nothing to support them but opinion. It is, therefore, on opinion
only that government is founded.
          HUME, *On the First Principles of Government*

The most superficial reading of history convinces one that all
the long-range forces are moral and all the short-range forces
physical. No victory of material force ever is final unless it
corresponds to an idea.   Comments of BAGSHOT

T HE arbitrament of force has bulked so largely in
man's history that the majority of men find it difficult
to contemplate its exclusion from the field of morals and
politics. We have been told that civilization itself rests
upon force; that the state possesses an indefectible right
to use force for its ends; that force is the ultimate sanction
of the rule of majorities; and even the thesis that 'might
is right' has been exhibited not as an absurd paradox
'Might is but as a sort of philosophical necessity. This last opinion
right' is no doubt arrived at by inquiring into the nature of
a 'right'. When we think of rights we perceive that
though they are in their intrinsic nature ethical entities
many of them have no effective existence without acts
or forbearances on the part of other people. A right of
this type therefore must be regarded as something which
can be enforced or as something which others must
concede; to be seized of a right may then easily appear
to be the same thing as to be seized of a power, and the
formula of rights degenerates into: "he shall take who
has the power and he shall keep who can." Now the
definition of a right in terms of the power to enforce it
is a mere sophism, the sophistic substitution of the one

idea for the other. A right may be of no use to me if others can prevent my enjoying it; but the fact that its exercise is inhibited, whether by physical or moral means, leaves it intact as a philosophic and moral conception. If I have the right to kill my would-be assassin, for example, it is not the right which changes places should he prove to be stronger than I. What does the possession of a moral right depend on? The possession of moral rights depends, like all moral things, upon moral forces. If there were not moral forces at work there would not of course be any such thing as the moral conception of rights—and that which creates them is also that which sustains them; no force except that exercized under the aegis of moral ideas could insure their existence.[1]

There is another argument, based upon force, which affects primarily not the notion of a right but the seat of authority, and is in this form:—Government and the executive powers of civilized polities can never be in the hand of those who lack the physical power to inforce their decisions, in the ultimate resort authority must be where the physical force is. Force is therefore the sole ultimate sanction of authority. Let us analyze this. What is physical force? If it consists in bodily strength, and perhaps in one kind of bodily strength rather than another, cannon would be still more effective. The various kinds of human strength can readily be enumerated—vitality, endurance, persistency, toleration of pain, physical weight, physical skill, and what may be called hit and kick strength—strength of the biceps muscle type. This last is efficient against a less strong biceps muscle, but not against several units possessing the same kind of strength; and authority could not belong to one strong man it would belong to all the strong men, to the totality of hit and kick. But it cannot repose there either; for if someone comes along with a few firearms muscle is

The seat of authority

[1] See *infra*, p. 363.

vanquished. Moreover if mere physical strength were the natural basis and appropriate sanction of authority human muscles would not be the deciding factor, elephants would have a much better right to determine how matters should go.[1] The difficulty which appeared to present itself is this: How can laws be executed against the refractory unless we have the physical force on our side? But to have the force on your side does not mean to have it on your persons. It is not the possession of force which matters, it is the command of force; and this can be as easily acquired maintained or lost by a physically weak man as by a strong, by a group of weak as by a group of strong men. The captain of a ship does not wield authority because he is stronger than the crew; and if the crew rises against him it is not called authority but mutiny. The officers of an army do not send the men to death because they are the stronger, nor does a government control the police because it is the stronger. What holds the general from invading the cabinet with his soldiers to protest against unwelcome orders? The monarchical principle is itself evidence enough that authority is not based upon the personal or collective possession of superior physical strength. Everywhere physical force is the servant and moral force the master.

Civilization therefore is not built upon force. The topsy-turvy aberration that the presence of physical (nay of muscular) force indicates the seat of moral

[1] If physical force, *as such*, has any rights and a man with a big biceps would have more right than a man with a smaller one, the argument that elephants are still stronger than men is as much in place as the argument which suggests that a prizefighter has more right to enforce his views than an Aristotle. But those who claim that stable government rests upon the possession of the greater physical force would not agree that elephants have any say in the matter. It is not mere force—they would tell us—that makes rights, but mere force which is essential to maintain them, and, *per contra*, no set of men in possession of superior physical force would consent to be dictated to by a group possessing less force. This certainly means that even when we leave out the elephant we are left with the prizefighter.

authority could not have maintained itself in a world where the psychological contribution of both halves of mankind had been equal. What is ultimately true is that force αὐτὴ καθ᾿ αὑτήν, itself by itself, οὐδενὸς μεῖον σθένει, is strong less than nothing.

There are people so impressed by the truth that civilization is not and cannot be built upon force that they think all exercise of physical force is worthy only of ages of barbarism. But the essential point about force is its coercive not its physical quality; it is because it coerces that it attains its ends. It is not easy to justify other forms of coercion and condemn every physical form. Coercion Moral coaction employed to subjugate (as distinct from persuading) another is essentially the same as physical coaction; indeed physical coaction leaves the character more free. In our human life and psychology there can be and is in fact no reason why every sort of moral and semi-moral coercion should be exercized, however despicable, and physical coercion be deemed always unworthy of us. The necessity for physical force lies in the nature of things; it is imposed by the fact of body, physical mass. We must use physical mass (or its equivalent) to carry or support physical mass—the sick, the helpless. It is not a question of using material force when spiritual force should do—physical bodies *must* deal with physical bodies by physical means. We dominate living things, as we dominate inanimate mass, by corporal mass; and, if not, by ruse and reins. One or other must be used to dominate the delirious, the epileptic, the sick man or animal. How then can the necessity for force There must halt before the man who is exerting his cruel unjust and always be greedy instincts? While the savage lasts—the morally physical sick man—force must last. We cannot look on at wrongs resistance to the innocent while we invoke his tormentor's moral reformation. It is natural to use our legs to run away from the mad bull, and as natural to use our arms to coerce the human mad bull. There are iniquities which no one can look upon; and the reformation of no one (even if it were a certainty) precedes in importance the checking of the evil he does.[1]   If we do this—if we coerce the mad-bull man and the evil man—how can we stop at using the same sort of force for good causes? For, by hypothesis, it is not against perfect governments we act but against imperfect. The thesis, in religion and ethics, of non-resistance is a monstrosity. Would the non-resister see a child assaulted, or a dog burned. Would he resist if the agent were mad or drunk?

Then why allow it to occur because he is evil and infamous?

There will not only always be physical resistance to major force but it is right that there should be. The weakest child uses what force it has against a big man; the weakest animal in the clutch of the strongest does the same. Force itself is indifferent; it is neither right nor wrong. Nevertheless it has a spiritual role; and if it can be the instrument of tyranny it is also the safeguard of justice. Force, then, is used for ideal ends when it sets itself against mightier injustice. It is this use of minority force which has an effective moral function: for there is a permanent difference in idea and in fact between militarism and militantism; the one represents the fight which might puts up against right, and the other that eternal fight which right puts up against might. The second kind of force is always in place; it forms part of the law that force is and always must be used apart altogether from the possession of superior force. You cannot make the unspiritual spiritual by coercing him, but you can make the unjust do justice—and it is the right way because it is usually the only way. Force in itself settles nothing, but force in itself provokes reforms,

Minority Force

[1] See Punishment, p. 367.

and the political recognition of right derives in nine times out of ten from a show of force. The courage of those who use such minority force is not so much that of the soldier as that of the martyr—not that of a hireling but of a witness. Major-force is in its nature nearly always aggressive, whereas the force of the rebel is used for defence even when it is offensive; and when the rebel breaks the law he breaks it for two of the best of all reasons; the one is that it is vile to remain under major-force, and the other that the supreme act of violence is the refusal of justice. If the use of force and resistance to wrong were abolished it would mean a toleration of vileness harmful to all. It has been said that unless there is some provision for orderly changes of the law it is little use to provide against breaches of it; and so far so good. But it is no use at all waiting for 'orderly changes' where there is no good-will. Good-will is essential—and where it exists force is unnecessary; it is simply because there is so much of ill-will that we want some sort of coercion to break it up.[1] It is perfectly true that intellectual (or moral) agreement affords the only permanent solution of human conflicts; but the ethical question is how long are we to wait for intellectual agreement where there is ill-will and injustice on the other side. Our resistance to major force and to the forces of ill-will and evil may not produce great results in our time, but it makes each of us the man we should be and it is the torch which is borne through the ages by the human spirit.

(margin note: Martyr force versus military force)

---

[1] Evil is then a poison which we seek to expel by a counter-poison. The objection that force begets force and that by employing it we are setting evil against evil is not in place here, because it is not only that the evil of major force begets the resort to minor force, but that it is part of the inherent injustice of evil that it necessarily begets evil. *Per contra* the toleration of political iniquity can be no part of moral law. Where there is the soul to condemn such evil there must be the spirit to resist it—'even to blood'.

The origin of the assumption that government acts through the physical coercion of one living being by another is to be found of course in the practice of getting our way by muscular strength. And in itself this notion

Physical force and barbarism

is a savage one. It is not a jungle notion for among wild animals skill and ruse exercize the control as often as muscle. To be ruled by a man because his muscles are strong is ethically indistinguishable from being ruled by him because he is drunk: those who are in the grip of the 'big strong man' are in the grip of barbarism. But mankind as a matter of fact—making exception for the element of war—has not been controlled by muscular force; even the heroes of physical fights and revolutions could not be classed among big strong bullies for the world's great captains have been insignificant or small men—Odysseus, Alexander, Caesar, Drake, Napoleon, Nelson, Wellington, Gordon, Lawrence of Arabia. And the Trojans left it on record that they had suffered more from the wits of Odysseus than from the brawn of Ajax. It is then character not stature, mind not muscle, which has moved the world, and this is as true of the hero in combat as of the intellectual hero. The world-movers have never been men of big stature.[1]

Power

Mankind therefore owes the least of its debts to 'the big strong man' and nothing at all to the use of mass force as such. We possess something of immeasurable value to put in their place. It is power. Power is the greatest of all forces and is founded in the emotion of the ideal: already it has everywhere played the paramount part in human affairs though the uses of force have

---

[1] Mind and genius have habitually operated in small bodies—Sokrates, Epicurus, Plato, Aristotle, Horace, Paul, Maimonides, Albertus Magnus, Dante, Francis, Michelangelo, Erasmus, Montaigne, Giordano Bruno, Spinoza, Newton, Voltaire, Gibbon, Goethe, Kant, Keats, Florence Nightingale, Wagner, Mazzini, Einstein, none are examples of 'big strong men', most of them were "great little men"; and it has been noted that the great Englishmen of the xvii[th] century were "all tiny".

blinded men to the fact. We owe to Benjamin Kidd the realization that power as the great ethical example of ideal emotion is the proprium of the femel. In her we get an emotion of the ideal which is at the same time associated with foresight and dissociated from self-interest, and in this type of action we possess the master power of the future. "The activities of the male mind rest on force"; "sacrifice is meaningless" to that "fighting male" who has always assumed that we have in the conflict for subsistence a universal law of development. The constant employment of physical force has itself aroused an emotion of the ideal peculiar to it which is destructive of vitalizing ideals:[1] for behind all major coercive force for whatever end it is employed, however good, there lurks a materialistic principle, a principle of spiritual death— and the ethical future depends entirely on whether the arbitrament is to rest with physical force or with ideal power.

No government can be stable; because it may always lose that moral hold on which depends the command of force. Its stability therefore never depended on the physical force behind it. What it wielded was a moral force.

The same truth explains legal right; which a man possesses not because he possesses physical force, and not first and foremost because any other persons possess it, but because public opinion or the legislator discerns this right for him. This is inshrined in law. And the only reason why physical force is ever its sanction is because there are gainsaying elements ready to deprive him of it. These elements may be moral or immoral, as legal right

Legal right and opinion

---

[1] See A muscular illusion, p. 293 and n.[1].

"The overpowering heredity of the fight" (Kidd): the ideal impulse of all male use of force is lust of domination; and force has been employed by the male in support of his inability to postpone present appetite to future good.

363

may be unjust or just, but when the gainsaying elements act simply by major-force they are always immoral.

The stronger majority will consent to the rules of the weaker minority in every society where ideas have more power than greeds. But that half of humanity which has relied chiefly upon aggressive force is slow to persuade itself that violence is not the principle of power.

XII. POLITICAL GOVERNMENT AND THE SOCIAL REGIMEN

Perhaps the terms 'political' and 'government' are both out of place. The necessity of government at all has been denied by philosophical anarchism, but the social system it advocates would still be a government—a government by public opinion. Or it might be pointed out that though civilization in Europe has been prevalently a political civilization, in China, as in the asian social system generally, it is social and philosophical rather than political. This tendency to derive the social regimen not from the polity but from a social philosophy, as in confucianism socialism fascism the soviet or naziism, is a highly interesting phenomenon, where the assumption is made that all government should represent ideal considerations beside its function of conciliating and protecting interests and administering justice.

The first and most important object of government is Security to provide security and at the same time embody the two principles of co-operation and liberty. Savages are savage either because of a complete failure to co-operate or because there is a too intense sacrifice of the men of the tribe to the interests of the tribe; and whether our liberty is flouted by the private member of society or by the community the evil is the same. The general problem of political government therefore, like the general problem of ethics, is the conciliation of order and liberty, the rights and duties of the group with the rights and duties of the individual.

The commonest method of government has always been autokracy, and like demokracy it does not embody a philosophy. It assumes that the rule of one (or of a few) over all is not only the best but is the only possible way of governing men. On the other hand the principle of demokracy is that all men should have a share in their own government. This is the inevitable trend of human society as soon as men emerge from ignorance and serfdom. But how is the will of the community to be tested? It has been universally agreed that this should be done by counting heads. The right of majorities is based, of course, upon the patent justice of satisfying the wants of the larger number. But it is a mischievous presumption of democratic thought that majorities in a state represent not only what is but what ought to be wanted. This is to underpin the inherent weakness of majority government. Since the majority now is proletarian, and will always consist of the average man, it can and will look after itself and the real risk is the stifling of finer needs and higher activities in minorities. For majorities as such do not represent moral value at all: if it is better to clothe a thousand naked persons than fifty, it is not equally true that it would be better to give effect to the inferior choice made by a thousand persons than to the choice of fifty persons capable of making a better one. Majorities, then, do not represent moral value; and they can never have absolute rights for the same reason that force cannot. Majority law, like the law of force, may easily become mob law. If majority rule is to be absolute the basis of *consent* goes; 10 consent and 4 are coerced. The whole meaning historically of the cry "rights of man" is to be found in the desire and the power of despotisms to defy these. As soon as despotism is defied (as it now is) it is no longer the rights of man but the rights of minorities which have to be considered.[1]

Majorities and the average man

Rights The foundation of the theory of rights indeed has

[1] Of the power of majorities De Tocqueville writes: "In our days the most absolute monarchs of Europe cannot prevent thoughts hostile to their authority from circulating in their states. . . . It is not so in America. So long as the majority is in doubt, men speak, as soon as it has pronounced itself everyone is silent, friends and enemies bind themselves to its chariotwheels."

never been truly laid. Some have said there are rights which men have power to exercize as god's delegates, or that all men are patient of natural rights; and others have carried the theory of human rights to the length of affirming that one man is worth another man because both are men, a proposition which has no element of truth in it at all. For equality is only to be found in men's needs not in their worth. No polity finds human rights in existence; it is as parts of political justice that we lay the foundation of them.[1]

The protection of society is the essential element in the exaction of penalties, and the essential justification for it. In the case of a child the skope of punishment as educational is clear: in the case of social penalties it has always been doubted whether other elements besides that of self-protection do not and should not enter into penal theory. Is punishment vindictive? should it be reformative? It is difficult to banish these elements completely for punishment is in fact the record of a moral judgment; the culprit realizes that society must wish to see his wrongdoing react upon himself; while if penalty is in no sense remedial not only is the vicious thrown back upon the community but the community is content to wipe its hands of him and inhumanly leave him to suffer again and again for his vices. How much is he responsible for the wrong he has done? The answer to that question may modify our notions of the vindictive and remedial aspects of punishment but will not affect in the least the principle that the objective of punishment is the necessary protection of society. Penalty must consist in the 2 elements of detention and inforced work.[2] To make the malefactor work—useful and untormenting work—is the only use

Penalties

---

[1] Men have always debated if there be any natural rights. There are natural liberties—and men lose some of these when they come to enjoy 'rights'.

[2] 'Prison' has been the method of punishment since the days of Khammurabi—the only alternative to deprivation of liberty would be outlawry.

367

of him perfectly just both vindictively and remedially.

Penalty and reward

If we take our stand upon a theory of human irresponsibility the denial that punishment is just would involve the denial of the justice of rewards. Yet it is clear that the recognition of merit in the polity is advantageous and fruitful, and if this is so the principle of penalties cannot be excluded: the society which wishes to have the means of rewarding its friends cannot be deprived of the means of castigating its foes. The grossest injustice has been perpetrated in the meting of both rewards and punishments, in both cases owing to men's tyranny prejudice and partizanship. But the self-advertisement of those who have acquitted themselves well is an evil which grows apace in demokracies and is a *lèse-devoir* which would not be countenanced in such a social system as the japanese. Our present excess of rewards is no makeweight to our present leniency in punishment.

Socialism

The evil side of industrialism and of the factory system called forth the doctrine known as socialism in that first half of the xix[th] century from which it also drew its political inspiration. This doctrine declares that the manual workman has a right to share in the value of what he helps to create, not merely to remunerative pay, and that the community has the right to commandeer work from everyone. All that "surplus value" for the sake of which the capitalist employer undertakes his business ought to be distributed among the workers— the profits of capitalism should be utterly abolished.

Karl Marx saw human history and the human character itself as the product of economic factors; and the inherent materialism of outlook in its philosophy of history clings to the remedies which socialism prescribes for the diseases of the world. But it also sets before itself a true idealistic philosophy since it requires a world of men which shall no longer be ruled by the pursuit of money, and of nations which shall no longer be opposed to each other in terms of war and material force. It is as a materialistic idealism that socialistic doctrine can best be understood and explained.

The fundamental concern of the socialistic society is the distribution of the fruits of labour and it requires that the immaterial wealth of the world should be distributed on the principle of equality also. For socialism is a state workhouse. Individuals have rights because of their needs but no individual has rights because of his worth; all that can be meant by a right is monopolized by the community, which becomes the distributor of every social asset in the proportion it judges fit for the individual. Socialism is obliged to disregard all the intangible forms of work in the sense that it cannot admit that a man who writes what his generation will not pay for is a productive worker. It is obliged to require the production of material wealth as a first charge upon the individual, and no socialistic society as such could afford to consider even the highest product of genius as of prior importance to the community.[1]

It can at once be seen what grave wrongs would be righted if the wealth of the world were so distributed that everyone would have sufficient for his needs. What socialism seeks to do is indeed utopian, and some utopias may be possible. We can never say: 'Let us plan so that everyone is happy', but socialistic doctrine declares that it would be possible to banish all economic wrongs. If this were possible something like half the miseries and injustices of the world might be ended. No one could be forced to live in anguish and dread lest tomorrow there should not be enough to eat; the man of genius and talent

Redressing of economic wrongs

---

[1] For man's damnation was economic and by economics he must be saved. This is a simple formula compared with the intricate difficulties of appraising immaterial output, especially when such output is a promise only.

would no longer be thwarted by penury; there could be no family feuds over property and legacies, and all the many moral wrongs in family and conjugal life which have economic roots would disappear as if by a magic wand. No one could persecute another using the weapon of his wealth, and even much slander would lose its sting, for the blackmailed (and one could still attempt blackmail) would be able to live even if he had enemies: riches and poverty would each cease to trouble as they have always troubled.   This is not the place to discuss whether the complicated and bureaukratic system of socialism, with its stranglehold on every member of the community, its inability to vary the economic reward with the value or valuelessness of the work, and its incapacity to change human nature either in the administrator or the recipient of its doles, is in fact feasible. But if it could be established and when established could succeed in making everyone work and everyone live on what he had earned, there would still remain criticism of another order.

The theory of work   And there is, first, the theory of work itself: Rathenau recognized that the inforced work required by socialism would perpetuate the evil of uncongenial toil. For marxian socialism had made work penal. Yet for one man to be enabled to do what he is pre-eminently fitted to do matters more than all the advantage to be gained by providing routine work for a thousand men with no special aptitudes. Socialism is all through a safety-first system—it leaves nothing to chance or choice, to capacity or superiority, to the wish to live dangerously perhaps. And safety-first is inevitably pedestrian, it makes no calls, and kindles no enthusiasm and no devotion. It is those who are not satisfied with 'safety-first' and a short working day who are probably the best elements in any community. Meanwhile though it is assumed that the brain-worker is a willing horse who can be set to manual work for a part of each day it is not supposed that the manual worker could be called on to put in a few hours of brain work. And when Rathenau came to believe that uncongenial work might be commended to the workman if it were alternated with mental occupations, it was rightly pointed out that the day is far hence when intellectual professions could be followed as a serious contribution to work by the millions of workers in factories. The day when the helot will have ceased to exist is also far hence; and it is not only "a complete change" in our present way of thought and "ethical outlook"[1] which is demanded as a prelude to socialism—the present helot populations of the world must also disappear.[2] When the helot ceases to exist—the man by nature fitted for lower work and fitted only for this—the proper means of getting uncongenial tasks done is by additional pay. Pay will always be useful for this purpose, and affords a considerably greater freedom to the workman than the compulsion of socialism.

Then there is the essential need to preserve a standard of the value of work. Great work is done for love but all work done from compulsion, safety-first work, my-interests-first, is hireling work and the worker is a hireling. The 'working-class' man has been forced to protect himself from shameless exploitation by combining with other workers in trades unions which forbid him to work more than certain hours or for less than a certain wage, and order him to "down tools" when called upon. But the class of worker who has 'hours' and who leaves off work, whatever stage it is in, when the clock strikes is the man who is doing the world's inferior work. *All* higher work is done by those who do not count their time, and who invariably contribute to the community

The value of work

---

[1] Rathenau. Who also said that without these things "hell" would be the description of a completely socialized society.

[2] The Prussian socialist Rodbertus thought that 500 years of ethical advance would be necessary before socialism could be fully realizable.

more than they get from it.[1] The 'working-class' man pulls his weight, but it is only with his hands. Without the contribution made by brains to industry and 'big business' (in which he is called upon to make his living) the business or industry would not exist. Under socialism, however, his contribution is the foundation of the 'right to maintenance' and the right to an equal share in the infinite material mental and social gifts and riches of the world. The assumption peculiar to socialism is that manual labour is the criterion of work, that it justifies every claim the workman can make on society, and that those who do not contribute to industrial work have no right to its fruits. As a plain fact the gifts which come either from industry or from mental labour are not 'deserved' by the man who does not actually produce them. But the fruits of material wealth can never be regarded as belonging only to those who create it, as no mental wealth is confined to its creators but becomes the wealth of the world. Who deserved most, the architect of Amiens cathedral or one of the skilful workers thereon? and if we say: the architect and the workers together divide the merit, then the share of a manual worker is about $\frac{1}{500}$th of the share of a mind worker. It has been thought that the cry of the ill-requited wage-slave is the most poignant cry of all. Against it should be placed the age-long martyrdom of the world's most precious human material. If the hand toiler has not been requited the man who has worked with soul and brain has never received what his contribution merited; and unlike the manual worker he has not only not received it but it could not be received. Only the lesser work can ever receive reward.

The other contribution

[1] It is mass-labour which is of importance in the case of the manual worker; but in the higher activities the individual is the person of importance: and he asks and can ask no freedom from hard and continuous toil. It is not reasonable that because the manual workman's work is disagreeable or hard he alone should be spared from doing much of it.

As mechanization develops, the role of the manual worker must become less not more important; the quality of work and the number of workers demanded both decrease. So that a working-class population breeding freely would become parasitic on the community. Even now the production of multitudes of articles which no one wants makes any population for which a living is provided on such terms parasitic—and the industrial magnates who work up such industries parasitic also— a class for which work has to be made and whose work is making what nobody requires. This consideration spoils the socialist thesis that the world's enormous wealth could and should be employed in supporting huge populations of workers in comfort.[1]

Excess population and excessive production

---

[1] The extent to which material production represents what is not required at all is not realized. Some 200 items laid before buyers a hundred years ago have grown it is said to 3200; and while labour's overproduction is artificially creating 'wants', in great producing areas the produce is being destroyed in order "to keep up the price" of the commodities.

We live at a time when many sincerely believe that to live on the interest of even a small amount of capital which you have lent to industry is to be parasitic on the community. But the man who lives on small dividends and is engaged in useful or highly important work is no more living on the community than the big (or small) wage-earner who is protected by trades unions, out-of-work pay or pensions, is insured by his employer against accident or death in his employment, and who enjoys free education, free medical inspection, free medical care,* and free hospitals for himself and every member of his family. Not one of these benefits accrues to the educated person in possession of a little saved wealth, however small. The civil servant with a pension is also in a better position than this 'capitalist'. The 'working-class' workman does not contribute (that is, earn) sufficient to hand on wealth; the dividend owner has generally earned his money or inherits from those whose mental or organizing business capacity could and did. For there are the 3 factors in industry, the mental factor, capital, and labour. And it was not till the present industrial situation had been created by 'big business', which is the product of the first two factors, that it would have been possible to conceive the socialist state. There is not, then, any reason why the life and standard of the higher workers should be levelled for the sake of maintaining an unlimited number of the lower workers to

---

* Half, or more, of the small subscription to this required by the state is paid by the employer.

373

Our western civilization is based on money. And its radical materialism is responsible for the relative materialism of the remedy which socialism proposes. But the **The change that is necessary** change that is of course essential from the complete liberty of economic factors which has issued as industrial anarchy should not be a passage from anarchy to tyranny. We do not want life to be seized upon by economic factors and this is what *laisser-faire* at one end and socialism at the other propose to do. Internationalization of production transport and distribution is a more reasonable fruitful and humane scheme than state control of work and of the production and distribution of wealth within the different states. Civilized men have shown a pigheaded indifference to the fact that the welfare of one nation is not to be obtained by sacrificing the prosperity of another though Voltaire enunciated it nearly 200 years ago. The accumulation of private wealth should be discountenanced beyond a certain amount; after that it should be taxed a hundred per cent and escheat to the public coffers. It should only be possible to possess a certain quantity of land, and to bequeath a moderate portion of wealth. The extremes of poverty and riches are a canker-spot in human societies and always would be so; and it is a disadvantage of each that they produce a materialistic outlook. The new tendency which is towards not equality but equalization seems to be the best solution—the abolition of all extremes of luxury and want while providing for the free play of individualism and individual effort and adventure. No one, as has already been suggested,[1] will henceforth possess huge tracts of land castles villages and forests, or direct material concerns which enables him to engineer monopolies and

be provided for by the equal distribution of material wealth. These are to spend so many hours a day 'working'; not liking work, not doing good work. All such time-work, indeed, is parasitic, and must damage the workman as well as the work.   [1] See Money, p. 329.

'corners'. And as is now the case with great houses so it may come to be that works of art of great value will pass out of the hands of individuals, and ceremony and *fasto* be found only in public places. The *respublica* may be gorgeous, not its private citizen. It seems, indeed, more civilized that where there is splendour it should be representative and of public importance.

If these are the proper principles of socialization the non-recognition of talent (as in Soviet Russia after 1917), equal reward for work good and bad which damns all work, and the 'equality' which grudges the clean man his cleanliness by thrusting your dirt upon him, are the false principles. The best thing for society to supply would be a minimum provision payable to every person when they have come to, say, 18 years of age with freedom to earn beyond this in the professions, public offices and services, art, science, and commerce. It should be hardly above a bare subsistence wage and should eventually belong to everyone like free physicking and free schooling for the 'working-class' now.[1] While there is great inequality in education and status the mere proletarian and small wage labourer might have a smaller provision; while well-to-do parents (those with adequate inherited or professional means) would be required to provide the suggested minimum provision for each child.[2] For those who squandered this provision (which would be the fruit of the work of the community) and could not maintain themselves houses of toil would be the remedy and penalty.[3] Complete socialization is not a panacea for

[1] Cf. Bertrand Russell's "vagabond's wage" in *Roads to Freedom*.

[2] This does not differ from the obligation to bequeath some part of parental estate to children which, whenever there is the right to bequeath, should be the law in all states. This would mean freeing the state during the parents' lives of the care of all children of the well-to-do, whose contribution would be paid to the state.

[3] The economic and social conditions would determine whether it would be necessary to get people to do some 'productive' work for this

mankind. The important and fertile personal element in all the relations of life is opposed to it.¹ And human development is a cerebral development which makes the human hive system uncongenial. Many elements of our material existence, however—water, air, minerals, oils—should not be left in private hands, and many could be administered (as some now are) by corporations under safeguards. We must not make a world which ignores the truth that people do things best for themselves and are the better for making their own position and their own mistakes.²

small living wage or whether a greatly decreased population and an enormously increased mechanical output would suffice for this and all other social services. We should not want to create a class of idle poor to replace the "idle rich". A small living wage might enable the great majority to live as the very small capitalist has lived—employing himself as he desired; but it might also create a large class which did little or no work at all—actual 'doletarians' as we have them in this and other countries now. At any rate the small wage would not enable people to breed children for the sake of it, for parents would be bound to maintain the child—i.e. bound to work for the children they brought into the world; the living wage of the two parents being forfeit if the children were not properly maintained. This has the great merit of making parents responsible for their acts, and is the only alternative to state support of children which must incidentally be state support of parents, unless the children belong to the state as in Plato's system. This system strikes at choice and liberty, and especially at the rights of the mother as nurturer. The small living wage would stimulate the brain worker and stimulate artistic output, but before it was given to everyone society would have to become more homogeneous. If it were necessary for most people to produce something of economic value I think the sanction of a very strong public opinion would be effectual. Walther Rathenau records that before the great war idleness among young Prussians of the official and noble classes was almost unknown as the result of a strong class opinion against it. Why not—if such work were called for economically—give some form of reward to workers, or to good workers, and a less subsistence-wage to the non-workers?

¹ The liking of all living things for variety opposes it also. Differences in beauty, amenity, and riches, are liked by all, poor as well as rich. For variety adds colour and glamour to life, provoking standards of comparison.

² Mechanization is a herd factor, and socialism is a sort of mechanization of mankind, which harnesses the individual to the community and makes him look to the community instead of to himself. Too much socialization sacrifices not only his liberty of action but his liberty of judgment, dis-

There is no more useful political truth to remember than that men are not born free, nor are they born slaves —and that the only real matter at issue is whether they are born so that they desire to attain freedom, and whether they ought to desire it. The future path of mankind—as a political animal—will certainly be the path of demokracy, liberty, responsibility, and individualism.

Now the ultimate assumption of demokracy is that the political vote by which assent or dissent is signified belongs to the citizen not necessarily because he has property or means or education but because he has interests. Therefore in a demokracy the function of government comes to be regarded as the representation of various interests in the community. But what are men's interests? The answer would tell us whether governments are to be regarded as mere registers of the interests of the average man or whether they should also represent certain 'overhead' social and other ideals. When we inquire, as we must, what sort of theory is behind the demokratic practice of giving everyone because he has personal interests a *lien* on the business of the commonwealth as a whole we shall find that there is no real answer—the only answer is that demokracy differs from all forms of government in demanding a high general standard in human beings, and never could have been outlined until some general standard had been attained. As yet it is only imperfectly attained, and the ideals of demokracy must suffer eclipse until we have this higher general standard of personal demands and personal ideals. But though demokracy can only have a halting success till the general level of mankind is definitely higher its principle is without doubt the right principle of human government. No government can be as strong as one broad-based upon the general will—upon the assent and consent of men and

Demokracy

interests and their representation

couraging the individual qualities which are demanded by every great and good thing. Cf. e.g., the gregarious instinct.

377

therefore upon their co-operation with the laws which rule them. The broadest basis for a demokracy is therefore the safest. Changing conditions of human society may modify the theories of government which in any case can never be perfect and never should be rigid; but it is certain that it will not be possible to govern one section of the human race in one way and another in a way which it considers less advantageous to itself as soon as those world contacts, mental and geographical, are made which have already begun. It will not be possible to rule some men by force and others by freedom; any more than it will be possible to teach some men that the globe stands upon an elephant, or that god made the sun to light men by day and the moon to light them by night, while other men are taught the results of astronomic knowledge. Hence personal collaboration with the laws which regiment society is a strict corollary to the growth of our own knowledge of and interest in the principles involved.

Advantages and disadvantages of demokracy
grossness
public opinion
Leadership

Demokracy, because it means some education for all and the growth of common interests throughout the community, has made the world more estimable. The grossness which pleased in the middle ages, in Shakespeare's age, and in Goethe's, is ceasing to please; it is decreasing with the increase in interests, in decent amusements, and as a result of the freeing of the lives of women: a self-governing people will not neglect morals. Without demokracy there is no public opinion, and public opinion is stronger than all physical force in the world; the determination of the citizens of a demokratic state being a more powerful thing both within and without its borders than any display of power by their government. But demokracy has inherent disadvantages (which need only discountenance if it were true that any other system is without them). It emasculates the strength of leadership and the principles of leaders, for in a demokratic state the lead is given by the people. Demokracy, then, inevitably undermines initiative, superiority, and indi- superiority viduality. It is a flat-rate system. Nevertheless it contains in itself the seed of the remedy which is closed to every other form of government. For the choice of the best is with the totality. Distinctions must always emerge in any mass of men; such things as character talent and skill will not remain undistinguished: so the remedy we have is aristokratic demokracy—the opinion in the community aristo- that the opinion of the best is the best opinion. kratic de-
mokracy

When Sokrates speaking to the politically-minded Athenians said that he himself was perhaps the only true politician in Athens it was ideal interests he had in mind —he had in mind the rule of the best. What sort of world would it be which took no notice of its best? There is no other principle of progress, no other alternative to stagnation, than the emergence of superiority; which is too important a factor in human affairs to be smothered by doctrines of equality however specious. Mere equality will never give superiority all that it requires, for a society must be willing and able to recognize value if it is to make room for it. Such good things as independence and courage do not seem to rise from masses of men—mass-weight is not courage—they are things fostered by originality; and capacity to rule belongs to this courage and not to mass-courage: it is proper to the aristokratic method to select the individual, while the demokracy affords skope for the mass. At present the modern 'working-class' is moved first and foremost by pity, stirred by the consciousness of its own deprivations. But the class which has had the command of means education and social amenity is moved rather by honour, and influenced by the idea of the public interest. It may and should be said that so it ought to be—they have had leisure means and education to look beyond themselves. But they *have* done so, and this political and social contribution is theirs, not that of the manual worker. It belongs to a true demokracy to welcome the safeguard provided by diversity of opinion, knowing that all *cannot* think alike, and in a healthy body corporate should not.   When we said, then, that the only principle of progress, the only alternative to stagnation, is by recognition of the best, we were recognizing that in society as in biology the change which leads to progress depends on the production of varieties, and not on a continuous and regular evolution of the elements given in a state of equilibrium. There is need of *per saltum* change, an irruption of fresh elements.[1]

Rebellion and Revolution

So it is that in the freedom of opinion there is safety. But is there room for rebellion, for revolution? The question more or less answers itself. Freedom of opinion is no permanent safety-valve if all action is shackled. Ferrero has called opposition the vital organ of the modern state, and where there is no provision for it the only outlet is revolt. Goethe himself was convinced that the people are never to blame for this; that rebellion is always the reaction to bad government.[2] Against naked despotism the modern mind certainly decrees rebellion. Despotism is itself lawlessness. The acts of despots are in form and substance anarchical. But modern systems of government regard all abuse of power as ground for revolt.[3] Rights and laws, we now believe, are not absolute, and are estimable only as parts of justice; and as parts of truth: for the attempt to rule men by dogma

[1] The principle of the emergence of something better, outstanding, individual, is far more deeply rooted in the nature of things than any democratic principle: and the tendency to psychological communism—the resistance to a better and a best—as the upshot of demokracy must not be lost sight of.

[2] Bad rulers, he said, withhold reform until it is imposed upon them from below; Sully in his *Mémoires* and Burke gave a similar verdict.

[3] Republicanism in France was declared to teach *la défiance du pouvoir* and to make *"son contrôle permanent un devoir"*. Against abuse of power insurrection is incumbent on the whole people and on each part of the people. (Art. 35 of the *Déclaration des Droits de l'Homme et du Citoyen.* Juin 24, 1793.)

provokes another kind of rebellion—revolutions in thought. Such change in the received ideas is itself a vital factor, *"toujours libérateur"*, as Amiel said; and a modern historian has argued that revolution may contain "a principle of stability more sure than tradition".[1] The sap of life is not to be found in the ordered and ordained; the progresses of civilization have not been obtained by loyalties, *esprit de corps*, and belief in the force wielded by constituted authority; and these progresses may sometimes have to be sought by ikonoclasm.[2] In Bagehot's happy phrase: What civilizes humanity is the formation of a *cake of custom* but what makes progress possible is the power *to break the cake of custom*.

We have to learn to trust men with responsibility—because when education is general and each has a voice in the state the old government *de haut en bas* is impossible. The only way out is to give responsibility, and to teach by giving it. And the best use to which men can put this experience of responsibility is to recognize the values of order, liberty, and superiority. The very worst thing we can do with a bad opinion is to suppress it. There is no known way in which the right opinion can stand on its own legs except by knowing the bad one: no ignorance is strong. When we go about with our eyes open we recognize evil as an intolerable tyranny; other men's goodness, other men's good things, may sometimes be tyrannous too, but here again freedom is the remedy. The development of civilized societies is towards liberty, equalization, and individuality,[3] for these 3 afford the

[1] John 1st lord Acton.
[2] Force, p. 360.
[3] A greek minister told a french audience (in 1927) that the 'individualism' of states was a thing of the past, and added that individual men would cease to have any existence except as part of the group. This would make one suppose that it is the individual who has counted hitherto. But it is not so. The tyrannies of family and tribe and all types of society through the savage tabu to despotic, theocratic, caste, feudal, and gild systems have

best guarantee of justice, the best security for talent, and the best soil for idealism.

made the individual the constant sport of the group. It is only in the past one or two hundred years that the conceptions of individual right and of freedom of thought have developed—and lo! in every country men are now asking for group-leading and standardization back again. Nevertheless it is the rights of individuals which have never yet been tried out.

SECTION III

HUMAN CHARACTER

BETTERMENT AND HAPPINESS

Uno itinere non potest perveniri ad tam grande secretum. SYMMACHUS

Alteri vivas oportet si vis tibi vivere. SENECA

Forces of the soul are the sense of beauty, the sentiment of justice, the disdain of worldly trivialities. AZORÍN

Quant aux fins et aux origines, ce n'est pas leur connaissance incertaine qui peut fournir la direction de la vie. BERTHELOT

SECTION III

HUMAN CHARACTER

Is human character good or bad?

HAS man a good character or a bad. The commonplace remark 'I believe in human nature' is bare of meaning; for you can certainly trust good human nature and with equal certainty you cannot trust bad. But what is meant by 'belief in human nature' is that men in the long run will decide right and go right; and for this there is no sort of evidence. Mankind has never as a whole gone right, thought right, or desired right, and has never embraced one single idealistic principle or agreed to any one principle of right conduct. Crowds are both cruel and sentimental, and are not to be moved by fine ideas. Philanthropists indeed have usually thought well of human nature, but those who have made it their study have exposed its frivolity and weakness, its self-interest and hypocrisy. No other opinion can be gathered from the world's spiritual leaders: the opinion of man in the Gospels is condemnatory; and though indian thought has more tolerance for human foibles and more pity than christian and hebrew—though the buddhist is more concerned with man's miseries and the gospel with man's trespasses—both see that he is the slave of passions and wrong desire. Both know also that there are blessed elements, wherein lies the hope of humanity. Human mentality in the future, no doubt, will decide that the defect in the outlook of the world's great spiritual men lay in their acceptance of an extreme dualism—the soul of man is desperately wicked and his misery inherent, the men of light are but a foil to this dark picture, and the religions of conviction of sin and appeal for celestial help and mercy are the consequence. But man in the mass has no such polarity of devil and angel; the truth about him and the difficulty also is that he cannot be fitted into round and square holes. The evil instincts lie in layers with the good ones, and more could be made of us if we were not such moral hybrids. For the moral hybrids are judged by men like themselves, who praise the 'showy' and pleasant virtues of their acquaintance and leave sterling values alone. Man's chief wretchedness is not 'sin', and the conception of his inherent misery has been partly formed upon data which are in no wise inherent in his condition. Ignorance heredity and stupidity are the irresponsible elements of man's bad nature, and if at one end of the line we have the foul and evil and at the other those with all the felicities of generosity and goodness the centre is made up of people who are neither bad nor good: those who form the left wing here learn little or nothing from life, they do not 'improve' and they often sin without knowing it; those who form the right wing are the only material upon which education, direct civilization, and the forces of religion and ethic can do their work. But indirect civilization—the civilization which exists round and about us—may and does do in time for this left wing what I think religions and moral education are not fitted to do. The importance to civilization of improvement in our surroundings was pointed out by Guizot, "the inward is reformed by the outward".[1] Man went without the best gifts of a material civilization for long aeons of his history. In its place were all those conditions of life which by making strong definite contrasts made also strong definite dualisms in religion and philosophy. (I think it is evidence of the influence on the human spirit of more amene general conditions that the terrific spectacle of war-lust and human failure during 1914–18 did *not* produce a crop of dualisms.) Between ignorance and fear man did not see himself as he really was; and it is the obvious improvement in his

The middle men—a left and a right wing

[1] "As the outward by the inward." "An external fact leads sooner or later to an internal fact."

386

material condition—the immensely greater security and his being no longer the mere helpless sport and prey of pestilence and disease, for example—which makes him able to view life and himself without extravagant despair or superstitious self-abasement.

It must be realized that the characters which it is common to describe as specifically human such as intellect and personality are not in fact proper to man as man but are rare to the point of being idiosynkratic. None of the finer things are usual things, if they were they would not be recognized as fineness. It would not appear that there have been profound differences of moral character between barbarians and modern races of men, and our raw material—the savage—presents instances in every quarter of the globe of tribes which are gentle peaceable and honest and of others which are quarrelsome lying and cruel. It has been affirmed without fear of contradiction that at least man has an innate sense of justice. Justice Justice however appears to be a very late arrival in human affairs. It has never held sway over the human mind. It is said that a child has a keen sense of injustice; but I see little relation between its sense of the wrong it suffers and man's presumed craving to render justice to other men. The child resents, as any animal does, the taking of its share, or the taking of its companion's share, and much more indignation is aroused as a rule for a small wrong suffered by itself or its companions than would be aroused by a much greater wrong suffered by an outsider. In the same way revenge is a revindication of outraged personal right, it is not "a rude justice"; and it too is felt most intensely when you alone are concerned or at most your tribe or clan. Justice in law and civilization has not emerged slowly from a fount of just thinking, but on the contrary any justice has been the result of a gradual elimination of the unjust sense of personal right. We have worked from a consideration of our own rights, not from the rights of others, through reflection sympathy and the notion underlying the 'golden rule', to an ultimate idea of justice. If it were otherwise human institutions would have shown it. Human institutions are not just because man has not cared for justice. And we cannot point to the great acts of justice performed by men because our whole history is riddled with the keen consciousness of rights and interests nourished by individuals as against other individuals, of trades and classes, of young against old and old against young. If man were just we could not explain the fraud and self-interest which characterize his actions. Justice can mean nothing unless it implies as much sense of what is due to others as of what is due to self. No one can contend that this is what man has been conspicuous for.[1]

Cruelty

Justice has not held sway over the mind of man, and what virtue has done so? But there are vices which have always swayed him, and one of these—in its horror and wantonness the worst of all—is cruelty. Against this invading ocean of evil the one only breakwater has been maternal sympathy and love. It is this ubiquitous compassion which is set at the opposite pole of life to the vice defined by Johnson as being "pleased with hurting others". Why and how cruelty acquired so great a hold on mankind is a mystery of human character. No instances of it need be cited for the press which might be searched for a year to find an example or two of pure justice provides us with daily instances of appalling cruelties. Man created cruelty, which stenches to heaven, but he calls it 'brutality'. *Per contra* he has adopted the word 'humanity' for the opposite practices. Humanity however has never characterized mankind. The word 'humane' has never described actual man it has only described an ideal man; and man may hope, in time, to

[1] Lecky points to the abolition of slavery as one of the 3 or 4 "perfectly virtuous acts" of humanity.

disown his creation and to follow in the lines traced by the other animals: it must certainly be said that if he does not it is not worth while that such a species should exist. Man's conception of hell and its torments is in fact all derived from what he pictures himself doing to man, and has done to man.[1]   The cruel instinct is equally aroused in the desire to cause mental suffering; and those who indulge it are equally far from the 'humane' ideal. Irritation and resentment, as well as worse passions, make a man wish to inflict mental cruelties; and this mental cruelty, like physical, is always perpetrated on the helpless or through some helplessness of others which gives us an advantage. Neither kind of cruelty stands up to an equal. Hence both are always essentially cowardly. Humanity, then, like justice, is not the proprium of Vanity mankind. On the other hand no quality is more widely diffused than vanity. It is so rooted in organic life that we are entirely unconscious of its influence upon us, and do not realize that it is a prime mover of opinion and conduct. It is ubiquitous because vanity is a symptom of self-love and self-love is ubiquitous. The salient example of how much we are affected by each other's vanity is seen in our distribution of praise and blame. It is not reasonable, not desirable, that we should lavish praise and shrink from expressing the appropriate blame. But it is obvious that all praise is readily accepted as true and any blame as readily felt to be undeserved. Because of men's vanity we dare not say: 'that was not done right', while unmeaning (because undiscriminating) praise is always in place. For vanity is the enemy of truth; to placate it we say more than is true. In ourselves it is an enemy to mental and moral achievement, hindering generosity and magnanimity to other men, and indeed

---

[1] The devil has been drawn in man's own likeness. "The lower animals, if they could devise a religion, would certainly represent the devil as a great white man" (Dean of S. Paul's, 1927).

being often the occasion for malevolence. Our vanity and self-love cause us to excuse ourselves and accuse others; and when we are not men enough to say 'I ought not to have said this, or done that' we put away from us mental sympathy and understanding and no reconciliation of mind can take place. That terrible desire to put ourselves in the better light and throw the rest to the wolves is the cruelty of self-love. And the lie which lurks in it also. For it is clear that the reflection which each of us sees of himself in the mirror of his vanity bears no more resemblance to truth than does each man's belief that his own family is a model to all the others. The vain man mistakes his powers and his effect on other men—there is no better evidence of its self-stultifying influence. There can be

Self-love necessary no doubt that a certain amount of self-love is a necessary moral protection; without it men would suffer a violation of personality and a weakening of what is most precious to virtue, self-respect. It is due too, no doubt, to our friends' defects as well as to our own that we may not be ready to avow ourselves in the wrong. Again, it is neither unreasonable nor objectionable that a man should be vain of his quality or his skill. What makes vanity a desperate weakness is that it is habitually present where there is no excuse for it. Those qualities, then, are precious which do not feed upon vanity, and self-respect should be one of these. On the other hand hu-

Humility and self-re-spect mility can never be and has never been the support to virtue which is found in self-respect. It is the staple quality (second only to fear) exploited by religion, to the hindrance of higher moral efforts. Large humility and small self-respect is a mixture which defies moral education; and humility has been constantly represented as a great spiritual achievement whereas it is one of the virtues convenient to other men and an obstacle to inconvenient self-development. It has played a mean role in christianity as a set off to the christian prevention that pride is vicious. But what is known as 'a proper pride' is among the very best of personal qualities. A high spirit is itself absolutely necessary if we are to work moral and social reforms and denounce moral and social wrongs. No people devoid of high spirit has ever effected these things and none but high spirited peoples can maintain their liberties: the common desire to dominate and the still commoner instinct of subalternism demand that this quality should be upheld in honour. A measure of self-love and even of vanity contributes, like self-respect, in maintaining a moral level of life; they are protections and bulwarks, not to be broken down. The true significance of humility is to be found in teachableness. And it has its place in all spiritual discerning. But like obedience and self-denial it is an *ad hoc* virtue. What we should extol rather than humility or pride (which are not virtues at all when in the vague) is intellectual modesty, which ought to be thought of (like contempt for personal vanity) as a part of self-respect.

A high spirit

No virtue in the whole range of moral excellencies has been so extolled as courage; and from classical times to our own it has always meant physical courage, courage where the hazard is physical pain or death. We speak indeed of moral heroism but the world's 'heroes' are the men who have answered this call upon themselves to face physical danger. Yet this quality which has taken so large a place in the conception of virtuous character and has seized upon the heart and imagination of man with unique force has contributed less to human happiness than any other; whereas, next to sympathy, nothing has brought more happiness than moral courage. It is *not* shameful to dread the pain and anguish of burning my hand in the fire; it *is* shameful to yield to the cowardice which refuses to stand up for the right or the wronged; and one of the permanent distinctions between moral and physical courage is that while physical courage,

Courage

however great, will not go a hairsbreadth towards endowing a man with moral courage, great moral courage is likely to help a man to find the physical courage necessary to carry out his moral behests.[1] Whenever physical courage is something more than 'animal spirits' recklessness or physical prowess (as in prize-fighting), it calls upon a moral quality which we describe as strength of mind or soul; and it is this strength of soul which never fails to secure approbation from *our* souls. The finest moral contribution here has been the martyr's courage, and the most important social asset is the courageous bearing of sickness; for in a world where great pain has to be borne the courage with which it is met tempers the suffering of those around us. Physical courage however has had an insignificant part in procuring justice for other men: it has been in fact so rarely employed to protect the helpless, in comparison with its aggressive and truculent uses, that it cannot be claimed for it that it has played a role in human happiness even as a weapon of defence. It might be maintained on the contrary that 'stoutness of heart' is nearly allied to deadness of moral sensibility, making a man ready to inflict what he is willing to bear. Besides this, a lack of imagination has much to do with temperamental courage; the unimaginative cannot feel the same dread of danger as the imaginative. And since

[1] Cardinal de Retz writes of the count de Soissons that he had that stoutness of heart commonly called valour in the greatest degree possible; but had not, even in the least degree, that strength of mind which is called resolution. The first is common, almost vulgar; the second is even more unusual than one would think. (*Mémoires*, Bk. i, 1613–43.)

In the war of 1914–18 there was a captain who had shown "the courage of a lion", and for his heroism was the spoilt person in the Paris hospital where he was nursed by English and American women. One evening he asked the American who relates the story for *jam*; she had been on her feet for 12 hours and procuring it gave her a long walk along stone corridors: at the door the ward sister reproached her; jam was not permitted. "Of course," she said, "I only brought it because captain K. asked for it." "Oh no! I didn't," he said, "I never asked for anything of the sort."

there is a great difference in sensitiveness to pain the really brave man is evidently the one who performs an act of courage at which his flesh shrinks. The glory which has surrounded physical courage is due to the past magnification of war, and to a criterion of valour and value contributed by one half only of the human race ("*andreia*"). Far from being a breeding-ground of the virtues, as we are taught to believe, physical courage is among the least fertile of all moral qualities: on the other hand it is one which can never be dispensed with where its exercise is called for—it is imperative for sentient organic beings as few other moral qualities can be said to be.

Moral courage, the power to stand up against hostile opinion and the loss of approbation of your fellows, against ridicule and contempt—this moral strength is the greatest of all the gifts of character. Is not the ease with which 'courage' has been accepted as perhaps the most important virtue due in part to the fact that without moral courage there is *no* 'virtue', nothing, that is, which is secure, or strong. It would mean nothing if I were full of benevolence just minded amiable or considerate, for without moral courage I possess these things without possessing them. No one can depend on them. I cannot depend on them myself. If my charity is so large that I would give my body to be burned but my moral courage is so little that I would let someone else be burned, what is my virtue? "Weakness is next to wickedness" means that the only foundation for a moral character is moral strength.[1] Physical fear makes men cruel, but moral fear is the most heartless cowardice of all. It is viler to do wrong from fear of each other than from physical fear. What we have to suffer from each other indeed is more than all the physical suffering flesh is heir to, but this is not why moral courage is rare; it is rare simply because

Moral courage

[1] Was not this the truth that Nietzsche had hold of? and set forth awry as a man may do when surrounded by servile doctrines.

moral weakness is much more common than physical weakness. Everywhere the first is condoned and discounted though it is among the greatest miseries of our relations with each other; for if there were more moral courage it would not be possible for men to work so much harm. The cult of physical courage has allowed us to forget that the necessity for moral courage in big things as in small is always present: we may have to display physical courage once, but moral courage is called for every day; all social courage being part of it.

The epoch when moral courage is valued and praised will be the great epoch, and till then all the great justices social and personal must wait: for the kingdom of this justice suffers moral violence, and the violent take it.

Fear Fear is universally shared by all organic beings high enough in the scale to experience it: fear of enemies, fear of the unknown, and of the unaccustomed. But in conditions of developed mentality, intense gregariousness, and helpless dependence on his fellows, human fear has become largely moral fear: fear of each other, fear of loss of reputation and fortune, fear of ridicule, fear of tomorrow, fear of death. The fear of other men's minds is the most ignoble and far-reaching cowardice of all, because while physical fear and shrinking are in part organic and self-protective instincts the "fear of man which bringeth a snare" offers the soul no protection it is good to accept, and substitutes human for divine respect.

Jealousy There is no passion so malignant as jealousy, and the jealous person is capable of any cruelty. Jealousy is so inrooted in human character (and indeed in the character of other animals) that in greek and semitic theology it is assumed to be an attribute of the gods. No doubt it is hard to suppress all jealous movements of the soul, but it is not hard to determine that jealous thoughts shall never under any circumstances whatever be converted into 'Jealous love' action. It is not true that jealousy is an essential ingredient of fond love, since its essence is our idea of our own demands and desires as lovers.　　Jealousy has a root in vanity and self-esteem, and is in this unlike envy which *Envy* by nature is a mean emotion though it need not, like jealousy, be always despicable. For it may be the stimulus to emulation. As for the hypocrite you can only denounce him, you cannot reform him. Hypocrisy is the worst of *Woe to* moral cankers because it makes all virtue impossible. *you, hypocrites!* There is a mental myopy which may breed this moral disease; for moral character is largely dependent on mental sincerity in reasoning, on wishing and intending to see clearly, so that there is a kind of hypocrite who may deceive even himself.

The clue to all the riddles of human character is its *Incompleteness* incompleteness and inconsistencies. Every personality *and inconsistencies* joins both good and bad and a man's single actions may *sistencies* not be referable to virtue alone or to vice alone. For he is the outcome of hazard, the hazard arrangement of that multitude of psychic characters which heredity bequeaths him. In him everything that matters is uncertain: heart, intellect, educability, mental vigour, strength of character, fineness of temperament. With which of these will he come endowed? and what potion among all the riches of the world can insure him quality of temperament? which *Temperament* is genetically the most important basis of character, innate, ineducable, unchangeable.

If moral life were not a conflict—if there were no *Life and* arena in which we are to put forth our powers in a conflict- *conflict* grip with evil and ugliness—the moral life would not be worth living and it would never have developed. The man who is not naturally moral but is morally teachable must exercise himself in such an *agôn*. The man who is not morally teachable is not a subject for it; he is made 'to learn' or at least to conform by other means. The man who is naturally moral—the man whom nature delights to produce—has not indeed to fight in the arena with the wild beasts of his own inclinations, but if he has seen the light on the eternal hills he can only make towards it by climbing. It is a law of life that a world simply "all right" for a humanity which had done nothing to make it so, would not be all right at all. It is part of the law which makes effort and not perfection our daily supersubstantial bread. It is part of the same law that we must dislike and condemn individuals for qualities over which they have no control (such as the feeble and feckless) and like and esteem others for qualities which they owe to their forebears: no standard and no progress would be otherwise possible. Gentle and forgiving methods can win the naturally good and sometimes the very bad, but what we have to deal with is the neutral masses of men, and the majority are only influenced by the firmness which knows what it wants and the tenacity which requires it; for we are nearly all of us 'slackers' in one way or another and if you let a thing pass most men will do it again.

The law of life

"The old is better"

It is held to be natural that men should look forwards —to the generation which will be represented by their own children; but history shows that there has been no such general tendency. Men have spent a large part of their energies in looking back to ancestors, and tradition has been more highly prized than ideas of progress. We may set down this factor in human mentality to the pressure of the authority of custom on mankind, supported as this has always been on defective knowledge and justified by the obvious insecurity of the unknown, and it has perhaps no absolute value whatever except as a makeweight to the crude naïveté which is ever ready to welcome the new as the true. For the conservative and the progressive are parallel factors in our mental make-up; they play a large part in the same personality, and must do so while old and new share together as man's legitimate human treasure. If there is no clinging to the old there is no affection, if there is no greeting for the new there is no illumination. The strangest obsession civilized man has to register is its constant inclination to regard the last generation as better than the present, and especially to believe that everything was better "when we were young". How do we come by this useless piece of mental furniture? The long arm of the paidagogue explains the belief that the way we have been taught is the right way: but this does not explain why each age extols the customs of its forebears and bewails those of its contemporaries. Instances are forthcoming that every age has branded the morals and habits of its own time and praised an earlier time when everything was better, when men were more religious, and the manners and upbringing of children exemplary. I can offer no explanation of mental judgments which are and must be so palpably false except that the achievement under our eyes is a constant reminder of how much it falls below the standards men pursue, whereas past achievement can be isolated in imagination from these irritating realities.

HUMAN BETTERMENT

CIVILIZATION—that which arises from the commerce of men in cities; the arts and crafts which separate man from the savage; letters, literature, and political instinct which divide the Greek from the barbarian: this is the meaning of the word. It does not mean a finished state of society, which has never existed. Guizot as we have seen had noted the two facts which constitute civilization—a moral improvement in man and an improvement in his external surroundings. Up to now no civilization has been free of savage and barbarous accompaniments, because the only moral factor capable of creating and upholding

Civilization

civilized society is a gentilization of the human spirit which has never taken place.

Whether it be viewed from the interior angle or the exterior civilization has never been a continuous process. The intellectual condition in the Europe of the vth century A.C. was not comparable with the intellectual condition of Greece in the vth century B.C.: and spiritual and moral uplift at times and places in the thousand years before 1500 was superior to the progress in material inventions and devices. Now, progress in these has become so spectacular that it might be supposed that civilization principally consisted in them. They are so far in advance of moral development that the contrasts they create in any community are much greater than the contrast between bad and good men. And these contrasts are the measure of our civilization. On the one hand citizens who spend many thousand pounds on clothes and motors and entertainments, and on the other a citizen living for three days in her room with a coffin which cannot be buried because it is christmas time; or a little family assembling for a meal at the table which is the only trestle for a corpse. Underground rooms dank and foul where five or more human beings sleep on one bedstead without covering; filthy slums in a great scotch town where the dwellings are infested with rats and toads and the men with body vermin; an irish cabin where an inmate was roasted on the hearth by her family as a witch. Half a million pounds asked for as state aid towards the London slums was not forthcoming, but in 1918 more than six and a half million pounds was spent every day in war.[1] Who is civilized while such things are possible? "Who is offended and I burn not?" But what civilization

---

[1] The 'Unknown Warrior' may have been a great blackguard; but if so he is receiving a tardy homage from civil society which had taken him by force from such 'homes' as these, and assassinated him. It had never done anything for him.

can there be where such things are no offence? They are no offence because they are, literally, unperceived by the fortunate who need not be offended by them.

The civilizations of the past were of three types. We had doctrinaire civilizations—such as those of China, Japan, and the Hindu, or as the modern state theories of socialism and fascism. And we had religious civilizations, such as that of Egypt became, as european civilization was for about a thousand years, and as Islam is. And there have been philosophic civilizations which, of course, have degenerated as superstition and formalism: buddhism would have introduced a purely philosophic civilization had such been possible. The Greek type was neither doctrinaire nor religious. The Roman developed out of the conception of law—*jus*. It is these two—the Greek and the later Roman—which were the most eklectic and adaptable of the civilizations which have gone to form modern civilization; as they were both also the least doctrinaire and the least religious in character. They were cultural civilizations.   It is remarkable that of these types none was determined by its material civilization—with the possible exception of later Rome. Today the march of civilization has reversed this. In an immensely larger population amenities and pleasures are at the service of a far greater percentage of the whole than has ever been seen in the world before; and at the same time the researches and discoveries of science have sensibly and insensibly changed the outlook for all these men. The two notes of modern civilization are scientific and mechanistic.

The resulting 'materialism', it is thought, is choking the spiritual channels of life and will be a check to higher civilization. But the very worst feature of materialism is that belief in force which has dominated civil life hitherto. It is not the perfection of material things which makes us 'materialists'. Some years before the war of 1914 a novelist was declaring that nothing but the most optimistic

Material-ism

view could be taken about the progress of society. In a few vivid sentences and with half a score of compelling instances she made this progress stand out before us as a living thing not to be gainsaid. Then the war came. She hastened to help—and died of heartbreak at the spectacle offered by civilization. A foremost english professor of philosophy and the best known belgian writer both regarded pre-war Germany as an example of high thinking and plain living, the model of a moral society. Yet philosophic Germany showed no superiority to a bellicose 'patriotism' and was incapable of opposing high principles to class pressure. And the same was true of the preachers. The sound foundations of civilization then were not present either there or elsewhere in Europe when the war broke out.   In our present spiritual outlook we are experiencing the law of compensation. Material luxury and distractions will suffocate the spirit, but so will a false 'spirituality': today there is more spirituality with less demand for spiritual leisure; it is the reaction against an unreal spiritual.[1] One of the greatest obstacles to the civilizing of the human spirit has, in fact, been not materialism but obscurantism, which is the dead fruit of superstition and blind custom and of man's lust of domination over his fellows. Men extol religions because they inculcate reverence; but it would be hard to prove that reverence has been more valuable to man than criticism.   The gist of the matter is that no one is free of materialism who uses spiritual things as though they were material goods; and no one is spiritual who does not possess things material as though he possessed them not.

The present generation sees that the shibboleths the older generation stood for before 1914 turned out to be no good, or small good. Never before in the history of the world had there been a large population both free and literate as critic of its blunders; never before had such

[1] Ethics and Religion, p. 95.

an immense disaster been enacted before such an audience:
and the indifference of this audience to the spiritual claims
of the past is a recognition conscious or unconscious that
something was wrong with all previous 'civilizations' and
that the elements of most importance to the building of
man's ideal city were still to seek.

Do the facts of history suggest that there has been Progress
a .principle of progress at work in human affairs—a
natural tendency, that is, to develop in the better and
stronger directions. Human progress in this sense was
an idea born in the modern world. Sokrates and Plato
did not envisage it, for it does not consist in the demand
for conditions in which men can explicate political justice
it consists in the belief that the history of man is a history
of progress in realizations sentiments and ideas.[1] Turgot
was the first to posit such an evolution before Darwin had
familiarized us with the same idea in biology. It was some
advance of the human spirit itself which gave us this idea
of progress and also of the things in which progress consists. When we consider the four permanent essentials
of civilized society—intellectual and spiritual activities,
beauty and amenity—we find, as has been seen, no
evidence of intellectual or cerebral evolution since the
age of Plato and Aristotle; the differences in this direction
can all be set down to the greater wealth of material on
which the human mind is exercized and to the larger
number of the educated. The factors of external progress
—beauty and amenity—often appear to be and to have
been present in inverse ratio. There remains spiritual
progress; and I think there has been a general advance
in tolerance, justice, humanity, and kindliness.[2] This is

[1] The theory of progress would make utopias not palliatives for the
natural defects of mankind but descriptions of an event to which the whole
race is moving.

[2] It may indeed be claimed that we are superior to all the ages before
us in having less coarseness grossness and cruelty, less superstition and less

largely due—at least in this country and in France—to political and school education which have brought with them reflection on the distribution of the social advantages—health comfort knowledge and wealth—which was always absent while those who enjoyed them were surrounded by an ignorant and subject population: the sentiment of humanity itself awaited a greater general amenity of men's lives; as the finest gospel in the world must wait till you have fed the starving sinner who is to hear it.   None of these general spiritual realizations reached the masses through religion or philosophy. Up to the most recent times there has been no common advance at all in kindliness and sympathy. Brutality, delight in seeing pain, a shameless exploitation of man by man, and religious and political intolerance, reigned in Europe till well into the xix[th] century. There was a prevailing poverty in the things which belong to spiritual growth—as there had been among the masses in the middle ages. The giant progress of the race, indeed, comes when the heart civilizes the head. For if a fool can have none but a poverty-struck hold on moral notions the poor of heart can have none at all. We shall be able to register a general advance in the human spirit only when it is realized that the principle of civilization is a gradual displacing of the appetites by the affections.

In what sense does the conception of progress help the race. As regards absolute values no belief in a future perfection can change even in the least degree the moral necessities here and now.[1] But this apart, the conception

ignorance—in a prevailing decency and humanity of sentiment which persists despite the reminder in 1914–18 that it needs more substantial foundations; and which were unknown to Greece or Rome, to the 'ages of faith', to the puritan age and after.

[1] Cf. A Teleology, pp. 430–1.

To let zeal for the race modify zeal for our neighbours makes us no better than James's false philanthropist: Be ye warmed and fed . . . as I rejoice to think all men in the future will be.

of human progress is to be recognized as ethically helpful;
it satisfies the human spirit better than an outlook on
finalities. The individual grows, and he would like to
believe he is part of growth: and when the conception
of progress was unknown men made idylls of the development of the soul in another world, or philosophers placed
it in a cycle of kosmic forces where it was gradually
purified of its separate existence. If you can alter men
your thoughts and acts are more fertile things: the conception of progress in humanity realizes an immortality for
the human spirit. It was the consciousness of this new conception which informed the philosophy of the xix[th] century
and for the first time since christians wrote the *graffiti* in
the catacombs raised the presumption that there might
be something better than personal survival and reunion.

The xviii[th]-century belief that reason is the supreme Ration-
instrument of civilization and morals, the best arbiter in alism and
progress
human affairs, has no basis in experience or psychology.
The rationalist hypothesis in fact hindered moral progress
throughout the xix[th] century because it concealed and
kept in the background the real sources of moral action.
It checked knowledge and a sound and fruitful psychology
by assuming a barrier between man's cerebration and that
of the other animals. It exaggerated human rationality
both in its extent and in its validity, and thus allowed the
(mischievous) presumption that men's decisions and pre-
ventions are founded in "reason" or have a "rational
basis".[1] The most important things in the world are not
derived from reason, not supported by any ratiocinative
process—love, beauty, sympathy, the sense of responsibility, spirituality, honour, and that wisdom which, unreasoned, is added to reason. Reason can never take the

[1] If rational means the valid use of reasoning then it is true to say that the
proprium of humanity is to be irrational: intelligence is not a general
human property, it is the want of it which is a general human property.
Indeed it is obvious that there is no subject about which "reasoning" leading to opposite conclusions is not put foward.

place of the passion and power which alone have authority to coerce the minds of men.[1]

Reasoning convinces no one. Men will always find reasons for acquitting and accepting where their sympathies are engaged. Outside the processes of pure formal philosophy reason is never the determinant.

Education   Education could have accomplished much more for human improvement than it has done. It cannot do the greatest things but it can do very great things, and should be more definitely directed against certain pitfalls from which it is competent to save us. It could parry the instinct of credulity, the painful or evil sentimentalism which is a travesty of sentiment, moral cowardice,[2] truculence,[2] and all want of consideration for others. Detraction has been called the *péché mignon* of mankind; but we should be made to understand as children that speaking against others is an indirect way—and a mean one—of praising oneself: the society of other children may put the boastful in his place but this vanity is a subtler egoism which never leaves us. These half-dozen things alone would mean for the adult a more humane and happier standard of life. 'Education' in Latin countries means a moral acquisition, 'instruction' a mental one. We use the same word for both without perhaps having a very firm grip upon either. The abiding merit of the *studium* is that it affords an opportunity for education in manners as well as in mind, and it is astounding that teachers anywhere (and perhaps especially those in elementary schools) should be chosen when they know

[1] Of all the ways of defining man, said a modern frenchman, "I think the worst is the one which makes him out a reasoning animal. Reason rarely dwells in common minds, but still more rarely in great ones."

[2] In educating, physical courage should be treated as ancillary to moral courage; and while it should not be extolled or even praised it should always be expected. What should be impressed upon us is the necessity for *fortitude*, which includes both kinds of courage.

nothing about manners. Individuality and idiosynkrasy, again, have hardly any place in a school curriculum; if they had, the lines of school work would be chosen not for what they lead to but because the student can make something of them and of himself. Education obviously has a twofold office; the one is its classic office of bringing forth what is in a youth; the other is remedial—it seeks to supply the defects of nature. Each is clearly as important as the other.   The day is now past when repression and exhibition of the power of elders were held to be the staple of education; and the problem of the child has become the problem of the man and the problem of society—to determine, that is, the relative spheres of freedom and discipline. Without self-discipline there is no education; without freedom no moral development. When we have admitted to the full that every member of a community must be in some respects standardized there is still a great space left for freedom. It is probable that the core of fact in the theory of the psycho-analysts is that repression of tendencies (in any case ruthless repression) —even of bad ones—lays a foundation of delinquency; and when not of delinquency of unhappiness. I think the one exception is cruelty. Freedom is not only a main condition of happiness it is the soil for character, which is an indefinitely more important element for the individual and for society than either cleverness or remissiveness. The unhappy dualism of the past set the mind and soul apart from the body like a jewel in a casket. Now it is understood that the soul may be educated through the body, and the body by the soul, and that the direction of life is not something to be imposed from without but is already traced for each of us—that choices, likes, dislikes, impulses, instincts, are signposts which cannot be lost sight of without missing the way.[1] Little discipline

Freedom and discipline

[1] Froebel and Montessori were anticipated by Plato (*Republic*, vii): "Bring not up your children in learning by compulsion and fear but by

should be exacted for its own sake; resolution and strength of will do not grow if nothing is left to a child's choice and if its opportunities are all supervised. That is to say that the constant goal is self-discipline. On the other hand self-discipline only comes from experiences; so that even if it be true that nothing in education is more noxious than an excess of discipline it would still be true that when we are inexperienced everything in education could be better left out than the lesson of discipline.[1]

Freedom and indivi- dualities When the middle ages are recognized as *magna parens virum* something must be put down to the catholic system, to admirable qualities in its psychology and principles of education; but more must be set down to the comparative ease with which great men could then make themselves felt. Where freedom rules it tends to make insignificant personalities conspicuous ones, and I see no remedy for this but a real tolerance (which has never yet existed) for original and significant personalities so that the better may be gauged by comparison with the commoner: for it will be found that the only permanent way of reform lies along the road of comparison not that of suppression. Those strange ribaldries and obscenities, the bizarre contrasts of the middle ages, suggest that rigidity of discipline and dogma does not in fact result in educating any but the best elements, and these generally make good whatever the system. In the time of Lady Jane Grey and again under the Puritans cruel discipline and repression had certainly an untoward effect on life and character; and it would appear that later still it was the brutalities and the artificial moral training in

playing and pleasure." See also *The School of the Future a school of manual work*, by G. Kerschensteiner, director of education of the city of Munich (1908) translated by T. C. Horsfall.

[1] Education is largely the forming of (right) habits; these are not formed by spontaneous uncoördinated impulses; and the necessary co-ordination and direction which results in right habits is discipline. It is common to us and the other animals.

schools which were responsible for the bullies and rakes of the period.

There has been a swing of the pendulum and the present tendency is to believe that the bad child has every right to exchange his dirty pinafore for his good brother's clean one, and sit at table, like the prodigal son, a shining example of the success of 'natural impulses'. No distinction is made between 'naughty' and bad; but while naughty only means rebellious and unlike other people it is inherited badness which cannot be allowed the freedom of its impulses.[1] No doubt what makes a child believe in natural kindness and goodness is worth more than discipline and is much more enlightening to its moral nature than "catechisms and the commandments";[2] but educational theory cannot be built up on the assumption that bad material is not as real a handicap in education as elsewhere.

Apart from improving the race by eugenic methods Breeding can any improvement be looked for from that type of breeding which is due to ancestry? Breeding, good or bad, is a real phenomenon in men as in all other domesticated animals; it was realized in Homer's time as we realize it now. But it cannot be made solely responsible for the production of 'the gentleman' since the moral (The qualities of a gentleman or the criteria offered us by gentleman) Confucius, Aristotle, Chaucer, or Bernard Shaw may be clearly independent of birth and education. The concept of the 'gentleman', however, represents the tradition of a standard and this tradition of a standard is its quota to

---

[1] If there is no inherited badness there is no inherited goodness—the alternative is the 'clean slate'. That, *ex hypothesi*, is neutral, and what is written upon it may be good or bad. So that the distinction of good and bad is not removed.

[2] This has nowhere been better put than in a daily newspaper a few years ago: "The tender memory of kindnesses when we were little is worth all the catechisms and the commandments for the formation of character and ennobling of mind."

social civilization. Ancestral breeding and nurture produce a type as clearly marked as the churl; and the
development which brought a new fitness amenity and
charm into social intercourse is due to it. France is the
creator of the highest social amenity and in France this
was produced by the union of ancestral breeding with
intellect and wit.[1] Wealth has nowadays replaced both
requirements. But this urbanity and grace of social
intercourse mark a real stage in human evolution. They
also suffice to differentiate the community: as much as
ignorance and uncouthness they introduce a class element
the more durable in its nature of the two. And the class
(and class) element which is produced by social urbanity may make
class inurbane. To put forth claims because of your
ancestors' breeding is contemptible, to presume upon it
shameful; for though your breeding acts as godparents
for your good behaviour, like godparents it is no substitute for it. There is only one principle which suffices
(*Noblesse* here, the french *noblesse oblige*; it will make us realize that
oblige) the man of birth without this sentiment is a snob, and the
man of wealth who takes much from the community and
returns little to it, a cad: the meaning of *noblesse oblige*
indeed is that privilege creates another kind of privy law
—the sense of a claim upon you. It is a self-respecting
axiom, it refuses to have without giving. It should not
be so difficult today to substitute esteem for this principle
for the adulation of fortune and rank, which in themselves deserve no consideration whatever. Of all kinds of
superiority it is true that *la supériorité oblige*, that because
of it something is to be rendered by me which need not
(Moral be rendered by others.   And a deeper current of
influence fine breeding must not be overlooked: in some terrific
of
breeding) crisis men have felt everything else fail them except the

[1] Not till then did fine society become a possibility. Intellectual France
rose into self-consciousness in the salons of the Frenchwoman; it waited on
the advent of the woman of intellect who was a great lady.

sense of a tradition which passed through them and beyond, which braced them to endure the fearful task and to scorn any faltering of the spirit.

As between classes so everywhere else nothing better awaits society than exchanging competition for co-operation. It will begin in the school; where we shall educate for a society in which co-operation is the goal. At present, it is competition which begins in the school—to succeed is to win by competing; and it is a sign of the coming civilization that the school *primus* has been abolished in Germany on the ground that rivalry is no part of education. Emulation in games studies and careers is I think often dubbed 'noble' because it is realized that there is little that is noble about it. In the civilizations of the past it was assumed that rivalry was always necessary as a sanction; the team-work most in evidence had rivalry as its obverse; it was co-operation for the sake of competition. *Esprit de corps* has in fact been overpraised: it has been willingly overlooked that its loyalties and complacencies are fosterers of narrowness and injustice. Its role has been to offset a type of civilization whose essential character was competition and privilege. What we have to reach is the ideal of general and international co-operation, and for this group-self-interest is no substitute. To the savage any team-work is easier than initiative and intelligent co-operation apart from the interests of one's group, which are better things than mere team loyalty when once we have stepped out of savage conditions.[1]

Competition and co-operation

'Noble emulation'

Esprit de corps

Better instruments than those of the past are then possible. It is possible to replace the armoury of prejudice

Public opinion

---

[1] President Woodrow Wilson of the United States said: "Disregard for the rights of others has no place in the councils of free men."

Competition in industry is proving a vain thing now that industrial processes are inter-dependent.

rivalry and jealousies by co-operation: and already the growth of a new instrument of government enables us to see that a wide education forges fresh tools for the work of civilization.

Plato's esteem for human nature did not increase with his knowledge of it; when he writes the *Laws* he looks for no improvement and, after education has done its work, depends on official oversight punishments and delation to secure social order: of public opinion as the growing sanction in human society Plato knows nothing.

Public opinion is indeed a very recent growth. It is first found in continental Europe, no doubt, with the french revolution and with the political conflict of the xviith century in England where it takes its place as the specific phenomenon of the xixth, becoming articulate in the agitation against slavery, the subjection of the masses and of women, and in the growing sentiment of humanity towards animals. It yet waits to be born in some other countries. But when it is born its sanction is stronger than any force on earth. Public opinion as a moral influence is not the prominence of herd opinion; on the contrary its organ is not the uneducated mass but the majority of the educated; it does not flourish in conditions of barbarism and cannot flourish in conditions of ignorance. Herd opinion is not opinion but custom and tabu; it is the public opinion which called Aspasia and Sokrates 'impious'. Public opinion rules as an enlightened force when the majority of the informed leads the herd.

As it is the strongest so it is certain that public opinion is the very best of social sanctions. But it can never be a
Its limitations substitute for the pioneer. It does not normally take account of the finest things and not often is it the vehicle of the finer sentiments. For men compacted together approve the glorified commonplace, since the approvers are the commonplace. What happens, however, is that the fine things which have been seen by the uncommon-

place become incorporated in the next generation, and their vehicle is then informed public opinion. Public opinion is the fruit of knowledge and liberty, part and parcel of human progress.

At the same time mass suggestion is a weapon of malign potency; indeed all suggestion tends to produce on the mind an undue impression, an impression out of all proportion to its credentials. Try as we will a false suggestion as to a person's character or actions clings to our notion of him and colours our thoughts against our will and reason. If when two people are being talked about we mistake one for the other and a supposed connexion of A with *x*—with which he has had nothing to do—has dwelt in our minds even for a moment, it will only be expelled with great difficulty: the more unlikely it is that such a man as A should be connected with such a thing as *x*, the more it will cling; for such is the effect of that associability of ideas which is at once the condition of our knowledge and a main source of our errors. We are the sport of suggestion. And then there is the false suggestion which is due to coincidence. We have been wisely warned to "believe nothing that we hear and only half what we see": the extraordinary tricks of coincidence are enough to make the gods laugh. For in life the impossible is the thing that happens, and the unbelievable is the thing that is true—the unlikely truth, part and parcel of those infinite absurdities of life *"le quali sfacciatamente non hanno neppure bisogno di parer verosimili; perchè sono vere"*.[1]

The printed journal is a force capable of creating mass suggestion on a colossal scale: the combined effect of all other propaganda—secular and religious—is now barely discernible in comparison with it. The newspaper has taken the place of the village pump and the popular preacher as centres of influence and magnified that in-

Suggestion and suggestibility

Coincidence

The Press

[1] Pirandello.

fluence tenfold. It is the first authoritative referee in the world. But the newspaper (in common with other demokratic institutions) though it forms public opinion leads by following. This is its strength as a force and its weakness as an influence. Like water and its source it never rises higher than its masters. So on the one hand we have the 'great man' paying his never-failing homage to the press—the harrow under which he too must come—and on the other we have the decisive factor for journalism in its economic dependence. Where competition is so intense even elect journalism must *kowtow* to what will 'pay'; yet if there were too few newspapers the moral evil of monopolies would arise, and when there are too many it means that thousands of citizens are acquiring a livelihood by making independent journalism impossible.

The 3 plagues are certainly dishonest partizanship, the uncritical submission of the ignorant many to the authority of the printed word, and the power to withhold the views and news of smaller sections of the public. Nothing effective on 'the other side' gets into newspapers unless such pressure be brought to bear that the insertion becomes good business. If when writing to the '*Despatch*' you refer to its magisterial utterance on the duty of the Churches or its weighty article on why women eat breakfast, your letter will be published; for constant repetition of the name of our newspaper in big print suggests to the public that their lives in some sort hinge on its daily appearance.

When the people want something better they will get it. That is how demokracies rule, and why press and parliament only reign. But it is the press which has helped mankind to realize its rights and powers—rights to know and so compare, to recognize the source of evils and the remedies. It is therefore the demokratic organ per excellency and missioner of that best reform of the modern world and our best remedy—the bringing things into the open. Secrecy and repression were the 2 methods of the past; wrongs innocence or vice were indiscriminately dealt with on these principles. We recognize now that knowledge and freedom are the conditions of safety and progress. No ruler can now be hedged round by men's ignorance of him; under the steady light of a fair press no body of men could pretend to monopolies of knowledge and skill. In fine, a complete and absolute liberty for the press is the complement of the new liberty of men; neither can exist without the other.[1]

The press is a new factor and its immense role for good Slander and evil has not yet been plumbed. Slander, however, is the oldest evil of the world, and it is curious that thousands of years of human civilization have not suggested to men any means of countering it.

We always oppose vices to virtues but we ought to oppose them to pleasures, because it is as a bastard sort of pleasure that nearly all vice, little and great, presents itself. The chief fact about detraction is that it is one of our *menus plaisirs*; slander also is a gratification but a purely malevolent one, it is moral murder; and that its encroachments upon us are so unquestioningly permitted must be due to a failing like that—whatever it may be— which keeps us the dupes of every kind of newspaper. "What did you slay him with?" asks Augustine; "with the sword of the tongue"—*gladio linguae*. When slander is aimed at benefiting the slanderer it is nothing but another form of blackmail, and it is helped along its proliferous existence by a sort of germ-carriers who though they may never have heard of the persons concerned make it their business to spread the infection.

[1] Limited only by the *beneplacitum* of the public. The freedom of the public, however, may be nullified if journalism is concentrated in the hands of a few persons who decide what pabulum shall be fed to it. The condition will then be licence on the one side and mental servitude on the other. The same conditions must apply to broadcasting—the access to the public mind must not be kept under lock and key by any set of men.

This is a good instance of human malevolence.   The pleasure of slandering will not be uprooted from human nature; the qualities intrenched in its behalf and the gregarious pleasures of gossip must prove too strong. But something could be done to discredit and weaken it. A slander is a stab in the back; but we let the slanderer approach us as if he were victim judge and jury in one and when he makes his usual shameless request "my name must not appear" we at once afford him cover. Then he shoots under cover at the unarmed man in the open. But on what principle should the slandermonger's tales be treated as confidential and himself as privileged, as the only person in fact who requires protection? It is not to the public interest that the hawking of slander should enjoy immunity. The effectual way of addressing ourselves to the scandalmonger is to tell him that you will repeat whatever he says to the person concerned, and if you do not know him you will in any case cite the slanderer's name as your authority on all occasions.

Slanders bear their charmed life because they are boxed about among people who may not even know the person attacked, and they are therefore hardly ever brought to the touchstone of persons and facts. The best remedy is to refuse cover to the slanderer.

INTER-
NATION-
ALISM
'Nations'

International co-operation has never been tried. What are nations? They are, we know, neither racial nor cultural unities; their only common factor is that all of them are political unities. But the fact that men find themselves in a geographical area and part of a political system though it may prove decisive for the individual cannot create any absolute moral obligation. The entire history of man has been a history of migrations and of new geographical racial and political ventures and combinations, above all of conquest and invasion; and the 'rights' of conquest and invasion are obviously destructive of the

sanctity of nationhood. Before american independence it
was thought heinous for any colony to rebel against the
parent-state. Now we realize that that theory was ludicrous. There is only one permanent reality in nationhood
and it is the desire to adhere together, and the only stable
unity consists in the consciousness of unity. If it were not
for that law of force which pertains exclusively to the
human jungle, and which humanity is now within sight
of disavowing, it would have been impossible for the
doctrines of the past to maintain themselves. One of these
doctrines is that political states alone of moral and social
forces owe no allegiance to any law higher than their
own view of their own interests; and another is that there
is no virtue higher than the love of country, and no duty
of a citizen higher than the duty of defending it. With
such moral maxims man has kept morality at bay. Why
should a state be an entity which in the nature of things
owes and can owe nothing to any law higher than itself?
The notion of the independent soveranty of states has no
better basis than the monarch's claim to use force, con-
sulting no rights and no interests but his own—which
has been for thousands of years the motor of national
and civil war.   A double conception of ethics has
always attended human development, and choked its
moral channels; what was right to do and forbear in your
own tribe never bound you outside it: this double standard as applied to nations must go, as the others have
gone, and there will no longer be 2 measures of right
because one man belongs to your nation and another to
mine. Internationalism does not mean indifference to What it is
your own nation and does not imply any weakening of not
public virtue; it means that the same code is recognized
as operating between nations as between groups of men
in the same nation, the disavowal of all special regard for
my nation because it is mine and for the rights of any It must
nation, as such, over others. With the universal habit of come

travel, the bringing together of peoples and sentiments by modern inventions and discoveries, and the scotching of the mental ignorance and contempt of each other which nationalism has fostered, internationalism is now inevitable and there can be no civilization without it. Four centuries ago the sickness of nationalism was not so acute; one religion and, when humanism arrived, one culture supplied a common intellectual and spiritual denominator, and achieved conditions which made an Erasmus at home in every country. But in the xvi^th century catholic christianity as a european idea ceased to exist, the work of a german peasant, an artizan's son from Picardy, and an english king. Commerce proved as little able to bind nations as religion;[1] and we have had to await the revelation of science which is now, as an Italian points out, the fiercest opponent of the narrow nationalism fostered by man's ignorance, and has made that nationalism "anti-natural": henceforth nations must cast about for barriers still more artificial than in the past if they would keep their neighbours at bay. In science the scientists have seen a higher denominator, overriding geographical and racial barriers and setting a term to local pride and self-sufficiency. For knowledge acts, as no religion has acted, by dispelling ignorances and prejudice.   This coming together of the nations of the earth through the Humanism revelations and inventions of science must be paralleled by a similar advance in the human spirit, a step which was actually first taken by Italy before the close of the xiv^th century: this advance is humanism, which is a cultivation and disposition of mind and spirit the best fitted to insure international civilization. It is the only trend of the human spirit which is both widening and enlightening, making for peace and mutual understanding: it includes

---

[1] Religion has at times provided men with a *lingua franca* of the soul, and catholicism did in Europe for a thousand years, without however securing peace on earth or good-will among men.

the humanistic and the humane, and is the one co-efficient capable of forming the international mind.[1]

Nationalism as modern nations have understood it has meant wars and the duty of glorifying your country. But for a thousand years wars had been due to dynastic pretensions or religious bigotries; it is modern war based on national pretensions which has produced so hard and strait a national spirit just as men had grown out of such motives for war as religion and dynastic rights. "Patriotism", they say, calls upon them to protect their country: and against what? Against the competitive nationalism which is the bogey of their own creation. There is no uglier feature of competitive nationalism than competitive populating, the motive for which is rivalry in wealth and war: for the strange perverse desire of nations has been to destroy the civilization and nationality of others; and war as the chief product of what Nietzsche called the nationality-mania[2] has done as much to improve the nations as wars of religion have done to improve religions. It is the low level of the masses which has been everywhere responsible for war and also for the separation of peoples; and the uplifting of the level of populations which is

[1] The Prime Minister of Egypt lately drew attention to the effect of an education at Oxford on a man of another race: the freedom of such a corporation implies the willing acceptance of standards "founded on common interests, discipline, and sympathies, which transcend political and racial differences".

[2] He looked on it as the sole cause of the morbid estrangement of nations in Europe. In the reign of Henri IV Sully wrote: "When I consider Europe as composed of civilized people I cannot but be astonished that it still continues to be governed by principles so narrow and so barbarous." 300 years later Rabindranath Tagore said to the english ambassador at Berlin after the european war: "No european realizes how small are the differences between european nations . . . whose main stock-in-trade consists of national antipathies."

That modern nationalism is a barrier to ethical thinking should be clear enough: no one has put it better than a modern writer (Philip Gibbs) —nations refuse to recognize any general law "which would enforce some surrender of their own selfishness". One cannot think that way nationally and be an ethical being individually.

becoming the note of Europe is the prelude to the fusion of nations. It is astonishing that it can be asserted that wars could be made to cease under the influence of religions, since religion has never had this effect.[1] Wars will cease when there is less distinction between the uninstructed masses and the rest of the community and the peoples have varied and wider interests. No religious teachers and no religious teaching will end war; its proper antidotes are of the psychological and sociological order.

What the world now wants—supremely—is a pooling of human faculties and resources; no national ideal can equal this in importance as harbinger of civilization.[2] Every nation has its great qualities and its great defects; no nation is alone 'great', and no nation's history is 'great' if greatness includes fair dealing within your borders and outside them. Races present a congeries of qualities which in our ignorance and darkness we have plumed ourselves on keeping unalloyed by the qualities of our neighbours. Nevertheless it is not the true theory of education that it should emphasize what has already been emphasized by nature, and the education of mankind itself will depend on this recognition. The in-eptitude of one race for government is as marked as the genius of another for ruling men. The most intellectual race of the modern world is the french, the most essentially artistic the italian; the foremost representative of a character people is the british, and of mental capacity and

The education of races

---

[1] Rare sects such as the Society of Friends in England which have joined peace among men to the religious ideal have invariably been despised for this very tenet. We see that the followers of their country's faith offer no objection to war, and in lands where there are numbers of spiritual contemplatives these retire into their shell and leave the world to fight it out.

[2] When Mazzini praised nationhood so highly the circumstances of his country made the rise of the nation the first great step on the road to the rights of the people. Nationhood, and the liberation of a nation, appeared as the stepping-stone to the ideals of humanity as such. The reverse is now true.

418

industry the german.¹ The british temperament is dull, the latin temperament brilliant, and there is a sombre asian temperament, a sombreness which qualifies the Latin in the Spaniard and has its part in the Russian. The American has acquired a new temperament, a very bright one, and deploys a higher mental energy than the English. He has sloughed english inaccessibility and reserve and is more direct and simple. He has exaggerated the english sense of humour and has no gallic wit. There are races always hurrying, and races always becalmed; passionate races, prey to their own imagination, which cannot understand phlegm, and races that can always count on themselves for a certain amount of phlegm and will never excuse passion. English and Germans are grown-up schoolboys—the Englishman tending to the sports and mindless order of schoolboy while the German always bears about with him the boy's romanticism and sentimentality: but Latins put away such childish things, and at the same time treat with a greater simplicity and are amused by small things, which appears to these ponderous class-ridden and romantic peoples to be childish.   Now it would be to the world's advantage if such racial characters and temperaments were distributed, and not all penned in geographical areas. In the present conditions of the world, with enormous populations and a general level of advantages, the age of the gifts of small nations disappears.² Great races still exist,

¹ The Scotch are, I think, the only people in any race where strength of character balances strength of intellect. English brain power is character power.

² Greece was the nation of greatest attainment and achievement in the past. That monopoly of human achievement occurred once only, and its fruits were lost to Europe because the roman empire fell. (The new empires, east and west, which then arose were built on theological foundations and were completely non-humanistic.) And Rome? It was the most kosmopolitan of all the agencies the world has seen. Throughout the imperial period it gave its colonials the same rights as itself—the roman citizenship; and it numbered natives of Spain Gaul and Africa among

but they are wanted as a leaven in the whole not as the monopoly of one family. When men are free of the force fetich and indued with a *lingua franca* of the spirit—which indeed has been hitherto muted by artifice—peaceful inmixing will take place as groups become ready for it.[1] The present nationalized man is ready to execrate such ideas; forgetful that nation-making in the past was the outcome of aggressions and conquest which he and his ancestors have tolerated. The qualities of races will not disappear, they will be found throughout the human community, the *propria* of individualities not of nations. Men in the future will not find that a national pleasure in their own limitations and the exclusive exercise of their own virtues compensate for a richer more varied and more humane experience of living. And there will be great compensations for the variety and contrast which races now present in the wider distribution of racial wealth. As men multiply and combine originality becomes even more precious, and ethnology shows us that racial admixture is the cradle of original and gifted men. The modern mind is (despite some appearances) as little captivated by a pretentious nationalism such as filled the xix[th] century as by the narrow geographical conception of religion.

its famous men and its greatest emperors. The genius of Rome was the genius of comprehensiveness, the roman people were the one people which spurned the ideas of nationalism and founded their greatness on the greatness and gifts of mankind. And it is from Rome that there issued the great conception of the *pax romana*—a universal peace.

[1] Since the sense of property is innate in living organisms, no group has more right to impinge on settled possessors of country than to impinge on any individual's hut or house. No large groups could come to occupied territory *and find a living there* unless they dispossessed by force—and force will not be used: but the sense of property never is and never should be illimitable and group 'right' to exclude every other group from all the territory round you cannot be sustained. It should not be a matter of "national soverarity" but a matter of the property and love rights of occupiers. In fine, all regrouping must depend largely and chiefly on a further equalization and homogeneity in civilized development.

420

We have no right to look back to any past time as The hope having proved itself adequate to the work of human humanity reform. From the way some people talk of the past, of the time, say, "before the war" or "before the reformation" or before the rise "of the rationalistic spirit", one would suppose that religious and moral teaching had achieved noble results in the masses of men and that these teachings, apart from hardly-won education and equally hardly-won social conditions, had gone on from strength to strength as the centuries rolled by. But the only hope for humanity is in the production of a larger number of men of better quality. If we continue to produce large masses of inferior moral and mental material laced with homœopathic doses of good, no reforms and no doctrines can save us. In the long run human nature alone is what makes the world bad or good.[1]

How is it, then, that amid a mass of men who would How never themselves initiate righteous ideals these ideals do justice and decency get spread? I think it is due to the power of the single are spread idea reiterated, pressed home, and forced upon the attention; and to the strength of character which belongs to

---

[1] The advantages of a non-increasing population cannot be exaggerated. In a stable population there are more adults and fewer children, and the editor of the *Observer* newspaper (writing on the census of 1931) made an original contribution by pointing out that that means "an immense increase in the range of possible activities". Stability of the population would be emphasized by the gradual increase in the higher age groups, making it possible for "quality to replace quantity"; and "tone of mind and body" which already count for more than numbers will count for much more in a world where men can "organize for clear aims".

In those favoured lands which have a diminished birth rate the haphazard existence of swarming millions which mankind hitherto has never had enough cohesion and coherence to criticize and condemn, will yield to the conscious and compact building up and maintaining of human welfare, physical and mental. It has always been the character of the few not the numbers of the many which has made a people great. But numbers can swamp even character. Individuality flourishes where there is room to move, and human progress will depend on men refusing to men the 'liberty' —which is no liberty but a preposterous licence—to breed as many children as they choose.

the pioneer. Men are driven by their interests but led by other men's ideas; and the real power which inheres in the right idea is the reason why the evil and self-interested have always been obscurantists.

HUMAN HAPPINESS

If we look at people's faces we shall see that mankind is not happy and is not miserable. Happiness is among the things which are not got by pursuing them, as we are our best self when we are least conscious of self. Men, indeed, look for pleasure, which is important and necessary to life; but pleasures and the pursuit of pleasure do not win happiness—their office is to supply a certain measure of satisfaction. *Le bonheur c'est être né joyeux*; and nothing that a man has if he has not a happy nature will make him quite happy, though with a happy nature he may be happy wanting everything. A man's nature, then, and not his ideals or his religion will make him most happy, so that if he is born with an unhappy nature his religion itself will be concerned with damnation and salvation and may bring him satisfaction but not happiness. Evil people, however, are not happy people: it is an interesting an unexpected and a delightful fact that the evil-natured man does not enjoy happiness; it belongs to him hardly more than blessedness which is what the good man can possess apart from it. The evil-natured take satisfaction from their courses but are not happy: and the fact hidden like a leaven in life, and bound up with its warp and woof, which sentimentalism has not created and cynicism cannot destroy, is that goodness is happiness. A man, that is, gets happiness from goodness. But this good man is no unruffled sea nor is he the man whose optimism lights his face with smiles. Complete happiness is not a good in a world like this; it would mean that we missed too much and knew too little. There must be unhappiness while there is discontent, and 'divine discontent' is far better than any contentment. Life, we see, is compact of contrasts, perception of opposites, conflicts—it is never of a uniform colour. A man who can say he has enjoyed every day of his life is the kind of man the true and faithful witness of the Apocalypse would have spewed out of his mouth.

But perhaps happiness and the moral life of man are bound up with what he can know or what he believes concerning the ends and purpose of life.   The ethical and spiritual may be thought of as ends in themselves; east and west have suggested kosmic or mystical explanations; and the other teleological possibilities appear to be exhausted in these two (1) that the human race is going towards a far higher terrestrial life—perfectibility, and (2) that it is the destiny of all the individuals of the human species to survive death and enjoy—some or all—a glorious immortality.

It has been usually supposed that philosophies had to account for the world in the state in which we find it, with the elements as we know them—a world of objects terrestrial and extra-terrestrial as they are perceived by us. But the philosopher is so far removed from men of ordinary clay that he has conceived a metaphysic denying the existence of things as we perceive them, or asserting the complete insubstantiality of the 'material' world, leaving mind as the only ultimate reality. After the philosopher science stepped in and gradually attenuated 'matter' in another way, going behind its gross manifestations to such forces as 'ether' and movement or protons and elektrons or the mathematical expressions of these. This resolution of matter has been seized upon by the dogmatic as bringing us nearer to a substance which is more akin to mind. But revolving elektrons protons and neutrons, even forces which may be still less

A TELEO-
LOGY?

423

accessible to man's senses than these, are no nearer to conscious intelligence, to spiritual or supernatural facts, than are the phenomena we ourselves discern. No more and no less. Spiritual truths if they are to be obtained are not to be obtained in this way, as though the spiritual were a sort of rarified dumpling; and man's life is too wonderful for him to take refuge in puerilities such as an alleged 'bankruptcy of science'. What science has made us able to realize is the profound inadequacy of the explanations which have been given without it. What science set out to seek it found; it found efficient causes for things; it discovered what things do in order to produce their effects. It did not set out to discover the final causes of the universe, or to tell us how the first parcel of psychic or physical stuff came to exist dowered with its properties: what science has to say about final causes is that to assert the existence of a first cause capable of producing the universe is not to explain the universe; such an assertion does not provide us with a final cause, it only dispenses us from seeking one.

The most satisfying philosophy of the meaning and process of life, owing nothing to knowledge and investigation, is the original buddhist philosophy of India. It is an impersonal doctrine; if there is no equivalent of individual mind in the kosmos *à fortiori* is human personality not absolute: everything which is separate, individual, is subject to change, and all living things in putting on individuality put on impermanence and contain in themselves the elements of their disintegration—all life is a *becoming*: absolute being is not life. That which has life is caught up for a space in the life-cycle, and while the individual end is nothingness—in as far as individual—the kosmic end is Being. Individuality involves limitation, limitation ignorance, and ignorance sorrow. All the elements of individuality are painful. This doctrine does not require us to think that existence is misery, but that wrong attachment is misery. It says that living can only be a noble experience if there is a certain emancipation in the treatment of it,[1] and the emancipation consists in a habit of mind. We can make ourselves free of ourselves; we alone can do so.

It was a completely different order of ideas which led to the belief in gods. Early thought about the kosmos led to the conception of great kosmic powers—the *elohim* of the book of Genesis. Into this idea personality and anthropomorphism did not enter—and further research is sure to confirm an original complete separation of the idea of the primal forces from the idea of divine persons: at first, men had no wish to project their gods into the skies. The first gods were men. They were those divine men who brought the great gifts to humanity; men at once of maternal and heroic mould—and skilful men. How did such divinities become sky gods? It is probably to be explained by the mystery of death which has played as large a part in man's career as the mysteries of life. The dead divine man was not dead— she was alive for evermore in the veneration and affection of those she had guided, and as she no longer tabernacled on earth she came in time to inhabit the sky, and to consort with the divine elohim.   Therefore for the first human philosophers the gods were not the origin of the things that are; this origin was sought for in such principles as fire and water and air; the gods exist but they do not usurp the place of kosmic forces.[2] Zeus if

Gods

---

[1] And any discipline is for the end of emancipation. Ascetic practices are painful, unprofitable, ignoble—they are not the path to freedom from the passions. The path to be taken is the Middle Path—not the *abrutissez-vous* of Pascal, not the abrutissez-vous of low enjoyments, but a path which opens the eyes, which gives understanding, brings insight and peace, and leads to the higher wisdom whose end and meaning is nirvana.

[2] In the indian *Gathas* the *daevas* are represented as the gods of the common people. Like the hebrew *elohim*, brahmă is neuter in sanskrit, and 'god' in anglo-saxon. None of them is equivalent to *deva*.

a 'father of men' is also himself created. But in Europe for many centuries only one solution of the mystery of the worlds has been tolerated, it is that god exists endowed with all the powers which would enable a great being to plan and execute the vast kosmos. With the present knowledge of our planet however, and its aeons of pre-human history, the solution of a design and a designer has not the cogency it had for our forebears. What part in the design was played during long thousands of years by the giant reptiles who occupied the earth? What part was played by a primitive type of *homo* during other aeons of time? The solution of a 'design' leaves unsolved the mystery of its worthwhileness to the designer. The teleological value, indeed, of the answer provided by 'a personal creator' is not higher than that of a *lusus divinus*; and the setting of men upon earth to start an unending career in which even the most unpromising subject here may develop his powers in a hereafter is in fact and radically nothing but a divine game—which need not have been played.

A design appears in the left margin beside the first paragraph.

Human mentality is ceasing to respond to the idea of god as purely transcendent, and it has tried to realize god as at once transcendent and immanent. In its turn that conception is losing its hold; the difficulties of an immanent divine are too great unless we accept pantheism and deny transcendence. So difficult is it to realize any form of theism which is not 'atheism'. It is to be supposed, again, that the conception of the supreme divine being revealing itself to man will come to be regarded as what it essentially is, purely anthropomorphic and devoid of spiritual and philosophic content: it is as though a foreigner were to introduce himself from another continent, or the ruler of another planet to open up communication with this one. Why should not we know god as we know love? There is nothing—except man's experience of his own acts of causation—to suggest that

The immanent god and *Revelation* appear in the left margin beside the second paragraph.

the explanation of the universe is only to be found by positing an anthropomorphic intelligence. This anthropo-morphic intelligence was at first expected to be the direct maker of all things from the moon to a beetle. But if there was no 'creator' of those things—no one who compacted the moon and formed the insect—it is as true to say that they made themselves as that god made them. There is no maker in such a process as the hurtling of a portion of a world into space which becomes in its turn a planet. The fables of creation are the outcome of our ignorance: had men known the facts they would not have imagined such gods. We men then are not left with no mystery— or with the great mystery solved—because we say "god made all". This throws the mystery a step further back but offers no solution of it.[1] God, uncreated, self-deter-mined, self-subsisting, is an infinitely greater mystery than the worlds in space.

'Creation'; a 'creator'

Philosophy and theology have supplied such answers as these to the riddle of the universe—Whence? Whither? But the belief in personal gods has always tended to reinforce a belief in the personal survival of men. Have we in the survival of individual personalities the real teleological answer to the riddle of the universe? The strongest bulwark of this belief is the mental tendency to assume that the existence of a desire is an earnest of the existence somewhere of what will satisfy it. We demand that there should be a purpose in human existence and

The personal survival of men

[1] Or rather it explains it as Cinderella's fairy does: god is a hypothesis like the fairy; the fairy could do it if there were such fairies.

Men have divinized their human reasoning faculties; so much has this been the case that unless you can see your way to anthropomorphize the ultimate causes european men will not allow that you 'believe in god'.

In a higher synthesis it might be that mind as we know it is not more wonderful than a nerve; and it cannot be legitimate to project the pheno-menon of the human mind into infinitude, and form of such elements the first and final cause of all that is. Whatever 'god' is or might be it is *not* some extension of the phenomenon of organic mind.

that it should satisfy ideas of justice. But no teleological doctrine has as yet satisfied these ideas. Justice is not satisfied if men are eternally damned for sins done by their forebears and made possible by an all-wise all-good and all-powerful god's permission of evil. No soul can deserve eternal glory or eternal hell (and if glory is attained by grace rather than merit why should the title to damnation be irremissible?). Moreover the fabric of european theology is an appeal to be saved from the consequences of a catastrophe in which you played no part. The same clumsy sense of injustice attaches to the notion that the deeds of your own few years of life determine an existence which must indure 'for ever and ever'. No one can picture what this means measured by time, and measured by intensity it is as difficult to adapt to what we know of man. Metempsychosis itself—the more philosophic conception of requital and development—is subject to the criticism that it is not fair to suffer for wrong which you are entirely unconscious of ever having committed.

If the moral equation here has been at fault so also has the philosophic. That Greek distinction between body soul and spirit, which was adopted by Paul, enables us to recognize that the 'soul' is our psychological self, the self we owe to heredity from other men, which had a beginning with our birth and will have an end when we die. We know nothing of each other apart from this soul and cannot for a moment imagine the spirit when we have subtracted the thousand elements which constituted it. But let us subtract a man's soul, and say that his spirit has survived: then shall we not say that it survives not because it is his but because it is not his, because it has not an individual existence but belongs to the universal. Even Paul had seen a truth like this; for even the mighty spirit of Christ was one day to be subsumed in god. The european doctrine that man was specially created as an immortal soul flouts all the psychological probabilities.

Body soul and spirit

428

It does not reckon with the wonder of the psychosis of the other animals. What is it that is immortal? For the other animals have life and personality, have intelligence, have love.[1] Some hold however that survival will only be for those who have special spiritual quality and desires; but how can we picture between man and man a difference so immense that the one should survive death and the other not. Personality is—or can be—a most glorious outcome of life, but the most magnificent personality cannot be conceived of as living eternally. Precisely the contrary is often maintained by those who believe in human survival—the life of fine and holy men, they think, suggests inevitably the hereafter. But as this hereafter is to be shared by every other sort of man it is more probable that fine men should cease to live than that every human specimen should survive.[2]

What is it we want to preserve? Our life, the living of life, living on? But is that any goal for the universe. Mere individuality and individual life has no intrinsic value or importance; and the natural astonishment of highly organized beings that they should one day cease to exist affords no evidence to the contrary. If we are to care for life for its value, then if what we should wish to see live in ourselves lives on, whether with us or without us, we have the eternal. We live, if the best in us lives. What else is there in the desire to survive except what is partly *indignum*? But this you say is for the more exalted and detached souls—only a few can reach so far. Why,

If the care is for value

---

[1] Was it not when discussing the immortality of the soul that Sokrates called himself "fellow-servant of the swans".

[2] One of the arguments against making survival of death depend on human fineness is that in general we are neither very fine nor entirely without fineness—we are in a middle path. The attempt to base a future life on the value, or even on the mere existence, of 'personality' brings us up against the fact (noticed elsewhere) that if we are to judge by the number of human beings who in our own or any epoch can be said to be personalities we must agree that far from personality being a proprium of human life it is merely its idiosynkrasy.

then, should heaven exist to accommodate the mediocre? For it is not goodness which claims a hereafter—goodness has no claims, it is its own reward, its own complete satisfaction.   I cannot believe that the purpose of the universe is the preservation of human individuality. No one has been absorbed in a work of the spirit—art or thought—without having at some time experienced a momentary losing of the consciousness of his own identity: even on earth, then, we can reach something better than the ego.[1] And a similar thing happens with the works of love. What can take from us the glory of having been 'sons of god' here. What extension of that can possibly matter in the all of things?

Perfectibility

If it does not appear that the significance of human life is the personal survival of all, or some, human individuals, can that significance be found in the perfectibility of the species—in the fact that the human race is going towards a far higher terrestrial existence. Man naturally looks for some fruit to his ideas and aspirations; we hope the young will benefit where we have failed; that since the good things did not come to the men of the past they will come to men in the future. Yet the future of the race can have no more (intrinsic) importance than its past. There can be no larger advantage in some millions of men a million years hence living fine lives than in millions of men doing so now; because there can be no better reason for and no more ethical quality in the happiness and goodness of some future man than there is for the happiness of those good men we have known and loved here and now. The future happiness and attainment of the race through the losses and suffer-

[1] As regards this abeyance of the consciousness of personal identity, Porphyry records that Plotinus had, on 2 or 3 occasions, the further experience of an abeyance of definite thought; a common experience of the mystics.

ings of those who went before them may become a fact but it cannot have the value of a moral purpose, something which is an end in itself. No doubt many people feel the strong solidarity of mankind; they can regard future generations as flesh of their flesh, the children they have begotten, the pledges they have themselves given to the future; and are able perhaps to feel that all has been worth while if the race improves, just as parents may feel that the gain of their children is a complete compensation for their own loss. But such a sentiment does not endow the achievement of those future generations with any higher moral or purposive significance. It remains true that—intrinsically—the future is no more important than the past. There is no necessity for the race to go on existing; and therefore that men in the future should be good and happy is an incidental not an absolute end— not, that is, an end which does or can represent the purpose of the universe.

But we cannot conceive perfection to be the goal of humanity. Perfection is a notion which inheres in all effort, all trial, all use of skill, and is present in ethical effort and ethical speculation also. Is it patience we think of or good temper—why should not we be perfectly patient or perfectly good tempered, not merely on this occasion or in this or that event; and so with all our dispositions.[1] We can and do envisage perfection in regard to every possible activity physical and mental. But the disposition of living things being what it is no perfection is to be looked for even in a remote future. The method of all organic life is by trial and error. And we value by contrast. So that if man were free of vice we should not value the virtues of our friends; were there no ugliness there would not be passionate appreciation of

The possibility of perfection

---

[1] We think how good it would be, and how easy, if such and such a good man would be this or do that—but he is not that and he does not do this. Such are the conditions of human nature, stopping short of perfection.

beauty; and even the delight we feel in the abundance of a fruitful season would go unfelt if no frost ever nipped the blossoms.

Since trial and error is the method of all organic things we owe more to the imperfection of our efforts than to their perfection. We never reach, or keep, the perfect except through the sense of the imperfect; it is the contrast which teaches. Mere perfection could never be the best thing that man can reach.

Purpose The meaning of life is to be found in life itself, it is disengaged from its processes and achievements. It is not necessary in order that life should have significance that this should be something laid down beforehand, that it should have been all predetermined by an 'intelligence' operating anthropomorphically. We do not suppose that nothing exists except what the human senses are capable of discerning, and a purpose would not be 'blind' though it were inaccessible to human reason.[1] But however much we regarded the life-process as simply an experience with a view to something else, it would unfailingly give us the material for a certain completeness; it would, and does, inevitably round itself off as being an end in itself.[2]

---

[1] The universe need not be meaningless because it does not correspond to the human conception of a meaning; and it is perhaps not realized how much a kosmic 'purpose' has already receded from human ken. There is no place for the notion of purpose in its relation to mankind when the immensities of space and time are brought into view. And it is not more satisfactory if the idea of 'purpose' which man has staged for his world be multiplied for the two million universes which may exist similar to ours. No teleology man has put forth offers data to explain such facts as these.

[2] There is in our intellectual activity obviously a *completeness* which no imaginable after life could utilize. How incredible, we think, that the stored up riches of a mind suddenly cease to exist, and become useless. But that is exactly what does happen; what use can be made of a great philologist's knowledge? To regard this life "not as intrinsically valuable in itself, but as merely a means of some final perfection ever beyond and yet ceaselessly to be pursued" would "reduce eternal life for God and man

432

There is a strengthening of virtue if life is held to be valuable for its own sake. If it is lived primarily in the interests of a man's own soul this interest will replace his generous impulse "to lose his own life" which the gospel told him was the best way of gaining it: it makes religious teleology encourage that lust of personal gain which is so overpowering in human affairs. Neither is it possible that the ideal of progress should loom large if this present life is only a stepping-off ground for the next; this ideal would always be felt to be supererogatory. And progress in fact is a modern ideal; in 'the ages of faith' there was no movement, lay or clerical, for the radical bettering of human conditions; men patched, they did not reform. That is the stultifying effect of belief in a final revelation.[1] When men believe that they possess what is perfect they cease to listen to the spirit which bloweth where it listeth. "Look, and make it according to the pattern"—men under the law learnt to look back not forward. Yet the efflorescence of early christianity had been no doubt largely due to the call it made upon men to look away from the stereotyped law and become interpreters of a spiritual law: and the idea that the 'eternal gospel' is the 'gospel of the spirit' is one that never fades from the hearts of men—it has always haunted the hearts of christians. The meaning of life is not then something stereotyped and stationary but, like life itself, it is something growing and becoming. No real meaning to life can be stationary.

alike to nothing better than an endless mirage". (James Ward, *Hibbert Journal*, January 1925.)

There is no satisfying goal to the pilgrimage of man, wrote R. L. Stevenson—"his soul is in the journey".

[1] It may be said of course that human ills are the consequence of sin and should be combated as a disfigurement of the creator's work and wishes: but in the 'ages of faith' evidences of diabolical agency were all valued for hortatory purposes, and they must be regarded as irremoveable factors in that spiritual scheme, blocking the conception of orderly human progress. Cf. Sin and forgiveness *infra*, p. 472.

Against this principle of a vital meaning to life—learnt in the living—there has been set the religious purpose of life which is bound up with man's moral conduct, so that his being good is dependent on his belief in the purpose.[1] Goodness therefore is never its own sanction and reward, or its own incentive, for it can only be expected of the self-interested and if a man has nothing to gain he will not be good. But religious teleology of this kind constrains us to ask ourselves whether indeed there can be any moral disposition at all except in believing that goodness is worth while for its own sake—that goodness is moral beauty, and that all beauty is worth while for its own sake, its own inherent loveliness.   If man should come to regard 'the life of the soul' and spiritual aspiration as the best thing in a life and the best that can be provided for humanity, will it be objected that in that case the belief in immortality would be a necessity? This objection could not mean, of course, that spiritual aspiration is only possible if we believe in the survival of our own identity? The religious life of the spirit does not change its quality because our spirit does

---

[1] Thomas More thought no one can be trusted to be good who does not believe he has a soul to be saved (*Utopia*, Bk. ii). It follows that without the hope of eternal reward or the fear of eternal punishment you will only do what is good and right because it jumps with your interests. But when your good actions are done with the hope of being eternally rewarded then you can be depended upon as a 'good man'.   Sidgwick also accepted survival as a sanction for conduct, because of the presumed necessity of "harmonizing duty and happiness", and Kant regarded survival of death as a useful hypothesis for the same reason. This is of course to make duty not what is owed but what is paid for.

If the ill-dispositioned and worldly were assured that there was no future personal life which depended on their conduct they might often act on the "eat, drink, for tomorrow we die" precept? That is to say they would throw over some of the restraints and principles they had kept to, and would become, in so far, less estimable. Their fresh doings however would not much affect the community, and in so far as they did it would be police-matter: as to their souls it is impossible to imagine any god who would not 'see through them'—to god their souls would be neither more hideous nor more beauteous than before.

not survive our flesh; and my personal destiny cannot affect the root matter of spirituality—which is that my spirit should reach as far as it can, though it die. The desire of immortality then for that which is best worth being immortal remains always the only desire which is admirable; the desire for the eternal life of the ideas which dignify soul rather than each one's desire to immortalize his own soul. It is not the belief that there is a purpose nor the belief in religious sanctions which insures moral life—nothing can insure it but its essential elements. No doubt it is a species of intellectual necessity for man to assume and to desire that purpose which governs his own operations is acting in those operations of the kosmos which surround his own ignorance. But though man has wondered and feared it would not be true to represent him as craving a sublime interpretation of the universe; only the very few in any age have done so.

The anthropomorphism which besets our ideas of purpose is not the only barrier to truth; there is a still subtler factory of fictitious conclusions. Things do not exist as perceived; which nowise implies that they do not exist unless perceived. What it implies is that our modality of perception may give an entirely false hint of reality and cannot guarantee a true one: we seek an explanation of the universe on the basis of our mental kategories, and it is more than probable that no final truth can be reached this way. Intelligence may itself be only one mode of mind; and thought may support itself only in a given mental 'atmosphere' as life in a given physical one, all that is beyond being too 'rarified' for our apprehension. Is 'psychical' fact 'physical' fact or 'spiritual' fact the clue to the universe. What is the meaning of the inquiry, Which came first? Panpsychism may be the answer. Or the process of life may be itself the only reality, and the intuition of life (the simple consciousness of life identical with life itself) the only creator of all

the modes of mentality and of existence.[1] Or is the outcome of all life buddhist being: if so, we whose life has
never been anything but a becoming can form no conscious part of it—to change this flux form of life for the
changeless life is to change ourselves out of ourselves.
But beside these transcendental life cycles, and beside
that perfectibility of species which may be called an
organic purpose to life, or the extraterrestrial destiny of
individuals, it is possible to conceive that there should be
not a particular but a universal spiritual purpose—that
the kosmical process of this earth in common with the
whole kosmos is working towards a spiritual goal and
achievement. The terms of such a conception are clearly
beyond all human ken and even all human participation.
It involves, also, a conception of time which is perhaps
radically false. But is not the whole idea of purpose
riddled through and through by this difficulty of ends in
an anthropocentric kategory of time? If there is no such
time. If it is only a kategory of intelligence—like space,
like dimensions in space, or causality. And this is where
the mystical solution touches reality as our everyday
intelligence must fail to do—for it is not a teleology at
all, it is not apokalyptic. It sets forth life as an intensive
experience, timeless, with no before or after. It suggests
a profound reconciliation of subjective and objective. As
to our own share, we have it now; and there is only one
due attitude for the individual towards any "far-off
divine event", If it comes it comes. What greater satisfaction is possible at the end of life than the thought that
it has been well-lived. It does not seem to me that any
expectation of reward or glory in a life to come would
or should outweigh this happiness.[2]

[1] Bergson.

[2] Either we are the result of kosmic forces (but their sport only in the
sense that they are unconscious) or we are the result of conscious creation.
What is the outlook for the soul? In the one case it is annihilation, it is impersonal; in the other, western religion sets before us a personal fate which

A doctrine of final ends is not demanded for life-happiness; what we crave is a satisfactory use of the powers with which we are endowed in the environment for which they are adapted. Man[1] sees his life necessarily as a constant pursuit of ends, whereas the kosmic process knows being only, in which all the elements (of 'space' and 'time') coexist. This kosmic process never forms part of the experience of living, and in the work which life—thus limited—sets before us failure to use the tools to our hand cannot be compensated by any extraneous source of satisfaction.[2]

Someone has said that the significance of christianity MYSTICISM is that the human is secretly endued with the divine. Some such words would I think fit not christianity but mysticism as a definition: for mysticism is the visible and tangible pervaded by the spiritual; but it is also more than this. The secret of nature is itself a mystical secret—

is one of eternal privilege or eternal suffering. And we did not ask to be here.

That something enters into being through a fine life which does not cease to exist is a much more momentous outcome of life than that this something should persist in the individual, and is the true sense of *non omnis moriar*: I shall not all die. It is also the significance of the buddhist condemnation of both 'eternalists' and 'annihilationists'; where there is the conception that when right life has formed the right *karma* 'the outcome of us on the universe' remains—ours for evermore in ceasing to be ours. Which is impossible for the wrong or the callous life.

[1] In common with other terrestrial living things.

[2] *Cui bono?* What use is any effort, any conflict, any achievement amidst the immensities where we and our planet are nothing? The question is posited because *for us* the outcome of the kosmic conditions is self-conscious individuality—and individuality provides a reply: the personality must always think its activities have meaning, it cannot deny its aims or think its goal profitless, whether it be an exercise of skill, or great art, or a great discovery, or great science, or great thought. It must think with Goethe (*infra*, p. 453). To fulfil the personality is a goal in itself, like art; what we can do that we want to do and must do. If conscious individuality is the mystery of the kosmos, it also gives the individual a permanent anchorage in the immensities; it is there, and can achieve fulfilment—it can only be fulfilled by disregarding the immensities.

because there is no dualism; and the mystic habitually lays hold of the oneness by spiritual methods and spiritual experiment, welding and fusing all experience into a new synthesis of oneness.   Sacramentalism, which makes the material become a channel of the spiritual, is then one aspect of mystical experience. The other is a pantheism— the divine is in all things and all things in the divine; and therefore the reality of the soul itself is to be found in being oned with the divine: the two permanent mystic truths are immanence (of the eternal), mergement (of the personal). For the mystic, god is never a being outside self, and self is never a being outside god; neither does the true mystic commune with a personal god: no matter what his creed, in his moments of clearest vision his soul escapes from the prison of such dualism. There has come to him, at some great moment, the revelation that "god shall be all in all"—whether it be mine or Thine, in the highest reaches of mysticism the personal is forgotten. "One knocked at the Beloved's door, and a voice said 'Who is there?' and he answered "It is I", and the voice said 'This House cannot hold Me and Thee'; and the door was not opened. Once more he knocks and to the question 'Who is there?' he answers "It is thyself!" and the door is opened.[1] While I hold self up as a barrier between me and what I seek, I understand nothing; only when we come to want what transcends self is the barrier removed. "Forgoing self the universe grows I." This teaching of the Buddha is the burden of all mystical knowledge, which is the recognition that no spiritual aspiration can have self as the term. "The lord being asked when the kingdom of heaven should come, said, When two shall be one, and that which is without as that which is within."[2] It is the barrier of self, with its neces-

---

[1] Sufi identification of the soul with the deity.

[2] The Lord's answer to Salome in the *Gospel of the Egyptians*, and quoted also in *Clement*, Cor. B. xii.

sary correlative the barrier of what is external to self, that always obstructs the divine vision. In the mystic way the soul tries to solve the signification, to resolve the anguish, of the self and not-self—and the solution it finds is that the distinction is illusory.

Mysticism is a splendid ethereal outcome of philosophy and spirituality, and it serves man's great need in making for him a way of escape from 'the letter which killeth' —that tyranny of the letter. But the religion of the mass could never be exchanged for the religion of the mystic: the gifts of the mystic are as singular as the gifts of the artist; and a mystic view of life which universalized the mystic way of life would be as impossible as it would be for the whole world to dwell in monasteries. Nevertheless none of us need renounce his right to some part in this splendid heritage of the soul.

Death is another way in which man envisages the GREAT merging of himself in the not-self. This is indeed the DEATH mystical equivalent of death.

That we are all born and all die are the only two things true of everyone without exception. But they suffice; to suffer life and suffer death covers the whole ground. The character of death compared with all life is its finality. And this final thing bulks on the human horizon —familiarly incredible. A condition of the world might one day be possible when disease would have ceased to be and—apart from accidents—there would be no sickness. But death would remain. And its bitterness lies upon all the sons of men. They must always occupy themselves in some degree with considerations to assuage the anguish of those two certainties—personal dissolution and the sting of bereavement.

When a man contemplates his own dissolution the help he gets from philosophy is derived from the very conditions of organic life: the most reconciling thing we can think about death is that it is part of life, not only is it organically part but the modality of all living is determined by the fact that *life has an end*. To understand this we have only to realize for a moment the change in every element of life if there were no end to living. Death then is the condition of life: if there is anything precious, achieving, compelling in our lives it is due to this condition. There could be no accomplishment of ends if there were no end. Without death "le monde serait insensible, immobile, et par rapport à notre conception des choses, anéanti".[1] Marcus Aurelius thought that since death is natural and universal it cannot be an evil. And another philosopher points out that there is no human passion which is not ready to despise death.[2]

The personal reflections do not differ from these: if we go before our life is fulfilled there is no comfort to offer, there is only a call on courage and virtue. But if life has been fulfilled, first or last, there is real consolation. And as we must die and can only die once it is the easier, if the great occasion offers for decision, not to wait till death becomes a meaner performance. Since dying is part of living there is every reason to set yourself free at that hour from fret and gloom which have no power to help you and which immeasurably increase the distress of those you are leaving to remembrance. Thomas More said the Utopians considered there was no better proof of a man's life than his cheerful dying. It is the last occasion for showing our quality.

What can I say to myself if I lose what I love. There is no personal comfort. Except this one—that what you bear alone is spared the one you love. For the anguish when one must go and the other remain is the only burden which shared is not diminished. There is another source

[1] Berthelot, *Le Jour des morts*, 1895.
[2] Francis Bacon, *Essays*.

of comfort—those we love are at rest. There is nothing more to trouble, nothing to apprehend: and because there is this goodness in the end there is greatness in death; it has no hurt. One of the highest consolations in bereavement has been the hope of reunion. But no part of the doctrine of survival is riddled with more insuperable difficulties than this. Sokrates was himself more sure of "going to gods" than of meeting hereafter other human personalities: it is the real survival of individuals about which he is uncertain. Indeed the platonic Sokrates bases the argument for survival itself on the doctrine of pre-existence. And clearly the doctrines of reincarnation into this world or of metempsychosis leave no room for reunion. What would be consolation, what would the outlook be, if we were parting from one we loved? The truth is that the expectation of meeting again is an expectation of recovering the conditions of life as we know it here—this is what the flesh cries out for and the soul: and this which is popularly demanded of a future life is something that can never be.[1]

We say to our hearts, If man could think thoughts which would spare the painful anticipation of death, make death come nearer to the ways of life. But our thoughts have no such power. Death though it is the condition of all life, all living, has no other truck with life. It is a vanishing. The best is that there should be un- We vanish consciousness of the end, that it may come when we have had our life or when some occasion makes us gladly part with it, or when we are too tired to live. Meanwhile death should have but a small share in life; *pace* stoic and christian, life has not space for it. There is nothing to prepare for; no call upon us except here. We are not dead nor asleep; we vanish—to ourselves and to others.

[1] If it could simply be realized that an after life must be a state and not a place; that there is no "place" "up there"; it would free minds of much lumber.

441

Annihilation is not dreadful for we are unconscious of it. We cannot fear what is imperceptible. And it is not loss, it is nothing.

The knowledge that the survival of individuality is not to be expected adds tenderness and depth to our relations with living loved things. It is part of their preciousness. So death heightens love and when it touches the loved embraces both—"it is the survivor who dies". Death lifts our comrades above us, so that they speak a language which is muted in living intercourse; the action of their life is lifted to a higher power, and we commune with a meaning—in themselves, in us —made sensible by an immense detachment. By death life is revalued, and if there were no death it would be for ever impossible for us who live to seize life in that wonderful perspective. They shed on us the light of their vanishing.

Future civilization can abolish some of the horrors of death—the one thing we should not allow it to be is horrible, and all our customs keep it so. Men have persisted in transferring to the dead body what belongs only to the soul-body. The body after death is not our body any more than it is our soul; and by permitting this transposition, by transferring the idea of those who have vanished to what has no part in them, we diminish their memory, and increase the gloom and darkness of death. No dead body should be the centre of a pageant, since nothing so little befits death as pomp. This horrid contrast is a creator of the macabre. The dreadful publicity about the transport of the dead enhances the horror of death whenever the blow is mortal for those who remain; and it should not be expected that these should take their private grief into the street. Neither when we commemorate the dead nor when we raise monuments to them should the dead body represent them: for a man's memory should be preserved where he has lived not where he is dead. In

The greatness of death

Funeralia

The soul-body

442

spite of all the morbid cult of death it is the smallest men who have secured the biggest tombs.[1]

We can do away with the horror and repulsion that surround death and are the relics of the barbarian in us. We can free it of all mere gloom and unloveliness. Simplicity (which is also the truest decency) and a refusal to make the dead body the lugubrious centre of sentiment —these things only can bring quiet of heart when the soul has vanished. When what is necessary is done, everything which centres round the dear dead body, or seeks to preserve it, is unwholesome and horrible, and shuts the soul away from us.[2]

Man's 3 good things are love, work, and prayer—and in this order. They represent the 3 elements which are worthy of attention in man's life, namely the affections, the activities, and reflection. Only some men can rest in the happiness offered by the mystic, but these three are the universal sources of happiness. Love is the best that life can give; the world holds nothing so good as to be born to love and to be loved, it is the source of supreme happiness. But if the affections are the very best life has to offer, work is the most necessary thing, the essential

THE THREE GOOD THINGS

Love, Work, and Prayer

[1] The whole world, said Perikles, is the tomb of famous men.

[2] Christendom added a weight of uncertainties to the certainties of death. It overwhelmed the imagination with bogies at a moment of supreme call upon our powers of self-adaptation. It insisted on the reality of a life after death where a man's fate remained in the balance up to the last moment of his existence. Gebhart does not exaggerate the religious horror created in the middle ages when he writes that men were *tourmentés sans trêve, et avec cette pensée désespérément triste, que la nature était scélérate, la vie mauvaise, Dieu hostile.*

Some years ago notes were made of 500 deaths by a professor of medicine at Oxford. Among these, one dying man, only, felt spiritual exaltation, and one, only, bitter remorse. 11 showed mental apprehension and 2 positive terror. Less than one in five suffered bodily. "For the great majority their death, like their birth, was a sleep and a forgetting." (It is sufficiently remarkable that the ratio of spiritual joy was $\frac{1}{500}$ths and of spiritual terror $\frac{13}{500}$ths.)

element in well-being happiness and satisfaction. We may live without love but we cannot live without work— which is the innate blessing of life, its marrow and its backbone. By work is meant fruitful activity and the exercise of energies. Everything is work which is not waste or play or rest. And work is that which is done for its own sake, whereas when we gratify the appetites it is for our own sakes. It is the condition not of happiness only but of efficiency that we should do the work we want and are fitted to do; for in all work as in all art a call is made on the worker's self; and the pleasure which it gives us is a better cozener of good work than duty or ambition or gain—this personal element in work being akin to the personal element for the artist, who cannot do good work merely for duty's sake if he knows that it is not *his* work. Life is not primarily service it is activity; service is contingent, work is absolute. There is of course work which is done from necessity; this is a law of all organic beings, a law of life and part of life. It is usually called a laudable and even a noble thing to earn your own living; but this cannot be an end to set before ourselves. If everyone should have work to do everyone's work should be what he wants to do, and there is nothing noble or worthy in supporting yourself—unless thereby you avoid exploiting others. Both work and the worker are prostituted if we are to regard putting bread into our own mouths as the most obvious reason for working. It would not matter at all where a Leonardo, a Michelangelo, a Dante, a Shakespeare, a Beethoven got the money which enabled them to live and work; and it is not a finer thing to do the world's work in order to maintain yourself than to be maintained in order to do the world's work. The growth of mechanism will free men from many hateful tasks; but it is when machinery replaces toil and when apprenticeship is no longer valued and over-populated countries present the problem of unemployment for masses of men[1] that we are in danger of forgetting the most important thing about work which is the worker's attitude to it. Modern work is spoilt by an undue regard for the unworthy susceptibilities of those employed in it: there is no profit in praising things men do well and letting things done ill go unnoticed. Praise, of course, supposes a standard, and if you only praise you never praise. Neither should the workman resent anger when he does wrongly. If we are to be so mawkish and vain that the work is of less consideration than a disturbance to our self-complacency then its dignity goes and our own with it. When work is done badly the individual or group responsible for it attracts a natural contempt; we feel it belongs to the nature of work that it should be well done, and this not simply because the workman owes a duty to his employer or because he is paid for his work. It would not be necessary to emphasize a workman's subordination if he worked with self-respect, that is, gave what he is paid for and a little more: when he does not do this he is a servile worker however he is treated personally. It is not the act of a free man to wish to elude his employer. The really sick symptom of present day society (especially in England) is a wrong attitude to work, the worker living his life outside that which it is a great part of life to do and do well. Such things can only be remedied by those who educate us from five to twenty-five years of age.   We see that there is always some work which must be done whether organic beings like it or not; and it may be that the true principle of all work is that it should be not the one thing always paid for but the thing that is never done for pay.[2]

Work then is in itself the main source of happiness,

The worker's attitude to work

Work as unpaid activity

---

[1] See Political Government, p. 373.

[2] The exception, of course, must always be the lowest classes of work. See Political Government, p. 371.

and it used to be understood (as a woman writer on medieval France has pointed out) that it is not a servitude but a way of enfranchisement for the soul. But if work is worth while apprenticeship is worth while. When you neglect apprenticeship you despise work.

Prayer

Activity and repose are the unchangeable alternations of life. Leisure is the obverse of work; and the third good thing is an inner and spiritual activity which in complete men is not ousted by the outer social activity. And like other physical and mental forms of life it cannot be fed upon nothing. By what name shall it be called? Let us call it prayer. Prayer is spiritual integration and spiritual spaciousness: it is the aspiration of the soul and its nourishment—it meditates, contemplates, reflects, and recollects.[1] Every day the soul descends into the market place and is cumbered with much serving that is futile and vain; prayer brings it home. It is said no man can realize his life unless he go outside himself; equally is it true that he cannot realize it entirely outside himself: and that kind of rest from without which is able to complete human life is 'prayer'.   Modern conditions put true leisure in a far background, its preciousness is forgotten, some of us never knew about it. Pauses in life then which are forced upon us by circumstances become a great good, and these are or can be part of prayer even when we have no gift for spiritual leisure. Without leisure no acquirements can serve us much. Without chewing of the cud there is no digestion. What is recognized today as the speed mania (due to the invention of road motor traffic) and those many other conditions of life which are keyed up to it—the constant distractions of spirit and the superficial view of what is seen, here this moment and gone the next—these are in a profound sense antisocial as well as antispiritual manifestations;

Spiritual leisure and spiritual spaciousness

[1] Jeremy Taylor says: "Prayer is the peace of our Spirit."

446

and they choke confuse and pervert the spirit. From constant distractions a certain amount of satisfaction can be got but not happy satisfaction; and if the conditions favoured it a large number of people would respond to something better. Happiness can be gained in work (when it is mental work it may be the highest satisfaction in life) and is given in love, but prayer takes us on a voyage of the intimate and unknown, and, as Meredith tells us, "he who has the fountain of prayer in him will not complain of hazards", for it will make him "flexible to change"; it casts out fear and tyrant custom and foolish pride.

Man's three good things each cause him to forget time and space and self—to lose the consciousness of self and its exigencies. If we love our work we do not feel hunger or fatigue. It is as with love. There are many who cannot love who cannot work who cannot pray—but each of these things is a primary good because each is so happy it takes us out of the self which is unhappy.

Would the happiness of a majority of men be increased A COMMON by a common cult: is a common cult now possible, and CULT? if so what should its elements be. Let us begin by asking whether there is an innate faculty for worship. There has certainly been an instinct to placate born of fear of the unknown and there has been the subaltern instinct to do homage to the stronger. No one can doubt that taking Is worship worship in its world-wide aspects ignorance and super- innate? stition have been by far its largest components, and, next to these, an attitude towards divine persons—deities— compounded of fear, deprecation and placation, contrition sometimes, and sometimes gratitude. But the common root is fear, fear for your welfare in this world, or fear for the future of your own soul. It has been maintained that these primeval emotions point to a spiritual reality and a spiritual law. Superstition and fear cannot however form any part of a true worship. Men no longer think of creating ruling and omnipotence as the divine attributes which should provoke their natural spiritual reverence; and adoration, which many will suppose to be the deepest instinct in worship, in fact is difficult to distinguish from the dulia rendered to despots. Man is indeed capable of adoration for the beautiful the good and the glorious, but these are highly civilized and spiritualized instincts and do not enter into cults which depend on fear, nor even upon wonder and awe. Awe and wonder concerning the *elohim* are the nearest kin to religious adoration, and the mystery surrounding us has hitherto nourished these sentiments to excess; but to the modern mind even the thought that we can never fathom the kosmic process does not suggest 'worship' in the real and proper sense.[1] The answer to the question, Has religious worship represented any ultimate necessity in the soul of man is not then so evident as it has generally been supposed to be. We may say that the instinct to placate is a necessity when the conditions of ignorance and fear of which it is the outcome are present, but it is an instinct which cannot be 'sublimated' into love of god, for this love belongs to another kind of man altogether. The instinct to worship is certainly the same whether for persons, supernatural persons, or ideas, but the highly developed worship of admiration and love has not grown out of the primitive worship of fear and superstition.

Elements of a cult   The answer to the question, Would a common cult increase happiness, must be that it can increase happiness in the same way as other vehicles of expression and representation can increase it. Purged of its archaic elements a common cult may still be possible based on the fundamental instincts of piety and on aspiration after the

---

[1] The sense of the 'mysterious' (awe and wonder as elements of religion) should be regarded as no more religious than is fear. See Ethics and Religion, p. 88.

spiritual as the common interest of men. Aspiration after unworldliness is no rare visitant in human nature, and is the katharsis of the soul. It may be strengthened by the contagion and support of a common cult. Thomas More wrote that in Utopia there was a common cult in which "nothing is seen or heard but that seemeth to agree indifferently with them all". But how many more elements would now have to be ruled out since he supposed such a possibility. Prayer in its anthropomorphic Prayer sense would not be possible, that prayer of petition which has been given first place as a spiritual instinct: for in so far as it is spiritual prayer is the obtaining of something not for yourself but from yourself. And with this would have to go a whole gamut of emotions which in the past have appeared natural to all but a few. Their place would be filled by sentiments less self-referring and less fearful. No common cult could in future supply our needs which did not place in the forefront the aspiration of moral Moral goodness towards our fellows and add to the spirit of goodness kindness which is the greatest grace of life. This element, conspicuous in the first christian church, has been left aside in nearly all rituals. On the other hand self-abasement has been fomented which has no power to foster human virtue: the wholesome sense of unworthiness however is both worth while in itself and worth while to feel among our fellows. And participation in a common act of aspiration can give us still more than a freedom from our worldliness; it can lift us above our everyday selves. We should not dispense with external imagery round The about us which has power to constrain and direct atten- external tion, suggesting what is undeviating compared with our own inequality in spiritual things: but if the external and symbolic have this grandeur they have also a tormenting futility, they cannot create what is not there nor give what is not given; and all external religion (apart from the satisfaction of superstition) leaves in us a sense of dissatisfaction due to its radical inequivalence to the spiritual. Cults since they tend to become the shrine of religion are always nigh to being its tomb.[1]

Mistaken assumptions Up to now it has been assumed that public worship was so good and pious a thing in itself that it was unnecessary to ask what needs it met, and whose. That is no longer possible.[2] And in the future a common cult must not assume that the spiritual is the sense of the supernatural, that to adore the *elohim* is essentially a religious act, that spirituality is dependent on the existence of an infinite spiritual person; and it will no longer ignore the striking truth in the history of religious sentiment that the Hebrew religion which was based on moral responsibility and Buddha's religion which was based upon a philosophy had no dependence on the notion of an after life. But a common cult though it need not depend on the sense of the supernatural nor on a relation to the personal makes its appeal directly to the sense of the **The numenous** numenous. The numenous? We may make abstraction of all that we call the supernatural, of all veneration for beings holy and dreadful, and the numenous will remain with us in the faculties of sublimity and spiritual exaltation. It was a Hindu who pointed out the spiritual flaw in the christians' attitude to god whom they regard "solely in his relation to his creatures" and as perpetually occupied in their affairs. Perhaps we are on the threshold of a new beholding; and perhaps it may be necessary in order to release all the treasures of the spirit that man should break down the barrier of his anthropomorphic conceptions, and that *quid pro quo* mentality which has companied with it.

[1] As an amateur of liturgies I have noticed that their loveliness bears a constant inverse ratio to the moral and spiritual barbarism of the peoples who employ them.

[2] For example, when it was asserted that the churches are the book and the theatre of the poor and that they feed the imagination, it is clear that these poor are no longer with us.

Since religious natures have been so rare it is not superfluous to inquire whether religions themselves have made for the happiness of mankind or not. Lucretius would have said not. But Christendom had other consolations to offer. It brought the hope of heaven, the inspiration of a perfect human character, and the joys of the interior life not for the few but for the many; while for the general no doubt the sense of forgiveness has been a solace, especially among the unself-reliant peoples. On the other hand spiritual despair has at times of the world's history been an immane menace to happiness, and christianity, above all other faiths, has exploited the fear of hell.[1] But having regard to the fact that religions have appealed to the strong human tendencies to superstition and symbolism, have provided an occupation which has been both the most important business of life and the most soothing passtime, and have never failed to arouse not only the emotional nature but the affections, I should place them definitely among the sources of happiness. When one has said this, however, it must not be forgotten that they have always fomented that plague of the mind credulity, and that obscurantism and the play upon superstitious fears are the secular blight upon every religion in the world. It is always true that a very great deal of attention to religion has been a tribute not to its consolations but to its terrors.

Has religion brought more happiness?

No such spiritual defect attaches to the pursuit of art; and in a world where man is constantly beset by himself and by his problems few life activities can be more perfectly satisfactory and satisfying than art—the creation of that beauty which is always complete as an end in itself. The arts are energies of expression and of presentation which is the art sense. As he works the artist is made to realize that a harmonious originality develops more

ART AND BEAUTY

The art sense

[1] Cf. p. 443 *n.*[2].

451

'The
freeing
influence
of a great
tradition"

freely along the lines of a great tradition, and he becomes the joyous reconciler of past authority and present liberty. The urge to expression and interpretation is what is common to all art, and the fact that art demands freedom of the personality shows us once more that apart from this freedom we do not receive gifts from men.   In

Artist and
mystic

soul energy artist and mystic stand opposed, the one demanding first and foremost an outward expression, the other an inward integration. But both these paths to interior harmony are protests against the ugliness of the world without and within, a seeking after the beautiful-in-itself.

SPIRI-
TUALITY
IN LIFE

Man is not a spiritual being as he must be said to be a moral being—a being compact of customs manners and conduct-actions. And his morality may be right or wrong. But though man, as such, is not a spiritual being it is by spiritual realizations that he reaches his highest life. Since the spiritual are conscious that the love of these things is the possession of them they do not entertain the self-ful expectation of future reward; having loved and desired what is lovable and desirable this love which is the not-self takes up the attributes of eternal life. Equally with the lover the philosopher disdains all measuring of pleasures; perceiving that to forgo one pleasure for the sake of another and to fear that by enjoying the one you will miss the other has nothing to do with virtue. Therefore what Sokrates called wisdom and Francis of Sales called love is the only true coin "for which all things ought to exchange"; and any other sanction differs in nothing from merchandize or 'the arm of the law'.[1] So man is left with his soul and his want of it, and the gulf is not bridged in this world or another.

---

[1] This is that distinction between those who love goodness for its own sake, those who would like to love it, and those who would never love it. See Human Character, pp. 395–6, and Individual and Species, pp. 116–17.

The divers powers of the soul are energies which with- The powers
draw us from ourselves and above ourselves, exalting and of the soul
dignifying life, and it is obvious that in them a real and
perdurable happiness is experienced comparable with
that which the soul may enjoy in recollecting that there
will be a hereafter. By these powers of the soul time and
space are overpassed, the future and the past are concentrated in the present which receives the qualities of
the eternal. So they bring us to that persuasion of
Lucretius that life can suffice for all its demands, and to
the truth realized by Goethe that the interest of things
is in themselves not in explaining them. The soul of
man is fitted for the life of man; it is all demanded of
him here. And the incentives to be found in life are
sufficient for every claim upon us.   We are left
with a present which is *unendlich lang*. Man looks back
and looks forward—at least as much backwards as forwards. He does this because he has missed satisfaction,
because of the terrific tragedies of life, because so many
fail in life from poor mental or physical endowment.
Thus has been created the cult of the past and of the
future—a future to redress the past. But there is no
remedy for life's failure. Who has ever suggested one?
Not even the Buddha. The call is always to those who
are able to hear.[1]

And as we walk along the great ways of the spirit and The affec-
of the powers of the soul we become aware that what tions and
the reason
enlightens is feeling and the experience of life. That

[1] If we demur to this, from the point of view of religious teleology, that
the well-endowed can no doubt make something of life but what of the
maimed and broken? The answer is that all over the globe the motley
which is man supplies examples of those whom no teaching will reach, of
whom modern man will say no more than this, but whom even the religions
of mercy and redemption have destined for some sort of hell or even for
endless torment. The answer is that the faiths and philosophies which tell
us that there is a final significance in all things mislead men. It is not true
that there is nothing without purpose or meaning, nor is it true that men
are what they will to be.

453

reason is ancillary to the other powers of the soul and not vicê versâ. This does not mean that the soul can do everything apart from reason but that reason can do nothing at all apart from the powers of the soul.[1] It is always the soul which argues; and our outlook on life is always bounded by our experience of it. Feeling, then, illumines; and the affections are the natural sanction against the preponderance of selfish interests; where they lack, no other sanction has ever yet been found to take their place.

Kindness   Kindness is an anglo-saxon word which has more moral and less social emphasis than 'gentilezza' and it connotes something which has a much greater share in lightening the misery of life than the advertized palliatives. It is the most important social virtue, the natural antidote to the human proclivity towards injustice, defrauding, and malice.

The stock of human happiness in fact depends upon ideas and habits of mind, not upon doctrines and principles.

The ethical content of life is something more than what is described as moral good and evil, right and wrong; since its elements are mind as a whole—discernments, feeling, fineness, felicity, all the reaches of thought. So that the true good and beauty of life may be summed in the platonic *kalokagathon*, that which is done finely and rightly, the right and the fine in all action. What is good or right is a spiritual and psychological unity each parcel of which is referred to some finer perception, to that understanding which is illumination: the platonic idea of the 'good' as the highminded teaches us therefore far more about conduct than the bare notion of moral trespass could ever teach us.[2]

[1] Take for example the truth that good reasoning depends upon the imagination; or take such capacities as the realizing imagination, observation, concentration, judgment—as the prelude to opinion and conduct. Cf. Rationalism and progress, pp. 403–4.

[2] The platonic idea of the 'good' cannot in fact be fitted into the simple

454

Now the education of all living things for life is an MANNERS
education in manners, not behaviour merely but right
behaviour: for some of us the teaching remains only as
a discipline, others it makes free of a kingdom. Goodness,
in fact, always demands that we should concern ourselves
with manner as well as matter; bare virtues are never
enough: it does not carry us far enough to have good
intentions, to be just, temperate, or self-denying, since
any good action or disposition may be made into an ugly
one by the way in which it is carried out. In the manner
of its doing the biggest thing may become poor and mean
and the smallest may dignify life—or sully it: here is
a daily power put into the hands of ourselves and the
'man in the street'. It must be evident if we think of it
that a great part of the virtue of organic beings necessarily
resides in their manners; and they are often the only soil
in which certain virtues can be reciprocally exercized.
Manners have been esteemed and cultivated—for example in the jesuit education of youth, as a fundamental
principle in China, and for their social value in France;
they have been considered the proper adornment of
religious training and a chief part of the urbanity and
amenity of life; but in nations and individuals they have
too often functioned as a substitute for morals, and their
rightful place as sheer moral matter has not been widely
discerned or sufficiently explored. Manners are morals;
good and fitting manners are moral gestures and actions,

idea of the 'moral', it is always more nearly rendered as the highminded.
Tò ἀγαθόν is really that which is right in its kind, and τὸ καλόν is that
which is right and fitting in its time and place. Plato's conclusion is that
"virtue is knowledge", or rather *to understand* (*epistēmē*) is to be virtuous:
and "evil is ignorance", for not to have learnt our lesson (*amathia*) is to be
vicious. But 'moral' virtue cannot be made co-terminous with knowledge,
and Plato does mean by 'virtue' (*aretē*) more than moral goodness—it
means the generally right and honourable treatment of life; which is what
it should mean.

"To do whatever you do with a part of virtue is virtue", Plato,
Menōn, 79.

and the mind behind them is a moral mind: good or bad they are born, like virtue and vice, of the soul, they wound and heal, and good men are more often detested for a defect in their manners than loved because of their virtues. I think that if virtue consisted with universally offensive manners and vice consisted with universally considerate manners it would result in men tolerating all the vice consistent with social security.

The prevalence in the future of a type of conduct which makes manners part of morals is of more importance than the formation of the religious or spiritual type of man. For it is the absence of the grace of manner which makes virtue sterile: had all the saints been as Catherine, Francis, or Clare (and with the freedom of two of these) the world would long ago have been converted to holiness. It is not virtue alone which is compelling.   In the long run it is impossible that humanity should put up with callousness and indifference as the norm of manners. We shall not consent for them to be removed from the things which demand the attention of the soul. Just now there is a tendency to set them aside as superfluous and above all as an insincerity. But this takes too short a view; for it is clear that whenever we give expression to genuine feeling (good or bad) it returns to us both heightened and deepened; and that by the expression of courtesy and kindness we help ourselves to live as much as we help others.

Then the essentially good act is not a simple act but the result of a psychological and spiritual unity in the actor. The really good man, as Plato saw, is not he who keeps the commandments or he who has been instructed in the ways of virtue; the wholeness of good which in and by itself can make life a splendid thing being neither learnt nor taught.[1]

[1] "The conclusion is that virtue comes to the virtuous by a divine fate." *Menōn*, 98.

We considered[1] whether fine breeding has anything to contribute to human betterment, and we are now going to consider whether and in what way human happiness may be increased by equality. Liberty in a state is a political achievement whereas equality is a social achievement—it derives from the social sentiment that we are all really equal or that we ought all to be equal. But there is no such thing as natural equality; there is and there can be nowhere in nature such inequalities as there are between men. Since we start with natural inequalities and can do nothing to render men really equal will the artificial creation of social equality procure greater happiness—equality, that is, in rank, in fortune, in education? History shows that nothing has been less desired and prized than equality, but it also shows that equality has been scorned in proportion to the social and educational inequalities among men. In the modern world however we are confronted by 2 conceptions of equality, the french and the american. In America equality means nothing but equal opportunity for all. When this has been enjoyed—or as much of it as is compatible with the unequal start we all make—no resulting inequality is an offence, and no injustice or shame to which equality of opportunity may lead comes amiss. The most worthless values and the most worthless men may go to the top and remain there determining world movements. This conception clearly dispenses with all ideality and is not truly humane. When A has made his big fortune his son B starts with an advantage as compared with C, just as much as in the case of privileges of birth. The fact that he has been able to use his opportunities to grow rich franks all his worthless descendants. Hence in America equality is not a sociological or philosophical postulate. What happened was this: the statement (which heads the American Constitution) that all men are born equal is so

[1] Human Betterment, p. 407.

manifestly untrue that an artificial equality was propounded, "the equality of opportunity". As a sociological and philosophical ideal equality is french. The French are the only people who really care for it; with them it is not merely a means to individual licence and the mounting-block to fresh inequalities.

But equality if in certain ways it is a guarantee of liberty is also an obstacle to it. Men are not equal and *Its relation* therefore equal treatment does not meet the requirements *to liberty* of liberty, and in an equalitarian state it is liberty which is liable to pay the costs. Again, unlike liberty, equality *and in-* may not favour individuality. It is admired, like col-*dividuality* lectivism, by those who have less marked characteristics. For collectivism and equalitarianism are not only or chiefly a protest against class injustice they are an outcrop and affirmation of herd mentality, of its lack of differentiation. The sociological basis for inequalities is to be found in the fact that it will always be the more highly developed who are individual by instinct and the poorly developed who are collectivist. A Frenchman has said, "What is equality but liberty for all?" And it is quite untrue. Not until societies are very much more homogeneous than at present can we insure against the inferior man's equality being the superior man's servitude. The equalitarian society, then, demands a homogeneous civilization —an equality in manners and in responsibility—only to be reached through education and the exercise of political duties and rights. And this has never yet been attained. In university societies where similarity of fortune corresponds with similarity in merit and moral responsibility, equality of fortune is well exemplified. But such conditions never can exist in mixed communities. Nevertheless the tendency of all social evolution is towards *The desire* equality as the norm. Are we to see in this desire for *for and the* *desirability* equality a legitimate social and spiritual defence. Is the *of equality* contention for equality a spiritual meanness, or rather is

458

it justified because it seeks to do away with fictitious excellencies; and is a general equality of states fortune and education in fact desirable? And if it should be contended that a conventional equality among men is liable to puff·up the mediocre, does not all inequality of this sort (as of money or birth) give the same result? There is only one answer to the problem here involved, and that is the acceptance of a real basis for superiority—which does not exclude, but rather perhaps implies, a general equality. What should the bases be? The antithesis to demokracy is aristokracy, the essential meaning of which is not the rule of the favoured few in a society but the rule of the few who are favoured by nature. The *charismata* of these few or many form a natural aristocracy and it will become evident as soon as education and the amenities of life are standardized that there can be no other.

I do not think that mere inequalities of status and fortune have been a general source of unhappiness in the past. But the absence of those social opportunities which play their part in placing men who would otherwise remain unplaced presses hardly on the unusual man. The conclusion is that the french conception of equality has a real social importance, and that a very large measure of equalization of fortune, education, and status would benefit society as a whole and the unusual man. In a far future of humanity it is probable that no fictitious standard of superiority will be able anywhere to maintain itself.

The congress of youth with youth and of the mature in age with their contemporaries is a pleasure evident throughout organic life. Amongst men however it leads to one MATURITY of our human misfits. Age and youth operate on the same AND YOUTH plane but the constant non-coördination of their mental and moral realizations is a despoiler of life and a thief

459

of its riches. Man has kept youth by his side where the animal has sent it forth, but he has the remedy for a misfit which is wholly due to human conditions. It is said that a young man cannot understand an older man, but the remarkable thing is that it can be said older men do not understand the young. What has happened to make men forget how they felt when they were young? What has happened is the fact of experience. The mature have *experienced* what the young have not experienced, and complete sympathy where this means feeling as those feel with whom you sympathize is not in fact possible, because the mature no longer feel or can feel like the immature. The kind of sympathy which is demanded for this human misfit is sympathetic understanding, which ought to be the basis of the reciprocal relation of maturity and youth. At present this does not exist; apart from relations of a parental nature, the staple is simply reciprocal tolerance. We see that human life as a whole has never been based on the natural and mental verities, it has never yet been regulated by sympathetic wisdom; the same bases should underlie the relation of youth and maturity which should underlie all other relations—understanding, and interdependence with individuality.

The impass which exists between youth and maturity indicates at the same time a natural interdependence; there is a permanent division of capacities in all human congress which is not that of birth and talent but that of age. In the old world it was considered that each generation existed for the last, and the modern world is inclined to ratify something as topsy-turvy; for is there not a sense of 'mirage' if every generation is to spend all its capacities for the sake of the succeeding one? There is incompleteness and acquiescence in incompleteness when men always look to the promise of the future rather than to achievement and fulfilment in the present: and a lesson should be taken from the sanity of the artist who works for art, works for himself—and the future profits as the result. Age in itself is not more 'venerable' than youth, and youth is not in itself 'glorious'. Both these are absurd *clichés*. Each age however has its special unhappinesses: age should not look with intolerant condemning eyes upon the many difficulties of youth—difficulties of mal-adjustment—and the youth should not strive to displace those who sit at the banquet prepared by themselves till he has gotten himself a wedding garment. One of the mistakes is to regard youth as the period of greatest happiness. Life is a happier thing than the cynics are wont to assert because this is not true. The forties and fifties are the prime of life, but there may be more happiness in the next two decades; and the contribution of these two decades cannot be anticipated. It is natural but unreasonable that the young should pity the grey-headed; it is understanding which causes the grey-haired man to look with pity upon the fatuities and crudeness of the young.

Aristotle wrote that the true nature of a thing is that which it is when its becoming is completed.

> ——"The best is yet to be
> The last of life, for which the first was made"

Nature does not stultify itself and place all the joy in the becoming and all disillusion in the fulfilling. No doubt there is a temperamental inclination to spring or autumn —some see the wonder of the one and miss the grandeur of the other; some only realize the activities of spring, to others autumn is the season of high emprise, described by the young Keats as "close-bosom friend of the maturing sun". The appreciation of mature life is a great help to young life; it helps us to realize that age is only relative and it gives us at the outset of life the freedom of men's city of the soul and mind. When 25 thinks 40 old all it means is 'older than me'. 10 of course thinks 20 'old', 20, 30 and 30, 40—each decade seeming old to the one before it, even half a decade. This gamut is complete proof that the notion of age is subjective: in a real sense adults all live on the same plane—between immaturity and senility—the vision of the young in this matter being myopic.[1] It is the young who are deceived since they will all come to be where the older man is and to look back as he does with those eyes of quickened vision which now seem to them unseeing eyes.

When I was 21 I made a friend 30 years my senior: during the 20 years and more of close friendship neither of us was ever aware of the difference in years; nor did she ever speak of her age, she let what she was be its measure. And the secret of these human relations which has never yet been learnt is that the generations should not exploit one another.[2] It is illegitimate for younger men while claiming for themselves every freedom to depend on older men to smooth their path. The relation between maturity and youth is not seldom wrecked by this complacent assumption: and our over-population increases the problem, it makes too many old men in the way and (what is just as much an obstacle) too many young ones on the way. The pressure makes us retire men at one end who are fitted for their work and foist in at the other those who are not yet fitted for it. It opens a breach in the natural harmonies. For here, as elsewhere, it is coöperation not competition between youth and maturity which is wanted.[3] The younger men have habits to form and older men have prejudices to slough—each keeps in touch with reality by contact with the other.

[1] How many young men would suppose it possible that Defoe was in his 60th year when he wrote Robinson Crusoe.

[2] See the Family, pp. 321–2.

[3] When population was small there was everywhere apprenticeship to work. It is no substitute for this to allow the younger to learn by taking the posts of older men. The work suffers, and goes round in a perennial circle, the inexperienced gaining just enough experience to carry on—not to carry further.

The superciliousness of experience and the arrogance
of inexperience must be done away with—those tempers
of the untried and the overtried wings. After all, it is
by experience, only, that men learn; someone else's
experience will not do. It is a natural phenomenon
therefore that as each individual can only learn by his
own experience each generation begins afresh, and the
next generation assimilates only a part of the experiences
stored by the preceding.[1] But if man learns by experience
he learns by standing on his feet not on his head, and to
call upon youth to rule, as a periodical in England did
during the war of 1914–18, is like standing a pyramid
on its apex. Experience is the basis of man's pyramid;
and the permanent distinction between the youth and
the mature man is that youth lacks the basis. When we
recall our own youth we know that however precocious
our intelligence, despite the thought we had at our dis-
posal, the lack of experience meant lack of judgment.
The generality of older men may be without judgment
based on experience, the young man must be. If, nevertheless, youth be more fitted than age, if all that is necessary is inexperience, then the process of human life is
entirely stultified—we proclaim that living is a failure
the end of which is and must be bankruptcy; all life is
lived in vain and all experience earned in vain. If with
such data we call upon youth it is no call of life and
promise but a *memento mori*—'as we are so you will be'.
What is the great lack of age? It is lack of faith to take
a plunge. But youth lacks wisdom in every direction
even in that of the plunge it is ready to take. When you
are 20 you believe that everything can be got from life:
if a man no longer believes this at 60 it does not mean
that he has compromised with it; it means that he has

---

[1] The story of Sisyphus is the story of mankind, and Sisyphus is an old
man only because men have always been at the task of rolling up the same
boulder—but it is a young man who has been doing it.

realized, what the youth does not realize, that progress and improvement depend on human character, and though the great ideas of the world can be tapped the character has to be made.   Experience is a rude teacher, and in nothing ruder than that it comes too late: but there is no other education of the soul. Few experiences are useless. Young people, even the very young, seldom choose companions unlike themselves, and well-conditioned children show amazing resistance to bad example. It is the weak (and the vicious) who cannot free themselves from it, and the weak are under tutelage all their lives.

Men, now, are not conscious of growing old, of laying aside interests, and renouncing enthusiasms. There is a quickening of the pulses of life due to the longer vista before them, and this affects not only the older but the younger man, since life appears far less cumbered with the atmosphere of declining power. 300 years ago people of 50 thought of themselves as nearing the end of their lives, and even 50 years ago they were considered old at 60, which today may only be the beginning of middle age. A change so remarkable must bring in its wake increased understanding between the young and the mature.[1]

It was a consequence of the war of 1914–18 that the young pitied, perhaps, rather than despised their elders whose complete moral ineptitude had let the world into it. And it is in fact an appeal to a different standard of conduct which is now demanded to take the place of the false values and false dignities which brought about that catastrophe because the politicians had taken too long to learn the lesson that force proves nothing. Neither the old nor the young could succeed with tools which shamelessly built up civilization on the two powers of force and money.

---

[1] It has not yet been realized how much more striking this change has been because of the heightened lives and interests of the women. It is they chiefly who have set the current away from old age.

Is pessimism or optimism the right frame of mind for life. The pessimist understands better and the optimist acts better, for valid action involves optimism; so that however great philosophic pessimism may necessarily be action requires us to put it aside. And this means that there is a place for philosophic optimism, or action would be only tilting at windmills. The analogy is with the problem of our 'freedom': we must and do think of ourselves as free; and we *are* free within the limits of determination. We can change the venue sufficiently not to alter human character but to alter the direction of our minds and our mental realizations.

Is there room for the sentiment of gratitude towards the universe? For gratitude towards a supreme person who has spared me and not spared my neighbour there is no place; but it has its place in our relation to the stuff of life, the risks and hazards of the delicate fabric, the balance which the universe holds so many chances of shattering in the lives of all we hold dear. It has held, it has not been shattered; the waves which might have raged have slipped away and left us in the golden calm. The sense of that is the sense of gratitude. Marcus Aurelius, Catherine of Siena, lived close to this sentiment, which helps those who have realized it—much or little— to face the many misfits and the many storms.   There is another gratitude—gratitude to each other. The generous are grateful; and it has been well said that there is no sacrifice so great but gratitude will render it bearable, and none too small to be magnified into a burden by absence of recognition.[1]

Virtues are not made attractive. An impatient nature being told of patience as a submissive resignation is disgusted; but if it were shown that the events of life must needs be encountered with some measure of patience, and that better things than submission result from it—such

[1] W. E. Norris, novelist.

as Pliny's recognition that indulgent patience is a part of justice[1]—the impatient would have a better chance of becoming more patient. 'More patient', for the course of life does not require that men should toe a line of virtues and temperament.[2]

Peace-mindedness — Patience and the peace-mind in general are hard, since natural dislikings and likings are inevitable and proper. Nevertheless we must become ready to cultivate the peace mind in our relations with all groups of human beings—from the narrowest to the widest—because this alone will make possible the fairness and willingness to co-operate which underlie all civilization.[3] And these things are far more attainable now than at any time in the history of the world. Never more will it be possible that "one half of the world" should not know "how the other half lives". Modern inventions have brought together lands and races, weakening antagonisms born of ignorance: it is in fact by understanding and by mental realizations only—not by systems and doctrines—that men can obtain the happiness of the peace-minded. An understanding of what is unlike self is an essential of all

Prejudice — progress. We are all of us influenced by prejudice in face of the new and untried, and there is no better remedy than common mutual experience. To realize that the tyrannies and absurdities of mere custom have every-

---

[1] Or Ruskin's that patience is the finest part of fortitude.

[2] Naturally, the attractiveness of virtue will make no appeal to stupid trivial and callous people but no religion no doctrine no philosophy has succeeded in making such people virtuous.

[3] Human history, since its iron age, has been one of constant provocation and reliance upon force; which has not been condemned by any form of christianity, with the one exception of 'quakerism'. Our daily language supports it. We say someone has "given in" to us when he has accepted our suggestion; and we are accustomed to refer in this vain and truculent way to many of our relations with our fellows. This language of rivalry and depreciation and domination (which we would not stand in regard to ourselves) is inimical to the peace-mind, and it has nothing to do with being spirited, rather is it the reverse.

where been the staple of human opinion is to take arms against prejudice.[1]

Until those great changes took place which are bringing peoples together the lay element in life had always been despised and the professional expert held in much honour; for there was no diffusion of knowledge and only a very small fraction of mankind was free of superstition. Hence the rule of priestcrafts in religion, in medicine, in law. It is not till the general torpor of ignorance is dispelled that the layman is able to criticize the professional, and to recognize that he is made for the layman and not the layman for him, and that the group-protection which has always accompanied the professions has done injury to lay requirements. For the goal of specialized knowledge is not the creation of the 'expert' state; no society should live in awe of the professional expert, and control by the lay mind will always be an affair of first importance in maintaining liberty and diffusing truth. The banefulness of the professional has consisted in his control of false doctrines—a charlatanry which has held the layman in thrall to those as ignorant as himself. The blessed laity has been both victim and debtor of the '3 learned professions'—and may continue to be both. But it is profoundly unlikely that anyone of the 3 will enjoy in the future the prestige of the past.[2]

Profession-alism and the layman

Though a very great deal has been said of the havoc wrought by sin little has been made of the havoc wrought by sins against the body: yet of all the sources of suffering

Health

[1] For example, it is not fashion, however ludicrous, but the unusual, however sensible, which attracts antipathy and ridicule.

[2] Professionalism is not of course confined to these 3, it has invaded most human activities; but it is these 3 which have wrought most havoc. The most suggestionable of them is the medical—its outlook is pathological—and suggestionability is not a valuable quality when we have passed the age of tutelage.

It was noted by Berthelot that the progress of the human spirit has never come from the academies—from professionalism, which is always unself-critical.

none perhaps is greater than the heredity and practice of physical intemperance in any direction. A man's body should be considered as the noble companion of his life— life which is itself an interaction of soul and body. Perhaps when once the relation of body and spirit (which help to maintain each other) is recognized as the root of all well-being, an ideal of health rather than an image of sickness will be uppermost—the classical rather than the post-classical outlook on life. The medicine-men, whether primitive or civilized, have been at one in discarding the wholesome and the reasonable; and it is strange enough to find that the modern medicine-man has been working on our fear for our bodies as the priest worked on our fear for our souls. Now the lay world is no longer ignorant and it will turn to the natural allies of health.[1]

The harmony of body and soul

Harmony and happiness in life will depend on accepting its basic elements as a whole and in a happy relation to each other; they are not the result of a moral philosophy which regards the 'physical' as a mean cumberer of the 'soul'. The best life, then, is a spiritual adventure which lifts soul and sense through vision and courage—integrating, because truth lies that way.[2]

The postponement of life

We diminish the happiness of life by the habit of neglecting the foreground, which is a defect, I think, of the middle years; life is foreshortened by postponing its quality. We look forward to enjoying tomorrow and let today pass unmarked. But life has nothing to yield but its quality and so its secret is held in the hours as they pass and not in the vista of years. It was no epicurean but the stoic emperor who said that if we would live what alone is our real life, that is the present, there would be less anxiousness, and we should be not less but more attentive

[1] This natural "regimen of healthfulness" was enunciated in the school of Salerno, only to be contemptuously cast aside by the medical faculty there.

[2] "This sameness (of the spiritual and the material) is the gate of all spirituality." Laô-Tsze.

to our good genius. If it be objected that all civilization requires postponement of the present to a future good, the answer is that we ought to conciliate human foresight as often as may be with the claims of here and now; it need not cause us to miss their quality.[1]

It is the same case with another despoiler of life— mechanization. Men come to resemble the machines they have made and readily regard purely mechanical ends as more momentous and interesting than all the richnesses of life. But life and mechanism are contraries, they do not meet at any point; and the trend will certainly be back to nature here also.

The mechanization of life

It will take the efforts of both halves of the race to clear the world of cant, and scorn of cant and the readiness to call things by their right names are among the best factors of modern mentality, promising both betterment and happiness. Civilized men have replaced the unflinching superstitions and conventions of uncivilized men by cant and hypocrisy: that they might maintain unjust social and political distinctions—that they might keep others in an inferior position only because it was inferior—they have inthroned lies and obscurantism and habitually repelled and suppressed truth; "in slave states the slave must rule".

Cant and com-promise

And the habit of cant in speech and writing may be a more insidious thing than hypocrisy. The hypocrite consciously feigns opinions and sentiments—different or superior to his own—in order to curry moral or material advantage. But cant is rather an affliction than a weapon; it is the consequence of embracing false sentiments and opinions, and it cannot be exorcized except by an unflinching respect for intellectual truth.

[1] Professor Sheldon Amos wrote that by referring all our activities and interests to something which is going to be we check the spontaneity and buoyancy which belong to the present and in so far denaturalize life.
I know of no other moralist who has made this point.

(Absolute
truth)

Which means intellectual honesty, and not the cult of the absolutely true. For men cannot live by absolute truth, and cannot even mete absolute justice; not because they are themselves only partially just but because their circumstances are never perfectly just. Hence men are accustomed to see the direct path and take a middle path —to compromise. In matters legal, compromise may be rank injustice, favouring the aggressor; but in the private and domestic relations of friendship and dwelling together it is the generally right path. What poisons compromise is the intellectual deception which can accept the half-truth for the whole truth, and the second best for the best. In intellectual matter and in the great decisions of life compromise has no role at all.

*Gnōthi
seauton*

There is a blindness like the blindness of our passions our appetites and our ignorance—it is the ignorance of ourselves. And when we recognize the material with which we have to work if there is to be a better and happier world, it is with ourselves that we are left face to face. "Know thyself" and we know not what manner of men we are. In a mirror of vain imaginings we have seen a person who does not exist. The last knowledge which a man acquires is knowledge of himself, and none has so many obstacles arrayed against it. It is easier, wrote Julian of Norwich, to come to the knowing of god than to know one's own soul. To a degree which would astonish any onlooker we ignore our defects and mistake our talents, pluming ourselves upon the quality we do not possess and blinding ourselves to the fault which all our friends behold in us. If it were realized that this ignorance of self is the original sin of mankind it would throw light on the doctrine of Plato that sin is ignorance. It is *not* true that if we knew the better we could not choose the worse, unless by 'knowing' we mean a spiritual understanding also; it *is* true that men choose

470

the worse because in the real sense they have not known the better. But the counsel *gnōthi seauton*[1] means something more immediate than this; it means that better knowledge of ourselves instructs us in the knowledge of good and bad, unmasking the mixed motives of good actions, and of bad, and preparing the mind to find within (and not without) the index of human conduct. This sincerity with yourself is by no means within reach of all; such desperate wounds as hypocrisy, our self-deception, our timidity where self-knowledge is concerned, bar the portals of the soul. But we might expect a moral reaction in the larger number of men if they ever came to recognize their own likeness: self-criticism would more often take the place now usurped by vain criticism of others; a stage would be reached on the road to that knowledge which is at least part of virtue.[2]

Self-knowledge is also a clue to right criticism of societies and nations; if we took trouble to understand the mainsprings of our own conduct the experience which is necessary to understand motives and character foreign to ourselves would be greatly strengthened. If we do not know ourselves, or rightly gauge the sources of our own actions, what sort of judges are we of characters and temperaments to which we have relatively so little access? To fear any knowledge is to show us its

---

[1] By 'know thyself' the Greek did not mean 'know thyself in relation to the kosmos'—mighty knowledge which all teaching since the greek age has concealed from us. This is knowledge, as Goethe saw, which cannot be obtained from mere knowledge of self; for if attained it attaches the personal consciously to the universal; it is the penetration into the personal consciousness of truths which are beyond personality, and beyond even the reach of organic life.

[2] People often know themselves better than we think they do; and there is a sense in which we know ourselves better than others know us—we know that we are not as bad as the judgment passed on us, and not as good. But to know your defects does not make it desirable often to speak of them. No one should be accustomed to hear himself vilify himself. We have to keep that self-respect which is essential to all good behaviour.

necessity; this which is true of our avoidance of what is
new and unlike ourselves is specially true of self-knowledge.

Nothing will affect the mentality of civilized man more
than an inevitable change in the notions of sin and forgiveness. The earliest conception of sin and wrong-doing
had to do with the individual's responsibility to his tribe.
Later, this responsibility was directed to a supreme person
—the god. But in both cases sin is what he has to suffer
for rather than what he is guilty of; it is something
objective, and does not involve voluntary action on a man's
part;[1] he may, for instance, injure his tribe if he happens
to encounter a snake on his path. Sin, then, is of the
nature of *tabu*, and the notion of *tabu* still persists when
the sense of responsibility comes to be directed towards
a deity. "Which man sinned, this man or his father?"
the Jew can ask Jesus; for he knows that Jahveh visits
the sins of the fathers on the children to the third and
fourth generation, thereby outraging the supposed responsibility of each conscience. Without willing, without
knowing it, a man becomes a malediction to his fellows
or himself; he is unfortunate or fortunate rather than
wicked or good; the mystery of his moral relations with
things and persons is the mystery of *tabu*. In the hebrew
scriptures 'uncleanness' is often represented as both
objective and involuntary; and in the early conception
of sin and the sinner the accursed and the sacred are
themselves not really separable: the sacred is the set-
apart not because it is too good but because it is too
dangerous—your tribe does not pursue you because you
are wicked but because you are noxious.

The change in man's moral relations from the abound-

---

[1] A primitive view of ethic which persisted in the great greek age—as
its drama shows. It was also inherent in the jewish religion, and in
pauline christology.

472

ing sense of personal responsibility for involuntary sin to the sense of personal or volitional guilt brings a new religious feature in its train. Henceforward wrong and right are subjective events; there is a moral law to which the conscience responds and which is consciously violated—and the new feature is the expectation of divine forgiveness by the trespasser. The interesting thing here is that though the consciousness of wrong has turned inward—a sense of responsibility for evil you have not willed being replaced by the prick of a guilty conscience— the reaction is not a more spiritual one. It cannot in fact be shown, in spite of the almost universal religious prejudice to the contrary, that there is any essential ethical significance in the idea of forgiveness.[1] Sin and forgiveness are to be considered as the false poles of the religious instinct; and if the energies of the human race had been spent on trying not to do wrong rather than on trying to be forgiven for doing it, men would no doubt have progressed further in moral apprehension. For it is not 'the conviction of sin' which matters or has mattered to the human race, much less that each man should somehow earn god's forgiveness of sin: what matters is the sense of responsibility for conduct as a constant spiritual activity.

The new inwardness was fresh soil which produced not a flower but a blight, that self-regardingness which made men desire forgiveness in preference to all other divine gifts. 'Sin' and not joy in goodness has been the burden of european religion and religious worship.[2] *The new inwardness*

When the offence to a supreme person, which may involve the loss of heaven, is the important thing no other ethical problem—either as regards oneself or society —can really matter: this supernal personal negotiation will claim precedence of all other ethical requirements and of all ethical progress. If ethical *growth* is demanded it *If growth is demanded*

[1] See Ethics and Religion, pp. 89–91.   [2] See ibid., p. 88.

473

is clear that we must make use of some other tool than the theological conscience.

The buddhist conception comparedThe other conception of 'sin' is the buddhist which regards the evil of human nature as binding man in his misery, from which he can escape by the denial of desire. This conception proved too abstract for the masses. It aims too high, it expects too spiritual a direction of thought for men in the misery of their ignorance their circumstances and their passions. With the theological conception of sin the terror of god's judgment acted as a police, reaching the unspiritual and lawless; but the buddhist conception offered man an escape for his misery provided that he was himself aware that he was miserable. This conception is of the highest possible moral value. Both have proved inadequate as methods to produce great social and political conceptions. Each is a development on the primitive tribal code of conduct, which has no regard to the evil or baseness of human nature.

The tribesman does not repent of the evil he brings upon his tribe, he is anguished by it. Ethically this is a stronger foundation than theological remorse in the sight of the god or gods. For the ethical character can A dual persuasiononly in fact be built on a dual persuasion: that the harm of my actions consists in the harm they bring to my neighbours (and *not* to me at the hands of god) and in the deterioration of my own character as an ethical being; and that the subjective inwardness which has developed out of an objective tribal code is concerned not with the reference of my sinfulness as an offence to god but with the spiritualization of myself as an ethical agent. The future must comport not the religion of man's relation to an offended god but the religion of development in the spiritualization of man.

Goodness has both roots and wings; its roots are in biology, its wings are the ideal. Sokrates had taught that a man should care for his soul; the christian teaches that he should be preoccupied with saving it. And the two precepts imply two different conceptions of spirituality. In the one the spiritual criterion is fineness and beauty, and virtue is only to be found in "those thinking beauti- Ideas of the fully". In the other a man without any beauty or fineness soul may yet save his soul. Now how a man regards his soul is how he will regard his conduct, and a new beholding of the spiritual will be a new ethical agent. The direction which ethical development must take is suggested by the astounding immorality and materialism with which moral instructors have cloyed the moral sense. Progress has been slow because the unethical has been set before men in the guise of the ethical.[1] Nothing else could be expected from the history of humanity, but the first step forward is that this should be understood—that man should know himself. That knowledge is being brought within his compass day by day; within and without all his conditions favour it. Never before has man been able to bring his past into so pregnant a relation with his future.

[1] Introductory, pp. 5 and 8–10.

INDEX OF PERSONAL NAMES

(Divinities and fictitious characters are in *italics*)

477

GENERAL INDEX

(*For* INDEX OF NAMES OF PERSONS *see p.* 477.)

The principal references are in black type

Rights 356–7; **366–7** not absolute
380   legal 363
Roads to Freedom 375 *n*
Roman catacombs 241; 403   law 29
Rome, its genius 420 *n*   its kosmo-
politanism 419–20 *n*
Running amok 282–3; 348 *n*   ex-
amples of 386–8
Russian mujik quoted 340

Sabine archpriest on morals 255
Sacramentalism 95 *n*³; 438
Sacred, the 472
Salerno, school of 468 *n*¹
Salons, french 408 *n*
Samuel, book of 177
Samurai 32; 35; 169
Sanction 92; 103   of custom 8; 14   of
honour 102; 103   of money 337
of punishment and reward 434 *n*
of public opinion 410
Sanctitas 52
Sanitary faculty 224 and *n*²
Satisfaction, not happiness, as self-
fulfilment 3; 33; 35; 80; 422   ex-
traneous sources of 437   and work
443–4
Savage Life in Central Australia 208 *n*³
Savagery (the savage) what it is 83;
179   customary lore and the savage
11   the higher mental activities and
22; 25–6   self-sacrifice and 32   and
team-work 409   and war 351; 352
Scrupulosity 95; 97
'Seed' 58 and *n*¹
Self-abasement 387; 449
Self-covetousness 118
Self-criticism 92; 286; 471
Self-cultivation 120 and ascetism 115;
116; and theologies 114
Self-discipline 111; 114–15; 405–6
Self-fulfilment 33; 80; **112–13**; 120
Self-interest 30 (see Religion)
Self-love 100–1; 120; 390; 391
Self-preservation 33; 72
Self-respect 32; 92; 100; 101; 103;
106; 390; 391; 471 *n*²
Self-sacrifice 113–14; 120 and its gifts
113; 120–1; 322 and women 221
Sense, organs of 19–20
Sentimentality 9; 242; 267 and *n*⁵;
276; 280; 404

Sermons of Bishop Butler 184 *n*
Sex, origin of 55–9
antagonism **219; 288**
biologically, sex freed the mo her
64
customs, and savagery 11
determination of 56; 62 *n*³
and the ideal man 296–7
pathology 211; 294
sex process, instability of 254
the sex relation, sympathy not inherent in 49; 155
not necessary to reproduction 58
and *n*¹ *n*²; 61   and *n*¹ *n*²; 63 *n*¹
sex restraint 80; 218 *n*¹; 250; 265;
294 and *n*¹
secondary characters 254
as the social nucleus 50; 261
traditions of a conflict **215–17;**
233 *n*
Sexes, approximation of 298
[and see Oversexualization]
Shame 13; 32
Sibylline Books 205
'Simple reflex arch' 18; 22
Simplicity 186; 320; 329
Sin **472–4**
'conviction of' 473
and ignorance (see ignorance and
evil)
and man's wretchedness 386
as the theological sense 90
[and see Forgiveness]
Sincerity 125; 140; 395; 471
Sire 58
Sister and brother 81; 171–2 and the
blood-tie 317; 324–5; 326
Skull 20–1; 212 *n*³
'Slackers' 396
Slander 413–14
Slime, primordial 17
Sociability 28; 49; 76–7
Socialism 399 seqq.
Sodom 145; 146
Solidarity, organic 16   christian 16
human 16; 431 and misfortune 32
and *n*² of women 217 *n*
Song of Creation 214 *n*¹ of Creatures
180 of Deborah 232 *n*² of Miriam
232 *n*² of 'Moses' 232 *n*² of the
Three Children 180
Song of the Celtic Women 299 *n*¹